Choice, Rules and Collective Action

The Ostroms on the Study of Institutions and Governance

Elinor Ostrom and Vincent Ostrom

Introduced and Edited by
Filippo Sabetti and Paul Dragos Aligica

© Elinor Ostrom and Vincent Ostrom 2014

Cover image – *Fotolia.com* © dedoma

Photographs courtesy of the Ostrom Workshop and Indiana University

Published by the ECPR Press in 2014

The ECPR Press is the publishing imprint of the European Consortium for Political Research (ECPR), a scholarly association, which supports and encourages the training, research and cross-national co-operation of political scientists in institutions throughout Europe and beyond.

ECPR Press
University of Essex
Wivenhoe Park
Colchester
CO4 3SQ
UK

Typeset by ECPR Press

Printed and bound by Lightning Source

British Library Cataloguing in Publication Data

A catalogue record for this book is available from the British Library

Paperback ISBN: 978-1-910-259-13-9
PDF ISBN: 978-1-910-259-15-3
Kindle ISBN: 978-1-910-259-16-0
ePub ISBN: 978-1-910-259-17-7

www.ecpr.eu/ecprpress

ECPR Press Series Editors:
Dario Castiglione (University of Exeter)
Peter Kennealy (European University Institute)
Alexandra Segerberg (Stockholm University)
Peter Triantafillou (Roskilde University)

ECPR Essays:

Croce, Gramsci, Bobbio and the Italian Political Tradition (ISBN: 9781907301995) Richard Bellamy

From Deliberation to Demonstration: Political Rallies in France, 1868–1939 (ISBN: 9781907301469) Paula Cossart

Hans Kelsen and the Case for Democracy (ISBN: 9781907301247) Sandrine Baume

Is Democracy a Lost Cause? Paradoxes of an Imperfect Invention (ISBN: 9781907301247) Alfio Mastropaolo

Just Democracy (ISBN: 9781907301148) Philippe Van Parijs

Learning About Politics in Time and Space (ISBN: 9781907301476) Richard Rose

Maestri of Political Science (ISBN: 9781907301193) Donatella Campus, Gianfranco Pasquino, and Martin Bull

Masters of Political Science (ISBN: 9780955820335) Donatella Campus, and Gianfranco Pasquino

The Modern State Subverted (ISBN: 9781907301636) Giuseppe Di Palma

ECPR Classics:

Beyond the Nation State (ISBN: 9780955248870) Ernst Haas

Citizens, Elections, Parties: Approaches to the Comparative Study of the Processes of Development (ISBN: 9780955248887) Stein Rokkan

Comparative Politics The Problem of Equivalence (ISBN: 9781907301414) Jan Van Deth

Democracy Political Finance and state Funding for Parties (ISBN: 9780955248801) Jack Lively

Electoral Change: Responses to Evolving Social and Attitudinal Structures in Western Countries (ISBN: 9780955820311) Mark Franklin,Thomas Mackie, and Henry Valen

Elite and Specialized Interviewing (ISBN: 9780954796679) Lewis Anthony Dexter

Identity, Competition and Electoral Availability: The Stabilisation of European Electorates 1885–1985 (ISBN: 9780955248832) Peter Mair and Stefano Bartolini

Individualism (ISBN: 9780954796662) Steven Lukes

Modern Social Policies in Britain and Sweden: From Relief to Income Maintenance (ISBN: 9781907301001) Hugh Heclo

Parties and Party Systems: A Framework for Analysis (ISBN: 9780954796617) Giovanni Sartori

Party Identification and Beyond: Representations of Voting and Party Competition (ISBN: 9780955820342) Ian Budge, Ivor Crewe, and Dennis Farlie

People, States and Fear: An Agenda for International Security Studies in the Post-Cold War Era (ISBN: 9780955248818) Barry Buzan

Political Elites (ISBN: 9780954796600) Geraint Parry

Seats, Votes and the Spatial Organisation of Elections (ISBN: 9781907301353) Graham Gudgin

State Formation, Parties and Democracy (ISBN: 9781907301179) Hans Daalder

System and Process in International Politics (ISBN: 9780954796624) Mortan Kaplan

Territory and Power in the UK (ISBN: 9780955248863) James Bulpitt

The State Tradition in Western Europe: A Study of an Idea and Institution (ISBN: 9780955820359) Kenneth Dyson

Please visit www.ecpr.eu/ecprpress for up-to-date information about new publications.

Contents

Part Three: Epistemic and Social Philosophical Perspectives

List of Figures and Tables

Acknowledgements

This project is a result of an invitation-challenge coming from Dario Castiglione, of The European Consortium for Political Research (ECPR) Press and it wouldn not have been possible without the strong and enthusiast support given by him, Laura Pugh and Kate Hawkins also from the ECPR Press.

Ionut Sterpan from George Mason University contributed in critical ways to the timely completion of the project. Mercatus Center at George Mason University has generously provided much needed logistical and technical assistance. Filippo Sabetti also wishes to acknowledge support for his work in this project by the Social Sciences and Humanities Research Council of Canada (SSHRC 410–2011–0698). We would like to express our deep gratitude to all of them.

We would also like to extend our thanks to the wonderful community of the Ostroms' Bloomington Workshop. Our special thanks to Patty Lezotte at the Workshop for helping us to secure the permission to publish the works of Vincent and Elinor Ostrom from the Vincent and Elinor Ostrom Workshop in Political Theory and Policy and the Indiana University Foundation. Patty's title there is Publications Manager but anyone who has read Lin's publications and has had any experience with the Workshop knows how foundational her help and memory are around the Workshop since its very creation in 1973. She generously responded to our repeated calls for help.

Last but not least, we would like to thank the copyright holders that have allowed us to reprint the texts included in this volume:

1. The *Public Administration Review* for Ostrom, Vincent and Ostrom, Elinor (1971) 'Public Choice: A Different Approach to the Study of Public Administration'. *Public Administration Review* 31(2): 203–16.

2. Dr. Robert B. Hawkins Jr, Publisher of ICS Press for Ostrom, Vincent (1991) 'Polycentricity: The Structural Basis of Self-Governing Systems'. In *The Meaning of American Federalism: Constituting a Self-Governing Society*, 223–44. San Francisco: ICS Press.

3. John Wiley & Sons Inc. for Ostrom, Elinor and Ostrom, Vincent (2004) 'The Quest for Meaning in Public Choice'. *American Journal of Economics and Sociology* 63(1): 105–47.

4. Springer Publishing for Ostrom, Elinor (1986) 'An Agenda for the Study of Institutions'. *Public Choice* 48(1): 3–25.

5. Cambridge University Press for Ostrom, Elinor (1998) 'A Behavioral Approach to the Rational Choice Theory of Collective Action'. *American Political Science Review* 92(1): 1–22.

6. The American Economic Association for Ostrom, Elinor, 2010, 'Beyond Markets and States: Polycentric Governance of Complex Economic Systems'. *American Economic Review* 100(3): 641–72.

7. Sage Publications for Ostrom, Elinor (1982) 'Beyond Positivism: An Introduction to This Volume'. In *Strategies of Political Inquiry*, edited by Elinor Ostrom, 11–28. Beverly Hills, CA: Sage Publications.

8. The Rowman & Littlefield Publishing Group for Ostrom, Vincent (1979) 'A Conceptual-Computational Logic for Federal Systems of Governance'. In *Constitutional Design and Power-Sharing in the Post-Modern Epoch*, edited by Daniel J. Elazar, 2–22. Lanham, MD: University Press of America.

9. The University of Michigan Press for Ostrom, Vincent (1997) 'Epistemic Choice and Public Choice'. In *The Meaning of Democracy and the Vulnerability of Democracies: A Response to Tocqueville's Challenge*, 89–116. Ann Arbor: The University of Michigan Press.

Paul Dragos Aligica and Filippo Sabetti
May 2014

Foreword

by Dario Castiglione

The rationale of this volume is ably explained in the editors' Introduction. Readers who would like to know more about the content of the essays by Elinor and Vincent Ostrom collected in this book should start from there. This Foreword is more modestly intended to explain the genesis of the volume and to offer a personal reflection on the place that Elinor and Vincent Ostrom and their Workshop occupy in political science and its traditions.

When five years ago the ECPR Press decided to start a series of 'Essays', hoping, amongst other things, to convince well established scholars to collect some of their own miscellaneous writings in single volumes organized by a connecting thread; Elinor Ostrom was one of the authors at the top of our list. She was a big name, whose work we greatly valued, and, in addition to various books, she had also published extensively in journals and edited collections. In short, she was an ideal author for our series. It so happened that I knew her personally, having met her in 2001 at a international conference on social capital I had organized at the University of Exeter. Like everyone else who came in contact with her, I immediately felt the warmth of her personality, the friendliness and kindness of her way of engaging with people, and the sheer enthusiasm she had for intellectual conversation and scholarly collaboration. Not only was she kind enough to participate in the conference, but she was extremely supportive with the ensuing publication and other initiatives that followed. Last time I saw Lin (as I learnt to call her in the more familiar way in which she liked to be addressed) was in 2011, when she gave the Stein Rokkan Lecture at the ECPR Joint Sessions in St. Gallen. In between my first and last meeting with her, I saw Lin a number of times on both sides of the Atlantic, something that always gave me great personal and intellectual pleasure. Through my acquaintance with Lin, I became increasingly aware of how much her work was interconnected in both substance and method with that of her husband, Vincent; and also of the distinctive contribution made to the study of politics by the community of scholars that Lin and Vincent had gathered around their Workshop in Political Theory and Policy Analysis at Indiana University, which was known as the Bloomington School.

When, at the end of 2009, I approached Lin for the 'Essays' series, it seemed only natural, therefore, to put to her three possible options: a selection of her own essays, a thematic selection of hers and Vincent's, and a selection of essays by members of the Workshop. In truth, I had no great expectation that she would answer affirmatively; for I knew how busy Lin was, and also that Vincent's health was frail. Moreover, her recent award of the Nobel Prize for Economic Sciences made it less likely that she could or would be able to accept our offer. In the event, Lin's reply was both gracious and enthusiastic, saying how pleased she was with our suggestions; but it was, inevitably, apologetic: 'I wish, she wrote, I could bite on one or the other but I don't dare'. As she explained, she had already agreed very similar projects with another publisher, and did not think she would have the time to add to them.

At the time, I did not expect to get back to the project, and, above all, I did not expect the sad circumstances – Lin's death in June 2012, followed three weeks later by Vincent's – that would make us return to it. We were not sure how far Lin had progressed with the publications she had mentioned in her reply, but since no collection like the ones we had suggested was in print, we decided eventually to contact the Workshop Directors, Tom Evans and Burney Fisher, asking for their opinion on resuming our original project. Their reply was both courteous and encouraging. There was a comprehensive collection of published and unpublished essays by Lin in the making, but the Workshop had no objection to us publishing a somewhat shorter and more focussed selection. With this in mind, we contacted Filippo Sabetti and Paul Dragos Aligica, who had been closely associated with the Bloomington School, and had separately written on its scientific and intellectual aspects, and asked whether they would be willing to act as the editors for the book. Happily, they agreed to take the challenge on. It was their idea to focus the selection on the more foundational, theoretical and epistemological, aspects of the research programs that both Lin and Vincent had pursued during their long academic careers. The book therefore purports to offer a view of the Ostroms' own conception of political research, of how this connects to social research at large, how it contributes to policy-making and institution building, and to the normative agenda behind their own work.

In reading these more theoretical essays, and reflecting on the Ostroms' contribution to several fields of political research such as collective action, common-pool resources, polycentric administration and self-governance, one is left with no doubt about the magnitude of their contribution to political studies. But a lingering question remains: what is the idea of politics underlying their research programs? Or, to put it differently, how does their contribution to political research fit in with the self-understanding of politics as a discipline? This is not an entirely trivial question. In spite of the international recognition of their scholarly and scientific work (prestigious prizes, journal editorships, honorary appointments), and in spite of their high standing in the profession (presidencies of scholarly societies), there is something that seems to set them apart from the more traditional canons of political science; something that made them 'the odd couple out', so to speak, in political studies. Arguably, this is not just a personal impression. A close associate of the Ostroms and former co-director of the Workshop, Michael McGinnis (2011), raises this very issue in his piece on Elinor Ostrom for a volume on '*maestri*' of political science that the ECPR Press published a few years ago. McGinnis notices how this question underlies a review symposium published by *Perspectives on Politics* (Isaacs *et al.* 2010) on Elinor Ostrom's *Governing the Commons*, which, significantly, took place after she won the Nobel Prize. While celebrating her achievements and praising the magnitude of her intellectual contribution to the field, most of the writers in that symposium seem to ask themselves whether Elinor Ostrom's work truly belongs to the canon of political science. In a similar fashion, the same question can be asked of Vincent Ostrom's work, particularly with respect to the subject of Public Administration. A recent piece by Paul Dragos Aligica (forthcoming 2014) suggests that Vincent's work was never properly assimilated by mainstream scholars in either Public Administration or Public Choice, a point implicitly made in an assessment penned by McGinnis and Elinor Ostrom herself for the *Public Administration Review*, a journal for which Vincent Ostrom acted as editor in the mid 1960s. So, the question for the reminder of this Foreword is where do the Ostroms stand in the study of politics?

There are two possible ways of approaching such a question, not only in order to answer it, but also to try to explain why it is posed at all. The first suggests that the strong interdisciplinary nature of their research programs, and the way in which their research interests sits in-between different sub-fields of politics, makes it difficult to assimilate their work to one definite area or tradition of political science. The second builds on this intuition by suggesting that their way of thinking about politics is not only interstitial between disciplines and sub-disciplines, but also pursues lines of research that tend to be peripheral to mainstream preoccupations. I wish to explore these possible answers in turn, even though I think there is more to the latter than to the former.

The interdisciplinary nature of the Ostroms' research programs can be assumed as one of the reasons why their work does not fit so easily within political science and its main sub-disciplines. Economic rationality plays a large role in the way in which they engage with political choice and organization. The awarding of the Nobel Prize to Elinor Ostrom, particularly for her work on collective action and common-pool resources, could be regarded as testimony to the fact that her work is as much that of a student of economics as of a political scientist. As Robert Axelrod (in Isaacs *et al.* 2010: 580) notices, although hers is 'an outstanding example of interdisciplinary research', showing how much political science can offer to other disciplines; her work can also be presented in the reverse form, as demonstrating how 'economic analysis can shed light on most forms of social organization' (Isaacs *et al.* 2010: 582, n. 2) – which is indeed the justification provided by the committee in conferring her the Nobel Prize. There is no denying that both Vincent and Elinor Ostrom emphasised the importance of applying economic reasoning to the study of political phenomena. Indeed, this is what they took to be the central contention and the shared concern of that community of scholars working on the '"No-name" fields of Public Administration', later to become Public Choice, with whom they originally identified their own work, as explicitly argued in the opening essay of this collection, written in 1971. But, for them, economic rationality was only the opening gambit of a series of moves that were meant to question both the idea of public organization and the forms of collective action required for those goods and resources shared by a community. As their respective research programmes took form, they started questioning some of the assumptions of economic rationality both in relation to empirical findings and to the norms of a science of association. This led Elinor Ostrom to call for a 'second generation' rational choice theory (*see* Chapter Five of this collection), while Vincent Ostrom drew attention to 'epistemic choice' (*see* Chapter Nine below) as a more complex way of thinking about the nature of public choice. As the editors of this volume explain in their Introduction, both essays show a certain disillusionment with the over-simplified assumptions made by mainstream studies in Public Choice and Rational Choice theory. Part of this disillusionment can be traced to the fact that Elinor and Vincent Ostrom were keen to point out that, though political research needed the powerful analytic tools provided by economic reasoning, such tools could not be deployed without due regard to the findings of empirical research; nor could they blind researchers to the diversity of normative values (not exclusively efficiency) that human beings bring into their actions and relationships. It is the recognition that a theory of collective action and socio-political organization must be congruent with empirical data that motivated the strong interdisciplinary program of the Ostroms, as they tried to assemble evidence from many disciplines, such as anthropology, sociology, law, as well as economics and politics; and from different methods of elaborating data: case studies, comparative analysis, experiments, abstract modelling. An interdisciplinary and multi-methods approach was central to the elaboration of what they understood as 'frameworks' for institutional analysis and development (IAD) and for the characterization of the variables determining either the micro-contexts or the broader socio-ecological systems that in combination provide the 'action situation' within which agents operate. As the Bloomington School took shape, their research became more interdisciplinary, and more self-consciously so. Similarly, some of the key ideas used for the assessment of the forms of social order and collective problem solving, such as polycentricity, self-governance, levels of choice, communication and learning, acquired as much a normative as an analytical purchase, thus making the boundaries between traditional sub-disciplines in politics more porous. If the interdisciplinary and interstitial nature of the Ostroms' research programs is the reason why they do not sound political enough, this may say more about the state of political studies – about a certain parochialism, which is the effect of increasing over-specialisation, and of the inability of many of its practitioners to communicate across disciplines and sub-disciplines – than on the Ostroms' own conception of what political research consists of.

But interdisciplinarity is only part of the story. As both the editors of this volume and Michael McGinnis (2011) in his piece on Elinor Ostrom makes clear, there is something more specific underlying the *marginality* of the Ostroms' research programs to political science. Indeed, the explanation – in a sense, the vindication of such marginality – can be found in two observations made by Vincent and Elinor Ostrom themselves. The first one is part of the critical remarks that Vincent Ostrom makes about mainstream Public Choice in Chapter Nine of this collection: 'work on the peripheries is where important advances at the frontier are most likely to occur'. The second is in the lecture that Elinor Ostrom delivered on the occasion of the award of the Nobel Prize (here reproduced as Chapter Six), where she talks about the 'intellectual journey' which she underwent in the process of recognizing the greater complexity of the motivational structure and capabilities that people have in solving social dilemmas. By taking these two elements, we may perhaps better understand what sets the Ostroms apart from more traditional political science, or, at least, why mainstream scholarship finds it difficult to assimilate them to the 'cores' of the discipline. In brief, their intellectual journeys took them to the periphery of the dominant discourses in political science, where, as Vincent Ostrom says, innovation seems to take place.

In a sense, the Ostroms' intellectual careers have mostly consisted in questioning and displacing some of central assumptions of political science and public administration, or even of those approaches, such as Public Choice, Rational Choice theory, and constitutional engineering in which they identified the basic tools for political analysis. Their very idea of politics, and hence what interested them in political research, may, strictly speaking, not be the dominant one, but it is nonetheless part of the canon of modern political science. It is less about the nature of power relations and the exercise of power, and more about problem solving and the ordering of things; less about command and obedience, and more about balancing and coordination; less about Machiavellian statecraft, and more about citizens' competence; less about Hobbesian sovereignty, and more about Tocquevillian democracy. Arguably, at least for a while, at the beginning of their intellectual journeys, Vincent and Elinor Ostrom found themselves swimming with the main currents in American political science. Vincent Ostrom's questioning in the early 1960s of the hierarchical and centralised view of state administration and his idea of polycentric governance could be seen as inscribed in what John G. Gunnell (2004) has described as the dominant paradigm (by the second half of the 20th Century) of American political science in the form of 'democratic pluralism'. Such a paradigm had started in the first half of the century as a rejection of a view of the 'state' as the exclusive, and monolithic, subject matter of politics. Whether Gunnell is right or not over the genesis and dominance of the 'pluralist' paradigm, there is no doubt that the Ostroms' view of polycentric organization and their embracing of self-governing forms of policy communities reflects that view of politics. Similarly, their embracing of economic rationality as a method to study the micro-processes of public decision making was, by the late 1960s and the 1970s a well established, if not yet fully dominant, discourse in political science. So, there is no doubt that, though the Ostroms' conception of politics was not the only one available at the start of their intellectual journey, it was nonetheless one of the core traditions in the discipline. But, looking closely at the topics that preoccupied their research, one starts recognizing their constant interest for challenging and gently subverting acquired views and concepts – a move from the core to the periphery of the canon of the discipline.

A few examples of this inclination to question accepted views will suffice. The Ostroms' rejection of the hierarchical, centralised and bureaucratic view of addressing public decision making was, at the bottom, a rejection of the simple dichotomy between state and market, while questioning the assumption, dominant in mid-century, that the two modes of organization applied respectively and exclusively to the public and private domains; but also questioning the contention, that persisted until much later, that their modes of operation could not be mixed. If one looks at Elinor Ostrom's reputation-making book (1990), one notices a similar challenge to established patterns of thought. Whereas the dominant view was that a coherent examination of the logic of collective action would result in the 'tragedy of commons', Elinor Ostrom instead demonstrated through empirical observation and judicious theorising and modelling of collective decision making, that the commons can be *governed*, and indeed this is the usual, though fragile, pattern in human affairs, showing a 'world of *possibility* rather than *necessity*' (*see* Chapter Five in this collection).

This line of investigation resulted in two significant departures from the canon of rational-choice influenced political research. In this the Ostroms were not isolated voices, but they greatly added to a growing literature that started questioning some of the axiomatic assumptions about rational agency, by introducing a number of important qualification such as bounded rationality, the use of heuristics and norm-oriented behaviour in decision making, the importance of iterated situations and the role of communication and reputational considerations in producing trust and reciprocity as contributing elements for collective action and for solving real life social dilemmas.

The second, and perhaps less remarked upon, development is the questioning of the simple dichotomy between pure private goods and pure public goods, the latter being defined by the joint characteristics of being neither excludable nor rivalrous. The introduction of different degrees of both excludability and subtractability makes it instead possible to distinguish at least four different kinds of goods and resources: besides public and private goods, also toll-goods (low in subtractability and relatively easy in terms of exclusion), and common-pool resources (high in both respects). This new matrix of types of goods and resources opens up an interesting research program not only about the technologies of collective decision making but also about different types of property rights, something that has often been obscured by the simple dichotomy between state and market, or public and private, but which is certainly rooted in the history of many vernacular legal systems, and which, as the Ostroms have indicated in their research, may have a crucial importance in addressing the kind of problems involved in the new global commons with regard to issues of ecological sustainability.

Finally, it is important to point out one central element in the Ostroms' conception of institutional analysis and evaluation, which is also remarked on by Aligica and Sabetti towards the end of their Introduction. This is the open-ended quality of the Ostroms' research programs, which has an epistemic support in the emphasis that particularly Vincent Ostrom's work puts on taking seriously the learning capacities of human beings in designing the institutional frameworks within which they can take collective decisions. This is an intrinsic element of what Vincent Ostrom calls the element of 'artisanship' that comes in the joint design of institutions, but also in the running of them. Human institutions are not spontaneous in the strict sense, though polycentric organization and development is better suited at accommodating human diversity and liberty. Institutions are the 'artifacts' of human beings, who jointly try to impress upon them their own conceptions, values and purposes, which may fundamentally differ from individual to another. But institutions are also populated by human beings who have knowledge, purposes, and values of their own and, crucially, are capable of learning. Understanding the endogenous nature of institutional development is as important as understanding the principles of institutional design: both exercises belong to a 'science of civics' (*see* Sabetti 2014). Thus, as the Ostroms conceive it, institutional analysis is by definition an open-ended exercise: a never ending intellectual journey that continuously challenges the canon of political science by offering views from its periphery.

References

Aligica, P. D. (forthcoming 2014) 'Public Administration, Public Choice and the Ostroms: The Achievement, the Failure, the Promise', *Public Choice*.

Gunnell, J. G. (2004) 'The Real Revolution in American Political Science', *PS: Political Science and Politics*, XXXVII, 1: 47–50.

Isaacs, J. C. *et al.* (2010) 'Review Symposium. Beyond the Tragedy of the Commons: A Discussion of *Governing the Commons*', *Perspectives on Politics*, 8, 2: 569–593.

McGinnis, M. D. (2011) 'Elinor Ostrom: Politics as Problem-Solving in Polycentric Settings', in (eds) D. Campus, G. Pasquino and M. Bull, *Maestri of Political Science*, volume 2, Colchester: ECPR Press.

Ostrom, E. (1990) *Governing the Commons: The Evolution of Institutions for Collective Action*, New York: Cambridge University Press.

Sabetti, F. (2014) 'Artisans of the Common Life: Building a Public Science of Civics', in (eds) P. Levine and K. Soltan, *Civic Studies*, vol. III, Washington DC: Bringing Theory to Practice, pp. 23–32.

Elinor and Vincent Ostrom
and the Workshop

This book, that Filippo Sabetti and Paul Dragos Aligica have put together, is a book of essays written, some together, some separately, by Elinor Ostrom and Vincent Ostrom. It is a book by them and not about them. It is a book about ideas (hard ideas at that) more than about people. But there are times when knowing the people, seeing the people, tells us something about their ideas.

Given the genesis of this book, the close relation that particularly Elinor Ostrom (Lin, as she was familiarly known) had with the ECPR, and given that, coming posthumously, this book is also a small tribute to the life and work of both Lin and Vincent; we always thought to include a picture of theirs inside the book. But, in searching amongst the photos that are available at the website of the Indiana University Workshop in Political Theory and Policy Analysis, which they founded in 1973 and which is now appropriately named after them, we became convinced that the pictures told an intellectual story that is integral to the ideas of this book. We have selected a few, some showing Lin and Vincent when they were younger, some together, some discussing with students and colleagues, and some of the meetings of people connected to the Workshop. The reader will make what he or she may want from them. We hope they offer a kind of visual testimony of Lin's and Vincent's style of intellectual leadership: warm, personable, open, enthusiastic, caring, and, in a sense, collective.

The Workshop, a truly diverse and multicultural meeting of people, ideas, and research projects, was an integral part of their academic life and legacy. It is difficult to imagine them without their Workshop, and them without each other.

Images courtesy of the Ostrom Workshop and Indiana University.
[*Note*: The Workshop was renamed after the Ostroms in May 2012.]

Elinor Ostrom: Manitoulin Island, Ontario, Canada, 1968.

Vincent Ostrom: Manitoulin Island, Ontario, Canada, 1968.

Vincent Ostrom (others unknown): early 1970s.

Roger Parks, Elinor Ostrom, Diane Eubanks: Workshop in Political Theory and Policy Analysis, Indiana University, Bloomington, 1977.

Elinor and Vincent Ostrom: Rome, Italy, 1978.

Vincent Ostrom: Workshop on the Workshop (WOW1) conference, Indiana University, Bloomington, 1994.

Elinor and Vincent Ostrom: Current and former Workshop graduate students, WOW2 (Workshop on the Workshop) conference, the Indiana University Memorial Union, Bloomington campus, 1999.

Elinor and Vincent Ostrom: Manitoulin Island, Ontario, Canada, 2003.

Elinor and Vincent Ostrom: WOW3 (Workshop on the Workshop) conference, the Indiana University Memorial Union, Bloomington campus, 2004.

Elinor and Vincent Ostrom: American Political Science Association (APSA) meetings, Washington, D.C., 2005.

Vincent Ostrom: (John Gaus Award and Lectureship), American Political Science Association (APSA) meetings, Washington, DC, 2005.

Elinor Ostrom: office, Workshop in Political Theory and Policy Analysis, Indiana University, Bloomington, 2009.

Elinor and Vincent Ostrom: campus, Indiana University, Bloomington, 2004.

Introduction

The Ostroms' Research Program for the Study of Institutions and Governance: Theoretical and Epistemic Foundations

Paul Dragos Aligica and Filippo Sabetti

This volume brings together a set of key writings of Nobel Prize in Economic Sciences co-recipient Elinor Ostrom and public choice political economy co-founder Vincent Ostrom, in which the two scholars introduce, elaborate and explain their approaches, conceptual frameworks and analytical perspectives to the study of institutions and institutional performance. The book brings together a number of texts representing the main analytical and conceptual vehicles articulated and used by the Ostroms and their collaborators in the creation of the so-called Bloomington School of public choice and institutional theory. The focus is hence on the conceptual lenses and theoretical apparatus that shaped the construction of their work; an attempt to illustrate them, via selected readings organized using a tentative interpretative framework. Its ultimate objective is not only to offer a direct introduction to the conceptual, theoretical and epistemic perspectives that shaped and inspired this prominent research program, but also to point out the fascinating intellectual avenues opened by the Ostroms' and that invite further exploration and investigation.

In other words, the volume is not a comprehensive overview of the Bloomington School. It does not offer an intellectual biography of how Vincent and Elinor Ostrom came to form their exceptional partnership in the adventure of life and work that started at the University of California at Los Angeles in the early 1960s and continued at Indiana University, Bloomington, where they were instrumental in creating an intellectual community around and beyond the today's celebrated Workshop in Political Theory and Policy Analysis. Other sources can be mined for that history which has yet to be written. Nor does this volume deal with the whole range of contributions – theories of governance, common pool resources, public economies, metropolitan reform, the in-depth and comparative case studies, applied institutional analysis etc., all inherent to that research tradition. Hence this volume is not and should not be seen as a substitute for the essential three volume *Readings from the Workshop in Political Theory and Policy Analysis* edited by Michael McGinnis (1999a, 1999b, and 2000), the two volumes honoring the intellectual contributions of Vincent Ostrom edited by Barbara Allen, Filippo Sabetti and Mark Sproule-Jones (Sabetti 2009; Sproule-Jones 2008) and the two volumes of Vincent Ostrom's collected unpublished essays edited by Barbara

Allen (2011 and 2012). At the same time, the volume does not delve into the more applied methodological, research design and execution, the technical research side of the Bloomington scholars' work. The Ostroms and their collaborators were pioneers in developing many innovative approaches to comparative case study, field work, operationalization, measurement and evaluation, mixed and multi-method research design and strategy. This volume is not dealing with that entire domain. In this respect, the ground has already been covered by Amy Poteete, Marco Janssen and Elinor Ostrom in *Working Together: Collective Action, the Commons, and Multiple Methods in Practice* (2010). That is to say, this book should not be viewed as a substitute for that excellent work.

In brief, this book detaches and focuses deliberately only on the theoretical approaches, on the conceptual frameworks and the epistemic foundations of the Bloomington School, as seen through the works of the founders and leaders of this research program, Elinor and Vincent Ostrom. Viewed from this angle, the idea animating the project may be considered a reflection of the Ostoms' own views about the centrality of theoretical thinking in social sciences and a natural continuation of their endeavours to 'reestablish the priority of theory over data collection and analysis' and to better integrate theory and practice. In their view, theory has to be something more basic and more central to social sciences than a mere set of logically connected statements over a set of statistically handled data. The creation of the Workshop in 1973 was in part built on the initial program of a series of working papers on political theory and policy analysis that Vincent edited in the late 1960s and to which several graduate students contributed. That series of working papers was based on the following assumption worth quoting in full:

> [...] theory is the only reasoned guide to research that is available. In the absence of theory, inquiry becomes uninformed trial and errors. Conversely, these papers are also based on an assumption that practical political experience reflecting situations relevant to theoretical considerations are appropriate circumstances to test the empirical relevance of theory. Political science, thus, represents a union of interests between political theory and policy analysis.

Echoing Vincent, Elinor Ostrom in one of her very few statements on the epistemological foundations of political science, observed that scientific inquiry should be based on '[...] references to the work of political philosophers, a recognition of the importance of history, an awareness of diverse philosophies of science, a basic concern with the central place of theory in the development of the discipline, the use of formal models and a recognition of the importance of rigorous methods in data analysis' (Chapter Seven). For the Bloomington scholars, social science evolves around theoretical and philosophical thinking without however, becoming too abstract or divorced from events in the world. In their own writings they tend to stay away from 'grand theory' as much as possible. Throughout their career they were sensitive to what they often referred to as 'problem of cognition' – the challenge of how to tie theoretical discourse to empirical inquiry mindful of how the language of discourse relates to the world of events characteristic of natural phenomena (V. Ostrom [1990] 1999); they strove to avoid what Walter Eucken (1951) described as 'the great antinomy' between abstract models and the empirical reality. For these reasons, they favoured mostly 'middle range theory' identifying and exploring 'social mechanisms' and political and institutional processes. As Elinor Ostrom put it, the growth of scientific knowledge is 'limited in scope to specific types of theoretically defined situations rather than sweeping theories of society as a whole' (Chapter Seven). This book illustrates how the Ostroms responded to these self-imposed parameters or intellectual standards.

Needless to say, these are important themes both in terms of the intellectual history of the Bloomington School and in terms of future research developments to take place on the intellectual lines defined by it. Always present, this theoretical concern penetrated the Ostroms' work in multiple ways. Their ongoing effort in this respect has always been tentative, partial and open to new alternatives. This volume documents that. One can see through it an underlying logic evolving, branching taking place in several directions, but at the same time the presence of evident elements of consistency.

The volume also shows that by focusing on their theoretical frameworks and approaches, one may trace and explore a combination of intellectual influences inspiring the Ostroms work, as well as their persistent attempt to frame those influences through their own experience and perspective. As Elinor Ostrom put it:

> The work that we have done at the [Bloomington] Workshop is deeply rooted in the central tradition of human and social studies. There is no better testimony for that than the questions that structure our work: How can fallible human beings achieve and sustain self-governing entities and self-governing ways of life? How can individuals influence the rules that structure their lives? Similar questions were asked by Aristotle and other foundational social and political philosophers. These were the concerns of Madison, Hamilton and de Tocqueville. Today these central questions unite political scientists, economists, geographers, sociologists, psychologists, anthropologists, and historians who study the effect of diverse rules on human behavior in various institutional contexts, countries or at different geographic scales (E. Ostrom in Aligica and Boettke 2009: 159; *see also* McGinnis 2011).

Rooted in an illustrious tradition in political studies and the then emerging analytics of public choice at whose creation they contributed as founding figures, alongside James M. Buchanan, Gordon Tullock and William H. Riker, the Ostroms' inquiries went beyond narrow disciplinarily boundaries. The volume presents the various attempts and modes by which they and their associates tried to capture the public/rational choice theory potential and how in the process, they went beyond it to the point of developing an original and unique comparative institutional analysis agenda. The revolutionary and radical nature of this agenda has not been fully grasped. Thus the present volume tries to convey some of the deepest epistemic assumptions and foundational views that inspired this intellectual evolution.

One of the most interesting aspects of the Ostroms' efforts is the fact that they did not seem to be driven by a doctrinaire philosophy, a rigid code about how social and political science should be done 'correctly' in accordance with some philosophical or epistemological canons. They simply did it, following problems and puzzles they considered interesting or important – to know how things work or do not work – and trying to apply to them systematic reasoning, erudition and empirical evidence, via the best practice available to them. That view of their approach is correct only up to a point. They had indeed a pragmatic spirit that at some deeper level may be suggesting an underlying pragmatist philosophy of scientific practice. Yet, besides and beyond that, at a closer look, one realizes that they in fact consistently reflected on the theories and approaches used in their practice, on their instruments and their epistemic parameters. Usually they did that in strong connection with the core research domain or theme at the center of their attention, typically something having to do with governance issues. That is to say, you don't find them engaged in long epistemological and methodological preparatory exertions only to leave to others the task of doing the substantive work. But – that being said – they did dedicate significant time and effort to theoretical and foundational questions. Their work is marked by constant attempts to specify and reflect on their theoretical apparatus and by interrogations and investigations on the nature, direction and results of their work. Examined carefully, it is possible to see in their work how the substantive empirical and normative research and the theoretical and foundational reflection coevolve.

In addition to being faithful to the spirit and letter of the Ostroms' theory-centered approach to social sciences, there are a couple of additional reasons motivating this volume: First of all, this collection of essays is probably the most effective way to go straight at the core of, and understand, the Bloomington school of institutionalism. It is definitely possible to become familiar with this research program via its governance studies, or the natural resources management, common pool resources, municipal reform etc. research. Yet, to gain an undiluted sense of the nature, dimensions and ambitions of the program, to get a sense of its core and intellectual engine, one has sooner or later to engage the writings that define, explain and elaborate the theoretical logic and framing of its overall approach. Before jumping to the insights and conclusions regarding governance or institutional design, we need to know how those insights and conclusions were produced, what was the conceptual apparatus leading to them. Second, it is important to note that this volume is the result of a kind invitation and a challenge. The invitation-challenge to put together this collection came from Dario Castiglione as the editor of the European Consortium for Political Research (ECPR) Press. Recognizing the significance of Elinor and Vincent Ostrom's work for political science and social sciences more generally, as well as the fact that the nature and relevance of that work is still not very well understood, the Press wanted to encourage the publishing of a book capturing some of the most universally valuable aspects of the Ostroms' scientific work. As Castiglione put it to us, the ECPR Press was keen to sponsor a volume that would make the case for the political science relevance of the Ostroms' views, unambiguously clear to an international audience of social scientists. In other words, he wanted to have distilled or pinpointed (beyond the inevitably US-driven intellectual and policy related facets of the Bloomington scholars work), a set of essential features of general scholarly relevance.

In thankfully accepting the challenge, we decided that there are two ways of responding to it. The first was to focus on the most general governance theory insights – on what one could learn from the Ostroms' work on governance systems, institutional design and public and non-profit administrative processes and on the directions for future work in this respect that are emerging from those insights. The other was to focus on the Ostroms' analytical and theoretical approach, on the conceptual instruments and the epistemic logic driving their investigations and perspective. Both ways are equally relevant and legitimate in representing the broad relevance of the Bloomington scholars' contribution to social sciences.

We decided to go with the second approach for several reasons: First, it is interesting and intriguing. As we discovered, the process of putting together the readings for the volume dealing with a combination of public choice, institutionalism (old and new), rational choice and behavioral decision theory – all inherent to their theoretical endeavours – is a truly thought-provoking intellectual challenge. Second, as already mentioned, the type of themes and considerations covered in this volume are, in an epistemological sense, more basic, more foundational. They seem to hold the keys to the entire research program. The governance research is framed and driven by them. The Ostroms themselves seemed to have an acute sense of this fact. Again and again, over time, they returned to further (re)define, explore, reframe and reconstruct or add new elements to this theory-and-approach component of their thinking. As a result, the more one becomes familiar with it, the more obvious becomes the character of the project, including its strikingly dynamic and open-ended nature.

Finally, this is not a domain or theme that has received sufficient attention so far in the growing literature dealing with (or building on) the Ostroms' work. The unique focus developed by the present book raises thus in itself an important challenge. In the light of this collection, readers will realize that the Ostroms indeed left behind a veritable work in progress. They opened the way not only for a series of remarkable empirical and applied investigations but also for a fascinating domain of theoretical and analytical explorations, inviting further developments and elaborations. This volume thus, ultimately, may be seen as a vehicle for a renewed and refocused engagement with this line of research. It is one possible way to introduce to the international community of social scientists the Bloomington school's intellectual approach and at the same time it is an invitation or challenge to further explore and develop this fascinating and ultimately practically relevant research program.

There is an additional set of challenges intrinsic to this volume, and it comes from seeing the Ostroms' research program as a case study of a successful social science research program worth a special investigation in order to understand the nature of its theoretical dynamics and the role the theoretical dimension has in its success. The fact that the Ostroms and their associates contributed in major and diverse ways to our understanding of social, political and economic order is uncontroversial. The respect and recognition their work receives from diverse communities of social scientists and even beyond the boundaries of that community is well documented. Their contributions on different topics and themes – positive and normative, explanatory, descriptive and interpretative – are models of social science research practice at its best. We have hence, by all accounts, an example of a successful research program in social sciences.

All of the above make for a very interesting case study. We have simultaneously a very successful research program and practice in contemporary social sciences, and, side by side, an ongoing intellectual effort to specify, meditate at and elaborate the theoretical lenses, social philosophy and epistemic principles recognised as pivotal to that practice. Hence the questions: How did they do it? How are we to place, more precisely, that work as a whole in the broader picture of the various traditions and perspectives of social science? What was the theoretical pivot and driver they used in their work and what was the epistemological status of their theoretical apparatus? What is the specific nature of their approach?

We know both from their own statements and from the scholars that commented on that issue that the Ostroms were deeply opposed to the mainstream positivist philosophy of science of their day as well as to the positivist ethos of formulaic empiricism lingering for decades in social sciences, long after the demise of that doctrine in the philosophy of sciences. We are thus led to ask, what does that mean for their theoretical frameworks and approaches? What are we to make of the fact that we have a solid, by all accounts thriving empirical, theoretical and normative research program that was successful somehow against the underlying epistemic tone of the milieu within which it operated. How did they succeed in this endeavour? What is going on in terms of theory and philosophy of science? If we all agree that the program is a success then the question is in what measure could we learn from its study as a case of 'best practice' something about the theoretical and epistemic ingredients of that success?

These questions raise a thought-provoking challenge: To see the Bloomington School as a case of scientific practice and try to investigate its success with a special view to its theoretical component. It is not easy to illuminate the relevant theoretical features and then chart how they were connected to practice and with what epistemic consequences. But the challenge may go in fact even deeper. It is well known that often there is a disjunction or incongruence between the 'philosophical' reconstruction and interpretation of scientific practices and approaches and the way the actual research is done. Even more, there is often a substantial gap between what scientists may say about the epistemological facets of their work or their cognitive practices and their work practices themselves. What scientists think they do, and what they actually do, may be markedly different things.

Hence, the contributions in this volume seek to address an additional challenge that comes in the form of several questions: In what measure the kind of theoretical and epistemic approach identified as essential for the Ostroms' work is indeed essential to it? Is the story of the success of the Bloomington program to be written on the theoretical and epistemic lines assumed and presented by its founders? Are there any other further elements or aspects to be considered? Is there any divergence between what they considered as essential and what an external, neutral observer may identify as essential? In this respect, this collection may also be seen as an instrument of an investigation on these lines. It provides a set of readings that, once seen in the light of the above questions, they become an open invitation to revisit and rethink the Ostroms' legacy from a fresh angle and, at the same time, they give us an instrument and vehicle in assisting that task.

To sum up, the readings besides offering an introduction to the more theoretical dimensions of the Ostroms' work, provoke us to think about how the Ostroms' concepts, theories, frameworks and analytical approaches can be extended, improved and applied. Moreover, they lead us to consider the relationship between a successful social scientific practice and the nature of the conceptual and theoretical logic involved in its success. Implicit in this task is the need to find the links that anchor their perspective to the other contemporary intellectual schools of thought and to the history of social and political sciences.

With these parameters and objectives in mind, we have selected a collection of nine pieces authored or coauthored by Elinor and Vincent Ostrom and organized them into three sections. The first section deals with the political economy and public choice roots of their work and with the ways they developed from those roots a distinctive branch of political economy. The second section focuses on the evolution of the public choice approach and the factors that led the Ostroms to go beyond mainstream public choice. The third section consists of three contributions reflecting on the foundational and epistemological perspectives of their work.

Public choice and political economy

The Ostroms were key participants in the resurgence of political economy starting in the 1960s. They arrived to that field coming mostly from the discipline of public administration and the empirical investigation of governance issues related to natural resources, public entrepreneurship, and service industries. The Ostroms built their work on basic public choice postulates. They extended later on that foundation an impressive research program that transmuted at one point into a new form of institutional theory. Yet, they used public choice theory as a background and reference point, even when subsequently they questioned, redefined or transcended it. While insisting that *homo economicus*[1] was too narrowly conceptualized to serve as basis for the viability of constitutional democracies over time, they retained from the work of James M. Buchanan and Gordon Tullock the importance of constitutional choice for establishing the logical foundations for constitutional democracies. That is the reason why any overview of the Bloomington program has to give it a preeminent place and why, consequently, the first part of the volume brings together three pieces that give a sense of the nature of the Ostroms' relationship to public choice, the evolution of their thought in this respect, as well as of their take on the meaning (or better said, multiple meanings) of public choice.

---

1. It may be worth nothing that 'homo' in Latin has no gender; that is, it refers to both man and woman.

The first paper of the selection is a major statement of the theoretical foundations of their research program, made at the very moment when their distinctive research agenda was truly taking off. They co-authored 'Public Choice: A Different Approach to the Study of Public Administration' published in *Public Administration Review* of 1971. We considered it important to have it featured in this volume because it provides a key reference point in the evolution of the Bloomington scholars' work and a reminder of the rather special location of that work at the boundary between the applied-oriented discipline of public administration and the public choice intellectual movement with its insistence on the importance of theoretical foundations. It is a statement of the first-generation public choice outlook and at the same time a programmatic effort to introduce into the field of public administration a new way of conceptualizing and analyzing public governance problems. The text reads as fresh today as it was when it was written, more than 40 years ago. We find in it the key elements of the nascent public choice movement and a very concise, clear and enduringly instructive introduction to it and a manifest interest in its application to concrete governance puzzles and problems.

More precisely, the text presents a novel (at that time) mode of analysis of non-market decision making, based on the theoretical assumption of interacting rational individuals that act strategically, within an environment defined by decision rules or decision-making arrangements and that have to deal with different 'structures of events' (some of them described as 'collective actions' or 'public goods'). As Vincent Ostrom synthetized it a couple of years later in his landmark book *The Intellectual Crisis in American Public Administration* (1973 [2008]), an approach on those lines leads to the conclusion that no single form of organization is 'good' for all circumstances and events. Any particular organizational or institutional form has certain capabilities and is subject to specific sources of weakness or failure. Given the problem of institutional weakness and institutional failure that plagues both market arrangements and bureaucratic hierarchies, the choice of decision rules that would enable a community or group of people to reduce these weaknesses by continuously adapting and adjusting the organizational patterns, in function of shifting circumstances and preferences, is essential. With that, we have identified thus a major underlying theme of the entire Ostroms' program. An entire conceptual and theoretical universe is pivoting on these observations. The analytical strategy associated to the exploration and development of these observations is straightforward and involves both a positive and a normative theory dimension:

> The essential elements in the analysis of organizational arrangements are to (1) anticipate the consequences that follow when (2) self-interested individuals choose optimizing strategies within the structure of a situation that has reference to (3) particular organizational arrangements applied to (4) particular structures of events (goods) in the context of (5) some shared community of understanding. The optimal choice of organizational arrangements would be that which minimizes the costs associated with institutional weakness or failure (V. Ostrom 1973 [2008]: 49).

The chapter opening the volume introduces and elaborates these and related ideas. In it one may see emerging the contours of a robust methodological individualist orientation and of a theoretical framework in which the problem of the nature and structure of the 'goods' and the associated 'collective action' problems are central. All these are elements that will define the core of the Bloomington school's research over time, up to the celebrated work on the governance of commons or the explorations of a behavioral rational choice approach to institutional analysis. In brief, one may see *in nuce* in this 1971 article an entire series of themes and research directions that become salient as time went by, as well as a concise introduction to a mode of thinking that has profoundly influenced the Ostroms even when they tried to transcend it.

The second article of the section presents the Bloomington school's most distinctive and innovative extension of the political economy and public choice perspective in the domain of governance studies, the notion of polycentricity. Vincent Ostrom's 'Polycentricity: The Structural Basis of Self-Governing Systems' (Chapter Nine of his 1991 *The Meaning of American Federalism*) is a concise introduction to the notion and the phenomenon in point. (For a longer, richer and more elaborated presentation *see* V. Ostrom, 'Polycentricity', in McGinnis 1999b). A polycentric system, explains Vincent Ostrom, is one in which 'many officials and decision structures are assigned limited and relatively autonomous prerogatives to determine, enforce and alter legal relationships' and in which the elements are allowed to mutually adjust to each other 'within a general system of rules where each element acts with independence of other elements'. Such systems have specific properties and given a certain set of conditions, polycentrism may generate a very special governance structure that fosters self-governance. The performance parameters of such systems may be easily extrapolated from the public goods analysis:

> [...] one may expect that the performance of any particular polycentric system depends on the measure in which the actual arrangements on the ground corresponded to the theoretically specified conditions for efficient performance such as: the correspondence of different units of government to the scales of effects for diverse public goods; the development of cooperative arrangements among governmental units to undertake joint activities of mutual benefit; and the availability of other decision-making arrangements for processing and resolving conflicts among units of government (V. Ostrom, 'Polycentricity', in McGinnis 1999b: 55–56).

The chapter gives a bird's eye view on a series of arguments that reconfirm the centrality of the notion of polycentricity in the structure of the Ostrom paradigm. Polycentricity is a complex multifaceted concept and it is yet to be fully and systematically elaborated as an analytical instrument. It has (1) a descriptive function (it describes the complex social reality of multiple decision centers and overlapping, multi-layered jurisdictions); (2) a heuristic function (it helps identify patterns of order amidst what otherwise may look as chaotic social systems); (3)

an explanatory function (it helps identify social mechanisms and causal processes in the complex concatenation of causes and effects of complex systems); and it also has (4) a normative function. In this latter respect, it introduces a rather original approach to the problem of optimal political structures, and the issue of determining what are the main features of a functional, desirable political structure.

In the light of an approach framed using the notion of polycentricity, such a structure involves: (a) separating the provision and production of public goods (since the economies of scale of production and those of provision often differ significantly); (b) decentralizing production on functional grounds rather than political ones (because various goods are best produced at rather different scales, while the political units have a given, fixed scale); (c) inducing a role for the political units mainly in provision rather than production that would allow a significant degree of flexibility including maintaining redistributive and welfare aspects and would preserve the competitive framework for production; and (d) organizing the political units in a multi-level and overlapping manner, creating a resilient and adaptive ecosystem of rules in which debates about provision aspects (what should or should not be provided) are settled by an agreeing-to-disagree process. All that takes place within various levels of collective preference aggregation that maintain learning by trial-and-error capacity of the entire system. In brief, even a cursory review shows that the notion of polycentrism combines constructively an entire set of political economy and public choice concepts, and elements of positive and normative theory in an innovative manner that generates a fresh vision and one of the trademarks of the Bloomington school.

The third and last piece of the first section is a fascinating overview of the field of public choice as seen from the unique perspective of the Ostroms, a perspective that diverges more than in one way from the mainstream public choice school canon. The article was co-authored for a special 2004 issue of the *American Journal of Economics and Sociology*, dedicated to 'The Production and Diffusion of the Public Choice Political Economy'. The title of the Ostroms' contribution is telling: 'The Quest for Meaning in Public Choice'. The article starts by anchoring the very idea of investigations and scholarship on public choice, public governance and collective action in the Western intellectual tradition of a search for the logical foundations of good governance and democracy. It then introduces and discusses the distinction between 'frameworks', 'theories' and 'models' in the study of public choice, a distinction that, in their view, has significant consequences for the research practice. The Institutional Analysis and Development (IAD) framework, another major contribution and trademark of the Bloomington school, is introduced. Its employment at multiple levels of analysis (constitutional, governmental and operational) is described, and examples of its application in concrete research settings are given. The conclusions of the chapter revert to the broader intellectual and philosophical themes that opened up the discussion. All in all, this piece is probably one of the most original and compelling overviews and interpretations of the domain of public choice, broadly defined, existent in the literature. In addition, there is an exceptional joint statement of the Ostroms regarding their take on the key problem of naturalism and social sciences: Can social studies be reduced to natural sciences? Their response, clear, concise and straightforward:

The quest for meaning in the constitution of order in human societies cannot rely on the methods of the natural sciences. Instead, we face the challenge of developing and working with what might be called 'the sciences of the artifactual' that are broadly applicable to the cultural and social sciences and the humanities.

Last but not least the chapter challenges us to be self-conscious about the method of normative inquiry we use as we confront the fundamental question that people aspiring to be self-governing engage when they seek to transform ideas into deeds: what are the logical and moral or normative foundations of constitutional democracy and social order?

Beyond mainstream public choice

The second section of the volume consists of three pieces written by Elinor Ostrom. They all reflect the different ways in which the initial public choice political economy approach evolved and was further developed into an institutional theory direction, fuelled on a variety of innovative elements ranging from a behavioral approach to collective choice, to a reconsideration of rules and rule-guided behavior in collective action and public choice theorizing.

The first piece, 'An Agenda for the Study of Institutions', published in *Public Choice* in 1986, was initially delivered as the Presidential Address at the Public Choice Society meeting in 1984. This text is important in the architecture of the volume for two reasons: first, because it marks a considerable shift away from the direction mainstream public choice was moving at that time and in the direction of a broader institutionalist perspective. Second, because it boldly advances a rule-focused approach to analysis, a second significant shift of focus in itself. Rules were important in the public choice worldview from the very beginning. Elinor Ostrom notes that 'an unstated assumption of almost all formal models is that individuals are, in general, rule followers'. Most public choice analyses include the rules in use, or working rules, and typical public choice theorists 'know' that 'multiple levels of analysis are involved in understanding how rules affect behavior'. But, warns Ostrom, this mostly tacit knowledge 'is not self-consciously built into the way we pursue our work'. Much attention is given to choices, incentives and sometimes to information and communication while the problem of rules is too often treated as a residual.

Elinor Ostrom understands that the logic of analysis, if consistently spelled out, requires a more systematic engagement with the issues of rules. To understand their nature and their implications for rule guided behavior is at least as important as spelling out formal models of rationality or strategic behavior. Moreover, the problem is central to any theory of institutions, and even more so if one makes out of the concept of rule a key element in defining the very idea of institution. Because little agreement exists, on what the term 'institution' means, argues Ostrom, the cumulative study of institutions is fraught with problems. She does not pretend to come with the 'right definition' but she makes a strong case for the analytical utility of one concept – that of rules – used as a referent for the term 'institution'. She distinguishes rules from physical or behavioral laws and discusses the prescriptive and normative nature of rules with a view to the analytical implications. She considers how rules are approached in public choice theory and draws attention to the configurational character of rules and to the multiple levels of analysis required for their systematic study.

In reading this piece, one key point in her argument should not be missed. Elinor Ostrom makes very clear that her position entails more than simply 'viewing rules as directly affecting behavior', a sort of naïve determinist and pseudo-behaviorist pre-analytical assumption common in the literature. She is emphatic that she views 'rules as directly affecting the structure of a situation in which actions are selected'. Rules 'rarely prescribe one and only one action or outcome'. Instead, 'rules specify sets of actions or sets of outcome'. This is not a minor point. As explicitly noted in the next chapter, that entails an entire paradigm or worldview: 'a world of possibility rather than of necessity'. Social actors 'are neither trapped in inexorable tragedies nor free of moral responsibility' for their individual or collective actions that create or change their institutional or organizational environment. This position entails a major epistemological, theoretical component. The intentionality and possibilist features of rules and rule-guided behavior, the multiple levels, nested systems that are intrinsic to them, require 'a self-conscious awareness of the methodological consequences'. We are moving thus further and further away from the positivist epistemology and methodology. The chapter ends up outlining an entire research agenda in institutional theory and public choice that instead of putting the main focus on the formal modelling of rationality in decision making and its algorithms, it focuses its main interest on the problem of rules and issues such as:

> the problem of the origin and change of rule configurations in use. How do individuals evolve a particular rule configuration? What factors affect the likelihood of their following a set of rules? What affects the enforcement of rules? How is the level of enforcement related to rule conformance? What factors affect the reproducibility and reliability of a rule system? When is it possible to develop new rules through self-conscious choice? And, when are new rules bound to fail?

In brief, the chapter lets us get a glimpse of an entire dimension of institutional theory and public choice analysis that is yet to be fully explored and developed. In other words, 'An agenda for the study of institutions' is a truly programmatic statement that deserves its place in a volume like this.

The next chapter of this section is Elinor Ostrom's 1997 American Political Science Association Presidential Address: 'A Behavioral Approach to the Rational Choice Theory of Collective Action' (Ostrom 1998). The importance of this contribution in the architecture of the book is hard to exaggerate. Ostrom discusses a new generation of rational choice models, and the need to expand the range of those models and about their use as foundations for the study of social dilemmas and collective action. The dominant theories of collective action do not provide convincing explanations of collective action. Still, the fact remains that the theory of collective action is the central subject of political science and crucial for any attempt to understand governance systems: 'If political scientists do not have an empirically grounded theory of collective action, then we are hand-waving at our central questions. I am afraid that we do a lot of hand-waving'. The point is evident: 'we need to formulate a behavioral theory of boundedly rational and moral behavior'.

The chapter reviews the accepted rational choice theory of the day and its application to the study of social dilemmas while discussing the problem of the models of rationality in the light of the results generated by extensive experimental research. It then turns to discussion of the empirical findings that show how individuals achieve results that are 'better than rational' by 'building conditions where reciprocity, reputation, and trust can help to overcome the strong temptations of short-run self-interest'. It considers the issue of second-generation models of rationality and develops a relevant theoretical scenario. Finally, it looks at the implications of 'placing reciprocity, reputation, and trust at the core of an empirically tested, behavioral theory of collective action'.

This chapter is a veritable tour de force. One cannot give enough justice to the wealth and density of ideas and insights it contains. There are at least three important implications of those insights that reveal how and why the theoretical core of the Ostrom program inspires a broader and deeper vision transcending the boundaries of the social scientific and academic universe. The first, already been mentioned, is the point about the potential for constituting social order drawing on the moral and social capital available, going beyond determinism and social traps. It is a basic postulate of a social philosophy of human freedom and responsibility:

> What the research on social dilemmas demonstrates is a world of possibility rather than of necessity. We are neither trapped in inexorable tragedies nor free of moral responsibility for creating and sustaining incentives that facilitate our own achievement of mutually productive outcomes.

Second is the fact that the theory of rationality suggested by Elinor Ostrom has rather momentous applied-level consequences. Reconsidering in a realistic manner both the limits and the capabilities of human rationality leads to a reconsideration of the structure and function of even the most familiar institutional arrangements. In the light of such an exercise, we may be compelled to adjust familiar views on familiar governance arrangements. For instance:

> A broader theory of rationality leads to potentially different views of the state. If one sees individuals as helpless, then the state is the essential external authority that must solve social dilemmas for everyone. If, however, one assumes individuals can draw on heuristics and norms to solve some problems and create new structural arrangements to solve others, then the image of what a national government might do is somewhat different. There is a very

considerable role for large-scale governments [...] But national governments are too small to govern the global commons and too big to handle smaller scale problems.

Finally are the implications for civic education, a corollary of all of the above, and a major theme of the Ostrom agenda. This is worthwhile emphasizing because usually this theme of major preoccupation for the Ostroms is rarely recognized as such by commentators:

> We need to translate our research findings on collective action into materials written for high school and undergraduate students. All too many of our textbooks focus exclusively on leaders and, worse, only national-level leaders. Students completing an introductory course [on political science] [...] will not learn that they play an essential role in sustaining democracy. [...] It is ordinary persons and citizens who craft and sustain the workability of the institutions of everyday life. We owe an obligation to the next generation to carry forward the best of our knowledge about how individuals solve the multiplicity of social dilemmas large and small – that they face.

The last chapter of the second section is a revised version of the lecture Elinor Ostrom delivered in Stockholm, Sweden, on December 8, 2009, when she received the Bank of Sweden Prize in Economic Sciences in Memory of Alfred Nobel. It was published in 2010 by *The American Economic Review*, under the title of 'Beyond Markets and States: Polycentric Governance of Complex Economic Systems'. In it, E. Ostrom describes the intellectual journey spanning more than half of a century from graduate studies in the late 1950s and early efforts working with Vincent Ostrom and Charles M. Tiebout on delineating features of polycentric systems at work in California, to the development of the Institutional Analysis and Development (IAD) framework enabling her and her colleagues 'to undertake a variety of empirical studies including a meta-analysis of a large number of existing case studies on common-pool resource systems around the world'. This chapter may be read as a personal self-effacing survey of the range of work done in the Bloomington tradition, both theoretically and empirically. The capstone of the sequence of six chapters, gives content to the first two sections of the book, adding to the picture a more substantive outlook of the empirical dimension of the program and its coevolution with the theoretical one. The chapter fittingly completes our overview thus far. At this point it is to be hoped that the reader will have a clear understanding of the nature, evolution and significance of the Ostroms research program and its theoretical dimension. We are now in the position to fully turn our attention towards the foundational and epistemic dimension.

Foundational and epistemological perspectives

The third section of the volume consists of three pieces that each reflects several defining aspects of this dimension. The first is an excerpt from Elinor Ostrom's introduction to her edited volume *Strategies of Political Inquiry,* published in 1982. The introduction is tellingly titled 'Beyond Positivism'. It is a piece in which we see Elinor Ostrom taking a direct stab at a philosophy of science and philosophy of research practice theme. The result is an anthological criticism of the mainstream views on the nature and foundations of political science, a spectacular statement in favor of a truly scholarly and nuanced theory-centred approach to political science.

Elinor Ostrom makes a forceful case against formulaic empiricism, and 'the heavy emphasis on descriptive, empirical, quantitative work' detrimental to real analytical and scholarly reflection. That misplaced focus 'may have resulted from the naive acceptance of a particular school of philosophy of science'. She is not shy of naming it: the logical positivist doctrine as the uniquely appropriate 'scientific method to form the foundation of the social sciences'. At the same time, she makes an equally forceful case in favor of the efforts to 're-establish the priority of theory over data collection and analysis' while warning that 'what constitutes proper theory is used differently here from the definition of theory articulated by logical positivists and accepted by many scholars in the discipline'. In just a handful of vivid anthological paragraphs she manages to capture the spirit of an entire epoch that has marked for better or for worse the evolution of contemporary political science:

> With the 'rock bottom' approach, as Popper calls it, scientific theories could not be constructed until political science had undertaken substantial hard-nosed empirical work to find the empirical laws to become the bedrock of the discipline. With missionary zeal, several generations of young colleagues went forth to collect data so that a political science could be constructed using their empirical findings as *the* foundation. Many of the early generations in this revolution were armed for the foray with minimal statistical training and no training in mathematics or logic. [...] The combined effect of this recruitment process interacting with this type of socialization may have produced a 'know nothing' era in the discipline.

Elinor Ostrom goes on to explain that fortunately, many scholars (obviously including the contributors to her edited volume) 'are taking major steps to reestablish the priority of theory over data collection and analysis'. They are thus inducing and reflecting 'a subtle change occurring across political science and the sister disciplines of economics, sociology, and psychology'. In what measure that change has been successful and where do things stand now in terms of the residual positivism and formulaic empiricism of nowadays, is a separate discussion in itself.

The second piece of the section is by Vincent Ostrom and was published in 1979 as an opening chapter in Daniel Elazar's *Constitutional Design and Power-Sharing in the Post-Modern Epoch.* The chapter, fittingly titled 'A Conceptual-

Computational Logic for Federal Systems of Governance', offers a glimpse at the less visible social philosophical thought that associates the theoretical and empirical endeavours of the Bloomington scholars. Vincent Ostrom discusses what he identifies as the fundamental methodological problems of 'the basic conceptions that are used to frame our inquiries' on federal systems and governance in general. Ingrained in his argument is the notion that clarifying the methodological problem requires clarifying an epistemological problem and that, in turn, requires clarifying an ontological problem.

He makes it clear why a methodological doctrine that grows and evolves independently of any ontological concerns may be sooner rather than later floating freely in a sphere that has less and less analytical and empirical relevance. Whether we like it or not, we have to 'raise questions about the nature of political and social phenomena'. It may not be fashionable to ask such questions but the fact is that 'if human beings, at least in part, create their own social realities', then sooner or later, the challenge that is facing us in our investigations 'is to reconsider the epistemological and metaphysical grounds on which we stand'. That is, observers need to learn to recognize that ordinary people can construct their own realities and fashion rules and norms that apply to the constitution of self-governing entities. The social world of institutions, constitutions and governance arrangements is a universe of artisanship that is ongoing, created and recreated by ideas and the actions inspired by these ideas. Unfashionable as it may be, it looks like one should consider the fact that 'to the degree to which choice is possible and alternative possibilities are available, we might anticipate that different conceptions may be used to design, construct, and maintain different social realities'. In revisiting the crisis of centralized American public administration in 2008, Vincent Ostrom reiterated the point this way: 'becoming aware that human beings can draw upon different conceptions and systems of ideas to fashion different social realities is a fundamental step to becoming a master artisan in public administration and in the study of human societies' (V. Ostrom 2008: xxix).

This is indeed a crucial observation about the phenomenon of interest: the realm of social and institutional reality is based on human agency and that agency is at least in part fuelled by ideas and deliberation. 'Human beings as artisans conceptualize alternative possibilities and work through the computational logics that enable them to realize different possibilities'. That should definitely have theoretical and methodological consequences.

In other words, this chapter reveals how the entire Ostromian research program rests on a firmly assured position in the grand debate regarding the nature of the social reality and the nature of social sciences. In this respect, Vincent Ostrom is as straightforward as Elinor Ostrom was in her above mentioned introduction to her edited volume *Strategies of Political Inquiry*. The dominant naturalism and positivism are a hindrance to understanding, making impossible a fruitful theoretical and methodological approach:

Political discourse in the twentieth century has been dominated by a presupposition that 'natural' tendencies exist in systems of governance where models of government are assumed to be unitary in character and the method of the natural sciences apply to the investigation of political phenomena. There is no point to intentionality in construing the meaning of political experience if that experience is viewed as only manifesting natural tendencies.

The application of the natural science methods to the study of political phenomena notes Ostrom, has meant 'the abandonment of any serious preoccupation with the critical problems of constitutional choice and the conceptual-computational logics that inform the artisanship inherent in the design and alteration of systems of governance as these are constituted and reconstituted'. The result is a compounded misunderstanding of the multiple functions and dimensions that 'political theory' has in building and understanding institutional order. Political science 'has become a science without an explicit understanding of the critical role of theory as a system of conceptual-computational logics that applies to the design of different systems of government'. To sum up, this chapter is an excellent illustration of an entire set of arguments and interpretations that reveal the remarkable, profound and subtle link between the foundational-philosophical side and the empirical and the applied side of the Ostromian program.

The last chapter, an excerpt from Vincent Ostrom's last book, *The Meaning of Democracy and the Vulnerability of Democracies: A Response to Tocqueville's Challenge* (1997) brings further evidence in this respect. The reflections entitled 'Epistemic Choice and Public Choice' is a return to the roots of the Bloomington school, revisiting some of the core themes of the public choice intellectual movement. Now, in the presence of three or four decades of cumulative efforts in the public choice tradition, how does one of its founders assess the prospects for the next generation? The text is an attempt to evaluate and reconsider the hard core and periphery of the program. In revisiting some key themes of the underlying philosophy of public choice, the chapter opens a new direction of inquiry that transcends the core first-generation models. His key observation is rather striking: the real potential of the program comes now from 'the diverse thrusts on the peripheries of work in the Public-Choice tradition rather than with efforts at the core of the tradition to apply "economic reasoning" to "nonmarket decision making," as the Public-Choice approach has been conceptualized by the mainstream of Public-Choice scholars'.

The public choice program, as we knew it, may be heading into a dead-end. A solution is to develop a more problem driven approach 'to address how basic anomalies, social dilemmas, and puzzles can be resolved in human affairs, rather than to apply economic reasoning, narrowly construed, to nonmarket decision making'. Yet, this solution raises new problems regarding the nature and coherence of public choice as a discipline. One may easily imagine that these issue-driven efforts at the periphery of the public choice approach will be 'only miscellaneous idiosyncratic accretions', 'fleeting fads' leading to a Tower of Babel. Would it be possible in such circumstances to reconstruct a cumulative investigation front, with lines of inquiry that are complementary to one another?

After framing the issue in these terms, Vincent Ostrom goes well beyond the mainstream and familiar public choice territory, discussing an entire range of issues that touch in profound ways precisely this 'periphery' identified as rich in potentialities. Once this intriguing idea is introduced, an equally intriguing corollary becomes evident: a scientific community is confronted with a special type of collective choice when making decisions about the directions and parameters of its common research program. They are coproducers and they need to coordinate on the nature of the product in cases and practices associated to it. It is a matter of 'public' choice at an epistemic level about what is worthy of inclusion in the corpus of knowledge. Hence, we have the idea of 'epistemic choice'. With it the tantalizing prospect that limiting the theory of choice at the lowest common abstract denominator, universally applicable, may not be the optimal epistemic strategy. One may have a multifaceted, heterogeneous theory of choice:

> [...] the principles of choice applicable to the warrantability of knowledge are different than the principles of choice applicable to a choice of goods in market and public economies. These are different than the principles of choice applicable to the constitution of rule-ordered relationships in accordance with standards of fairness. Principles of consensus among participants can apply to each, but the criteria of choice vary among different types of choice.

The chapter starts with the problem of epistemic choice, 'the choice of conceptualizations, assertions, and information to be used and acted on in problem-solving modes' and then 'relate that problem to the arraying of elements in a framework implicit in the Public-Choice tradition'. It is a captivating overview of themes and insights some of which are not usually directly associated to the public choice paradigm. Yet, in Vincent Ostrom's broad and reflective discussion that ties them together, one realizes that theorizing in the public choice tradition is more than a technical or pure analytical approach. We get a better sense why Vincent Ostrom is fully entitled to claim that the next stage in our ongoing efforts to better understand collective action, public choice, governance and institutions we 'need to go back to basics to reconsider the human condition and what it means to be a human being relating to other human beings in the world in which they live'.

To sum up, the nine chapters of this volume, once seen in conjunction, offer a comprehensive, consistent and nuanced introduction to the Ostroms' work, along the lines of the theoretical dimensions of their program. The closer we get to the core ideas of the program, the better we realize the open-ended nature of the Ostrom enterprise: a fascinating work in progress, exploring the realm of human institutions, governance and collective action with the view to the institutional design and citizenship implications of the insights thus gained.

References

Aligica, P. D. and Boettke, P. J. (2009) *Challenging Institutional Analysis and Development: The Bloomington School,* New York: Routledge.

Allen, B. (ed.) (2011) Vincent Ostrom, *The Quest to Understand Human Affairs: Natural Resources Policy and Essays on Community and Collective Choice,* Vol 1., Lanham, MD: Lexington Books.

— (ed.) (2012) Vincent Ostrom, *The Quest to Understand Human Affairs: Essays on Collective, Constitutional and Epistemic Choice,* Vol 2., Lanham, MD: Lexington Books.

Eucken, W. (1951) *The Foundations of Economics,* Chicago: University of Chicago Press.

McGinnis, M. D. (ed.) (1999a) *Polycentric Governance and Development: Readings from the Workshop in Political Theory and Policy Analysis,* Ann Arbor: The University of Michigan Press.

— (ed.) (1999b) *Polycentricity and Local Public Economies: Readings from the Workshop in Political Theory and Policy Analysis,* Ann Arbor: The University of Michigan Press.

— (ed.) (2000) *Polycentric Games and Institutions: Readings from the Workshop in Political Theory and Policy Analysis,* Ann Arbor: The University of Michigan Press.

— (2011) 'Elinor Ostrom: Politics as Problem Solving in Polycentric Settings' in D. Campus, G. Pasquino and M. Bull (eds) *Maestri of Political Science* vol. 2, Colchester: ECPR Press, pp. 137–158.

Ostrom, V. [1973] (2008) *The Intellectual Crisis in American Public Administration,* 3rd edn, Tuscaloosa: The University of Alabama Press.

— [1990] (1999) 'Problems of Cognition as a Challenge to Policy Analysts and Democratic Societies', in M. D. McGinnis (ed.) (1999) *Polycentric Governance and Development: Readings from the Workshop in Political Theory and Policy Analysis,* Ann Arbor: The University of Michigan Press, pp. 394–415.

— (1991) *The Meaning of American Federalism: Constituting a Self-governing Society,* San Francisco: Institute for Contemporary Studies Press.

Poteete, A., Janssen, M. A. and Ostrom, E. (2010) *Working Together: Collective Action, the Commons, and Multiple Methods in Practice,* Princeton: Princeton University Press.

Sabetti, F., B. Allen and M. Sproule-Jones, (eds) (2009) *The Practice of Constitutional Development: Vincent Ostrom's Quest to Understand Human Affairs,* Lanham, MD, Lexington Books.

Sproule-Jones, M., B. Allen and F. Sabetti, (eds) (2008) *The Struggle to Constitute and Sustain Productive Orders: Vincent Ostrom's Quest to Understand Human Affairs,* Lanham, MD: Lexington Books.

Part One

Public Choice and Political Economy

Chapter One

Public Choice: A Different Approach to the Study of Public Administration[1]

Vincent Ostrom and Elinor Ostrom

In November 1963, a number of economists and a sprinkling of other social scientists were invited by James Buchanan and Gordon Tullock to explore a community of interest in the study of nonmarket decision making. That conference was reported in *Public Administration Review* as 'Developments in the "No-Name" Fields of Public Administration' (vol. 24, March 1964, pp. 62–63). A shared interest prevailed regarding the application of economic reasoning to 'collective', 'political' or 'social' decision making, but no consensus developed on the choice of a name to characterize those interests. In December 1967 the decision was taken to form a Public Choice Society and to publish a journal, *Public Choice*. The term 'public choice' will be used here to refer to the work of this community of scholars. The bibliography following this article refers to only a small fraction of the relevant literature, but will serve to introduce the reader to public choice literature.

The public choice approach needs to be related to basic theoretical traditions in public administration. As background, we shall first examine the theoretical tradition as formulated by Wilson and those who followed. We shall next examine Herbert Simon's challenge to that tradition which has left the discipline in what Dwight Waldo has characterized as a 'crisis of identity' (Waldo 1968). The relevance of the public choice approach for dealing with the issues raised by Simon's challenge will then be considered.

The traditional theory of public administration

Woodrow Wilson's essay, 'The Study of Administration', called for a new science of administration based upon a radical distinction between politics and administration (Wilson 1887: 210). According to Wilson, governments may differ in the political principles reflected in their constitutions, but the principles of good administration are much the same in any system of government. There is '[...] but one rule of good administration for all governments alike', was Wilson's major thesis (Wilson 1887: 218). 'So far as administrative functions are concerned, all

1. Published initially in *Public Administration Review*, vol. 31 (no.2, Mar–April 1971), pp. 203–216.

governments have a strong structural likeness; more than that, if they are to be uniformly useful and efficient, they must have a strong structural likeness' (Wilson 1887: 218).

Good administration, according to Wilson, will be hierarchically ordered in a system of graded ranks subject to political direction by heads of departments at the centre of government. The ranks of administration would be filled by a corps of technically trained civil servants '[...] prepared by a special schooling and drilled, after appointment, into a perfected organization, with an appropriate hierarchy and characteristic discipline [...]' (Wilson 1887: 216). Perfection in administrative organization is attained in a hierarchically ordered and professionally trained public service. Efficiency is attained by perfection in the hierarchical ordering of a professionally trained public service. Wilson also conceptualizes efficiency in economic terms: '[...] the utmost possible efficiency and at the least possible cost of either money or of energy' (Wilson 1887: 197).

For the next half-century, the discipline of public administration developed within the framework set by Wilson. The ends of public administration were seen as the 'management of men and material in the accomplishment of the purposes of the state' (White 1926). Hierarchical structure was regarded as the ideal pattern of organization. According to L. D. White, 'All large-scale organisations follow the same pattern, which in essence consists in the universal application of the superior-subordinate relationship through a number of levels of responsibility reaching from the top to the bottom of the structure' (White 1926: 33).

Simon's challenge

Herbert Simon, drawing in part upon previous work by Luther Gulick, (Gulick and Urwick 1937) sustained a devastating critique of the theory implicit in the traditional study of public administration. In his *Administrative Behavior*, Simon elucidated some of the accepted administrative principles and demonstrated the lack of logical coherence among them. (Simon 1964) Simon characterized those principles as 'proverbs'. Like proverbs, incompatible principles allowed the administrative analyst to justify his position in relation to one or another principle. 'No single one of these items is of sufficient importance', Simon concluded, 'to suffice as a guiding principle for the administrative analyst' (Simon 1964: 36).

After his indictment of traditional administrative theory, Simon began an effort to reconstruct administrative theory. The first stage was 'the construction of an adequate vocabulary and analytic scheme'. Simon's reconstruction began with a distinction between facts and values. Individuals engage in a consideration of facts and of values in choosing among alternative possibilities bounded by the ordered rationality of an organization. Simon envisioned the subsequent stage of reconstruction to involve the establishment of a bridge between theory and empirical study 'so that theory could provide a guide to the design of "critical" experiments and studies, while experimental study could provide a sharp test and corrective of theory' (Simon 1964: 44).

One of Simon's central concerns was to establish the criterion of efficiency as a norm for evaluating alternative administrative actions. Simon argued that the 'criterion of efficiency dictates that choice of alternatives which produce the largest result for the given application of resources' (Simon 1964: 179). In order to utilize the criterion of efficiency, the results of administrative actions must be defined and measured. Clear conceptual definitions of output are necessary before measures can be developed.

No necessary reason existed, Simon argued, for assuming that perfection in hierarchical ordering would always be the most efficient organisational arrangement (Simon 1962: 1969). Alternative organisational forms needed to be empirically evaluated to determine their relative efficiency. Simon's own work with Ridley on the measurement of municipal activities represented a beginning effort to identify the output of government agencies and to develop indices to measure those outputs. (Ridley and Simon 1938)

The work of the political economists

During the period following Simon's challenge, another community of scholars has grappled with many of these same intellectual issues. This community of scholars has been composed predominantly of political economists who have been concerned with public investment and public expenditure decisions. One facet of this work has been manifest in benefit-cost analysis and the development of the PPB system (U.S. Congress, Joint Economic Committee, Subcommittee on Economy in Government, 1969). PPB analysis rests upon much the same theoretical grounds as the traditional theory of public administration. The PPB analyst is essentially taking the methodological perspective of an 'omniscient observer' or a 'benevolent despot'. Assuming that he knows the 'will of the state', the PPB analyst selects a program for the efficient utilization of resources (i.e., men and material) in the accomplishment of those purposes. As Senator McClelland has correctly perceived, the assumption of omniscience may not hold; and, as a consequence, PPB analysis may involve radical errors and generate gross inefficiencies (Wildavsky 1966).

Public choice represents another facet of work in political economy with more radical implications for the theory of public administration. Most political economists in the public choice tradition begin with the individual as the basic unit of analysis. Traditional 'economic man' is replaced by 'man: the decision maker'.

The second concern in the public choice tradition is with the conceptualization of public goods as the type of event associated with the output of public agencies. These efforts are closely related to Simon's concern for the definition and measurement of the results of administrative action. In addition, public choice theory is concerned with the effect that different decision rules or decision-making arrangements will have upon the production of those events conceptualized as public goods and services. Thus, a model of man, the type of event characterized as public goods and services, and decision structures comprise the analytical variables in public choice theory. Our 'man: the decision maker' will confront certain opportunities and possibilities in the world of events and will pursue his relative advantage within the strategic opportunities afforded by different types of decision rules or decision-making arrangements. The consequences are evaluated by whether or not the outcome is consistent with the efficiency criterion.

Work in public choice begins with methodological individualism where the perspective of a representative individual is used for analytical purposes (Brodbeck 1958). Since the individual is the basic unit of analysis, the assumptions made about individual behavior become critical in building a coherent theory (Coleman 1966a, 1966b). Four basic assumptions about individual behavior are normally made.

First, individuals are assumed to be self-interested. The word 'self-interest' is not equivalent to 'selfish'. The assumption of self-interest implies primarily that individuals each have their own preferences which affect the decisions they make, and that those preferences may differ from individual to individual (Buchanan and Tullock 1965).

Secondly, individuals are assumed to be rational. Rationality is defined as the ability to rank all known alternatives available to the individual in a transitive manner. Ranking implies that a rational individual either values alternative 'A' more than alternative 'B', or that he prefers alternative 'B' to alternative 'A', or that he is indifferent as between them. Transitivity means that if he prefers alternative 'A' to alternative 'B', and 'B' is preferred to 'C', then 'A' is necessarily preferred to 'C'. (Boulding 1966; Eulau 1964).

Third, individuals are assumed to adopt maximizing strategies. Maximization as a strategy implies the consistent choice of those alternatives which an individual thinks will provide the highest net benefit as weighed by his own preferences (Wade and Curry 1970). At times the assumption of maximization is related to that of satisfying, depending upon assumptions about the information available to an individual in a decision-making situation (Simon 1957).

Fourth, an explicit assumption needs to be stated concerning the level of information possessed by a representative individual. Three levels have been analytically defined as involving certainty, risk, and uncertainty (Knight 1965; Luce and Raiffa 1957). The condition of certainty is defined to exist when: (1) an individual knows all available strategies, (2) each strategy is known to lead invariably to only one specific outcome, and (3) the individual knows his own preferences for each outcome. Given this level of information, the decision of a maximizing individual is completely determined. He simply chooses that strategy which leads to the outcome for which he has the highest preference (Fishburn 1964).

Under conditions of risk, the individual is still assumed to know all available strategies. Any particular strategy may lead to a number of potential outcomes, and the individual is assumed to know the probability of each outcome (Arrow 1951). Thus, decision making becomes a weighting process whereby his preferences for different outcomes are combined with the probability of their occurrence prior to a selection of a strategy. Under risk, an individual may adopt mixed strategies in an effort to obtain the highest level of outcomes over a series of decisions in the long run.

Decision making under uncertainty is assumed to occur either where (1) an individual has a knowledge of all strategies and outcomes, but lacks knowledge about the probabilities with which a strategy may lead to an outcome, or (2) an individual may not know all strategies or all outcomes which actually exist (Hart 1965; Radner 1970). Uncertainty is more characteristic of problematical situations than either certainty or risk. Under either certainty or risk, an analyst can project a relatively determinant solution to a particular problem. Under conditions of uncertainty, the determinateness of solutions is replaced by conclusions about the range of possible 'solutions' (Shackle 1961).

Once uncertainty is postulated, a further assumption may be made that an individual learns about states of affairs as he develops and tests strategies. (Simon 1959; Thompson 1966) Estimations are made about the consequences of strategies. If the predicted results follow, then a more reliable image of the world is established. If predicted results fail to occur, the individual is forced to change his image of the world and modify his strategies (Ostrom 1968). Individuals who learn may adopt a series of diverse strategies as they attempt to reduce the level of uncertainty in which they are operating (Cyert and March 1963; Stigler 1961).

The nature of public goods and services

Individuals who are self-interested, rational, and who pursue maximizing strategies find themselves in a variety of situations. Such situations involve the production and consumption of a variety of goods. Political economists in the public choice tradition distinguish situations involving purely private goods as a logical category from purely public goods (Davis and Winston 1967; Samuelson 1955; 1954). Purely private goods are defined as those goods and services which are highly divisible and can be (1) packaged, contained, or measured in discrete units, and (2) provided under competitive market conditions where potential consumers can be excluded from enjoying the benefit unless they are willing to pay the price. Purely public goods, by contrast, are highly indivisible goods and services where potential consumers cannot be easily excluded from enjoying the benefits (Breton 1966). Once public goods are provided for some, they will be available for others to enjoy without reference to who pays the costs. National defence is a classic example of a public good. Once it is provided for some individuals living within a particular country, it is automatically provided for all individuals who are citizens of that country, whether they pay for it or not.

In addition to the two logical categories of purely private and purely public goods, most political economists would postulate the existence of an intermediate continuum. Within this continuum, the production or consumption of goods or services may involve spill-over effects or externalities which are not isolated and contained within market transactions (Ayres and Kneese 1969; Buchanan and Stubblebine 1962; Davis and Winston 1962; Mishan 1967). Goods with appreciable spill overs are similar to private goods to the extent that some effects can be subject to the exclusion principle; but other effects are like public goods and spill over onto others not directly involved (Coase 1960). The air pollution which results from the production of private industry is an example of a negative externality. Efforts to reduce the cost of a negative externality is the equivalent of providing a public good. The benefits produced for a neighbourhood by the location of a golf course or park is a positive externality.

The existence of public goods or significant externalities creates a number of critical problems for individuals affected by those circumstances (Buchanan, 1968; Head 1962; Phelps 1965). Each individual will maximize his net welfare if he takes advantage of a public good at minimum cost to himself (Demsetz 1967). He will have little or no incentive to take individual action where the effect of individual action would be to conserve or maintain the quality of the good that each shares in common. Each individual is likely to adopt a 'dog-in-the-manger' strategy by pursuing his own advantage and disregarding the consequences of his action upon others. Furthermore, individuals may not even be motivated to articulate their own honest preferences for a common good. (Demsetz 1970; Musgrave 1959; Thompson 1968) If someone proposes an improvement in the quality of a public good, some individuals may have an incentive to withhold information about their preferences for such an improvement (Schelling 1963). If others were to make the improvement, the individual who had concealed his preference could then indicate that he was not a beneficiary and might avoid paying his share of the costs. If voluntary action is proposed, some individuals will have an incentive to 'hold-out', act as 'free-riders', and take advantage of the benefits provided by others (Cunningham 1967; Hirshleifer, DeHaven and Milliman 1960). Garret Hardin had indicated that these strategies typically give rise to 'the tragedy of the commons' where increased individual effort leaves everyone worse off (Hardin 1968).

The effect of decision structures upon collective action

The Problem of Collective Inaction. The problem arising from the indivisibility of a public good and the structure of individual incentives created by the failure of an exclusion principle is the basis for Mancur Olson's *The Logic of Collective Action* (Olson 1965). Olson concludes that individuals cannot be expected to form large voluntary associations to pursue matters of public interest unless special conditions exist (Musgrave 1939). Individuals will form voluntary associations in pursuit of public interests only when members will derive separable benefits of a sufficient magnitude to justify the cost of membership or where they can be coerced into bearing their share of the costs (Burgess and Robinson 1969; Garvey 1969; Leoni 1957). Thus, we cannot expect persons to organise themselves in a strictly voluntary association to realize their common interest in the provision of public goods and services. An individual's actions will be calculated by the probability that his efforts alone will make a difference. If that probability is nil, and if he is a rational person, we would expect his effort to be nil.

Constitutional choice and collective action

The analysis of Mancur Olson would lead us to conclude that undertaking collective actions to provide public goods and services such as national defence, public parks, and education is not easily accomplished. If unanimity were the only decision rule that individuals utilized to undertake collective action, most public goods would not be provided (Bator 1958). Yet, individuals do surmount the problems of collective inaction to constitute enterprises which do not rely strictly upon the voluntary consent of all who are affected. Buchanan and Tullock begin to develop a logic that a representative individual might use in attempting to establish some method for gaining the benefits of collective action (Buchanan and Tullock 1965). While many students of public administration would not immediately see the relevance of a logic of constitutional decision making for the study of public administration, we feel that it provides an essential foundation for a different approach to the field. Using this logic, public agencies are not viewed simply as bureaucratic units which perform those services which someone at the top instructs them to perform. Rather, public agencies are viewed as means for allocating decision-making capabilities in order to provide public goods and services responsive to the preferences of individuals in different social contexts.

A constitutional choice is simply a choice of decision rules for making future collective decisions. Constitutional choice, as such, does not include the appropriation of funds or actions to alter events in the world except to provide the organisational structure for ordering the choices of future decision makers. A representative individual wanting to create an organization to provide a public good would, according to Buchanan and Tullock, need to take two types of costs into account: (1) external costs – those costs which an individual expects to bear as the result of decisions which deviate from his preferences and impose costs upon him – and (2) decision-making costs – the expenditure of resources, time, effort, and opportunities foregone in decision making (Buchanan 1969).

Both types of costs are affected by the selection of decision rules which specify the proportion of individuals required to agree prior to future collective action (Tiebout and Warren 1961).

Expected external costs will be at their highest point where any one person can take action on behalf of the entire collectivity. Such costs would decline as the proportion of members participating in collective decision making increases. Expected external costs would reach zero where all were required to agree prior to collective action under a rule of unanimity. However, expected decision-making costs would have the opposite trend. Expenditures on decision making would be minimal if any one person could make future collective decisions for the whole group of affected individuals. Such costs would increase to their highest point with a rule of unanimity.

If our representative individual were a cost minimize, and the two types of costs described above were an accurate representation of the costs he perceives, we would expect him to prefer the constitutional choice of a decision rule where the two cost curves intersect. When the two cost curves are roughly symmetrical, some form of simple majority vote would be a rational choice of a voting rule. If expected external costs were far greater than expected decision-making costs, an extraordinary majority would be a rational choice of a voting rule. On the other hand, if the opportunity costs inherent in decision making were expected to be very large in comparison to external costs, then reliance might be placed on a rule authorizing collective action by the decision of one person in the extreme case requiring rapid response. An optimal set of decision rules will vary with different situations, and we would not expect to find one good rule that would apply to the provision of all types of public goods and services.

Majority vote and the expression of social preferences

Scholars in the public choice tradition have also been concerned with the effect of decision rules upon the expression of individual preferences regarding the social welfare of a community of individuals (Arrow 1963; Bowen 1943; Bradford 1970; Downs 1960). Particular attention has been paid to majority vote as a means of expressing such preferences (Downs 1957; Farquharson 1969; Hinich, Ordeshook 1970; Plott 1967; Riker 1958; 1962; Rothenberg 1970). Duncan Black in *The Theory of Committees and Elections* has demonstrated that if a community is assumed to have a single-peaked preference ordering, then a choice reflecting the median preference position will dominate all others under majority vote, providing the numbers are odd (Black 1958; Black and Newing 1951). Edwin Haefele and others have pointed out that this solution has interesting implications for the strategy of those who must win the approval of an electorate (Davis and Hinich 1966; 1967; Haefele 1972). If representatives are aware of their constituents' preferences, the task of developing a winning coalition depends upon the formulation of a program that will occupy the median position of voter preferences, providing that voters are making a choice between two alternatives. Under these circumstances, persons in political or administrative leadership would have an incentive to formulate a program oriented to the median preference position of their constituents. Voters would then choose the alternative, if presented with a choice, which most closely approximates the median position (Downs 1961; Hotelling 1929). Single peakedness implies a substantial homogeneity in social preference with the bulk of preferences clustering around a single central tendency. Such conditions might reasonably apply to a public good for which there is a relatively uniform demand in relation to any particular community of interest. Substantial variations in demand for different mixes of public goods, as might be reflected in the differences between wealthy neighbourhoods and ghetto neighbourhoods in a big city, would most likely not meet the condition of single peakedness when applied to the provision of educational services, police services, or welfare services. Majority voting under such conditions would fail to reflect the social preference of such diverse neighbourhoods if they were subsumed in the same constituency.

Bureaucratic organization

If the essential characteristic of a bureaucracy is an ordered structure of authority where command is unified in one position and all other positions are ranked in a series of one-many relationships, then we would assume from the Buchanan and Tullock cost calculus that a constitutional system based exclusively upon a bureaucratic ordering would be an extremely costly affair. Presumably, an ordered system of one-man rule might sustain considerable speed and dispatch in some decision making. However, the level of potential deprivations or external social costs would be very high. If external costs can be reduced to a low order of magnitude, then reliance upon a bureaucratic ordering would have considerable advantage.

The possibility of reducing expected external costs to a low order of magnitude so that advantage might be taken of the low decision costs potentially inherent in a bureaucratic ordering can be realized only if (1) appropriate decision-making arrangements are available to assure the integrity of substantial unanimity at the level of constitutional choice, and (2) methods of collective choice are continuously available to reflect the social preferences of members of the community for different public goods and services. The rationale for bureaucratic organization in a democratic society can be sustained only if both of these conditions are met.

In the political economy tradition, two different approaches have been taken in the analysis of bureaucratic organisations. R. H. Coase in an article on 'The Nature of a Firm' has developed an explanation for bureaucratic organization in business firms (Coase 1937). According to Coase, rational individuals might be expected to organise a firm where management responsibilities would be assumed by an entrepreneur, and others would be willing to become employees if the firm could conduct business under direction of the entrepreneur at a lesser cost than if each and every transaction were to be organised as market transactions. The firm would be organised on the basis of long-term employment contracts, rather than short-term market transactions. Each employee would agree, for certain remuneration, to work in accordance with the directions of an entrepreneur within certain limits. The employment contract is analogous to a constitution in defining decision-making arrangements between employer and employee.

Coase anticipates limits to the size of firms where the costs of using a factor of production purchased in the market would be less than adding a new component to the firm to produce that added factor of production. As more employees are added, management costs would be expected to increase. A point would be reached where the saving on the marginal employee would not exceed the added costs of managing that employee. No net savings would accrue to the entrepreneur. If a firm became too large, an entrepreneur might also fail to see some of his opportunities and not take best advantage of potential opportunities in the reallocation of his work force. Another entrepreneur with a smaller, more efficient firm would thus have a competitive advantage over the larger firm which had exceeded the limit of scale economy in firm size.

Gordon Tullock in *The Politics of Bureaucracy* develops another analysis using a model of 'economic man' to discern the consequences which can be expected to follow from rational behavior in large public bureaucracies (Tullock 1965). Tullock's 'economic man' is an ambitious public employee who seeks to advance his career opportunities for promotions within the bureaucracy. Since career advancement depends upon favourable recommendations by his superiors, a career-oriented public servant will act so to please his superiors. Favourable information will be forwarded; unfavourable information will be repressed. Distortion of information will diminish control and generate expectations which diverge from events sustained by actions (Niskanen 1970). Large-scale bureaucracies will, thus, become error prone and cumbersome in adapting to rapidly changing conditions. Efforts to correct the malfunctioning of bureaucracies by tightening control will simply magnify errors.

Coase's analysis would indicate that elements of bureaucratic organization can enhance efficiency if the rule-making authority of an entrepreneur is constrained by mutually agreeable limits and he is free to take best advantage of opportunities in reallocating work assignments within those constraints. Both Coase and Tullock recognize limits to economies of scale in bureaucratic organization (Williamson 1967). No such limits were recognized in the traditional theory of public administration. Bureaucratic organization is as subject to institutional weaknesses and institutional failures as any other form of organisational arrangement.

Producer performance and consumer interests in the provision of public goods and services

The problem of collective inaction can be overcome under somewhat optimal conditions provided that (1) substantial unanimity can be sustained at the level of constitutional choice, (2) political and administrative leadership is led to search out median solutions within a community of people which has a single-peaked order of preferences, and (3) a public service can be produced by an enterprise subject to those constraints. Some difficult problems will always remain to plague those concerned with the provision of public goods and services.

Once a public good is provided, the absence of an exclusion principle means that each individual will have little or no choice but to take advantage of whatever is provided unless he is able to move or is wealthy enough to provide for himself (Tiebout 1956). Under these conditions, the producer of a public good may be relatively free to induce savings in production costs by increasing the burden or cost to the user or consumer of public goods and services. Shifts of producer costs to consumers may result in an aggregate loss of efficiency, where the savings on the production side are exceeded by added costs on the consumption side. Public agencies rarely, if ever, calculate the value of users' time and inconvenience when they engage in studies of how to make better use of their employees' time. What is the value of the time of citizens who stand in line waiting for service as against the value of a clerk's time who is servicing them? (Kafoglis 1968; Warren 1970; Weschler, Marr and Hackett 1968). If the citizen has no place else to go and if he is one in a million other citizens, the probability of his interest being taken into account is negligible. The most impoverished members of a community are the most exposed to deprivations under these circumstances. A preoccupation with producer efficiency in public administration may have contributed to the impoverishment of ghettos.

This problem is further complicated by conditions of changing preferences among any community of people and the problem of changing levels of demand in relation to the available supply of a public good or service. No one can know the preferences or values of other persons apart from giving those persons an opportunity to express their preferences or values. If constituencies and collectivities are organised in a way that does not reflect the diversity of interests among different groups of people, then producers of public goods and services will be taking action without information as to the changing preferences of the persons they serve. Expenditures may be made with little reference to consumer utility. Producer efficiency in the absence of consumer utility is without meaning. Large per capita expenditures for educational services which are not conceived by the recipients to enhance their life prospects may be grossly unproductive. Education can be a sound investment in human development only when individuals perceive the effort as enhancing their life prospects.

Similar difficulties may be engendered when conditions of demand for a public good or service increase in relation to the available supply. When demands begin to exceed supply, the dynamics inherent in 'the tragedy of the commons' may arise all over again (Mohring 1970; Nelson 1962; Rothenberg 1970; Seneca 1970; Williamson 1966). A congested highway carries less and less traffic as the demand grows. What was once a public good for local residents may now become a public 'bad' as congested and noisy traffic precludes a growing number of opportunities for the use of streets by local residents (Buchanan 1970). In short, the value of public goods may be subject to serious erosion under conditions of changing demand.

Finally, producer performance and consumer interests are closely tied together when we recognize that the capacity to levy taxes, to make appropriate expenditure decisions, and to provide the necessary public facilities are insufficient for optimality in the use of public facilities. One pattern of use may impair the value of a public facility for other patterns of use. The construction of a public street or highway, for example, would be insufficient to enhance the welfare potential for members of a community without attention to an extensive body of regulations controlling the use of such facilities by pedestrian and vehicular traffic. As demand for automobile traffic turns streets into a flood of vehicles, who is to articulate the interests of pedestrians and other potential users, and allocate the good among all potential users?

The interests of the users of public goods and services will be taken into account only to the extent that producers of public goods and services stand exposed to the potential demands of those users. If producers fail to adapt to changing demands or fail to modify conditions of supply to meet changing demands, then the availability of alternative administrative, political, judicial, and constitutional remedies may be necessary for the maintenance of an efficient and responsive system of public administration. Efficiency in public administrations will depend upon the sense of constitutional decision making that public administrators bring to the task of constituting the conditions of public life in a community.

Most political economists in the public choice tradition would anticipate that no single form of organization is good for all social circumstances (Ashby 1962; 1960). Different forms of organization will give rise to some capabilities and will be subject to other limitations. Market organization will be subject to limitations which will give rise to institutional weaknesses or institutional failure. Bureaucratic organization will provide opportunities to develop some capabilities and will be subject to other limitations. Those limitations will in turn generate institutional weakness or institutional failure if they are exceeded. A knowledge of the capabilities and limitations of diverse forms of organisational arrangements will be necessary for both the future study and practice of public administration.

Toward new perspectives in the study of public administration

Our prior analysis has been largely, though not exclusively, oriented toward a circumstance involving calculations relative to the provision of a single public good. If we proceed with an assumption that we live in a world involving a large variety of potential public goods which come in different shapes and forms, we may want to consider what our representative individual as a self-interested calculator pursuing maximizing strategies would search out as an appropriate way for organising an administrative system to provide an optimal mix of different public goods and services. Would a representative individual expect to get the best results by having all public goods and services provided by a single integrated bureaucratic structure subject to the control and direction of a single chief executive? Or would he expect to get better results by having access to a number of different collectivities capable of providing public services in response to a diversity of communities of interest? (Bish 1968; Duggal 1966; Haefele 1970; Hirschman 1967; McKean 1965; Pauly 1970).

If the answer to the first question is 'no' then the presumptions inherent in Wilson's theory of administration and in the traditional principles of public administration will not stand as a satisfactory basis for a theory of administration in a democratic society. If the answer to the second question is 'yes' then we are confronted with the task of developing an alternative theory of public administration that is appropriate for citizens living in a democratic society (Lindblom 1965).

If a domain that is relevant to the provision of a public good or service can be specified so that those who are potentially affected can be contained within the boundaries of an appropriate jurisdiction and externalities do not spill over onto others, then a public enterprise can be operated with substantial autonomy, provided that an appropriate structure of legal and political remedies are available to assure that some are not able to use the coercive powers of a collectivity to deprive others of unlawful rights or claims (Hirsch 1968; 1963). Even where such conditions could not be met, solutions can be devised by reference to overlapping jurisdictions so that the larger jurisdictions are able to control for externalities while allowing substantial autonomy for the same people organised as small collectivities to make provision for their own public welfare.

In the traditional theory of public administration, the existence of overlapping jurisdictions has often been taken as *prima facie* evidence of duplication of effort, inefficiency, and waste. If we contemplate the possibility that different scales of organization may be appropriate to different levels of operation in providing a particular type of public service, substantial advantage may derive from the provision of services by overlapping jurisdictions (Dawson 1970; Hirsch 1964; Williams 1966). For example, local police may not be very proficient in dealing with organised crime operating on a state, interstate, national, or international basis. Large-scale national police agencies may be a necessary but not sufficient condition for dealing with such problems. Control over the movement of traffic in and out of urban centres may pose problems of an intermediate scale in policing operations. Crimes in the street, however, may reflect the absence of police services responsive to local neighbourhood interests.

Once we contemplate the possibility that public administration can be organised in relation to diverse collectivities organised as concurrent political regimes, we might further contemplate the possibility that there will not be one rule of good administration for all governments alike. Instead of a single integrated hierarchy of authority coordinating all public services, we might anticipate the existence of multi-organisational arrangements in the public sector that tends to take on the characteristics of public-service industries composed of many public agencies operating with substantial independence of one another (Ostrom and Ostrom 1965). Should we not begin to look at the police industry, (Ostrom 1971; Shoup 1964) the education industry, (Barlow 1970; Holtmann 1966; Machlup 1962) the water industry, (Bain, Caves and Margolis 1966; Schmid 1967; Weschler 1968) and other public service industries on the assumption that these industries have a structure that allows for coordination without primary reliance upon hierarchical structures? (Warren 1966). Once we begin to look for order among multi-organisational arrangements in the public sector, important new vistas will become relevant to the study of public administration (Bish 1971). So-called grants-in-aid may take on the attributes of a transfer of funds related to the purchase of a mix of public services to take appropriate account of externalities which spill over from one jurisdiction to another (Breton 1971; Weldon 1966).

A combination of user taxes, service charges, intergovernmental transfers of funds, and voucher systems may evoke some of the characteristics of market arrangements among public service agencies (Breton 1967; Buchanan 1968; Dales 1968; Ostrom 1969; Tiebout and Warren 1961). Instead of a bureaucratic hierarchy serving as the primary means for sustaining legal rationality in a political order as Max Weber has suggested, we should not be surprised to find that legal rationality can be sustained by recourse to judicial determination of issues arising from conflicts over jurisdiction among administrative agencies. Given the high potential cost of political stalemate for the continuity and survival of any administrative enterprise, we should not be surprised to find rational, self-interested public administrators consciously bargaining among themselves and mobilizing political support from their clientele in order to avoid political stalemate and sustain the political feasibility of their agencies (Lindblom 1955). Perhaps a system of public administration composed of a variety of multi-organisational arrangements and highly dependent upon mobilizing clientele support will come reasonably close to sustaining a high level of performance in advancing the public welfare.

References

Arrow, K. F. (1951) 'Alternative Approaches to the Theory of Choice in Risk-Taking Situations', *Econometrica*, 19:404–437.

— (1963) *Social Choice and Individual Values*, 2nd edition, New York: John Wiley & Sons.

Ashby, W. R. (1962) 'Principles of the Self-Organising System', in H. Von Foerster and G. W. Zopf (eds) *Principles of Self-Organization*, New York: The Macmillan Co., pp. 255–278.

— (1960) *Design for a Brain*, 2nd edition, New York: John Wiley & Sons.

Ayres, R. U. and Kneese, A. V. (1969) 'Production, Consumption and Externalities', *American Economic Review*, 59:282–297.

Bain, J. S., Caves, R. E. and Margolis, J. (1966) *Northern California's Water Industry: The Comparative Efficiency of Public Enterprise in Developing a Scarce Natural Resource*, Baltimore: The Johns Hopkins Press.

Barlow, R. (1970) 'Efficiency Aspects of Local School Finance', *Journal of Political Economy*, 78:1028–1040.

Bator, F. (1958) 'The Anatomy of Market Failure', *Quarterly Journal of Economics*, LXXII:351–379.

Bish, R. L. (1968) 'A Comment on V. P. Duggal's "Is There an Unseen Hand in Government?"', *Annals of Public and Cooperative Economy*, XXXIX:89–94.

— (1971) *The Public Economy of Metropolitan Areas*, Chicago: Markham Publishing Company.

Black, D. (1958) *The Theory of Committees and Elections*, Cambridge: Cambridge University Press.

Black, D. and Newing, R. A. (1951) *Committee Decisions with Complementary Valuation*, London: William Hodge.

Boulding, K. E. (1966) 'The Ethics of Rational Decision', *Management Science*, 12:161–169.

— (1963) 'Towards a Pure Theory of Threat Systems', *American Economic Review*, 53: 424–434.

Bowen, H. R. (1943) 'The Interpretation of Voting in the Allocation of Economic Resources', *Quarterly Journal of Economics*, LVIII: 27–48.

Bradford, D. V. (1970) 'Constraints on Public Action and Rules for Social Decision', *American Economic Review*, 60:642–654.

Breton, A. (1966) 'A Theory of the Demand for Public Goods', *Canadian Journal of Economics and Political Science*, XXXII:455–467.

— (1967) *Discriminatory Government Policies in Federal Countries*, Montreal: The Canadian Trade Committee, Private Planning Association of Canada.

— (1965) 'A Theory of Government Grants', *Canadian Journal of Economics and Political Science*, XXXI:175–187.

Brodbeck, M. (1958) 'Methodological Individualism: Definition and Reduction', *Philosophy of Science*, 25:1–22.

Buchanan, J. M. (1968) 'A Public Choice Approach to Public Utility Pricing', *Public Choice*, 5:1–17.

— (1969) *Cost and Choice: An Inquiry in Economic Theory*, Chicago: Markham Publishing Company.

Buchanan, J. M. and Stubblebine, W. C. (1962) 'Externality', *Economica*, XXIX:371–384.

— (1970) 'Public Goods and Public Bads' in J. P. Crecine (ed.), *Financing the Metropolis*, Beverly Hills: Sage Publications.

Buchanan, J. M. and Tullock, G. (1965) *The Calculus of Consent: Logical Foundations of Constitutional Democracy*, Ann Arbor, MI: University of Michigan Press.

— (1968) *The Demand and Supply of Public Goods*, Chicago: Rand McNally.

Burgess, P. M. and Robinson, J. A. (1969) 'Alliances and the Theory of Collective Action: A Simulation of Coalition Processes', *Midwest Journal of Political Science*, XII:194–219.

Campbell, C. D. and Tullock, G. (1965) 'A Measure of the Importance of Cyclical Majorities', *Economic Journal*, 75:853–857.

— (1966) 'The Paradox of Voting: A Possible Method of Calculation', *American Political Science Review*, LX:684–685.

Coase, R. H. (1937) 'The Nature of the Firm', *Economica*, 4: 386–485.

— (1960) 'The Problem of Social Cost', *Journal of Law and Economics*, III:1–44.

Coleman, J. S. (1966a) 'Foundations for a Theory of Collective Decisions', *American Journal of Sociology*, 71:615–627.

— (1966b) 'Individual Interests and Collective Action', *Papers on Non-Market Decision Making*, 1:49–63.

Cunningham, R. L. (1967) 'Ethics and Game Theory: The Prisoners Dilemma', *Papers on Non-Market Decision Making*, 2:11–26.

Cyert, R. M. and March, J. G. (1963) *A Behavioral Theory of the Firm*, Englewood Cliffs, NJ: Prentice Hall.

Dales, J. H. (1968) *Pollution, Property and Prices: An Essay in Policy-Making and Economics*, Toronto: University of Toronto Press.

Davis, O. A. and Hinich, M. (1966) 'A Mathematical Model of Policy Formation in a Democratic Society', *Mathematical Applications in Political Science*, 11:175–208.

— (1967) 'Some Results Related to a Mathematical Model of Policy Formation in a Democratic Society', *Mathematical Applications and Political Science*, III:14–38.

Davis, O. A., Hinich, M. and Winston, A. (1962) 'Externalities, Welfare and the Theory of Games', *Journal of Political Economy*, 60: 241–262.

— (1967) 'On the Distinction Between Public and Private Goods', *American Economic Review*, 57:360–373.

Dawson, D. A. (1970) *Economies of Scale in the Public Secondary School Education Sector in Ontario*, Hamilton, Ontario: McMaster University, Department of Economics, Working Paper No. 70–04.

Demsetz, H. (1967) 'Private Property, Information and Efficiency', *American Economic Review*, LVII:347–360.
— (1970) 'The Private Production of Public Goods', *Journal of Law and Economics*, XII:293–306.
Downs, A. (1957) *An Economic Theory of Democracy*, New York: Harper & Row.
— (1961) 'In Defence of Majority Voting', *Journal of Political Economy*, LXIX: 192–199.
— (1960) 'Why the Government Budget is Too Small in a Democracy', *World Politics*, XII:541–564.
Duggal, V. P. (1966) 'Is There an Unseen Hand in Government?', *Annals of Public and Comparative Economy*, 37:145–150.
Eulau, H. (1964) 'Logic of Rationality in Unanimous Decision Making', in C. J. Friedrich (ed.) *Nomos VII: Rational Decision*, New York: Atherton Press, pp. 26–5.
Farquharson, R. (1969) *Theory of Voting*, New Haven: Yale University Press.
Fishburn, P. C. (1964) *Decision and Value Theory*, New York: John Wiley & Sons, Inc.
Garvey, G. (1969) 'The Political Economy of Patronal Groups', *Public Choice*, VII:33–45.
— (1966) 'The Theory of Party Equilibrium', *American Political Science Review*, LX:29–38.
Gulick, L. and Urwick, L. (eds) (1937) *Papers on the Science of Administration*, New York: Columbia University, Institute of Public Administration.
Haefele, E. T. (1970) 'Coalitions, Minority Representation, and Vote-Trading Probabilities', *Public Choice*, VII:75–90.
— (1972) 'Environmental Quality as a Problem of Social Choice' in *Environmental Quality Analysis: Theory and Method in the Social Sciences*, Washington D.C.
Hardin, G. (1968) 'The Tragedy of the Commons', *Science*, 162:1243–1248.
Hart, A. G. (1965) *Anticipations, Uncertainty and Dynamic Planning*, New York: Augustus M. Kelley.
Head, J. G. (1962) 'Public Goods and Public Policy', *Public Finance*, 17: 197–219.
Hinich, M. J. and Ordeshook, P. (1970) 'Plurality Maximization vs. Vote Maximization: A Spatial Analysis with Variable Participation', *American Political Science Review*, 64:772–791.
Hirsch, W. Z. (1963) 'Urban Government Services and Their Financing' in W. Z. Hirsch (ed.)*Urban Life and Form*, New York: Holt, Rinehart and Winston, pp. 129–166.
— (1964) 'Local Versus Areawide Urban Government Services', *National Tax Journal*, 17:331–339.
— (1968) 'The Supply of Urban Public Services' in H. S. Perloff and L. Wingo (eds) *Issues in Urban Economics*, Baltimore: Johns Hopkins Press, pp. 477–526.
Hirschman, A. O. (1967) 'The Principles of the Hiding Hand', *The Public Interest*, 6.

Hirshleifer, J., DeHaven, J. C. and Milliman, J. W. (1960) *Water Supply Economics*, Technology, and Policy Chicago: The University of Chicago Press.

Holtmann, A. G. (1966) 'A Note on Public Education and Spillovers through Migration', *Journal of Political Economy*, 74:524–525.

Hotelling, H. (1929) 'Stability in Competition' *Economic Journal*, 39:41–57.

Kafoglis, M. L. (1968) 'Participatory Democracy in the Community Action Program', *Public Choice*, V:73–85.

Knight, F. H. (1965) *Risk, Uncertainty and Profit*, New York: Harper and Row.

Leoni, B. (1957) 'The Meaning of "Political" in Political Decisions', *Political Studies*, V:225–239.

Lindblom, C. E. (1955) *Bargaining: The Hidden Hand in Government*, Santa Monica: The Rand Corporation.

— (1965) *The Intelligence of Democracy: Decision Making through Mutual Adjustment*, New York: The Free Press, 1965.

Luce, R. D. and Raiffa, H. (1957) *Games and Decisions: Introduction and Critical Survey*, New York: John Wiley & Sons.

McKean, R. L. (1965) 'The Unseen Hand in Government', *American Economic Review*, 55:496–506.

Machlup, F. (1962) *The Production and Distribution of Knowledge in the U.S.*, Princeton, NJ: Princeton University Press.

Mishan, E. J. (1967) *The Casts of Economic Growth*, New York: Frederick A. Praeger.

Mohring, H. (1970) 'The Peak Load Problem with Increasing Returns and Pricing Constraints', *American Economic Review*, 60:693–705.

Musgrave, R. (1939) 'The Voluntary Exchange Theory of Public Economy', *QIE*, LIII:213–237.

— (1959) *The Theory of Public Finance*, New York: McGraw-Hill.

Nelson, J. C. (1962) 'The Pricing of Highway, Waterway, and Airway Facilities', *American Economic Review*, 52:426–435.

Niskanen, W. A. (1970) *Bureaucracy and Representative Government*, review draft, Arlington, Va.: Institute for Defence Analysis.

Olson, M. (1965) *The Logic of Collective Action*, Cambridge, Mass.: Harvard University Press.

Ostrom, E. (1971) 'Institutional Arrangements and the Measurement of Policy Consequences in Urban Affairs', *Urban Affairs Quarterly*.

— (1968) 'Some Postulated Effects of Learning on Constitutional Behavior', *Public Choice*, V:87–104.

Ostrom, V. and Ostrom E. (1965) 'A Behavioural Approach to the Study of Intergovernmental Relations', *Annals of the American Academy of Political and Social Science*, 359:137–146.

Ostrom, V. (1969) 'Operational Federalism: Organization for the Provision of Public Services in the American Federal System', *Public Choice*, VI:1–17.

Ostrom, V., Tiebout, C. M. and Warren, R. (1961) 'The Organization of Government in Metropolitan Areas: A Theoretical Inquiry', *American Political Science Review*, 55:831–842.

— (1968) 'Water Resource Development: Some Problems in Economic and Political Analysis of Public Policy' in A. Ranney (ed.) *Political Science and Public Policy*, Chicago: Markham Publishing Company.

Pauly, M. V. (1970) 'Optimality, "Public Goods and Local Governments: A General Theoretical Analysis"', *Journal of Political Economy*, 78:572–585.

Phelps, E. (1965) *Private Wants and Public Needs*, New York: W. W. Norton.

Plott, C. R. (1967) 'A Notion of Equilibrium and its Possibility Under Majority Rule', *American Economic Review*, 57:787–806.

Radner, R. (1970) 'Problems in the Theory of Markets under Uncertainty', *American Economic Review*, LX:454–460.

Ridley, C. E. and Simon, H. A. (1938) *Measuring Municipal Activities*, Chicago: The International City Manager's Association.

Riker, W. H. (1958) 'The Paradox of Voting and Congressional Rules for Voting on Amendments', *American Political Science Review*, 52:349–366.

— (1962) *The Theory of Political Coalitions*, New Haven: Yale University Press.

— (1965) 'Arrow's Theorem and Some Examples of the Paradox of Voting', *Mathematical Applications in Political Science*, I.

Rothenberg, J. (1970) 'The Economics of Congestion and Pollutions: An Integrated View', *American Economic Review*, LX:114–121.

Samuelson, P. A. (1955) 'Diagrammatic Exposition of a Theory of Public Expenditure', *Review of Economics and Statistics*, XXXVII:350–356.

— (1954) 'The Pure Theory of Public Expenditure', *Review of Economics and Statistics*, XXXVI: 387–389.

Schmid, A. A. (1967) 'Nonmarket Values and Efficiency of Public Investments in Water Resources', *American Economic Review*, LVII:158–168.

Seneca, J. J. (1970) 'The Welfare Effects of Zero Pricing of Public Goods', *Public Choice*, VII:101–110.

Schelling, T. C. (1963) *The Strategy of Conflict*, Cambridge, Mass.: Harvard University Press.

Shackle, G. L. S. (1961) *Decision, Order and Time in Human Affairs*, Cambridge, England: Cambridge University Press.

Shoup, C. S. (1964) 'Standard for Distributing of Free Government Service: Crime Prevention', *Public Finance*, 19:383–392.

Simon, H. A. (1957) *Models of Men, Social and Rational*, New York: Wiley and Sons.

— (1959) 'Theories of Decision-Making in Economics and Behavioural Science', *American Economic Review*, XLIX:253–283.

— (1962) 'The Architecture of Complexity', *Proceedings of the American Philosophical Society*, 106:467–482.

— (1964) *Administrative Behavior: A Study of Decision-Making Processes in Administrative Organisations*, New York: Macmillan.

— (1969) '*The Sciences of the Artificial*', Cambridge, Mass.: The M.I.T. Press.

Stigler, G. J. (1961) 'The Economics of Information', *Journal of Political Economy*, LXIX:213–225.

Thompson, E. A. (1966) 'A Pareto-Optimal Group Decision Process', *Papers on Non-Market Decision Making*, I:133–140.

Thompson, W. (1968) 'The City as a Distorted Price System', *Psychology Today*, pp. 28–33.

Tiebout, C. M. (1956) 'A Pure Theory of Local Expenditures', *Journal of Political Economy*, 64:416–424.

Tullock, G. (1970) 'A Simple Algebraic Logrolling Model', *American Economic Review*, LX:419–426.

—   (1965) *Politics of Bureaucracy*, Washington, D.C.: The Public Affairs Press.

—   (1967) 'The General Irrelevance of the General Impossibility Theorem', *Quarterly Journal of Economics*, 81:256–270.

U.S. Congress, Joint Economic Committee, Subcommittee on Economy in Government, (1969) *A Compendium of Papers on the Analysis and Evaluation of Public Expenditures: The PPB System, three volumes*, Washington, D.C.: U.S. Government Printing Office.

Wade, L. L. and Curry, R. L., Jr. (1970) *A Logic of Public Policy: Aspects of Political Economy*, Belmont, Calif.: Wadsworth Publishing Company.

Waldo, D. (1968) 'Scope of the Theory of Public Administration' in J. C. Charlesworth (ed.) *Theory and Practice of Public Administration: Scope Objectives, and Methods*, Philadelphia: The American Academy of Political and Social Science.

Warren, R. (1970) 'Federal-Local Development Planning: Scale Effects in Representation and Policy Making', *Public Administration Review*, XXX:584–595.

—   (1966) *Government in Metropolitan Regions: A Reappraisal of Fractionated Political Organization*, Davis, Calif.: University of California, Davis, Institute of Governmental Affairs.

Weldon, J. C. (1966) 'Public Goods and Federalism', *Canadian Journal of Economics and Political Science*, 32:230–238.

Weschler, L. F., Marr, P. D. and Hackett, B. M. (1968) *California Service Centre Program*, Davis, Calif.: University of California, Davis, Institute of Governmental Affairs.

—   (1968) *Water Resources Management: The Orange County Experience*, Davis, Calif.: University of California, Davis, Institute of Governmental Affairs.

Wheeler, H. J. (1967) 'Alternative Voting Rules and Local Expenditures: The Town Meeting vs. City', *Papers on Non-Market Decision Making*, 2:61–70.

White, L. D. (1926) *Introduction to the Study of Public Administration*, New York: The Macmillan Company.

Wildaysky, A. (1966) 'The Political Economy of Efficiency', *Public Administration Review*, XXVI: 292–310.

Williams, A. (1966) 'The Optimal Provision of Public Goods in a System of Local Government', *Journal of Political Economy*, 74:18–33.

Williamson, O. E. (1967) 'Hierarchical Control and Optimum Firm Size', *Journal of Political Economy*, 75:123–138.

— (1966) 'Peak Load Pricing and Optimal Capacity under Indivisibility Constraints', *American Economic Review*, LVI:810–827.

Wilson, W. (1887) 'The Study of Administration', *Political Science Quarterly*, II:197–222.

Chapter Two

Polycentricity: The Structural Basis of Self-Governing Systems[1]

Vincent Ostrom

[It] was asserted that traditional patterns of metropolitan government make up a 'polycentric political system', in which there exist many decision-making centres, formally independent of each other. To the extent that these political jurisdictions take each other into account in competitive relationships, enter into contractual and cooperative relationships, or turn to central mechanisms to resolve conflicts, they may exhibit coherent, consistent, and predictable patterns of behavior and may be said to function as a 'system'. These assertions referred to units of government in the context of metropolitan areas. They raise the question of whether general sets of relationships can exist where multiple units, formally independent of one another, can function interdependently as polycentric systems capable of yielding emergent patterns of order. Systems of governance occur wherever complementary arrangements for formulating, using, monitoring, judging, and enforcing rules exist.

If the conditions applicable to polycentric orders can be generalized to apply to all patterns of order in a society, we might then meet the conditions specified by Madison in essay 51 of *The Federalist* where he suggests that 'this policy of supplying by opposite and rival interests, the defects of better motives, might be traced through *the whole system of human affairs, private as well as public*' (Hamilton, Jay, Madison 1788: 337, my emphasis). If the whole system of human affairs is capable of being organized on principles of polycentricity rather than monocentricity, we could have human societies that no longer depend upon a unity of power to achieve coherence. Such an idea is of radical proportions; but this is what Madison is saying in what I would regard as the single most important assertion about the organizing principle of American federalism to be found in *The Federalist*. This assertion, then, is fully consistent with Tocqueville's observation that American democracy is a self-governing society: 'there society governs itself for itself' (Tocqueville [1835] 1945, 1: 57).

If we view a federal society as a covenanting society capable of generating rich assemblages of associations, we would expect to see social units of one sort or another, formally independent but choosing to take each other into account, functioning in mutually accommodating ways to achieve many different patterns

---

1. Initially published in Vincent Ostrom's *The Meaning of American Federalism: Constituting a Self-Governing Society*, (1991) 223–44. San Francisco: ICS Press.

of order. How these patterns of order are constituted is, at least in part, an empirical question. In any general system of polycentric order, we would expect particular patterns of polycentricity to be interdependently related to other such patterns.

The appearance of disorder that prevails at the surface, to paraphrase Tocqueville, may upon further inquiry reveal coherent patterns of order. Conversely, the appearances of order that are presumed to exist may be seriously misleading. A bureaucracy, for example, cannot function as the basis for a rational legal order, as Max Weber presumed, when those who exercise the prerogatives of rulership use their discretion to waive the requirements of law. The founder of the Ming dynasty discovered that holding the reins of rulership taut yields oppression, while relaxing them yields corruption (Dardess 1983). The Faustian bargain inherent in the constitution of order in human societies does not allow perfection.

Aspects of polycentricity are likely to arise in all systems of social order because human beings are capable of thinking for themselves and acting in ways that take account of their own interests. When power is used to check power, careful attention should be paid to the way that polycentricity serves as a structural basis for the emergence of actual self-governing arrangements. If such a system is to be extended literally 'through the whole system of human affairs', including the 'distribution of the supreme powers of the State' (Hamilton, Madison, Jay 1785: 338), it is necessary to explore the application of polycentricity to the realm of international affairs as well. When we contemplate how the principles of polycentricity might apply to the whole system of human affairs, we are exploring the fuller implications of the American experiment.

The concept of polycentricity

As formulated by Ostrom, Tiebout, and Warren (1961), a poly-centric political system would be composed of (1) many autonomous units formally independent of one another, (2) choosing to act in ways that take account of others, (3) through processes of cooperation, competition, conflict, and conflict resolution. The resolution of conflict need not depend upon 'central mechanisms' as stated in that formulation. Noncentral mechanisms for conflict resolution also exist.

It was not until after the essay just cited had been published that I became aware of the prior use of the concept of polycentricity by Michael Polanyi in *The Logic of Liberty* (1951). Polanyi distinguishes between two different methods for organizing social tasks, methods that are constitutive of two different types of social order. One is referred to as a 'deliberate' or 'directed' social order, coordinated by recourse to an ultimate authority exercising control through a unified command structure. I presume that this type of order is equivalent to Hobbesian sovereignty, in which there is a single ultimate authority exercising a monopoly over rulership prerogatives and the instruments of coercion in a society.

The other type of order for organizing social tasks is identified by Polanyi as 'spontaneous' or 'polycentric'. It is conceptualized as an order where many elements are capable of making mutual adjustments to one another within a general system of rules where each element acts independently of the other elements.

Within a set of rules, autonomous decision-makers are free to pursue their own interests subject to the constraint inherent in those particular rules being enforced.

I have difficulty with the use of the term 'spontaneous' in the development of social orders. When juxtaposed with the term 'deliberate', as it is by Polanyi, the term 'spontaneous' implies that a development has occurred without the intention of those involved. I readily recognize that such possibilities may exist. Whether vehicles in meeting one another on the same roadway move to the right or to the left probably derived from experiences in which the rule accrued with significant spontaneity at different places in human history. However, a great deal of deliberateness may be required to establish a federal system of governance where power is used to check power amid opposite and rival interests. A polycentric political system, where rule-ruler-ruled relationships are organized by reference to many autonomous decision structures within each unit of government, requires a good deal of deliberateness in order to function. Anyone who has read Madison's 'notes' on the Philadelphia Convention of 1787, not to mention *The Federalist*, will appreciate that formulating the rules for the federal union called the United States of America did not occur spontaneously, nor was it an edict issued by a supreme authority.

As Jean Piaget ([1932] 1969) demonstrates, children at play can, in light of their accumulated experiences and maturation, learn to modify and create games by formulating mutually agreed upon rules that they themselves proceed to enforce. But such capabilities depend upon a sophistication about rule-ordered relationships that must be added to the skills needed for shooting marbles or playing ball.

To expect a democratic society not only to emerge spontaneously, but to modify and sustain itself in the same way, is not plausible in light of the problems of and probable threats to the viability of democratic institutions. I prefer, then, to presume that polycentric systems of order depend upon a good deal of deliberateness in their creation, operation, and maintenance over time. Yet Polanyi, F. A. Hayek (1973) and others who use the language of 'spontaneity' in referring to social orders are emphasizing points that have considerable merit. Such systems depend upon accumulated experience and cannot be laid down by simply putting words on paper, whether in the form of constitutions, statutory enactments, or the edicts of an autocrat. They depend upon people who know what they are doing and have acquired workable standards by which they can measure successes and failures. We can expect more failures than successes to accrue from the type of 'spontaneity' that might be associated with trial and error. Liberty and justice are performance criteria that cannot be measured in the same way as net monetary return.

The autonomous character of polycentric systems implies self-organizing capabilities. The many autonomous elements or units seek to order their relationships with one another rather than by reference to some external authority. Self-organizing systems become democratic self-governing systems when those being governed have equal liberty and equal standing in the constitution of an order where rulership prerogatives are subject to effective limits among multiple agents, each exercising a limited public trust. I assume that the rules of such associations are open to public scrutiny, to constrain the organization of unlawful conspiracies.

In a theory of polycentric orders I further assume that individuals are the basic units of analysis. Individuals will occupy positions where decisions are taken on behalf of the interests of others in the exercise of agency and trust relationships. Business firms, units of government, agencies of government, legislative bodies, political parties, courts, and nation-states may also be used as units of analysis having to do with relationships at incremental levels of analysis. Societies then become richly nested assemblages of associations that include the diverse forms of association developed within and among units of government.

Diverse autonomous units can then be subject to analysis in relation to specifiable rules of association. The rules of association within business firms at one level of analysis need then to be explored in relation to the rules of association pertaining to market relationships at another level. But markets, electoral contests, and international relations may involve such different strategic calculations that, when polycentric systems of orders apply through the whole system of human affairs, few predictable inferences can be made regarding units of all types. Most inferences will apply to the relationships of particular types of units functioning in particular forms of polycentric order characterized by particular types of rules and payoff functions. If the whole system of human affairs were subject to systems of poly-centric orderings, it would be as though all patterns of order in a society were conceptualized as a series of simultaneous and sequential games. A general system of polycentric ordering, then, would be one where each actor participated in a series of simultaneous and sequential games and where each act had the potential for being construed as a move in simultaneous games. Time out in the play of any one game might be taken to reach resolution of disagreements and conflicts.

We might further anticipate that general systems of polycentric orderings applicable to whole systems of human affairs would take on the characteristics of competitive games: contestability, innovative search for advantage, and convergence toward successful strategies. If the whole system of human affairs were organized in this way, we would expect to see the emergence of a civilization with greater evolutionary potential than can be achieved by those who call for revolutionary change.

The emergence of patterns of order in polycentric structures

In this section I shall consider the patterns of polycentric orderings as these apply to (1) competitive market economies, (2) competitive public economies, (3) scientific inquiry, (4) law and adjudicatory arrangements, (5) systems of governance with a separation of powers and checks and balances, and (6) patterns of international order. The challenge is to understand how patterns of polycentricity might extend to the whole system of human affairs.

Competitive market economies. Since Adam Smith's *Wealth of Nations* (1776), competitive market economies have been celebrated as systems of economic order that manifest patterns of polycentricity and significant degrees of spontaneity. Competitive markets are open systems where anyone is free to enter as a trader subject to the condition of conducting exchange relationships by mutual agreement. The ordering of market relationships responds by mutual adjustments to the activity of others. Competition occurs in the exercise of choice among the alternative options available. Exchange is itself a cooperative relationship between particular buyers and sellers.

Voluntary agreement implies that each party to an exchange is left better off by consummating the exchange. Competition implies that those offering a similar product for sale must meet the terms offered by their competitors. The buyer has incentives to take advantage of lower prices for any given quantity or quality of a good. The combination of these circumstances means that no single producer is free to maximize profits. Competition reduces returns to producers and increases returns to consumers.

These results are both counterintentional and counterintuitive. Each producer may seek to maximize profits, but instead his profits will be reduced by the presence of competitive alternatives. Consumer surplus is proportionately increased. It is consumers who benefit from competitive markets. Selfishness in seeking private advantage yields public benefits. It is this relationship that was dramatized in Mandeville's *The Fable of the Bees* ([1714] 1970).

Furthermore, the idiosyncratic pursuit of self-interest yields not chaos but a predictable system of order with tendencies to drive toward an equilibrium of supply and demand at a point where marginal price covers marginal costs. Such a system of relationships offers optimal opportunities for the alleviation of scarcity in human societies. Investment is no longer justified when costs of economic activities exceed benefits, for when they do the net effect is to leave people worse off. The best results are achieved where benefits are equal to or marginally greater than costs. Societies cannot hope to improve upon such conditions given comparable technologies, human skills, levels of knowledge, and access to information.

Given producer motives to maximize profit, incentives exist in any market economy for established producers to collude, restrict entry, reduce competition, and set prices to allow for a more favourable rate of return. To the extent that such strategies are successful, the competitiveness of market systems is reduced. So long as producers can turn to political authorities to fix the terms of trade and enforce cartel agreements among producers, the equilibrating tendencies of market arrangements shift to the advantage of producers and to the disadvantage of consumers. There are conditions where the equilibrating tendencies of an open (free) competitive market economy cannot be maintained and distortions can be expected to occur. A knowledgeable awareness of these conditions is essential to the maintenance of competitive market arrangements as a polycentric order. If courts treat cartel agreements as valid contracts, they are using their prerogatives to impair the competitive viability of a market economy. The viability of any polycentric order depends upon the maintenance of appropriate limits. Such structures are vulnerable to dominance strategies.

Market arrangements work effectively in relation to goods that are subject to exclusion, and are marketable in units that are both measurable and specifiable in equivalent quantities and/or qualities. Markets are facilitated by commensurate institutions pertaining to private property, the enforcement of contracts, the existence of a reliable monetary system as a medium for exchange and as a measure of value, and access to appropriate public infrastructures pertaining to open spaces, roadways, and public utilities.

A competitive market economy contributes to the emergence of public information about the comparative prices of a vast array of goods and services. It is this information that provides participants in market relationships with an awareness of relative advantage that may accrue to entrepreneurial efforts and innovative potentials. It is the accretion of public information that enables each participant successfully to coordinate his or her pursuit of opportunities in relation to others, and to function in a system of order that works by mutual accommodation among the participants.

The contestability of markets offers rewards to those who discover innovative potentials including the use of new ideas, the development of new technologies, and whatever advantage is to be had from local knowledge. The significance of these rewards for innovations is given recognition in patent and copyright laws that allow an innovator to gain monopoly advantage for fixed periods of time because innovations are not easily appropriable as private property. Whenever a competitor gains an advantage from innovative potentials, all other competitors functioning in the same market have an incentive to acquire them. There is, in other words, a convergence toward successful innovations. The most important factors contributing to the success of competitive market economies are their information-generating features and incentives for innovation. Market economies, as Hayek and the Austrian economists have emphasized, appropriately constrained by patent laws, can then be viewed as facilitating processes of discovery and innovation. Appropriate constraining institutions are therefore necessary to the maintenance of competitive market conditions.

Competitive public economies. Competitive *public* economies can emerge in highly federalized systems of government where substantial fragmentation and overlap exists among diverse government units. These latter, in arranging for the provision of public goods and services, function as collective consumption units. The competitive rivalry in public economies cannot be expected to achieve equilibration between marginal cost and marginal price that economists expect from a 'perfectly' competitive market economy. We would expect, however, that there would be similar pressures toward enhanced efficiency where diverse communities are organized as collective consumption units, and where competitive alternatives exist among production units. So long as the communities of beneficiaries bear the costs of providing public services and there is an appropriate fit between the nature of the good and the boundaries of the collective consumption unit, we can expect increased sensitivity to benefit-cost calculations so that benefits cover costs. The structures of incentives under these conditions work in the proper direction. Such structures can be expected to yield different results from what would be achieved by supplying public services through a system of public administration organized in the kind of unified command structure characteristic of an integrated public bureaucracy. The more highly federalized a political system, the higher the degree of competitive viability that can be expected to exist in fitting patterns of demand to patterns of supply.

It is in achieving a fit between consumption and production functions that configurations of relationships need to be established among the government units responsible for each. Size economies applicable to the consumption of collective goods and services can function independently of economies-of-scale in transforming factors of production into outputs. To assume that overlapping jurisdictions yield wasteful duplication of services fails to take account of collective consumption functions that need to be organized in public economies as distinguished from market economies. The existence of overlap among collective consumption and production units means that competitive options become available. Contestation is then facilitated in circumstances where increasing information on comparative performance can be expected to emerge, where incentives for innovation occur, and where participants become knowledgeable about the successful and unsuccessful arrangements that become available. Patterns of order are maintained by mutual adjustment among informed participants choosing from among the alternatives that are available to them.

Scientific inquiry. Polanyi's *The Logic of Liberty* (1951) draws heavily upon the organization of scientific communities as manifesting the characteristics of a polycentric order. To engage in the pursuit of scientific inquiry, Polanyi argues, requires that any particular investigator take account of the achievement of others. Whatever it is that becomes problematical is so in light either of some anomaly that arises between a theoretical formulation and the consequences that follow from acting upon it, or of the existence of some alternative way of addressing some problematical situation. An awareness of either of these circumstances depends upon an awareness of the formulations and achievements of others. The merit of any new formulation turns first upon its public reproducibility. The particular formulation and the results achieved, if appropriately formulated and acted upon, are not idiosyncratic to particular human personalities but are presumed to be publicly reproducible by others possessing comparable skills and knowledge.

There are, then, basic presuppositions about the essential coherence of a universal order that enable scholars eventually to resolve puzzles or dilemmas and to choose among competing conjectures. The act of choosing accrues to others in the scientific community. Presumably, some 'advantage' must accrue to a new 'discovery' as an alternative way of addressing a problematical situation before others can be persuaded by its merit.

This taking account of the work of others and advancing alternative formulations presumes that 'the scientific community is held together and all its affairs are peacefully managed through its joint acceptance of the same fundamental scientific beliefs. These beliefs, therefore, may be said to form the constitution of the scientific community and to embody its ultimate sovereign will' (Polanyi 1951: 26). The 'sovereign will', in this case, is the concurrence of others in the scientific community rather than some ultimate authority who exercises monopoly control over rulership prerogatives and instruments of coercion. Polanyi explicitly recognizes that a polycentric order among scientific investigators entails normative presuppositions that respect the search for truth, desire justice, and maintain mutual respect and reciprocity in their relationships with one another.

The tensions inherent in the work of the scientific community are, however, exceptionally high because every belief is potentially contestable. Inquiry in the scientific tradition represents, then, a challenge to every form of orthodoxy. Further, there is a danger that scientific investigators may abandon modesty, presume to know the Truth, and create their own form of orthodoxy, while engaging in sweeping rejections of other forms of belief and failing to pursue the merit of the arguments that may be at issue. Dogmas advanced in the name of science are no less dogmatic than other dogmas. Efforts to destroy or silence others is a manifestation of dominance strategies that are repugnant to polycentricity in scientific communities. A repudiation of religion, as such, fails to indicate an appreciation of those who teach that nature is the creation of a transcendent order. The study of nature as God's creation can provide scientific investigators with an appreciation for the existence of an order that gives coherence to all other forms of order. This is consistent with a presumption that a universe exists.

Science as a polycentric order depends, then, upon an autonomous pursuit of inquiry that requires a reciprocal respect for the autonomy of others. Contestability in the realm of ideas is an essential feature of science as such an order. Tensions must necessarily exist in such circumstances, but the reward for participating in contestable arguments in respectful ways is to reap the fruit of tilling the field of knowledge as civilization advances. The civilization advances only when innovations in human knowledge offer others opportunities to achieve net gains in the advancement of human welfare. It is the free professions and the institutions for the transmission of learning to each new generation that provide the essential links between those working at the frontiers of inquiry and the accessibility of knowledge to other members of a society. These institutional arrangements are potentially as open to a polycentric system of order as the scientific community itself. The rules of conduct applicable to these orders may be breached when the modesty appropriate to human fallibility is abandoned for the presupposition that omniscient observers can know what is good for others. Polycentric orders allow others to speak and act for themselves in light of the emergence of new ideas and the accretion of new knowledge.

Law and adjudicatory arrangements. Polanyi conceives of law courts and the larger legal community as forming a polycentric order. The judiciary and members of the legal profession are viewed as participating in processes to elucidate information and articulate contending arguments as means of resolving conflicts and rendering judgments; they do so under conditions where each participant exercises an independence of action in relation to each other participant, subject to common rules of evidence, procedure, and argumentation.

The possibility of conceptualizing courts and the judicial process as a polycentric order will depend upon the development of (1) legal concepts and terms that can be known in a public interpersonal context, (2) legal criteria that can be used as a basis for judgment, and (3) methods of legal reasoning that can be used to organize thoughts and array evidence for the same purpose. Unless a community of agreement (in other words, substantial consensus) can exist regarding legal concepts, criteria for choice or judgment, and methods of legal reasoning, there can be no basis for a polycentric ordering.

A fundamental tension exists between conceptualizing law as command and law as rules grounded in consensus. When the emphasis is placed upon law as command by those who exercise rulership prerogatives, the correlative relationship on the part of those who are ruled is to obey and submit to the rule. Where law is conceptualized as rules grounded in consensus, those subject to the rules are free to contest how they are formulated and applied. The point of contestation is to allow for resistance and an opportunity to challenge either the formulation of a rule or its application. It is the emergence, then, of contestation with this end in view that has been critical in the emergence of an independent judiciary and the development of rules of procedure that allow for a polycentric legal order. Harold Berman, in *Law and Revolution* (1983), provides an account of the origin of Western law with the papal revolution evoked by the dictate of Pope Gregory VII in 1075, when he was attempting to establish the independence of the Church from secular authorities in Western Christendom. The conception of a basic tie between God's law and secular law served as the basis upon which ecclesiastical authorities could judge whether the conduct of secular authorities conformed to religious precepts. A fundamental breach of God's laws and disobedience to the Church in ecclesiastical affairs were grounds for the excommunication of secular authorities, as church members from the Church itself. Excommunication was an act of banning an offender from partaking in the Christian community.

From the time of Pope Gregory VII onward, issues about the proper structure of authority relationships have been contestable in Western Christendom, and it is the persistence of this contestation that has led to the emergence of the systems of law characteristic of Western jurisprudence. The development of the Protestant tradition was an extension of principles of contestation as these applied to the organization of authority relationships in both the ecclesiastical and the secular realms.

The achievement of polycentricity in the function of the judiciary and the maintenance of a rule of law was an important step in the development of Western civilization. The natural response to any offense, unjust deprivation, or threat is to move toward a fight set. Threats or offenses yield a response by counterthreats or counteroffenses (Boulding 1963). Peaceful communication is breached; hostility easily escalates to destructive fighting; and the peace of the community is threatened. The judicial process affords a way, then, to have recourse to intermediaries who seek to do justice, maintain the peace of the community, and search for a constructive resolution of existing conflicts when adversaries are no longer on speaking terms with one another.

The road to justice depends upon suspending judgment and having recourse to a process where the adversaries have their say in mobilizing evidence and advancing arguments bearing upon the matters at issue. The parties are presumed to stand as equals before the bar of the court and are entitled to seek justice through a due process of law. Judges are obliged to do justice by conforming to the requirements of a due process of law. The method of normative inquiry inherent in the Golden Rule is the methodological foundation for principles of equity.

Adherence to principles of polycentricity in the function of the judiciary and in the maintenance of the rule of law is important to the maintenance of polycentricity in other systems of order. Market mechanisms depend upon the existence of property rights, the enforcement of contracts, and the maintenance of a just system of commercial law. This requires a knowledgeable understanding of the appropriate limits that apply to a valid contract. Otherwise, established producers who enter into contracts to form cartels will call upon courts to enforce such contracts against new competitors. Not every contract can be a valid contract – only those that conform to valid principles of polycentric ordering.

Systems of governance. This same principle of polycentricity applies to the scope of judicial authority in systems of governance as polycentric orders. If the whole system of human affairs, including the distribution of rulership functions traditionally ascribed to a sovereign are subject to principles of polycentric ordering, then any controversies at issue pertaining to those functions must become contestable and justiciable. These in fact are the grounds for the development of a constitutional jurisprudence in the American federal system. A legislature that acts beyond the scope of its constitutional authority is presumed to be acting in circumstances that are without authority, that is, null and void. Such enactments are not entitled to enforcement; they cannot establish the basis for lawful claims, as Alexander Hamilton argued in essay 78 of *The Federalist* and as the U.S. Supreme Court asserted in *Marbury v. Madison*.

When the Supreme Court concludes that it has no grounds for establishing limits to the substantive powers assigned by the Constitution to the U.S. Congress, it is drawing limits to the application of the principles of polycentricity that apply to the American federal system of government. Constraining either the jurisdiction of an independent judiciary or limiting the independent standing of that judiciary has a significant bearing, then, upon the degree of polycentricity that can apply through 'the whole system of human affairs'. It may even result in arbitrary rules becoming incontestable.

Polycentricity in each unit of government, then, is essential to the maintenance of polycentricity in 'the whole system of human affairs'. Law acquires a publicness and a justness in proportion as it withstands critical scrutiny under conditions allowing for contestability in diversely structural political processes. Although provisional decisions can be taken by minimum winning coalitions, they can still be contested through diverse political processes that contribute to an understanding of their implications.

In the evolution of Western law, distinctions have long been made between the exercise of legislative, executive, and judicial authority. Such distinctions imply that there is a conceptual basis for distinguishing the different processes applicable to rule-ruler-ruled relationships. Distinguishable legislative, executive, and judicial instrumentalities exist in all Western nations organized through 'republican' institutions. The critical controversies have pertained not to the distribution of authority as such, but to the patterns of dominance among the diverse instrumentalities of government. The doctrine of parliamentary supremacy, for instance, implies that parliament as a legislative assembly is supreme. The corollary of such a doctrine is a limitation upon judicial authority placing enactments of parliament beyond judicial scrutiny. Another correlative development in Westminster-type parliamentary systems, a development not consistent with parliamentary supremacy, is that of executive privilege associated with the oaths of secrecy taken by ministers by virtue of their membership in a privy council. This tradition is reinforced by acts to preserve official secrecy. The executive privilege of privy councillors interposes severe limits upon the supremacy of parliaments as representative assemblies while creating opportunities for establishing conspiracies of silence among those who exercise executive prerogatives. The doctrines of parliamentary supremacy and ministerial confidentiality are incompatible. Where an independent judiciary is denied jurisdiction with regard to the exercise of public authority, and its authority is confined to 'civil law' as distinguished from 'administrative law', even greater opportunities exist to establish conspiracies of silence.

If parliamentary supremacy is to yield responsible government, then a proper accounting must be given to limits upon the judiciary and to the existence of executive privilege. A critical scrutiny of how authority relationships are constituted always needs to take account of opportunities to usurp authority and pervert justice. In much of Latin America, limits upon the creation and maintenance of an independent judiciary create a pattern of executive privilege in which the military presume to be the ultimate guardians of the peace. There, parliamentary supremacy is little more than a pretence that gives way to the privileged standing of the military to assert supreme authority.

When the logic of American federalism is viewed from the perspective of a system of polycentric ordering, we can begin to understand how fragmentation of authority accompanied by contestation and innovation yields resolutions that achieve consensus among the members of society. [...] Stalemates occur, but those stalemates are indicative of the need to struggle with one another in a search for a better understanding of the way that conflicting interests yield to a community of relationships.

Any such system of polycentric order is, however, vulnerable to the pursuit of strategies in which some will take advantage of opportunities to gain dominance over others. Politicians may have incentives to form coalitions to gain dominance over political structures in the same way that merchants have incentives to form cartels. Such strategies came to fruition in the United States following the Civil War. If politicians could dominate the slating process and offer slates of candidates for all legislative, executive, and judicial offices, the ones who controlled the winning slate could then exercise dominance over all instrumentalities of government and override the checks and balances inherent in the constitutional separation of powers. A surprising degree of success in putting together such coalitions was achieved during the era of machine politics and boss rule.

So long as competitive rivalry exists among political parties, they can contribute to maintaining polycentricity as part of the system. In those circumstances, politicians will attempt to advance proposals for collective action that will offer sufficient appeal to voters to win them the next election. Contestation yields information and critical assessments of alternative proposals. Tendencies exist to converge toward an appeal to median voters.

But success in gaining dominance over all decision structures can also yield extreme corruption, as revealed in the era of machine politics and boss rule. The method pursued by the Progressive reform movement was to reestablish conditions of polycentricity by constitutional modification of electoral arrangements in each of the states. With the introduction of systems of primary elections, which allowed any dissident to challenge the candidates offered by party leaders, and other electoral reforms, contestation was reestablished in electoral processes and strategies of dominance were sharply constrained. Every system of polycentric ordering is potentially vulnerable to circumstances where some achieve dominance at the cost of others. Spontaneity is not a sufficient condition for the maintenance of polycentric systems of order. A self-governing people need to understand when failures occur and how to reform their systems of order.

If polycentric arrangements were spontaneous systems of order, we might expect peace to occur spontaneously among the nations of the world. I do not expect that to occur. Rather, we can expect struggles for dominance to occur. We do, however, confront a challenge: If conditions of polycentricity were to apply through 'the whole system of human affairs', how might such a system of relationships apply to all the nations of the world? As we turn to this question, we will also be exploring some of the implications that follow from the American experiment in constructing a federal system of governance.

Patterns of international order. Over the course of the past one thousand years the nations of Western Christendom have achieved some important degrees of polycentricity in their patterns of relationships with one another. I ascribe these developments, in their origin, to the quest by the Western clergy to establish the conditions for God's peace by renouncing retribution and to their efforts to establish the conditions of peace in the Western reaches of the Roman Empire after the fall of Rome. The papal revolution elicited by the dictate of Pope Gregory VII can be construed as one such effort to establish God's peace in Western Christendom. The constitution of the Holy Roman Empire evolved over a period of nearly a thousand years through processes of oath-taking mediated through the Church amid struggles for papal and imperial supremacy. The rituals of investiture in both ecclesiastical and secular offices involved the acknowledgment of obligations to others. Struggles over authority relationships were sustained both within the ecclesiastical realm, and within the *secular* realm as well as between these two realms. Popes, bishops, monks, and parishioners engaged these issues with reference to the governance of the Church just as emperors, kings, princes, dukes, counts, merchants, and villagers did with reference to secular affairs.

Wars persisted; but the presumptions of God's peace interposed limits against violating churches as places of refuge, of assembly, and of worship, and in establishing the presumption that rules of war applied among knights as the warriors of Western Christendom. Church officials, in their exercise of secular prerogatives, were not immune to participating in warfare, but they had an important place in maintaining a balance of power among contestants who aspired to imperial dominance.

Even such a limited system of order was marked by significant achievements. The basic contestability of the European balance of power system was marked by important advances in economics, science, and technology. In turn, authority relationships were continuously being altered in the struggles for empire mediated by balance-of-power strategies. While some of these struggles were marked by efforts to achieve dominance that might appropriately be labelled 'absolutism', others were marked by successful forms of resistance. The American federal system, much like Bismarck's Second Reich, can be regarded as a by-product of struggles for imperial dominance. The Americans were successful in resisting imperial dominance; and the Germans, in identifying the future of Germany with a system of imperial dominance, fashioned the Second and Third Reichs. The Swiss maintained their *Eidgenossenschaft* by resisting Austrian, French, and German imperialism. 'Whether Europe will be able to achieve constitutional arrangements under which its whole system of human affairs is ordered by principles of polycentricity remains to be seen'.

The mediating place of polycentric systems of order in Western Christendom requires some comparative sense of proportion. The casualties – unarmed peasants – in Stalin's campaign to collectivize Soviet agriculture were as numerous as the total Russian casualties in World War II. Hitler's effort to create a Third Reich was met by an organized resistance that prevailed in a relatively few years against his imperial aspirations.

The world still faces the problem of achieving a peaceful order among its nations. The instruments of autocratic rule have been sufficiently well perfected that a so-called dictatorship of the proletariat exercised in the name of the workers of the world proved feasible for an extended period of time. But such a system of autocracy can be achieved only under conditions of servitude. Societies that place substantial reliance upon polycentric patterns of order present contestable options that must necessarily challenge systems organized on autocratic principles. The world cannot remain half free and half in servitude. Each is a threat to the other.

The irony is that the liberation of the world cannot be achieved by strategies of dominance: the world cannot be made safe for democracy by warfare. Liberation can be achieved only by building polycentric systems of order that can emerge in ways that, in Madison's words, apply through the 'whole system of human affairs'. There is no one strategy and no one way for building systems of polycentric ordering. We cannot expect such systems either to be constructed or to work in only one way. They have too much spontaneity and creativity to conform to a single mould. The American federal system suggests that polycentric systems can generally apply in human societies: human societies can exist without a monopoly of authority relationships. It is possible for societies to become self-governing rather than state-governed. The state, in such circumstances, withers away even when agents who may exercise limited authority are nominally designated as 'heads of state'.

If relationships among societies are to be achieved by extending principles of polycentricity through the whole system of human affairs, these conditions cannot be achieved when governments presume to govern other governments. Principles of poly-centricity require critical attention to the equal standing of individuals with one another in a system of lawful relationships that meet the conditions of equal liberty and justice. The American way, however, is not the only way to achieve polycentric systems of order. Polycentric orders are open systems that manifest enough spontaneity to be self-organizing and self-governing. But the maintenance of such orders depends upon a sufficient level of intelligent deliberation to correct errors and reform themselves.

Conclusion

We can rule out the possibility that a polycentric system of order among the nations of the world will emerge spontaneously. Instead, it is necessary, as Tocqueville suggested, to draw upon a science and art of association in learning how to put polycentric systems of order together. Such systems can be expected to work well only under limited conditions. All are vulnerable to strategies of dominance. Difficulties arise because all polycentric systems of order are subject to counterintentional and counterintuitive patterns of relationships. The appearance of disorder, which is presumed to prevail at the surface, can be expected to generate emergent patterns of order that require deeper investigation.

Economists have long engaged in praise of competitive markets as systems of spontaneous order. But markets, like any other such systems, are vulnerable to the strategies of those who seek to acquire dominance over economic relationships. When the structure of human societies is conceptualized in terms of markets and states, there is strong reason to believe that the formal structure of economic relationships will succumb to dominance strategies pursued in collusion with state officials. Principles of polycentricity need to be extended through the whole system of human affairs. This applies to public economies as well as to market economies, to the constitution of particular units of government and to federal systems of government, to the conduct of elections and to the organization of political parties, to the operation of open public realms, to the deliberations of legislative bodies, to the function of executive instrumentalities, to communities of scholarship, to spiritual affairs, to institutions of education, and to the practice of professions – in short, to all of the conditions of life.

The radical implication of American federalism can be appreciated only if principles of polycentricity are to apply through the whole system of human affairs. It is then that we can begin to appreciate how that experiment was an effort 'to construct society upon a new basis', why theories 'hitherto unknown or deemed impracticable' were to have a special significance, and why that experiment was 'to exhibit a spectacle for which the world had not been prepared by the history of the past'. Tocqueville was one of the few observers who in the conduct of his analysis showed an appreciation for the way that principles of federalism, viewed as principles of polycentricity, might apply through the whole system of human affairs.

It is in that context, then, that I interpret his observation about the need for 'a new science of politics' for 'a new world' (Tocqueville [1835] 1945, 1: 7). We cannot rely upon spontaneity alone. Instead, human beings need to draw upon an art and science of association that will enable them to recognize the essential limits to every system of polycentric ordering, and see how strategies of dominance always pose threats. Contestation, innovation, and convergence toward mutually productive arrangements are the most likely ways to achieve progress in human societies. Once we accept this, we can begin to appreciate why the use of power to check power need not yield deadlock, stalemate, and immobility. Sufficient degrees of spontaneity exist to yield counterintuitive results. But such systems of order are always vulnerable to circumstances where bonds of mutual respect and methods of normative inquiry give way to efforts to gain dominance over others and to enjoy the fruits of victory by exploiting others.

References

Berman, H. (1983) *Law and Revolution: The Formation of the Western Legal Tradition,* Cambridge, Mass.: Harvard University Press.

Boulding, K. E. (1963) 'Toward a Pure Theory of Threat Systems', *American Economic Review* 53 (May): 424–34.

Dardess, J. W. (1983) *Confucianism and Autocracy: Professional Elites in the Founding of the Ming Dynasty,* Berkeley and Los Angeles: University of California Press.

Hamilton, A., Jay, J. and Madison, J., *The Federalist,* New York: Modern Library, (First published in 1788)

Hayek, F. von (1973) *Rules and Order,* vol. 1 of *Law, Legislation and Liberty,* Chicago: University of Chicago Press.

Mandeville, Bernard (1970) *The Fable of the Bees,* New York: Penguin. (First published in 1714)

Ostrom, V., Tiebout, C. M. and Warren, R. (1961) 'The Organization of Government in Metropolitan Areas: A Theoretical Inquiry', *American Political Science Review* 55 (Dec.): 831–42.

Piaget, J. (1969) *The Moral Judgment of the Child,* New York: Free Press. First published in 1932.

Polanyi, M. (1951) *The Logic of Liberty: Reflections and Rejoinders,* Chicago: University of Chicago Press.

Smith, A. *The Wealth of Nations,* London: Ward, Lock & Tyler. (First published in 1776)

Tocqueville, Al. de *Democracy in America,* New York: Knopf. (First published in 1835 and 1840)

Chapter Three

The Quest for Meaning in Public Choice[1]

Elinor Ostrom and Vincent Ostrom

Logical foundations of democracies

In our efforts to understand the logical foundations of constitutional democracy, we both found that *The Calculus of Consent* (Buchanan and Tullock 1962) gave us basic tools for acquiring some analytical leverage in addressing particular problems that people are required to address about public affairs. Vincent had, for example, served as a consultant to the Alaska constitutional convention, working with others in committees and subcommittees to prepare the draft of Article VIII on Natural Resources. The principle of conceptual unanimity gave meaning to what he had observed and what was accomplished. The physical and cultural exigencies of Alaska loomed large in considering the juridical principles of property relationships to apply to the appropriation of natural resources in the public domain.

Elinor explored the way that pumpers in West Basin, California, used equity jurisprudence to engage efforts to craft public enterprises for governing and managing groundwater basins as common-pool resources. The processes of equity jurisprudence sought to achieve conceptual unanimity in establishing the nature of the problem, in adjudicating water rights, in formulating the rules that were constitutive of water user associations, the way they related to one another, and in monitoring performance.

Adjudicating water rights, establishing pump taxes, and developing exchange relationships suggested efforts to minimize the costs of time and effort to be expended and potential deprivation costs. Public enterprises capable of levying taxes and enforcing regulations became the essential complement of private for-profit enterprises and voluntary nonprofit enterprises. Public entrepreneurs in the Southern California region crafted numerous, diversely constituted enterprises to facilitate the development of that region. Water supply depended on extensive analytical capabilities worked out in different political arenas (E. Ostrom 1965 1990).

These tiny events in the sea of human endeavours impelled us to explore efforts to address the logical foundations for order in human societies. In addition to

1. Ostrom, Elinor, and Ostrom, Vincent (2004) 'The Quest for Meaning in Public Choice'. *American Journal of Economics and Sociology* 63 (1): 105–47. Special Invited Issue: The Production and Diffusion of Public Choice Political Economy: Reflections on the VPI Center (Jan., 2004).

reading what authors had to say, we devoted ourselves to efforts to understand the logic and the presuppositions that authors were using in what they had to say. The authors of *The Federalist* (n.d. [1788]) developed and used a theory of constitutional choice to explain the draft constitution formulated by the constitutional convention held in Philadelphia in 1787. The essays initially prepared as newspaper articles were addressed 'To the People of the State of New York' as an effort to inform their deliberations about the ratification of the Constitution of the United States. Vincent's *The Political Theory of a Compound Republic* (1987 [1971]) is an effort to expound the theory used by Alexander Hamilton and James Madison as they sought to address themselves to the theoretical architecture of a federal republic known as the United States of America.

The works of Thomas Hobbes, John Locke, the Baron de Montesquieu, David Hume, Emmanuel Kant, Adam Smith, and many others provide a longer-standing tradition of inquiry about the logical foundations of order in human societies. All of these efforts sought to contribute to and elaborate a *calculus of consent*. In many ways, Hobbes's *De Cive or the Citizen* (1949 [1642]) and *Leviathan* (1960 [1651]) are remarkable efforts to deal with the logical foundations of political order. His treatment of the human condition, the place of language in understanding the human condition, and the dilemma of individuals who seek their own good and who in the presence of scarcity wind up fighting with one another and enduring the misery of war are efforts to clarify the logical foundations of commonwealths.

Hobbes's way of resolving the dilemma of those who seek their own good but realize the misery of war was to consider how men might achieve peace as an alternative to war. His resolution was to use the Golden Rule – '*Do not that to another, which thou wouldest not have done to thyself*' (1960 [1651]: 103); emphasis in original – as a method of normative inquiry to establish the basic principles that would serve as the articles of peace. This is a method for making interpersonal comparisons and striving for conceptual unanimity.

> [If,] when weighing the actions of other men with his own, they seem too heavy [...] put them into the other part of the balance, and his own into their place, that his own passions, and self-love, may add nothing to the weight; and then there is none [of the conditions of peace] that will not appear unto him very reasonable. (*Ibid.*)

These articles of peace, also referred to as 'natural laws' and 'God's law', were clearly insufficient because words alone cannot bind people to perform without means of enforcement: 'And Covenants, without the sword, are but words, and of no strength to bind a man at all' (p. 109). Hobbes expounded a theory of a unitary sovereign, presuming that the unity of law and the unity of a commonwealth depended on the unity of a sovereign representative. It follows that Hobbes's sovereign is the source of law, is above the law, and cannot be held accountable to law. His theory of democracy in which an assembly of citizens would exercise sovereign prerogative was clearly inadequate. *Rule by assembly* cannot occur in the absence of a common understanding about the *rules of assembly*. Such a common understanding to prevail would need to meet the requirement of conceptual unanimity. Indeed, the play of any game marked by winning and losing is viable only when the players agree on the rules of the game. A sense of justice depends on standards of fairness that apply to human relationships.

Locke, Montesquieu, Hume, Smith, Kant, and the American federalists were able to conceptualize aspects in the logical foundation of constitutional democracies. Montesquieu expressed the basic anomaly in a straightforward way. Virtue is the basic motive governing republics in which each individual is presumed to be self-governing and the legislative power is presumed to reside in the whole community. But to prevent the abuse of power, it is necessary that the architecture of authority relationships be fashioned on the principle that 'power should be used to check power'. Madison in Essay 51 of *The Federalist* expressed the same principle in the following language:

> This policy of supplying, by opposite and rival interests, the defect of better motives, might be traced through the whole system of human affairs, private as well as public. We see it particularly displayed in all the subordinate distributions of power, where the constant aim is to divide and arrange the several offices in such a manner as that each may be a check on the other – that the private interest of every individual may be a sentinel over the public rights. These inventions of prudence cannot be less requisite in the distribution of the supreme powers of the State (n.d.[1788]: 338).

Dilemmas confronting human beings can be resolved to mutual advantage, but all resolutions are subject to threats. Wherever we turn, human beings are plagued by many of the following anomalies:

- Languages greatly enhance human capabilities for learning that can be accrued across successive generations, but language can also be used to create false illusions, deceive, misinform, and amplify errors.
- The amplification of knowledge and action possibilities creates potential for chaos unless the language of rule-ordered relationships can be used to establish mutual expectations about how to behave in hypothetical situations.
- To make rules binding in human relationships requires that some be assigned authority to impose sanctions (evils) on others. All human societies are Faustian bargains; potentials for doing evil are necessary to achieving the common good.
- The rule-ruler-ruled relationship is the most fundamental source of inequalities in human societies.
- If the unity of law depends on a single ultimate centre of authority, then those who are the source of law cannot themselves be held accountable to a rule of law.
- Those who exercise the prerogatives of rulership and control the instruments of coercion in a society are in a position to dominate the allocation of values and to use the instruments of ruler-ship to oppress and exploit those who are subject to those rulership prerogatives.

- The quest for rule-ordered relationships creates opportunities for oppression and tyranny.
- The character of this Faustian bargain leaves human beings in a difficult dilemma. They have the choice of submitting to those who are their rulers or to try to find ways to bind those who exercise rulership prerogatives to a rule of law.
- Submission to dominance is destructive of innovative potentials. Immobility prevails.
- The long-standing quest to achieve a just state and covenantal system of governance turns on placing enforceable limits on the exercise of rulership prerogatives by allocating agency relationships subject to veto capabilities.
- Any system subject to an assignment of limited authority is vulnerable to stalemate.
- Strong incentives exist for some individuals in the presence of recurrent stalemates to form organisations to slate candidates, fabricate slogans, mobilize votes, win elections, dominate the various instrumentalities of government, and enjoy the fruits of victory. Systems grounded in limitations on power associated with such concepts as separation of powers, checks and balances, and federal distributions of authority give way to machine politics and boss rule.

What was expounded by Alexander Hamilton as a general theory of limited constitutions remained to be construed by Alexis de Tocqueville in his *Democracy in America* (1990 [1835, 1840]). He recognized the innovative and experimental character of the undertaking in the concluding remarks at the end of the chapter on the physical features of the North American continent:

> In that land the great experiment of the attempt to construct society upon a new basis was to be made by civilized man; and it was there, for the first time, that theories hitherto unknown, or deemed impracticable, were to exhibit a spectacle for which the world had not been prepared by the history of the past (*Ibid.* 1: 25).

Tocqueville referred to the aggregate structure of the great experiment to construct society on a new basis as a *self-governing society*: 'there society governs itself for itself' (1: 57). Larry Siedentop in his biography entitled *Tocqueville* asserts that '[b]y writing *Democracy in America* [1835] Tocqueville attempted something extraordinary – the overturn of the established European idea of the state' (1994: 41). Rather than a state-governing society, the possibility exists of societies governing themselves for themselves.

The principle of using power to check power might be reiterated in all their political experiments with processes of *constitutional choice* setting the terms and conditions of *collective choice* and carried through to the *operational choices* that people make in their everyday life. Buchanan and Tullock's *The Calculus of Consent* (1962) helped to clarify the logical foundations of constitutional democracy if extended throughout the whole system of human affairs.

By contrast, Milovan Djilas, writing in the 1950s, observed in his analysis of the Soviet experiment:

Everything happened differently in the U.S.S.R. and other Communist countries from what the leaders – even such prominent ones as Lenin, Stalin, Trotsky, and Bukharin – anticipated. They expected that the state would rapidly wither away, that democracy would be strengthened. *The reverse happened.* They expected a rapid improvement in the standard of living – there has been scarcely any change in this respect and, in the subjugated Eastern European countries, the standard has even declined. In every instance, the standard of living has failed to rise in proportion to the rate of industrialization, which was much more rapid. It was believed that the differences between cities and villages, between intellectual and physical labor, would slowly disappear; instead these differences have increased. Communist anticipations in other areas – including their expectations for development in the non-Communist world – have failed to materialize.

The greatest illusion was that industrialization and collectivization in the U.S.S.R. and destruction of capitalist ownership, would result in a classless society. In 1936, when the new Constitution was promulgated, Stalin announced that the 'exploiting class' had ceased to exist. *The capitalist and other classes of ancient origin had in fact been destroyed, but a new class, previously unknown to history, had been formed* (1957: 37–38; emphasis added).

The viability of American experiments in Tocqueville's analysis was subject to certain risks marked by the collusive efforts of politicians to gain dominance over all decision structures. These efforts came to fruition in the post–Civil War era with the reign of machine politics and boss rule. Constitutional remedies were achieved by the Progressive Reform Movement during the late 19th and early 20th centuries. Tocqueville was convinced that if citizens act on their natural inclinations that centralization of government and the abandonment of self-governing capabilities would be the result; and that the exercise of self-governing capabilities would depend on the exercise of an artisanship grounded in an art and science of association. Maximizing utility without attention to the way that ideas shape deeds leads people to trample civilization underfoot.

F. A. Hayek in his essay on 'The Use of Knowledge in Society' (1945) advanced the thesis that all artisanship requires the application of generalities to time and place specificities. The logical foundation of constitutional democracy requires that generalizations be applied to the specificities of time and place exigencies. Local knowledge is a necessary complement to the generalities that accrue from scientific knowledge.

The specificities associated with contingencies of time are subject to dynamic patterns of change. Tocqueville, for example, in the opening paragraphs of his 'Introduction' to *Democracy in America* advances the conjecture that 'a great democratic revolution' was occurring in western Christendom. Efforts to apply the logical foundation of constitutional democracy to heterogeneous time and place exigencies and to avoid the manifold threats to the viability of democratic undertakings will assume such complexities that they will exceed human understanding. Karl Popper in *The Open Society and Its Enemies* presents a comparable assertion when he writes that '[t]he open society can be described as one of the deepest revolutions through which mankind has passed' (1963 [1945] 1:175). The meaning of deepness is suggested by Tocqueville when he writes that the 'great democratic revolution' is marked by basic long-term transformations in human societies:

> Gradually enlightenment spreads, a reawakening of the taste for literature and the arts became evident, intellect and will contributed to success, knowledge became an attribute of government, intelligence a social force; the educated man took part in the affairs of state. (*Ibid.* 1: 4)

Harold Lasswell and Abraham Kaplan (1950) have suggested that the different social sciences apply to different aspects of the same social reality. Alexander Hamilton had raised the question of whether good government could be shaped by reflection and choice. James Buchanan (1979), in turn, suggested that the character of individuals is an artifactual creation fashioned by reflection and choice.

Frameworks, theories, and models for studying public choice

Explaining the anomalies presented above, the multiple levels of analysis, and the complexities and dynamic aspects of public choices depend on theoretical work undertaken at three levels of specificity that are often confused with one another. These essential foundations include: (1) frameworks, (2) theories, and (3) models. Analyses conducted at each level provide different degrees of specificity related to particular problems.

The development and use of a general *framework* help to identify the elements, and relationships among these elements, that one needs to consider in doing any analysis. Frameworks organise diagnostic and prescriptive inquiry. They provide the most general list of variables that should be used to analyse all types of institutional arrangements. Frameworks provide a metatheoretic language that can be used to compare theories. They attempt to identify the *universal* elements that any theory relevant to the same kind of phenomena would need to include. Many differences in surface reality can result from the way these variables combine with or interact with one another. Thus, the elements contained in a framework help the analyst generate the questions that need to be addressed when first conducting an analysis.[2]

The development and use of *theories* enable the analyst to specify which elements of the framework are particularly relevant for certain kinds of questions and to make general working assumptions about these elements. Thus, theories include elements of a framework and make specific assumptions that are

---

2.   This section draws on E. Ostrom (1999).

necessary for an analyst to diagnose a phenomenon, explain its processes, and predict outcomes. Several theories are usually compatible with any framework. Economic theory, game theory, public choice theory, transaction cost theory, covenantal theory, and theories of public goods and common-pool resources are all compatible with the Institutional Analysis and Development (IAD) framework that has been developed over the years at the Workshop in Political Theory and Policy Analysis at Indiana University (Kiser and E. Ostrom 1982; Oakerson 1992; E. Ostrom, Gardner, and Walker 1994).

The development and use of *models* make precise assumptions about a limited set of parameters and variables. Logic, mathematics, game theory, experimentation and simulation, and other means are used to explore systematically the consequences of particular assumptions on a limited set of outcomes. Multiple models are usually compatible with any one theory. Slight changes in the assumptions made about the shape of a production function or the payoff function of a particular player change the structure of a model without changing the structure of the broader theory generating the model.

For policy makers and scholars interested in issues related to how different governance systems enable individuals to solve problems democratically, the IAD framework helps to organise diagnostic, analytical, and prescriptive capabilities. It also aids in the accumulation of knowledge from empirical studies and in the assessment of past efforts at reforms. Markets and hierarchies are frequently presented as fundamentally different 'pure types' of organisation. Such a view precludes the use of a more general explanatory framework and closely related theories that help analysts make cross-institutional comparisons and evaluations.

Without the capacity to undertake systematic, comparative institutional assessments, recommendations of reform may be based on naive ideas about which kinds of institutions are 'good' or 'bad' and not on an analysis of performance. One needs a common framework and family of theories in order to address questions of reforms and transitions. Particular models then help the analyst to deduce specific predictions about likely outcomes of highly simplified structures. Models are useful in policy analysis when they are well tailored to the particular problem at hand. Models can be used inappropriately when applied to the study of problematic situations that do not closely fit the assumptions of the model.

The institutional analysis and development (IAD) framework

As indicated earlier, an institutional framework should identify the major types of structural variables present to some extent in *all* institutional arrangements but whose values differ from one type of institutional arrangement to another. The IAD framework is a multi-tier conceptual map (*see* Figure 3.1). One part of the framework is the identification of an action arena, the resulting patterns of interactions and outcomes, and evaluating these outcomes (*see* right half of Figure 3.1). The problem could be at an operational tier where actors interact in light of the incentives they face to generate outcomes directly in the world.

Figure 3.1: A Framework for Institutional Analysis

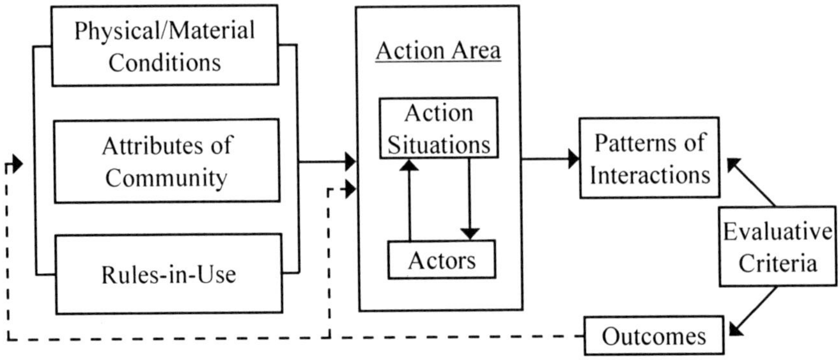

Source: E. Ostrom (1999: 42).

The problem could also be at a policy (or collective-choice) tier where decision makers repeatedly have to make policy decisions within the constraints of a set of collective choice rules. The policy decisions then affect the structure of arenas where individuals are making operational decisions and thus impacting directly on a physical world. The problem could as well be at a constitutional tier where decisions are made about who is eligible to participate in policy making and the rules that will be used to undertake policy making.

The first step in analysing a problem is to identify a conceptual unit – called an *action arena* – that can be utilized to analyse, predict, and explain behavior within institutional arrangements. Action arenas include an *action situation* and the *actors* in that situation. An action situation can be characterized using seven clusters of variables: (1) participants, (2) positions, (3) outcomes, (4) action-outcome linkages, (5) the control that participants exercise, (6) information, and (7) the costs and benefits assigned to outcomes. An actor (an individual or a corporate actor) includes assumptions about four clusters of variables:

1. the *resources* that an actor brings to a situation;
2. the *valuation* actors assign to states of the world and to actions;
3. the way actors acquire, process, retain, and use *knowledge contingencies and information*; and
4. the processes actors use for *selection* of particular courses of action.

An action arena refers to the social space where individuals interact, exchange goods and services, solve problems, dominate one another, or fight (among the many things that individuals do in action arenas). Considerable theoretical work in the public choice tradition focuses only on one arena and takes the variables specifying the situation and the motivational and cognitive structure of an actor as givens. The task of analysis is then to predict the behavior of individuals, assuming that some kind of equilibrium is likely in a fixed situation.

Two additional steps could also be taken. One step digs deeper and inquires into the factors that affect the structure of an action arena. From this vantage point, the action arena is viewed as a set of variables dependent upon other factors. These factors affecting the structure of an action arena include three clusters of variables: (1) the rules used by participants to order their relationships, (2) the attributes of states of the world that are acted upon in these arenas, and (3) the structure of the more general community within which any particular arena is placed (*see* Kiser and E. Ostrom 1982). This step is examined in the next section of this paper. Then one can move outward from action arenas to consider methods for explaining complex structures that link sequential and simultaneous action arenas to one another (*see* the left side of Figure 3.1).

Diagnosis and explanation within the frame of an action arena

As mentioned earlier, the term *action arena* refers to a complex conceptual unit containing one set of variables called an *action situation* and a second set of variables called an *actor*. One needs both components – the situation and the actors in the situation – to diagnose, explain, and predict actions and results.

An action situation

The term *action situation* is used to refer to an analytic concept that enables an analyst to isolate the immediate structure affecting a process of interest to the analyst for the purpose of explaining regularities in human actions and results, and potentially to reform them. A common set of variables used to describe the structure of an action situation includes: (1) the set of participants; (2) the specific positions to be filled by participants; (3) the set of allowable actions and their linkage to outcomes; (4) the potential outcomes that are linked to individual sequences of actions; (5) the level of control each participant has over choice; (6) the information available to participants about the structure of the action situation; and (7) the costs and benefits – which serve as incentives and deterrents – assigned to actions and outcomes. In addition, whether a situation will occur once, a known finite number of times, or indefinitely affects the strategies of individuals. When explaining actions and cumulated results within the framework of an action arena, these variables are the 'givens' that one works with to describe the structure of the situation. These are the common elements used in game theory to construct formal game models.

The actor: theories and models of the individual

The *actor* in a situation can be thought of as a single individual or as a group functioning as a corporate actor. The term *action* refers to those human behaviours for which the acting individual attaches a subjective and instrumental meaning. All analysts of microbehaviour use an implicit or explicit theory or model of the actors in situations in order to derive inferences about the likely behavior of each actor in a situation (and, thus, about the pattern of joint results that may be produced). The analyst must make assumptions about what and how participants value; what resources, information, and beliefs they have; their information-processing capabilities; and the internal mechanisms they use to decide upon strategies.

For many problems, it is useful to accept the classical political economy view that an individual's choice of strategy in any particular situation depends on how he or she perceives and weighs the benefits and costs of various strategies and their likely outcomes (Radnitzky 1987). The most well-established formal model of the individual used in public choice is *homo economicus*, which assumes that actors have complete and well-ordered preferences, complete information, and that they maximize the net value of expected returns to the actor. All of these assumptions are controversial and are being challenged on many fronts. Many institutional analysts tend to use a broader conception of individual actors. Many stress that perceived costs and benefits include the time and resources devoted to establishing and maintaining relationships (Williamson 1979), as well as the value that individuals attach to establishing a reputation for being reliable and trustworthy (Breton and Wintrobe 1982).

Alternatively, one could assume that the individuals who calculate benefits and costs are fallible learners who vary in terms of the number of other persons whose perceived benefits and costs are important to them and in terms of their personal commitment to keeping promises and honouring forms of reciprocity extended to them (E. Ostrom 1990). Fallible learners can, and often do, make mistakes. Settings differ, however, as to whether the institutional incentives involved encourage people to learn from these mistakes. Fallibility and the capacity to learn can thus be viewed as assumptions of a more general theory of the individual. One can then presume that the various institutional arrangements that individuals use in governing and managing common-pool resources (or other problematic situations) offer them different incentives and opportunities to learn.

When fallible, learning individuals interact in frequently repeated and simple situations, it is possible to model them as if they had complete information about the relevant variables for making choices in those situations. In highly competitive environments, we can make the further assumption that the individuals who survive the selective pressure of the environment act as if they are maximizers of a key variable associated with survival in that environment (e.g. profits or fitness) (Alchian 1950; Dosi and Egidi 1987). When individuals face a relatively simple decision situation where institutions generate accurate information about the variables relevant to a particular problem, that problem can be adequately represented as a straightforward, constrained maximization problem.

Many of the situations of interest in understanding public choices about common-pool resources, however, are uncertain, complex, and lack the selective pressure and information-generating capabilities of a competitive market. Therefore, one can substitute the assumption of bounded rationality – that persons are intendedly rational but only limitedly so – for the assumptions of perfect information and utility maximization used in axiomatic choice theory (*see* Simon 1965, 1972; Williamson 1985; E. Ostrom, Gardner and Walker 1994: ch. 9). Information search is costly, and the information-processing capabilities of human beings are limited. Individuals, therefore, often must make choices based on incomplete knowledge of all possible alternatives and their likely outcomes. With incomplete information and imperfect information-processing capabilities, all individuals may make mistakes in choosing strategies designed to realize a set of goals (V. Ostrom 1986). Over time, however, they can acquire a greater understanding of their situation and adopt strategies that result in higher returns. Reciprocity may develop, rather than strictly narrow, short-term pursuit of self-interest (Oakerson 1993; E. Ostrom 1998).

Predicting outcomes within an action arena

Depending upon the analytical structure of a situation and the particular assumptions about the actor used, the analyst makes strong or weak inferences about results. In tightly constrained, one-shot action situations under conditions of complete information, where participants are motivated to select particular strategies or chains of actions that jointly lead to stable equilibria, an analyst can frequently make strong inferences and specific predictions about likely patterns of behavior and outcomes.

When there is no limit on the number of appropriators from a common-pool resource or on the amount of harvesting activities they undertake, for example, one can develop a mathematical model of an open-access, common-pool resource (*see*, for example, E. Ostrom, Gardner and Walker 1994). When the net benefits of harvesting to each entrant increase for the initial set of resource units sought and decrease thereafter, each appropriator acting independently tends to make individual decisions that jointly yield a deficient (but stable) equilibrium. A model of an open-access, common-pool resource generates a clear prediction of a race to use up the resource, leading to high social costs. Both field research and laboratory experimental research strongly support the predictions of overuse and potential destruction of *open-access*, common-pool resources where appropriators do not share access to collective-choice arenas in which to change the open-access structure they face (E. Ostrom, Gardner and Walker 1994).

Many arenas, however, do not generate such unambiguous results. Instead of completely independent decision making, individuals may be embedded in communities where initial norms of fairness and conservation may change the structure of the situation dramatically. Within these situations, participants may adopt a broader range of strategies. Further, they may change their strategies over time as they learn about the results of past actions. The analyst examining these more open, less-constrained situations makes weaker inferences and predicts the patterns of outcomes that are relatively more or less likely to result from a particular type of situation. In laboratory experiments, for example, giving subjects in a common-pool resource situation opportunities to communicate generally increases the joint outcomes they achieve (*see* E. Ostrom, Gardner and Walker 1994 and cites contained therein). In field settings, multiple studies have shown that individuals have far more capabilities to change rules to reduce the incentives to overproduce and in many cases achieve sustainable use of renewable resources (Tang 1992; Bromley *et al.* 1992; Lam 1998).

In field settings, it is hard to tell where one action arena starts and another stops. Life continues in what appears to be a seamless web as individuals move from home to market to work (action situations typically characterized by reciprocity, by exchange, or by team problem solving or command). Further, within arenas, choices of actions *within* a set of rules as contrasted to choices *among* future rules are frequently made without recognizing that the level of action has shifted. So, when a 'boss' says to an 'employee', 'How about changing the way we do X?', and the two discuss options and jointly agree upon a better way, they have shifted from taking actions *within* previously established rules to making decisions *about* the rules structuring future actions. In other words, using IAD language, they have shifted to a constitutional choice or a collective-choice arena.

Evaluating outcomes

In addition to predicting outcomes, public choice theorists may also evaluate the outcomes that are being achieved, as well as the likely set of outcomes that could be achieved under alternative institutional arrangements. Evaluative criteria are applied to both the outcomes and the processes of achieving outcomes. While there are many potential evaluative criteria, let us briefly focus on (1) economic efficiency, (2) equity through fiscal equivalence, (3) redistributional equity, (4) accountability, (5) conformance to general morality and (6) adaptability.

Economic efficiency

Economic efficiency is determined by the magnitude of the change in the flow of net benefits associated with an allocation or reallocation of resources. The concept of efficiency plays a central role in studies estimating the benefits and costs or rates of return to investments, which are often used to determine the economic feasibility or desirability of public policies. When considering alternative institutional arrangements, therefore, it is crucial to consider how revisions in the rules affecting participants will alter behavior and, hence, the allocation of resources.

Fiscal equivalence

There are two principal means to assess equity: (1) on the basis of the equality between individuals' contributions to an effort and the benefits they derive and (2) on the basis of differential abilities to pay. The concept of equity that underlies an exchange economy holds that those who benefit from a service should bear the burden of financing that service. Perceptions of fiscal equivalence or a lack thereof can affect the willingness of individuals to contribute toward the development and maintenance of resource systems.

Redistributional equity

Policies that redistribute resources to poorer individuals are of considerable importance. Thus, although efficiency would dictate that scarce resources be used where they produce the greatest net benefit, equity goals may temper this objective, resulting in the provision of facilities that benefit particularly needy groups. Likewise, redistributional objectives may conflict with the goal of achieving fiscal equivalence.

Accountability

In a democratic polity, officials should be accountable to citizens concerning the development and use of public facilities and natural resources. Without accountability, actors can engage successfully in the various strategic behaviours. Concern for accountability need not conflict greatly with efficiency and equity goals. Indeed, achieving efficiency requires that information about the preferences of citizens be available to decision makers, as does achieving accountability. Institutional arrangements that effectively aggregate this information assist in realizing efficiency at the same time that they serve to increase accountability and to promote the achievement of redistributional objectives.

Conformance to general morality

In addition to accountability, one may wish to evaluate the level of general morality fostered by a particular set of institutional arrangements. Are those who are able to cheat and go undetected able to obtain very high payoffs? Are those who keep promises more likely to be rewarded and advanced in their careers? How do those who repeatedly interact within a set of institutional arrangements learn to relate to one another over the long term?

Adaptability

Finally, unless institutional arrangements are able to respond to ever-changing environments, the sustainability of resources and investments is likely to suffer. Rural areas of developing countries are often faced with natural disasters and highly localized special circumstances. If an institutional arrangement is too inflexible to cope with these unique conditions, it is unlikely to prosper. For example, if an irrigation system is centrally controlled and allocates only a specific amount of resources for annual and periodic maintenance, it may not be able to meet the special needs associated with a major flood that destroys a section of the canal system.

Trade-offs are often necessary in using performance criteria as a basis for selecting from alternative institutional arrangements. It is particularly difficult to choose between the goals of efficiency and of redistributional equity. The trade-off issue arises most explicitly in considering alternative methods of funding public projects. Economically efficient pricing of the use of an existing resource or facility should reflect only the incremental maintenance costs and any external or social costs associated with its use. This is the well-known, efficiency-pricing principle that requires that prices equal the marginal costs of usage. The principle is especially problematic in the case of goods with non-subtractability attributes. In such instances, the marginal cost of another user utilizing the good is zero; hence, the efficient price is also zero. Zero user prices, however, require that all sources of resource mobilization are tax-based, which induces other kinds of perverse incentives and potential inefficiencies. Evaluating how institutional arrangements compare across overall criteria is quite a challenge. Analytical examination of the likely tradeoffs between intermediate costs is valuable in attempting to understand comparative institutional performance (*see* E. Ostrom, Schroeder and Wynne 1993: ch. 5).

Explanation viewing action arenas as dependent variables

Underlying the way analysts conceptualise action arenas are implicit assumptions about the *rules* individuals use to order their relationships, about attributes of *states of the world and their transformations*, and about the *nature of the community* within which the arena occurs. Rules, states of the world, and the nature of the community all jointly affect the types of actions that individuals can take, the benefits and costs of their attributes to these actions and resulting outcomes, and the likely outcomes achieved.

The concept of rules

Rules are shared understandings among those involved that refer to enforced prescriptions about what actions (or states of the world) are *required, prohibited,* or *permitted*. All rules are the result of implicit or explicit efforts to achieve order and predictability among humans by creating classes of persons (positions) who are then required, permitted, or forbidden to take classes of actions in relation to required, permitted, or forbidden states of the world (Crawford and E. Ostrom 1995; V. Ostrom 1991).

In an open and democratic governance system, there are many sources of the rules that individuals use in everyday life. It is not considered illegal or improper for individuals to self-organise themselves and craft their own rules, if the activities they engage in are legal. In addition to the legislation and regulations of a formal central government, there are apt to be laws passed by regional, local and special governments. Within private firms and voluntary associations, individuals are authorized to adopt many different rules for who is a member of the firm or association, how profits (benefits) are to be shared, and how decisions will be made. Each family constitutes its own rule-making body.

When individuals genuinely participate in the crafting of multiple layers of rules, some of that crafting will occur using pen and paper. Much of it, however, will occur as problem-solving individuals interact trying to figure out how to do a better job in the future than they have done in the past. Colleagues in a work team are crafting their own rules when they might say to one another: 'How about if you do A in the future, and I will do B, and before we ever make a decision about C again, we both discuss it and make a joint decision'. In a democratic society, problem-solving individuals do this all the time. They also participate in less fluid decision-making arrangements, including elections to select legislators.

Thus, when we do a deeper institutional analysis, we attempt first to understand the working rules that individuals use in making decisions. Working rules are the set of rules to which participants would refer if asked to explain and justify their actions to fellow participants. While following a rule may become a 'social habit', it is possible to make participants consciously aware of the rules they use to order their relationships. Individuals can consciously decide to adopt a different rule and change their behavior to conform to such a decision. Over time, behavior in conformance with a new rule may itself become habitual (*see* Shimanoff 1980; Toulmin 1974; Harré 1974). The capacity of humans to use complex cognitive systems to order their own behavior at a relatively subconscious level makes it difficult for empirical researchers to ascertain what the working rules for an ongoing action arena may be.

Once we understand the working rules, then, we attempt to understand where those rules come from. In a system governed by a 'rule of law', the general legal framework in use will have its source in actions taken in constitutional, legislative, and administrative settings augmented by decisions taken by individuals in many different particular settings. In other words, the rules-in-form are consistent with the rules-in-use (Sproule-Jones 1993). In a system that is not governed by a 'rule of law', there may be central laws and considerable effort made to enforce them, but individuals attempt to evade rather than obey the law.

Rule-following or conforming actions are not as predictable as biological or physical behavior explained by scientific laws. All rules are formulated in human language. As such, rules share problems of lack of clarity, misunderstanding, and change that typify any language-based phenomenon (V. Ostrom 1980, 1997). Words are always simpler than the phenomenon to which they refer.

The stability of rule-ordered actions is dependent upon the shared meaning assigned to words used to formulate a set of rules. If no shared meaning exists when a rule is formulated, confusion will exist about what actions are required, permitted, or forbidden. Regularities in actions cannot result if those who must repeatedly interpret the meaning of a rule within action situations arrive at multiple interpretations. Because 'rules are not self-formulating, self-determining, or self-enforcing' (V. Ostrom 1980: 312), it is human agents who formulate them, apply them in particular situations, and attempt to enforce performance consistent with them. Even if shared meaning exists at the time of the acceptance of a rule, transformations in technology, in shared norms, and in circumstances more generally change the events to which rules apply. 'Applying language to changing configurations of development increases the ambiguities and threatens the shared criteria of choice with an erosion of their appropriate meaning' (*Ibid.*).

What rules are important in public choice? A myriad of specific rules are used in structuring complex action arenas. Scholars have been trapped into endless cataloguing of rules not related to a method of classification most useful for theoretical explanations. But classification is a necessary step in developing a science. Anyone attempting to define a useful typology of rules must be concerned that the classification is more than a method for imposing superficial order onto an extremely large set of seemingly disparate rules. The way we have tackled this problem is to classify rules according to their impact on the elements of an action situation.

Rule configurations

A first step toward identifying the working rules can be made, then, by overtly examining how working rules affect each of the variables of an action situation. A set of working rules that affect these variables should constitute the minimal but necessary set of rules needed to offer an explanation of actions and results based on the working rules used by participants to order their relationships within an action arena. Because states of the world and their transformations and the nature of a community also affect the structure of an action situation, working rules alone never provide both a necessary and sufficient explanation of the structure of an action situation and results.

Adopting this view of the task, seven types of working rules can be said to affect the structure of an action situation. These are: *entry and exit rules, position rules, scope rules, authority rules, aggregation rules, information rules,* and *payoff rules*. The cumulative effect of these seven types of rules affects the seven elements of an action situation.

Entry and exit rules affect the number of *participants*, their attributes and resources, whether they can enter freely, and the conditions they face for leaving. Position rules establish *positions* in the situation. Authority rules assign sets of *actions* that participants in positions at particular nodes must, may, or may not take. Scope rules delimit the *potential outcomes* that can be affected and, working backward, the actions linked to specific outcomes. Authority rules, combined with the scientific laws about the relevant states of the world being acted upon, determine the shape of the decision tree the *action-outcome linkages*. Aggregation rules affect the level of *control* that a participant in a position exercises in the selection of an action at a node. Information rules affect the *knowledge contingent information sets* of participants. Payoff rules affect the *benefits and costs* that will be assigned to particular combinations of actions and outcomes and establish the incentives and deterrents for action. The set of working rules is a *configuration* in the sense that the effect of a change in one rule may depend upon the other rules-in-use.

The problem for the field researcher is that many rules-in-use are not written down. Nor can the field researcher simply be a survey worker asking a random sample of respondents about their rules. Many of the rules-in-use are not even conceptualized by participants as rules. In settings where the rules-in-use have evolved over long periods of time and are understood implicitly by participants, obtaining information about rules-in-use requires spending time at a site and learning how to ask non-threatening, context-specific questions about rule configurations.

Physical and material conditions

While a rule configuration affects all of the elements of an action situation, some of the variables of an action situation are also affected by attributes of the physical and material world. What actions are physically possible, what outcomes can be produced, how actions are linked to outcomes, and what is contained in the actors' information sets are affected by the world being acted upon in a situation. The same set of rules may yield entirely different types of action situations depending upon the types of events in the world being acted upon by participants.

The attributes of states of the world and their transformation are explicitly examined when the analyst self-consciously asks a series of questions about how the world being acted upon in a situation affects the outcome, action sets, action-outcome linkages, and information sets in that situation. The relative importance of the rule configuration and states of the world in structuring an action situation varies dramatically across different types of settings. The relative importance of working rules to attributes of the world also varies dramatically within action situations considered to be part of the public sector. Rules define and constrain voting behavior inside a legislature more than attributes of the world. Voting can be accomplished by raising hands, by paper ballots, by calling for the ayes and nays, by marching before an official counter, or by installing computer terminals for each legislator on which votes are registered. However, in regard to organising communication within a legislature, attributes of the world strongly affect the available options. The principle that only one person can be heard and understood at a time in any one forum strongly affects the capacity of legislators to communicate effectively with one another (*see* V. Ostrom 1987).

Let us consider several attributes that are frequently used to distinguish public goods and services. Goods that are generally considered to be 'public goods' yield non-subtractive benefits that can be enjoyed jointly and simultaneously by many people who are hard to exclude from obtaining these benefits. Common-pool resources yield benefits where beneficiaries are hard to exclude but each person's use of a resource system subtracts units of that resource from a finite total available for harvesting.

Excludability and the free-rider problem

When it is difficult or costly to exclude beneficiaries from a good once it is produced, it is frequently assumed that such a good must be provided publicly, rather than privately. When the benefits of a good are available to a group, whether or not members of the group contribute to the provision of the good, that good is characterized by problems with excludability. Where exclusion is costly, those wishing to provide a good or service face a potential free-rider or collective-action problem (Olson 1965). This is not to say that all individuals will free-ride whenever they can. A strong incentive exists to be a free-rider in all situations where potential beneficiaries cannot easily be excluded for failing to contribute to the provision of a good or service.

Public sector provision of common-pool resources or infrastructure facilities raises additional problems in determining preferences and organising finances. When exclusion is low-cost to the supplier, preferences are revealed as a result of many *quid pro quo* transactions. Producers learn about preferences through the consumers' willingness to pay for various goods offered for sale. Where exclusion is difficult, designing mechanisms that honestly reflect beneficiaries' preferences and their willingness to pay is complex, regardless of whether the providing unit is organised in the public or the private sphere. In very small groups, those affected are usually able to discuss their preferences and constraints on a face-to-face basis and to reach a rough consensus. In larger groups, decisions about infrastructure are apt to be made through mechanisms such as voting or the delegation of authority to public officials where the difficulties of translating preferences into collective choices that adequately reflect individual views are present (Arrow 1951; Shepsle 1979).

Subtractability of the flow

The withdrawal of a quantity of water from an irrigation canal by one farmer means that there is that much less water for anyone else to use. Most agricultural uses of water are fully subtractive, whereas many other uses of water – such as for power generation or navigation – are not. Most of the water that passes through a turbine to generate power, for instance, can be used again downstream. When the use of a flow of services by one individual subtracts from what is available to others and when the flow is scarce relative to demand, users will be tempted to try to obtain as much as they can of the flow for fear that it will not be available later.

Effective rules are required if scarce, fully subtractive service flows are to be allocated in a productive way. Charging prices for subtractive services obviously constitutes one such allocation mechanism. Sometimes, however, it is not feasible (or legal) to price services. In these instances, some individuals will be able to grab considerably more of the subtractive services than others, thereby leading to noneconomic uses of the flow and high levels of conflict among users.

Allocation rules also affect the incentives of users to provide and maintain a system. Farmers located at the tail end of an irrigation system that lacks effective allocation rules have little motivation to contribute to the maintenance of that system because they only occasionally receive their share of water. Similarly, farmers located at the head end of such a system are not motivated to provide maintenance services voluntarily because they will receive disproportionate shares of the water whether or not the system is well maintained (E. Ostrom 1996b).

Consequently, for common-pool resources whose flows are highly subtractive, institutional arrangements related to the allocation of the flow of services are intimately tied to the sustainability of the resource. It is highly unlikely that one can achieve sustainability without careful attention to the efficiency, fairness, and enforceability of the rules specifying who can appropriate how much of the service flow, at what times and places, and under what conditions. Furthermore, unless responsibilities are linked in a reasonable fashion to benefits obtained, the beneficiaries themselves will resist efforts to insist that they take responsibilities.

Additional attributes

In addition to these general attributes of physical and material conditions that affect the incentives of participants, resource systems are also characterized by a diversity of other attributes that affect how rules combine with physical and material conditions to generate positive or negative incentives. Whether resource units are *mobile* or *stationary* and whether *storage* is available somewhere in a system affect the problems that individuals governing and managing common-pool resources face (Schlager, Blomquist and Tang 1994). The problems of regulating a lobster fishery, for example, are much simpler than those of regulating a salmon fishery. Similarly, allocating water in a predictable and efficient manner is easier to achieve when there is some storage in the system than when it is a run-of-the-river system.

The size of a resource system can also have a major impact on the incentives facing participants. The length and slope of a main canal of an irrigation system not only affects the cost of its maintenance but also the strategic bargaining that exists between headenders and tailenders on an irrigation system (Lam 1998; E. Ostrom 1996b). Increasing the number of participants is associated with increased transaction costs. How steeply the costs rise depends, to a large extent, on the rules-in-use and the heterogeneity of the users.

The productivity, predictability, and patchiness of a resource affects the likelihood that private-property arrangements will be successful and enhances the likelihood that common-property arrangements will be necessary (Netting 1982). Similarly, the resilience of a multispecies ecosystem affects the sensitivity of the system to both the rules used to govern the particular system and to changes in economic or environmental conditions elsewhere (Holling 1994).

Attributes of the community

A third set of variables that affect the structure of an action arena relates to the community. The attributes of a community that are important in affecting the structure of an action arena include the norms of behavior generally accepted in the community, the level of common understanding potential participants share about the structure of particular types of action arenas, the extent of homogeneity in the preferences of those living in a community, and the distribution of resources among those affected. The term *culture* is frequently applied to this bundle of variables.

For example, when all appropriators from a common-pool resource share a common set of values and interact with one another in a multiplex set of arrangements, the probabilities of their developing adequate rules and norms to govern resources are much greater (Taylor 1987). The importance of building a reputation for keeping one's word is important in such a community, and the cost of developing monitoring and sanctioning mechanisms is relatively low. If the appropriators of a resource come from many different communities and are distrustful of one another, the task of devising and sustaining effective rules is substantially increased.

Whether individuals use a written vernacular language to express their ideas, develop common understanding, share learning, and explain the foundation of their social order is also a crucial variable of relevance to institutional analysis (V. Ostrom 1997). Without a written vernacular language, individuals face considerably more difficulties in accumulating their own learning in a usable form to transmit from one generation to the next.

Multiple levels of analysis

As all public choice theorists have learned from the work of Buchanan and Tullock, all rules are nested in another set of rules that define how the first set of rules can be changed. The nesting of rules within rules at several levels is similar to the nesting of computer languages at several levels. What can be done at a higher level depends on the capabilities and limits of the rules (or the software) at that level and at a deeper level. Whenever one addresses questions about *institutional change*, as contrasted to choices within institutional constraints, it is necessary to recognize the following:

Changes in the rules used to order action at one level occur within a currently 'fixed' set of rules at a deeper level.

Changes in deeper-level rules usually are more difficult and more costly to accomplish, thus increasing the stability of mutual expectations among individuals interacting according to a set of rules.

It is useful to distinguish three levels of rules that cumulatively affect the actions taken and outcomes obtained in any setting. *Operational rules* directly affect day-to-day decisions made by the participants in any setting. *Collective-choice rules* affect operational activities and results through their effects in determining who is eligible and the specific rules to be used in changing operational rules. *Constitutional-choice rules* affect operational activities and their effects in determining who is eligible and the rules to be used in crafting the set of collective-choice rules that in turn affect the set of operational rules. There is even a 'metaconstitutional' level underlying all the others that is not frequently analysed.

At each level of analysis there may be one or more arenas in which the types of decisions made at that level will occur. In the collective-choice, constitutional, and metaconstitutional situations, activities involve prescribing, invoking, monitoring, applying, and enforcing rules (Lasswell and Kaplan 1950; Oakerson 1994). The concept of an 'arena' as described earlier does not imply a formal setting, but can include such formal settings as legislatures and courts. Policy making (or governance) regarding the rules that will be used to regulate operational-level choices is usually carried out in one or more collective-choice arenas, as shown in Figure 3.2.

Uses of the IAD framework

The IAD framework is thus a general language about how rules, physical and material conditions, and attributes of community affect the structure of action arenas, the incentives that individuals face, and resulting outcomes. It has been used extensively in teaching (*see*, for example, the syllabi for the year-long Workshop seminar at our website: http://www.indiana.edu/~workshop). In the early 1970s, when the IAD framework was first being developed, we were simultaneously trying to understand how the diverse paradigms in political science affected the way we conceptualized public administration and metropolitan organisation (*see* V. Ostrom and E. Ostrom 1971; E. Ostrom 1972). Then, for a decade and a half, we used the nascent framework as a foundation for the conduct of an extensive number of empirical studies of police service delivery in metropolitan areas. During the past 15 years, the IAD framework has been used as the language to develop a theory of common-pool resources and link formal models of appropriation and monitoring with empirical work conducted in an experimental laboratory and in field settings.

In crafting empirical studies using the IAD framework, a key question has always been the appropriate units and levels of analysis for any particular type of question (*see* Gregg 1974). For example, when we studied police services, the police department was only one of the units of analysis included in our work. Rather, we tried to understand who the actors involved were in diverse service situations such as immediate response services, homicide investigation, laboratory analysis, training, and communication services.

We found different sets of actors involved in each of the service situations. In some, citizens as well as police officers as street-level bureaucrats were key participants. In others, we found participants from many different urban service agencies. We had to examine interorganisational arrangements to understand patterns of interaction and results. Using this perspective, we found highly

Figure 3.2: Levels of Analysis and Outcomes

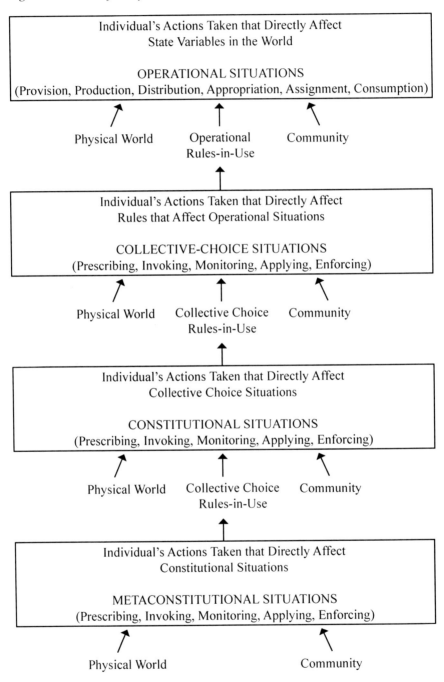

Source: E. Ostrom (1999: 60)

structured patterns of relationships where others had found only chaos. The highest levels of police performance existed, for example, in those metropolitan areas where small-scale, immediate-response units worked along with large-scale investigatory, laboratory, and communication units (Parks 1985). Ongoing research by Roger B. Parks in the Indianapolis area is providing strong evidence that many of the patterns we observed in the 1970s and 1980s are still in evidence in the 1990s. Efforts to understand who was involved in producing public safety led us to formulate a theory of co-production of urban public services (Parks *et al.* 1982; Percy 1984; Kiser 1984; Lam 1996; Whitaker 1980). The theory of co-production has now been applied to a wider set of phenomena (E. Ostrom 1996b). In light of the extensive empirical research, colleagues were able to achieve a far better understanding of the patterns of metropolitan organisation and local government more generally (ACIR 1987, 1988; V. Ostrom, Bish and E. Ostrom 1988; Oakerson and Parks 1988; Parks and Oakerson 1989; Stein 1990).

The second broad area in which the IAD framework has played an important organising role has been the study of common-pool resources. In the early 1980s, the National Academy of Sciences organised a research panel on the study of common property. Ronald Oakerson (1992) wrote a framework paper for the panel that was used in the organisation of a series of case studies of how diverse peoples had devised institutional arrangements related to common-pool resources (*see also* Thomson, Feeny and Oakerson 1992; E. Ostrom 1992). Oakerson's presentation of the framework has influenced an untold number of studies of common-property regimes in many diverse sectors in all regions of the world. The intellectual productivity stimulated by the work of the NAS panel has led to the formation of an International Association for the Study of Common Property (IASCP).

Colleagues at Indiana University have developed a theory of common-pool resources and a series of theoretical models of appropriation from a common-pool resource and tested these in experimental laboratory settings (*see* E. Ostrom, Gardner and Walker 1994; E. Ostrom, Walker and Gardner 1992; Walker and Gardner 1992; Hackett, Schlager and Walker 1994). When laboratory subjects are not allowed to communicate, their behavior closely approximates the behavior that is predicted using finitely repeated, non-cooperative game theory. When allowed to communicate or to use sanctioning mechanisms, the behavior observed in the lab is not consistent with these theoretical models but is similar to what we have observed in field settings. We have consequently developed a theory of how boundedly rational individuals use heuristics such as 'measured responses' to stabilize agreements achieved in settings where there are no external enforcers to impose rules on participants (E. Ostrom, Gardner and Walker 1994).

The IAD framework has now been used to develop three major databases related to the study of common-pool resources and diverse property regimes. The first 'CPR Database' drew on the cases produced for the NAS panel and on the extremely large number of individual case studies that we discovered had been written by historians, sociologists, engineers, political scientists, anthropologists, and students of environmental science (Hess 1999). We used the IAD framework overtly to create a structured database for appropriation and collective-choice arenas. Schlager (1990, 1994) and Tang (1991, 1992) studied approximately 50 in-shore fisheries and irrigation systems, respectively, and were able to isolate key rules that were positively associated with higher performance levels. In *Governing the Commons* (E. Ostrom 1990), I was able to draw on the framework and on an analysis of the extensive case studies we were all reading at that time to elucidate some aspects of a theory of common-pool resources. In particular, I examined the key design principles that characterized robust, self-organised institutions for achieving sustainable resource use of very long periods of time as well as developing an initial theory of institutional change.

The second database focused entirely on irrigation systems and has been used to code more than 175 irrigation systems in Nepal (Benjamin *et al.* 1994). That database has enabled us to test many propositions growing out of both our own theoretical efforts and those of development scholars more generally (*see* Schweik, Adhikari and Pandit 1997; Lam 1994; E. Ostrom, Lam and Lee 1994; E. Ostrom and Gardner 1993; E. Ostrom 1994, 1996a). We have been able to challenge many of the empirical assumptions used by development scholars who have presumed that farmers are unable to self-organise and engage in costly collective action without the imposition of rules from external authorities (*see also* Thomson 1992). We have found that farmer-managed irrigation systems in Nepal are able to outperform agency-managed systems in regard to agricultural productivity when we have controlled for factors such as size of group, length of canal, and type of terrain (Shivakoti and Ostrom 2002).

The third database is an integral part of the International Forestry Resources and Institutions (IFRI) research program, which is a major ongoing research program of the Workshop and of the Centre for the Study of Institutions, Population, and Environmental Change (CIPEC).

This research program is designed to address knowledge and information gaps about how institutions affect the incentives of forest users and result in substantial levels of deforestation in some locations while forest conditions are improving in other locations. Collaborative research centres are now functioning in Bolivia, Guatemala, India, Kenya, Nepal, Tanzania, and Uganda and several more are under consideration (*see* Gibson, McKean, and E. Ostrom 2000). In Uganda, Banana and Gombya-Ssembajjwe (2000) have shown in their initial studies that the only forests where deforestation is not extensive are where local institutional arrangements are viewed by local residents as legitimate and are monitored extensively. In India, Agrawal (2000) provides an empirical challenge to the presumption of many scholars that collective action becomes progressively more difficult as the size of the group increases from a very small face-to-face group. He shows that moderately sized villages are better able to generate the labour needed to protect local forests than are very small villages. Schweik (2000) has examined the geographic distribution of *Shorea robusta*, a highly valued species. He found that neither population density of the villages adjacent to the three forests he studied in Nepal nor predictions from optimal foraging theory adequately predict the spatial distribution of the species. The most robust explanation for the distribution of this species relates to the institutional rules that allow higher-caste villagers to access their 'own' forests as well as forests located near villages where lower-caste villagers live but not vice versa.

In addition to these research programs, the IAD framework has also influenced a variety of other studies, including those developing models of social-choice situations and then subjecting them to empirical tests in experimental laboratories (Herzberg 1986; Wilson and Herzberg 1987; Herzberg and Wilson 1988; Herzberg and V. Ostrom 1991); other empirical questions include the study of rural infrastructure in developing countries (E. Ostrom, Schroeder and Wynne 1993); privatization processes (S. Walker 1994a, 1994b); development processes more generally (V. Ostrom, Feeny and Picht 1993; Wunsch and Olowu 1995); constitutional dynamics in the American federal system (Jillson and Wilson 1994; V. Ostrom 1987, 1991) as well as in the Canadian federal system (Sproule-Jones 1993); linking local and global commons (McGinnis and E. Ostrom 1996; Keohane and Ostrom 1995; E. Ostrom *et al.* 1999; Dolšak and Ostrom 2003); and how rules, norms, and equilibrium strategies are related (Crawford and E. Ostrom 1995).

Conclusion

The quest for meaning in the constitution of order in human societies cannot rely on the methods of the natural sciences. Instead, we face the challenge of developing and working with what might be called 'the sciences of the artifactual' that are broadly applicable to the cultural and social sciences and the humanities. Herbert Simon has addressed what we call the sciences of the artifactual in *The Sciences of the Artificial* (1981[1969]). We prefer the term *artifactual* to *artificial*. He addresses the basic issues that need to be emphasized. The architectonics that apply to the constitution of open, democratic, self-governing societies involve extraordinary complexities confronting both scholars and those engaged in entrepreneurial efforts to create the enterprises necessary to address common problems confronting people in discrete ecological niches.

The condition of openness implied by the term *res publica* facilitates opportunities for an awareness of contingencies bearing on human interest evoking satisfaction, indifference, or dissatisfaction. Potentials for human communication allow discussion, contestation, and the use of the human imagination to stimulate innovation and conflict resolution. Such processes establish the grounds for reflection and choice in the realization of both objective and subjective potentials.

The availability of alternatives set in the context of multifaceted contingencies that vary in scope and depth is still subject to critical scrutiny in light of consequences realized. When ideas are used to realize potentials and the reverse happens, a negative test of hypotheses would suggest a refutation of the conjectures that shaped the work of those undertaking the endeavour. This is especially difficult when those engaged in the undertaking propose to use the instruments of violent force to save the oppressed from their oppressors. Such Faustian bargains yield oppression instead of liberation. Moral hazards abound. Misconceptions reinforced by oppression transform relationships into networks of lies.

The conditions of open societies are where democratic citizens develop analytical capabilities that are commensurate with the complexities that abound in human relationships that reach from the specificities of everyday life to global proportions. No theory or model will suffice. Instead, we face the problem of dealing with frameworks, theories, and models used in comparative assessment of human endeavours.

Human societies endure across decades, centuries, and millennia. Citizens in democracies are mortal and endure only for a generation, so to speak. Memory, knowledge, and skills are erased with death. Open, democratic, self-governing societies face the challenge of transmitting information, knowledge, and skills from one generation to the next. Civic knowledge is necessary to sustain the continuity of civil relationships in the conduct of civic affairs by both drawing on past achievements and realizing new potentials. Human rationality is grounded in the condition of fallibility, with potentials for learning. How to realize such potentials will engage each of us in our quest for meaning about the conditions of life that we share with others.

References

Advisory Commission on Intergovernmental Relations (R. J. Oakerson) (1987) *The Organisation of Local Public Economies*, Washington, DC: ACIR.

Advisory Commission on Intergovernmental Relations (R. J. Oakerson, Roger B. Parks, and Henry A. Bell) (1988) *Metropolitan Organisation: The St. Louis Case*. Washington, DC: ACIR.

Agrawal, A. (2000) 'Small is Beautiful, But is Larger Better? Forest-Management Institutions in the Kumoon Himalaya, India', in Clark, C. Gibson, M. A. McKean, and E. Ostrom (eds) *People and Forests: Communities, Institutions, and Governance*, Cambridge: MIT Press.

Alchian, Armen A. (1950) 'Uncertainty, Evolution, and Economic Theory', *Journal of Political Economy*, 58 (3): 211–21.

Arrow, Kenneth (1951) *Social Choice and Individual Values*, 2nd ed. New York: Wiley.

Banana, A. Y. and Gombya-Ssembajjwe, W. (2000) 'Successful Forest Management: The Importance of Security of Tenure and Rule Enforcement in Ugandan Forests', in Clark C. Gibson, M. A. McKean, and E. Ostrom (eds) *People and Forests: Communities, Institutions, and Governance*, Cambridge: MIT Press.

Benjamin, P., Lam, Wai, F., Ostrom, E. and Shivakoti, G. (1994) *Institutions, Incentives, and Irrigation in Nepal*. Decentralization: Finance & Management Project Report. Burlington, VT: Associates in Rural Development.

Breton, A. and Wintrobe, G. (1982) *The Logic of Bureaucratic Conduct: An Economic Analysis of Competition, Exchange, and Efficiency in Private and Public Organisations*, Cambridge: Cambridge University Press.

Bromley, D. W. *et al.* (eds) (1992) *Making the Commons Work: Theory, Practice, and Policy*, San Francisco: ICS Press.

Buchanan, J. M. (1979) 'Natural and Artifactual Man', in *What Should Economists Do?*, Indianapolis: Liberty.

Buchanan, J. M. and Tullock, G. (1962) *The Calculus of Consent: Logical Foundations of Constitutional Democracy*, Ann Arbor: University of Michigan Press.

Crawford, S. E. S. and Ostrom, E. (1995) 'A Grammar of Institutions', *American Political Science Review* 89 (3): 582–600.

Djilas, M. (1957) *The New Class: An Analysis of the Communist System*, New York: Praeger.

Dolšak, N. and Ostrom, E. (eds) (2003) *The Commons in the New Millennium: Challenges and Adaptations*, Cambridge, MA: MIT Press.

Dosi, G. and Egidi, M. (1987) 'Substantive and Procedural Uncertainty: An Exploration of Economic Behaviours in Complex and Changing Environments', Paper prepared for the International Workshop on Programmable Automation and New Work Modes, Paris, April 2–4.

Gibson, C., McKean, M. and Ostrom, E. (eds) (2000) *People and Forests: Communities, Institutions, and Governance,* Cambridge: MIT Press.

Gregg, P. M. (1974) 'Units and Levels of Analysis: A Problem of Policy Analysis in Federal Systems', *Publius* 4 (4): 59–86.

Hackett, S., Schlager, E. and Walker, J. (1994) 'The Role of Communication in Resolving Commons Dilemmas: Experimental Evidence with Heterogeneous Appropriators', *Journal of Environmental Economics and Management* 27:99–126.

Hamilton, A., Jay, J. and Madison, J. (n.d.[1788]) *The Federalist,* Edward, M. E. (ed.) New York: Modern Library.

Harré, R. (1974) 'Some Remarks on 'Rule' as a Scientific Concept', in T. Mischel (ed.) *Understanding Other Persons,* Oxford: Basil Blackwell.

Hayek, F. A. von (1945) 'The Use of Knowledge in Society', *American Economic Review* 35 (September): 519–30.

Herzberg, R. (1986) 'Blocking Coalitions and Policy Change', in G. C. Wright, L. Rieselbach and L. Dodd (eds) *Congress and Policy Change,* New York: Agathon Press.

Herzberg, R. and Ostrom, V. (1991) 'Votes and Vetoes', in F.-X. Kaufmann (ed.) *The Public Sector – Challenge for Coordination and Learning,* Berlin and New York: de Gruyter, W.

Herzberg, R. and Wilson, R. (1988) 'Results on Sophisticated Voting in an Experimental Setting', *The Journal of Politics* 50 (2): 471–86.

Hess, C. (1999) *A Comprehensive Bibliography of Common-Pool Resources.* (CD-ROM) Bloomington: Indiana University, Workshop in Political Theory and Policy Analysis.

Hobbes, T. (1949[1642]) *De Cive or the Citizen,* in S. P. Lamprecht (ed.) New York: Appleton-Century-Crofts.

— (1960[1651]) *Leviathan or the Matter, Forme and Power of a Commonwealth Ecclesiasticall and Civil* in M. Oakeshott (ed.) Oxford: Basil Blackwell.

Holling, C. S. (1994) 'An Ecologist View of the Malthusian Conflict', in K. Lindahl-Kiessling and H. Landberg (eds) *Population, Economic Development, and the Environment,* New York: Oxford University Press.

Jillson, C. C. and Wilson, R. K. (1994) *Congressional Dynamics: Structure, Coordination, and Choice in the First American Congress, 1774–1789.* Stanford, CA: Stanford University Press.

Keohane, R. O. and Ostrom, E. (eds) (1995) *Local Commons and Global Interdependence: Heterogeneity and Cooperation in Two Domains,* London: Sage.

Kiser, L. L. (1984) 'Toward an Institutional Theory of Citizen Coproduction', *Urban Affairs Quarterly* 19 (4): 485–510.

Kiser, L. L. and Ostrom, E. (1982) 'The Three Worlds of Action: A Metatheoretical Synthesis of Institutional Approaches', in E. Ostrom (ed.) *Strategies of Political Inquiry,* Beverly Hills: Sage.

Lam, W. F. (1994) 'Institutions, Engineering Infrastructure, and Performance in the Governance and Management of Irrigation Systems: The Case of Nepal', PhD diss., Indiana University.

— (1996) 'Institutional Design of Public Agencies and Coproduction: A Study of Irrigation Associations in Taiwan', *World Development* 24 (6): 1039–54.

— (1998) *Governing Irrigation Systems in Nepal: Institutions, Infrastructure, and Collective Action*, Oakland, CA: ICS Press.

Lasswell, H. D. and Kaplan, A. (1950) *Power and Society: A Framework for Political Inquiry*, New Haven: Yale University Press.

McGinnis, M. and Ostrom, E. (1996) 'Design Principles for Local and Global Commons', in O. R. Young (ed.) *The International Political Economy and International Institutions,* Volume II, Cheltenham, UK: E. Elgar.

Netting, R. McC. (1982) 'Territory, Property, and Tenure', in R. McC. Adams, N. J. Smelser and D. J. Treiman (eds) *Behavioural and Social Science Research: A National Resource*, Washington, DC: National Academy Press.

Oakerson, R. J. (1992) 'Analysing the Commons: A Framework', in D. W. Bromley *et al.* (eds) *Making the Commons Work: Theory, Practice, and Policy*, San Francisco: ICS Press.

— (1993) 'Reciprocity: A Bottom-Up View of Political Development', in V. Ostrom, D. Feeny, and H. Picht (eds) *Rethinking Institutional Analysis and Development: Issues, Alternatives, and Choices*, San Francisco: ICS Press.

— (1994) 'The Logic of Multi-Level Institutional Analysis', Paper presented at the 'Workshop on the Workshop' conference, Indiana University, Workshop in Political Theory and Policy Analysis, Bloomington, Indiana, June 15–19.

Oakerson, R. J. and Parks, R. B. (1988) 'Citizen Voice and Public Entrepreneurship: The Organisational Dynamic of a Complex Metropolitan County', *Publius* 18 (Fall): 91–112.

Olson, M. (1965) *The Logic of Collective Action: Public Goods and the Theory of Groups,* Cambridge: Harvard University Press.

Ostrom, E. (1965) 'Public Entrepreneurship: A Case Study in Ground Water Management', PhD diss., University of California, Los Angeles.

— (1972) 'Metropolitan Reform: Propositions Derived from Two Traditions', *Social Science Quarterly* 53 (Dec.): 474–93.

— (1990) *Governing the Commons: The Evolution of Institutions for Collective Action*, New York: Cambridge University Press.

— (1992) 'The Rudiments of a Theory of the Origins, Survival, and Performance of Common-Property Institutions', in D. W. Bromley *et al.* (eds) *Making the Commons Work: Theory, Practice, and Policy*, San Francisco: ICS Press.

— (1994) 'Neither Market Nor State: Governance of Common-Pool Resources in the Twenty-First Century', International Food Policy Research Institute Lecture Series No. 2, presented June 2, 1994, Washington, D.C.

— (1996a) 'Crossing the Great Divide: Coproduction, Synergy, and Development', *World Development* 24 (6): 1073–87.

— (1996b) 'Incentives, Rules of the Game, and Development', *Proceedings of the Annual World Bank Conference on Development Economics 1995*, Washington, DC: World Bank.

— (1998) 'A Behavioural Approach to the Rational Choice Theory of Collective Action', *American Political Science Review* 92 (1): 1–22.

— (1999) 'Institutional Rational Choice: An Assessment of the Institutional Analysis and Development Framework', in P. A. Sabatier (ed.) *Theories of the Policy Process*. Boulder, CO: Westview Press.

Ostrom, E., Burger, J., Field, C., Norgaard, R. B. and Policansky, D. (1999) 'Revisiting the Commons: Local Lessons, Global Challenges', *Science* 284 (5412) (April 9): 278–82.

Ostrom, E. and Gardner, R. (1993) 'Coping with Asymmetries in the Commons: Self-Governing Irrigation Systems Can Work', *Journal of Economic Perspectives* 7 (4): 93–112.

Ostrom, E., Gardner, R. and Walker, J. (1994) *Rules, Games, and Common-Pool Resources,* Ann Arbor: University of Michigan Press.

Ostrom, E., Lam, Wai, F. and Lee, M. (1994) 'The Performance of Self-Governing Irrigation Systems in Nepal', *Human Systems Management* 14 (3): 87–108.

Ostrom, E., Schroeder, L. and Wynne, S. (1993) *Institutional Incentives and Sustainable Development: Infrastructure Policies in Perspective,* Boulder, CO: Westview Press.

Ostrom, E., Walker, J. and Gardner, R. (1992) 'Covenants with and without a Sword: Self-Governance Is Possible', *American Political Science Review* 86 (2): 404–17.

Ostrom, V. (1980) 'Artisanship and Artifact', *Public Administration Review* 40 (July/Aug.): 309–17.

— (1986) 'A Fallabilist's Approach to Norms and Criteria of Choice', in F.-X. Kaufmann, G. Majone and V. Ostrom (eds) *Guidance, Control, and Evaluation in the Public Sector*, Berlin and New York: Walter de Gruyter.

— (1978[1971]) *The Political Theory of a Compound Republic: Designing the American Experiment*, 2nd edn. San Francisco: ICS Press.

— (1991) *The Meaning of American Federalism: Constituting a Self-Governing Society*, San Francisco: ICS Press.

— (1997) *The Meaning of Democracy and the Vulnerability of Democracies: A Response to Tocqueville's Challenge*, Ann Arbor: University of Michigan Press.

Ostrom, V., Bish, R. and Ostrom, E. (1988) *Local Government in the United States*, San Francisco: ICS Press.

Ostrom, V., Feeny, D. and Picht, H. (eds) (1993) *Rethinking Institutional Analysis and Development: Issues, Alternatives, and Choices*, 2nd edn., San Francisco: ICS Press.

Ostrom, V. and Ostrom, E. (1971) 'Public Choice: A Different Approach to the Study of Public Administration', *Public Administration Review* 13 (March/April): 203–16.

Parks, R. B. (1985) 'Metropolitan Structure and Systematic Performance: The Case of Police Service Delivery', in K. Hanf and T. A. J. Toonen (eds) *Policy Implementation in Federal and Unitary Systems*, Dordrecht, the Netherlands: M. Nijhoff.

Parks, R. B., Baker, P. C., Kiser, Larry, L., Oakerson, R. J., Ostrom, E., Ostrom, V., Percy, S. L., Vandivort, M., Whitaker, G. P. and Wilson, R. (1982) 'Coproduction of Public Services', in R. C. Rich (ed.) *Analysing Urban-Service Distributions*, Lexington, MA: Lexington Books.

Parks, R. B. and Oakerson, R. J., (1989) 'Metropolitan Organisation and Governance: A Local Public Economy Approach', *Urban Affairs Quarterly* 25 (1): 18–29.

Percy, S. L. (1984) 'Citizen Participation in the Coproduction of Urban Services', *Urban Affairs Quarterly* 19 (4): 431–46.

Popper, K. (1963[1945]) *The Open Society and Its Enemies*, 2 vols., New York: Harper and Row.

Radnitzky, G. (1987) 'Cost-Benefit Thinking the Methodology of Research: The 'Economic Approach' Applied to Key Problems to the Philosophy of Science' in G. Radnitzky and P. Bernholz (eds) *Economic Imperialism: The Economic Approach Applied Outside the Field of Economics*, New York: Paragon House.

Schlager, E. (1990) 'Model Specification and Policy Analysis: The Governance of Coastal Fisheries', PhD diss., Indiana University.

— (1994) 'Fishers' Institutional Responses to Common-Pool Resource Dilemmas', in E. Ostrom, R. Gardner and J. Walker (eds) *Rules, Games, and Common-Pool Resources*, A. Arbor: University of Michigan Press.

Schlager, E., Blomquist, W. and Tang, S. Y. (1994) 'Mobile Flows, Storage, and Self-Organised Institutions for Governing Common-Pool Resources', *Land Economics* 70 (3): 294–317.

Schweik, C. M. (2000) 'Optimal Foraging, Institutions, and Forest Change: A Case from Nepal' in C. G. Clark, M. A. McKean and E. Ostrom (eds) *People and Forests: Communities, Institutions, and Governance*, Cambridge: MIT Press.

Schweik, C. M., Adhikari, K. and Pandit, K. N. (1997) 'Land-Cover Change and Forest Institutions: A Comparison of Two Sub-Basins in the Southern Siwalik Hills of Nepal', *Mountain Research and Development* 17 (2): 99–116.

Shepsle, K. A. (1979) 'The Role of Institutional Structure in the Creation of Policy Equilibrium' in D. W. Rae and T. J. Eismeier (eds), *Public Policy and Public Choice*, Sage Yearbooks in Politics and Public Policy, vol. 6. Beverly Hills: Sage.

Shimanoff, S. B. (1980) *Communication Rules: Theory and Research*, Beverly Hills: Sage.

Shivakoti, G. and Ostrom, E. (eds) (2002) *Improving Irrigation Governance and Management in Nepal,* Oakland, CA: ICS Press.

Siedentop, L. (1994) *Tocqueville,* Oxford and New York: Oxford University Press.

Simon, H. A. (1965[1947]) *Administrative Behavior: A Study of Decision-making Processes in Administrative Organisation,* New York: Free Press.

— (1972) 'Theories of Bounded Rationality' in C. B. McGuire and R. Radner (eds) *Decision and Organisation: A Volume in Honor of Jacob Marschak,* Amsterdam: North Holland.

— (1981[1969]) *The Sciences of the Artificial,* 2nd edn., Cambridge, MA, and London: MIT Press.

Sproule-Jones, M. (1993) *Governments at Work: Canadian Parliamentary Federalism and Its Public Policy Effects,* Toronto: University of Toronto Press.

Stein, R. (1990) *Urban Alternatives: Public and Private Markets in the Provision of Local Services,* Pittsburgh, PA: University of Pittsburgh Press.

Tang, S. Y. (1991) 'Institutional Arrangements and the Management of Common-Pool Resources', *Public Administration Review* 51:42–51.

— (1992) *Institutions and Collective Action: Self-Governance in Irrigation,* San Francisco: ICS Press.

Taylor, M. (1987) *The Possibility of Cooperation,* New York: Cambridge University Press.

Thomson, J. T. (1992) *A Framework for Analysing Institutional Incentives in Community Forestry,* Rome, Italy: Food and Agriculture Organisation of the United Nations, Forestry Department, Via delle Terme di Caracalla.

Thomson, J. T., Feeny, D. and Oakerson. R. J. (1992) 'Institutional Dynamics: The Evolution and Dissolution of Common-Property Resource Management', in D. W. Bromley *et al.* (eds) *Making the Commons Work: Theory, Practice, and Policy,* San Francisco: ICS Press.

Tocqueville, A. de (1990 [1835, 1840]) *Democracy in America.* 2 vols, B. Phillips (ed.) New York: A. A. Knopf.

Toulmin, S. (1974) 'Rules and Their Relevance for Understanding Human Behavior' in T. Mischel (ed.) *Understanding Other Persons,* Oxford: Basil Blackwell.

Walker, J. and Gardner, R. (1992) 'Probabilistic Destruction of Common-Pool Resources: Experimental Evidence', *Economic Journal* 102 (414): 1149–61.

Walker, S. T. (1994a) *Crafting a Market: A Case Study of USAID's Fertilizer Sub-Sector Reform Program,* Decentralization: Finance & Management Project Report. Burlington, VT: Associates in Rural Development.

— (1994b) *Pitfalls of Privatization: A Case Study of the European Community's Programme Spécial d'Importation d'Engrais,* Decentralization: Finance & Management Project Report. Burlington, VT: Associates in Rural Development.

Whitaker, G. P. (1980) 'Coproduction: Citizen Participation in Service Delivery', *Public Administration Review* 40 (4): 309–17.

Williamson, O. E. (1979) 'Transaction Cost Economics: The Governance of Contractual Relations', *Journal of Law and Economics* 22 (2): 233–61.

— (1985) *The Economic Institutions of Capitalism*, New York: Free Press.

Wilson, R. and Herzberg, R. (1987) 'Negative Decision Powers and Institutional Equilibrium: Experiments on Blocking Coalitions', *Western Political Quarterly* 40 (4): 593–609.

Wunsch, J. S. and Olowu, D. (eds) (1995 [1990]) *The Failure of the Centralized State: Institutions and Self-Governance in Africa*, 2nd edn., San Francisco: ICS Press.

Part Two

Beyond Public Choice: Institutions,
Rules and Governance Systems

Chapter Four

An Agenda for the Study of Institutions[1]

Elinor Ostrom[2]

The multiple meanings of institutions

Recently, public choice theorists have evidenced considerable interest in the study of institutions. William Riker (1982: 20) recently observed, for example, that 'we cannot study simply tastes and values, but must study institutions as well'. Little agreement exists, however, on what the term 'institution' means, whether the study of institutions is an appropriate endeavour, and how to undertake a cumulative study of institutions.

Riker defines institutions as 'rules about behavior, especially about making decisions' (1982: 4). Charles Plott also defines institutions to mean 'the rules for individual expression, information transmittal, and social choice [...]' (1979: 156). Plott uses the term 'institutions' in his effort to state the fundamental equation of public choice theory. Using $\oplus$ as an unspecified abstract operator, Plott's fundamental equation is:

$$\text{preferences} \oplus \text{institutions} \oplus \text{physical possibilities} = \text{outcomes (1)}$$

Plott himself points out, however, that the term institution refers to different concepts. He ponders:

> Could it be, for example, that preferences and opportunities *alone* determine the structure of institutions (including the constitution)? These questions might be addressed without changing 'the fundamental equation' but before that can be done, *a lot of work must be done on determining exactly what goes under the title of an 'institution'*. Are customs and ethics to be regarded as institutions? What about organizations such as coalitions? These are embarrassing questions

1. I appreciate the support of the National Science Foundation in the form of Grant Number SES 83–09829 and of William Erickson-Blomquist, Roy Gardner, Judith Gillespie, Gerd-Michael Hellstern, Roberta Herzberg, Larry Kiser, Vincent Ostrom, Roger Parks, Paul Sabatier, Reinhard Selten, Kenneth Shepsle, and York Willbern who commented on earlier drafts.
2. This paper was delivered as the Presidential address at the Public Choice Society meetings, Phoenix, Arizona, March 30, 1984. It was initially published in *Public Choice* 48 (1), 1986, pp. 3–25.

[me - Inst = normative, regulative, cognitive]

which suggest the 'fundamental equation' is perhaps not as fundamental as we would like (Plott 1979: 160; my emphasis).

Plott's questions are indeed embarrassing. No scientific field can advance far if the participants do not share a common understanding of key terms in their field. In a recent volume entitled *The Economic Theory of Social Institutions*, Andrew Schotter specifically views social institutions as standards of behavior rather than the rules of the game. What Schotter calls 'social institutions':

> are not rules of the game but rather the alternative equilibrium standards of behavior or conventions of behavior that evolve from a given game described by its rules. In other words, for us, institutions are properties of the equilibrium of games and not properties of the game's description. We care about what the agents do with the rules of the game, not what the rules are (Schotter 1981: 155).

Schotter sees his enterprise as a positive analysis of the regularities in behavior that will emerge from a set of rules and contrasts this with a normative approach that attempts to examine which rules lead to which types of behavioural regularities. Schotter draws on a rich intellectual tradition that stresses the evolution of learned strategies among individuals who interact with one another repeatedly over a long period of time (Menger 1963; Hayek 1976; 1978; *see also*, Ullman-Margalit 1978; Taylor 1976; Nozick 1975). Rawls characterizes this view of how individuals come to follow similar strategies over time as 'the summary view of rules' (Rawls 1968: 321).

Still another way of viewing 'institutions' is equivalent to the term 'political structure'. This view differs from that of Schotter in that it does not equate institutions with behavioural regularities. It differs from that of Riker and Plott in that it does not focus on underlying rules. Institutions, defined as political structure, refer to attributes of the current system such as size (Dahl and Tufte 1973), degree of competition (Dye 1966; Dawson and Robinson 1963), extent of overlap (ACIR 1974) and other attributes of a current system.

The multiplicity of uses for a key term like 'institution' signals a problem in the general conception held by scholars of how preferences, rules, individual strategies, customs and norms, and the current structural aspects of ongoing political systems are related to one another. Over time we have reached general agreement about how we will use such key theoretical terms as 'preferences', 'actions', 'outcomes', 'coalitions' and 'games'. Further, we have a general agreement about how these concepts are used in our theories to generate predicted outcomes.

The multiple referents for the term 'institutions' indicate that multiple concepts need to be separately identified and treated as separate terms. We cannot communicate effectively if signs used by one scholar in a field have different referents than the same sign used by another scholar in the same field. As scholars, we are in our own game situation – a language generating game. The 'solution' is the result of our choice of strategies about the use of a set of terms to refer to the objects and relations of interest in our field.

No one can legislate a language for a scientific community. Scholars begin to use a language consistently when terms are carefully defined in a manner perceived by other scholars as useful in helping to explain important phenomena. In this presentation, I do not try to resolve the debate over which of the definitions of institution is the 'right definition'. Instead, one concept –that of rules– is used as a referent for the term 'institution', and defined. I distinguish rules from physical or behavioural laws and discuss the prescriptive nature of rules. Then I show how theorists use rules in public choice analysis. Two methodological issues are raised. One relates to the configurational character of rules. A second relates to the multiple levels of analysis needed for the systematic study of rules. In the last section, I propose an alternative strategy that takes into account the configurational character of rules and the need for a self-conscious study of multiple levels of analysis.

What is meant by rules

Focusing specifically on the term 'rule' does not immediately help us. Even this narrower term is used variously. Shimanoff (1980: 57) identified over 100 synonyms for the term 'rule' (*see also* Ganz 1971). Even among political economists the term is used to both refer to personal routines or strategies (e.g. Heiner 1983) as well as to a set of rules used by more than one person to order decision making in interdependent situations. In game theory, 'the rules of the game include not only the move and information structure and the physical consequences of all decisions, but also the preference systems of all the players' (Shubik 1982: 8).

Rules, as I wish to use the term, are potentially linguistic entities (Ganz 1971; V. Ostrom, 1980; Commons, 1957) that refer to prescriptions commonly known and used by a set of participants to order repetitive, interdependent relationships. Prescriptions refer to which actions (or states of the world) are required, prohibited, or permitted. Rules are the result of implicit or explicit efforts by a set of individuals to achieve order and predictability within defined situations by: (1) creating positions (e.g. member, convener, agent, etc.); (2) stating how participants enter or leave positions; (3) stating which actions participants in these positions are required, permitted, or forbidden to take; and (4) stating which outcome participants are required, permitted, or forbidden to affect.

Rules are thus artifacts that are subject to human intervention and change (V. Ostrom 1980). Rules, as I wish to use the term, are distinct from physical and behavioural laws. I use the term differently than a game theorist who considers linguistic prescriptions as well as physical and behavioural laws to be 'the rules of the game'. If a theorist wants only to analyse a given game or situation, no advantage is gained by distinguishing between rule on the one hand, and physical or behavioural laws, on the other hand. To change the outcomes of a situation, however, it is essential to distinguish rules from behavioural or physical laws. Rules are the means by which we intervene to change the structure of incentives in situations. It is, of course, frequently difficult in practice to change the rules participants use to order their relationships. Theoretically, rules can be changed while physical and behavioural laws cannot. Rules are interesting variables precisely because they are potentially subject to change. That rules can be changed by humans is one of their key characteristics.

That rules have prescriptive force is another characteristic. Prescriptive force means that knowledge and acceptance of a rule leads individuals to recognize that, if they break the rule, other individuals may hold them accountable (*see* Harré 1974). One may be held accountable directly by fellow participants, who call rule infraction to one's attention, or by specialists – referees or public officials – who monitor performance. The term 'rules' should not be equated with formal laws. Formal laws may become rules when participants understand a law, at least tacitly, and are held accountable for breaking a law. Enforcement is necessary for a law to become a rule. Participants may design or evolve their own rules or follow rules designed by others.

An unstated assumption of almost all formal models is that individuals are, in general, rule followers. Even when theorists like Becker (1976) have overtly modelled illegal behavior, some probability is presumed to exist that illegal actions will be observed, and if observed by an enforcer, that penalties will be extracted. Most public choice analysis is of the rules in use – or working rules as John R. Commons (1957) called them. Many interesting questions need exploration concerning the origin of rules, the relationship of formal laws to rules, and processes for changing rules. But, these topics cannot be addressed here.

Considerable dispute exists over the prescriptive force of 'permission'. Ganz (1971) and Shimanoff (1980) argue that prescriptive force is restricted to 'obligation' and 'prohibition' and does not include 'permission', while Commons (1957), von Wright (1968), V. Ostrom (1980) and Toulmin (1974) all overtly include 'permission' in their conception of rules. Part of this difficulty stems from efforts to predict behavior directly from specifying rules rather than viewing rules as a set of variables defining a structured situation. In this rule-structured situation, individuals select actions from a set of allowable actions in light of the full set of incentives existing in the situation.

Instead of viewing rules as directly affecting behavior, I view rules as directly affecting the structure of a situation in which actions are selected. Rules rarely prescribe one and only one action or outcome. Rules specify sets of actions or sets of outcomes in three ways:

1. A rule states that some particular actions or outcomes are forbidden. The remaining physically possible or attainable actions and outcomes are then permitted. The rule states what is forbidden. A residual class of actions or outcomes is permitted. (Most traffic laws regarding speed are of this type. The upper and lower bounds of the permitted speed are delimited by forbidding transit above and below specific speeds.)

2. A rule enumerates specific actions or outcomes or states the upper and lower bound of permitted actions or outcomes and forbids those that are not specifically included. (Most public agencies are authorized to engage

in only those activities specifically enumerated in the organic or special legislation that establishes them.)

3.   A rule requires a particular action or outcome. (Recent efforts to constrain judicial discretion are rules of this type. A judge must impose a particular sentence if a jury concludes that a defendant is guilty of a particular crime.)

Only the third type of rule requires that an individual take one and only one action rather than choose from a set of actions. The third type of rule is used much less frequently to structure situations than the first two.

In the everyday world, rules are stated in words and must be understood (at least implicitly) for participants to use them in complex chains of actions. For analysis, however, rules can be viewed as relations operating on the structure of a situation. Rules can be formally represented as relations, whose domain are the set of physically possible variables and their values, and whose range are the values of the variables, in the situation under analysis. (*See* below for further elaboration.) Viewing rules as directly affecting the structure of a situation, rather than as directly producing behavior, is a subtle but extremely important distinction.

How rules are used in public choice theory

Most public choice theorists 'know' that multiple levels of analysis are involved in understanding how rules affect behavior. But this tacit knowledge of the multiple levels of analysis and how they intertwine is not self-consciously built into the way we pursue our work. Plott, for example, has been engaged in a sophisticated research program related to the theoretical and experimental study of rules. Yet, as discussed above, he poses the central question of our discipline as a single equation, rather than as a set of equations. We have not yet developed a self-conscious awareness of the methodological consequences of the multiple levels of analysis needed to study the effects of rules on behavior and outcomes.

Most public choice theorists also 'know' that configurations of rules rather than single rules, jointly affect the structure of the situations we analyse. Again, this tacit knowledge is not reflected in the way we proceed. Most of our theoretical work has proved theorems about the expected results of the use of one rule in isolation of other rules as if rules operated separably rather than configurationally.

To illustrate the multiple levels of analysis and the configurational character of rules, I will use several examples from public choice literature. The first example combines the work of several scholars who have studied how citizen's preferences for public goods are translated through two arenas - an electoral arena and a bargaining arena - into an agreement that a bureau will produce a particular quantity of goods for a particular budget. The second example is from an experimental study of Grether, Isaac and Plott (1979) of the combination of default condition rules used in conjunction with aggregation rules. The third example is from McKelvey and Ordeshook (1983) who conducted an experimental study of the conjunction of three rules.

Rules as they affect outcomes in electoral and bargaining arenas. In a classic model of the election arena, Anthony Downs (1957) concludes that electoral procedures based on plurality vote will constrain a governing party to select (and therefore produce) the output-cost combination most preferred by a median voter within a community. The Downsian model predicts an optimal equilibrium in terms of allocative efficiency. Downs's prediction of optimal performance results from his analysis of the behavior of elected officials under the threat of being voted out of office by a competing party. It is the presence of a competitor ready to snatch any advantage that pushes the government party toward constant attention to what citizens prefer.

When William Niskanen (1971) examines how bureaucracy affects the linkage between citizen preferences and government performance, he focuses on the process of bargaining between the team of elected officials (called the sponsor by Niskanen) and bureau chiefs assigned the responsibility to direct agencies producing the desired goods and services. Niskanen assumes that a bureau chief attempts to obtain as large a budget as possible in order to secure the most private gain and to produce the most goods and services for a community. Niskanen's elected officials, like Downs's, know the preferences of the citizens that elect them. So do the bureau chiefs. However, elected officials do not know the production costs of the bureau. The equilibrium predicted by Niskanen is not responsive to citizen preferences since more than optimal levels of output are produced. The predicted result is technically efficient, but unresponsive to the preferences of those served.

Niskanen's model is based on an assumption that bureau chiefs could threaten elected officials with no output if the officials did not agree to the initial demand. Romer and Rosenthal (1978) argue that a more realistic assumption would be that the budget reverts to the status quo budget (the one used for the previous year) if the officials (or, the general public in a referendum) did not agree to the initial budgetary request. Changing this assumption in the model, Romer and Rosenthal continue to predict that the equilibrium budget-output combination represents a nonoptimal, oversupply. Their predicted outcome is, however, less than that predicted by Niskanen.

A dramatic change in assumptions is made by McGuire, Coiner and Spancake (1979) who introduce a second bureau to compete with the monopoly bureau chief in the bargaining arena.[3] Whatever offer is made by one bureau can then be challenged by the second bureau. Over time the offers will approach the same optimal level as predicted by Downs. If one bureau proposes too high a budget, the other will be motivated to make a counteroffer of a more optimal budget-output combination. As the number of bureaus increases beyond two, the pressure on all bureaus to offer an optimal budget-output combination also increases.

---

3. Niskanen had himself suggested that an important structural change that could be made to improve bureau performance was to increase the competition between bureaus.

The above models focus primarily on the structure of an operational situation and only indirectly on the rules yielding that structure. Without explicit analysis of the rules and other factors affecting the structure of a situation – such as the attributes of goods and the community – implicit assumptions underlying the overt analysis may be the most important assumptions generating predicted results.[4] In the analysis of electoral and bargaining arenas, all theorists used similar assumptions about the nature of goods and community norms. Goods are modelled as divisible in production and subject to a known technology. In regard to norms, all presume a high level of cutthroat competition is acceptable. These assumptions are not responsible for the differences among predicted outcomes.

The models have, however, different implicit or explicit assumptions about some of the rules affecting the situation. The models developed by Niskanen and by Romer and Rosenthal both give the bureau chief the capacity to make a 'take it or leave it' offer. Both of these models assume an authority rule giving the bureau chief full control over the agenda. Both models also assume that the aggregation rule between the bureau chief and the sponsors is unanimity. The models differ, however, in regard to the default specified in the aggregation rule. Niskanen presumed this rule would allow the budget to revert to zero. No agreement – no funds! An aggregation rule with such a default condition can be formally stated as:

$B_{t+1} = \{B_{bc}$ iff $B_{bc} = B_s$; 0 otherwise$\}$, where $\qquad$ (2)
$B_{t+1} = $ the budget-output combination for the next period,

$B_{bc} = $ the budget-output proposal of the bureau chief,
$B_s = $ the budget-output proposal accepted by the sponsor.

In other words, the aggregation rule affecting the structure of this situaction requires unanimity among the participants and sets the budget for the next time period to zero if such agreement is not reached. The first part of this rule states the outcome when there is unanimous agreement. The second part of this rule states the outcome when there is no agreement, or the default condition.

Romer and Rosenthal presumed the rule would be to continue the budget in effect for the previous year. No agreement - continuance of the status quo! Their rule can be formally stated as:

$B_{t+1} = \{B_{bc}$ iff $B_{bc} \neg B_s$; B_t otherwise$\}$ $\qquad$ (3)
where B_t is the level of the current budget-output combination.

Niskanen and McGuire, Coiner, and Spancake agree on unanimity and the default condition of the aggregation rule, but differ on the boundary rules allowing

---

4. *See* Kiser and E. Ostrom (1982) for a discussion of how rules, goods, and attributes of a community all contribute to the structure of a situation.

entry of potential producers into the bargaining arena. Once a position rule has defined a position, S_i, such as a bureau chief, a formal boundary rule consistent with the Niskanen model could be stated as:

Let $S_i = \{1\}$ (4)

A boundary rule consistent with the McGuire, Coiner, and Spancake model would be the following:

Let $S_i = \{1, \ldots, n\}$ (5)

    Assuming that the other rules are similar, we can array the configuration of rules that differ in the various analyses as shown in Figure 4.1. The Downsian model is placed in the upper left cell since he made a similar assumption about the default condition of the aggregation rule as Romer and Rosenthal (*see* Downs 1957: 69), but had to assume implicitly that elected officials controlled the agenda in their bargaining relationships with bureau chiefs (*see* Mackay and Weaver 1978). Consequently, the difference in the results predicted by Downs, by Niskanen, and by Romer and Rosenthal can be related to changes in authority rules and aggregation rules holding other rules constant.

    McGuire, Coiner, and Spancake accepted the Niskanen presumption of a zero reversion level while changing the boundary rules allowing producers to enter the bargaining process. This change in boundary rules generates a different situation leading to a prediction of relatively optimal performance as contrasted to Niskanen's prediction of nonoptimality. The change in boundary rules opens up a new column of potential operational situations under varying conditions of authority and aggregation rules. An effort that Parks and Ostrom (1981) made to examine the effect of multiple producers in metropolitan areas upon the efficiency of public agencies is closely related to the rule conditions specified in the upper right-hand cell. The implications of the situations created by the other combinations of rules represented in the second column have not yet been explored.

    In this discussion I wanted to illustrate what I meant by a 'rule configuration'. Figure 4.1 presents a visual display of the configuration of rules that are consistent with the models of Downs, Niskanen, Romer and Rosenthal, and McGuire, Coiner and Spancake. The results predicted in a situation, using one rule, are dependent upon the other rules simultaneously in force. Both Niskanen, and Romer and Rosenthal assume that only one bureau can be present in the bargaining. The boundary rule is the same. Their different results stem from the variation in the default condition of the aggregation rule. Both Niskanen and McGuire, Coiner, and Spancake agree on the default condition, but differ in regard to the boundary rule. Different results are predicted dependent on the configuration of rules, rather than any single rule, underlying the operational situation.

    Second, I wanted to illustrate the multiple levels of analysis involved. The overt models presented by these theorists are all at one level. By examining the rules affecting the structure of these models, I have focused on a second level of analysis.

Figure 4.1: Predicted Equilibrium Budget/Output Combinations Under Different Rule Configurations

Authority rules	Boundary rules	
Aggregation rules	Entry to bargaining process restricted to one bureau.	Allow multiple bureaus to enter bargaining process.
Open agenda Reversion level is status quo	Downs (1957) Equilibrium is the most preferred budget/output combination of the median voter. Thus, preferences of median voter dominate decision.	Parks and E. Ostrom (1981) Even if no direct competition between two producers serving same jurisdiction, presence of comparison agencies in same urban area will reduce costs of monitoring and increase pressure toward equilibrium producing the highest net value for the community.
Reversion level is zero budget	No model yet developed for this combination of rules.	No model yet developed for this combination of rules.
Restricted agenda controlled by bureau chief Reversion level is status quo	Romer and Rosenthal (1978) Equilibrium is the highest budget/output combination that provides the median voter with at least as much value as the status quo.	No model yet developed for this combination of rules, but given McGuire, Coiner, and Spancake (1979) status quo reversion level can only enhance tendency of equilibrium to move forward highest net value for the community.
Reversion level is zero budget	Niskanen (1971; 1975) Equilibrium is the largest budget/output combination capable of winning majority approval in an all-or-nothing vote. Preference of median voter is only a constraint.	McGuire, Coiner, and Spancake (1979) Equilibrium tends over time toward budget/output combination producing the highest net value for the community.

Committee decisions under unanimity and varying default conditions. A second example of the study of rules by public choice theorists is a recent set of experiments conducted by Grether, Isaac and Plott (1979) who examine the effect of various rules for assigning airport slots. Under one experimental condition, the Grether, Isaac and Plott situation involves a committee of 9 or 14 individuals that had to divide a discrete set of objects ('cards' or 'flags') using a unanimity rule. Three default conditions are used if unanimity is not reached:

1. If the committee defaulted, each committee member received his/her 'initial allocation' of slots that was unambiguously specified and known before the meeting began.

2. If the committee defaulted, slots were allocated randomly.

3. If the committee defaulted, slots were taken at random only from those with large initial allocations and given to those with small or no initial allocation (Grether, Isaac and Plott 1979: V-2).

All three of these rules can be stated in a form similar to that of equations (2) and (3) above.

While Romer and Rosenthal make a theoretical argument that the particular default condition used as part of an unanimity rule affects the predicted outcomes, Grether, Isaac and Plott provide evidence that default conditions markedly affect behavior. The decisions about slot allocations reached by committees tended to shift directly to the value specified in each of the default conditions.

> In summary, the committee decisions are substantially influenced if not completely determined by the consequences of default. Under the grandfather arrangement, 'hardnosed' committee members will simply default rather than take less than the default value. Social pressures do exist for those with 'large' initial endowments to give to those with 'small' endowments, but even if there is no default because of concessions to social pressure the final outcome is not 'far' from the `grandfather' alternative. On the other hand, when the consequence of default is an equal chance lottery, the slots will be divided equally, independent of the initial allocation [...] Default values literally determine the outcomes in processes such as these (Grether, Isaac and Plott, 1979: V-7).

It has frequently been presumed that aggregation rules varied unidimensionally across one continuum from an 'any one' rule to a unanimity rule (Buchanan and Tullock 1962). What should now be recognized is that most prior analysis of aggregation rules has implicitly or explicitly assumed only one of the possible default conditions that work in combination with the voting rule to yield incentives in the operational situation. There is nothing inherently conservative about a unanimity rule unless the default condition is the status quo.

Cumulative knowledge from the analysis of these diverse situations requires that we understand that Romer and Rosenthal and Grether, Isaac and Plott are examining the effect of variations of the same rule given the preferences of participants. If some participants strongly prefer other outcomes to that stated in a default rule, a strong bargainer can threaten them with the default unless the final outcome is moved closer to his own preferred outcome. But when some participants prefer the outcome stated in the default rule, they can afford to block any proposals that do not approach this condition (*see* Wilson and Herzberg 1984).

To enhance cumulation, we need to develop formal representations for rules themselves as well as for the action situations on which rules operate. Most formal analyses loosely state the rules affecting the structure of the action situation: (1) in the written paragraphs leading up to the formal representation of the situation, (2) in footnotes justifying why the presentation of the situation is modelled in a particular manner, or (3) even worse, leave them unstated, as implicit assumptions underlying the formal analysis of the situation itself.[5]

PMR, germaneness, and open versus closed information rules. An experiment conducted by McKelvey and Ordeshook strongly demonstrates the configurational relationships when pure majority rule (PMR) is combined with one 'germaneness' rule and two information rules. PMR and a loose operationalization of a germaneness rule – a change in outcome can be made in only one dimension on any one move – is used throughout the experiment.[6] McKelvey and Ordeshook use a closed or an open information rule. Under their 'closed' rule, members of a five-person committee can speak only if recognized by the chair, can address only the chair, and can make comments solely related to the particular motion immediately being considered. Under their 'open' rule, participants can speak without being recognized, can talk to anyone, and can discuss future as well as present motions.

McKelvey and Ordeshook find that the distribution of outcomes reached under the closed information rule, when used in combination with PMR and their germaneness rule, to be significantly different than the distributions of outcomes reached under the open information rule. The experiment is a good example of how rules operate configurationally.

Rules affecting communication flow and content affect the type of outcomes that will be produced from PMR combined with a particular germaneness rule. McKelvey and Ordeshook, however, interpret their own results rather strangely. Their overt hypothesis is 'that the ability to communicate facilitates circumventing formal procedural rules' (p. 8). A close examination of their series of experiments finds no evidence of participants breaking the rules laid down by the experimenters. What they do test is whether a rule giving capabilities or assigning limitations on

---

5. It is surprising how often one reads in a public choice article that prior models had implicit assumptions that drove the analysis. A recent example is in Mackay and Weaver (1978: 143) where they argue that:

> Standard demand side models of the collective choice process, in which fiscal out-comes are considered representative of broad-based citizen demands, implicitly assume not only that a 'democratic' voting rule is employed to aggregate citizen-voters' demands but also that the agenda formation process is characterized by both free access and unrestricted scope.

6. They do not specifically mention that they intend to operationalize the concept of germaneness, but it would appear from the 'dicta' that they think they have done so. However, as Shepsle (1979a; 1979b) conceptualized this rule, decisions about one dimension of a policy space would be made sequentially. Once a decision about a particular dimension had been reached, no further action on that dimension would be possible. Allowing members to zig-zag all over the policy space, one dimension at a time, is hardly a reasonable operationalization of the germaneness rule as specified by Shepsle.

communication patterns changes the way in which PMR and their germaneness rule operate. They test the configurational operation of rule systems. And, they find that the operation of one rule depends upon the operation of other rules in a rule configuration.

Consequences of the configurational character of rules on the appropriate strategies of inquiry

These three examples provide strong evidence for the configurational or, nonseparable, attribute of rules. This leads me to argue against an implicitly held belief of some scholars that what we learn about the operation of one rule in 'isolation' from other rules will hold across all situations in which that rule is used. I will characterize this view as a belief in the separable character of rules. I presume that rules combine in a configurational or interactive manner. If rules combine configurationally rather than separably, this dramatically affects the scientific strategy we should take in the study of rules and their effects.

A key example of the problems resulting from the view of the separable character of rules is the way theorists have approached the study of PMR as an aggregation rule. Many scholars, who have studied PMR, have self-consciously formulated their models in as general a manner as possible. By proving a theorem in a general case, it is presumed that the theorem will hold in all specific cases that contain PMR.

The penchant for generality has been interpreted to mean a formulation devoid of the specification of any rule, other than PMR. A set of N individuals somehow forms a committee or legislature. Position rules are rarely mentioned. The implicit assumption of most of these models is one and only one position exists - that of member. No information is presented concerning boundary rules. We do not know how the participants were selected, how they will be retained, whether they can leave, and how they are replaced. The participants compare points in n-dimensional space against one point in the same space called the status quo. We have no idea how that policy space came into being and what limits there may be on the policies that could be adopted. (One might presume from the way such general models are formulated that no constitutional rules protect against the taking of property without due process or prohibiting infringements on freedom of speech.) Authority rules are left unstated. We must guess at what actions individual participants are authorized to take. From the way that the models are described, it appears that any participant can make any proposal concerning movement to any place in policy space. We do not know anything about the information rules. Everyone appears to be able to talk to everyone and provides information about their preferences to everyone. PMR is the only rule specified.

In this general case, in which only a single rule is formulated, theorists typically make specific assumptions about preference orderings. This suggests that the concepts of 'generality' and 'specificity' are used arbitrarily. Specific assumptions about preference orderings are accepted as appropriate in general models, while efforts to increase the specificity of the rules in these same models are criticized because they are too specific.

The search for equilibria has occurred predominantly within the context of such 'general' models. And, in such 'general' models, equilibria are virtually nonexistent and are fragile to slight movements of preferences or the willingness of participants to dissemble (Riker 1981). McKelvey and Ordeshook (1983: 1) are willing to state that 'the principal lesson of social choice theory is that preference configurations which yield majority undominated outcomes are rare and almost always are fragile and thus are unlikely to be found in reality'.

If rules combine in a configurational manner, however, theorems proved about a 'zero' institutional arrangement will not necessarily be true when other rules are fully specified. Shepsle and his colleagues at Washington University have repeatedly shown that when several other rules are overtly combined with PMR, equilibria outcomes are more likely. Shepsle and Weingast (1981) have summarized the effects of:

1. Scope rules that operate to limit the set of outcomes that can be affected at a node in a process, e.g. amendment control rules (Shepsle 1979a; 1979b), 'small change' rules (Tullock 1981), rules requiring the status quo outcome to be considered at the last decision node, and rules requiring a committee proposal to be considered at the penultimate decision node.

2. Authority rules that operate to create and/or limit the action sets available to participants in positions, e.g. rules that assign a convener special powers to order the agenda (McKelvey 1979; Plott and Levine 1978; Isaac and Plott 1978), rules that assign a full committee, such as the Rules Committee in the House of Representatives, authority to set the procedures for debate and even to exclude a bill from consideration, and rules that constrain the action sets of members in regard to striking part of a motion, adding a part of a motion, and/or substituting a part of a motion (Fiorina 1980).

Structure-induced equilibria are present in many situations where scope rules, that limit the outcomes that can be reached, or authority rules, that constrain the actions of the participants in particular positions, are combined with PMR. This leads to an optimistic conclusion that equilibria are more likely, than previously argued, in committees and assemblies using majority rule to aggregate individual votes. This substantive optimism is, tempered somewhat when one recognizes the methodological consequences of rejecting the belief that rules can be studied as separable phenomena.

The methodological problem rests in the logic of combinatorics. If we were fortunate enough to be studying separable phenomena, then we could simply proceed to study individual rules out of context as we have done with PMR. We could then proceed to study other rules, out of context, and derive separable conclusions for each type of rule. Eventually, we could add our results together to build more complex models. This is an appropriate scientific method for the study of separable phenomena.

However, if the way one rule operates is affected by other rules, then we cannot continue to study each rule in isolation from others. A simple, scientific program is more difficult to envision once the configurational nature of rules is accepted. A configurational approach affects the way we do comparative statics. Instead of studying the effect of change of one rule on outcomes, regardless of the other rules in effect, we need to carefully state which other rules are in effect which condition the relationships produced by a change in any particular rule. We cannot just assume that other variables are controlled and unchanging. We need to know the value of the other variables affecting the relationship examined in a comparative statics framework.

Thus, we have much to do! It is more comforting to think about proving theorems about the effects of using one particular rule out of context of the other rules simultaneously in effect. If, however, combinations of rules work differently than isolated rules, we had better recognize the type of phenomena with which we are working and re-adjust our scientific agenda. We do, however, need a coherent strategy for analysing and testing the effects of combinations of rules. How can we isolate a key set of generally for mutated rules that provide the core of the rules to be studied? How can we build on the results of previous analytical work in our field?

Multiple levels of analysis and alternate strategy of inquiry

I have no final answers to these questions, but I do have an initial strategy to propose. This strategy relates to my earlier stress on the multiple levels of analysis involved in the study of rules. We have a relatively well developed body of theory related to the study of situations such as markets, committees, elections, and games in general. Thus, we already know what variables we must identify to represent one level of analysis. We can build on this knowledge as we develop the second level of analysis.

The structure of an action situation

The particular form of representation differs for neoclassical market theory, committee structures, and games in extensive form. However, in order to analyze any of these situations, an analyst specifies and relates together seven variables that form the structure of a situation.

1. The set of positions to be held by participants.

2. The set of participants (including a random actor where relevant) in each position.

3. The set of actions that participants in positions can take at different nodes in a decision tree.

4. The set of outcomes that participants jointly affect through their actions.

5. A set of functions that map participant and random actions at decision nodes into intermediate or final outcomes.

6. The amount of information available at a decision node.

7. The benefits and costs to be assigned to actions and outcomes.

These seven variables plus a model of the decision maker must be explicitly stated (or are implicitly assumed) in order to construct any formal model of an interdependent situation. We can consider these seven to be a universal set of necessary variables for the construction of formal decision models where outcomes are dependent on the acts of more than a single individual. This is a minimal set in that it is not possible to generate a prediction about behavior in an interdependent situation without having explicitly or implicitly specified something about each of these seven variables and related them together into a coherent structure. I call the analytical entity created when a theorist specifies these seven variables an action situation.

The most complete and general mathematical structure for representing an action situation is a game in extensive form (Selten 1975; Shubik 1982). The set of instructions given to participants in a well-constructed laboratory experiment is also a means of representing an action situation. Using these variables, the simplest possible working model of any particular type of situation whether a committee, a market, or a hierarchy can be constructed.[7] A change in any of these variables produces a different action situation and may lead to very different outcomes. More complex models of committees, markets, or other interdependent situations are constructed by adding to the complexity of the variables used to construct the simplest possible situations.[8]

---

7. The simplest possible representation of a committee, for example, can be constructed using the following assumptions:
    1) One position exists; that of member.
    2) Three participants are members.
    3) The set of outcomes that can be affected by the member contains two elements, one of which is designated as the status quo.
    4) A member is assigned an action set containing two elements: (a) vote for the status quo and (b) vote for the alternative outcome.
    5) If two members vote for the alternative outcome, it is obtained; otherwise, the status quo outcome is obtained;
    6) Payoffs are assigned to each participant depending on individual actions and joint outcomes.
    7) Complete information is available about elements (1) through (6).
    For this simplest possible representation of a committee, and using a well-defined model of the rational actor, we know that an equilibrium outcome exists. Unless two of the members prefer the alternative outcome to the status quo and both vote, the status quo is the equilibrium outcome. If two members do prefer and vote for the alternative outcome, it is the equilibrium outcome. The prediction of outcomes is more problematic as soon as a third outcome is added. Only when the valuation patterns of participants meet restricted conditions can an equilibrium outcome be predicted for such a simple committee situation with three members and three potential outcomes using majority rule (Arrow 1966; Plott 1967).
8. A more complex committee situation is created, for example, if a second position, that of

An action arena: Models of the situation and the individual

In addition to the seven universal variables of an action situation, an analyst must also utilize a model of the individual, which specifies how individuals process information, how they assign values to actions and outcomes, how they select an action, and what resources they have available. The model of the individual is the animating force that allows the analyst to generate predictions about likely outcomes given the structure of the situation (Popper 1967). When a specific model of the individual is added to the action situation, I call the resulting analytical entity an 'action arena'. An action arena thus consists of a model of the situation and a model of the individual in the situation (*see* E. Ostrom 1985).

When a theorist analyses an action arena, the model of the situation and the model of the individual are assumed as givens. At this level of analysis, the task of the analyst is viewed as one of predicting the type of behavior and results, given this structure. Questions concerning the presence or absence of retentive, attractive, and/or stable equilibria and evaluations of the efficiency and equity of these results are pursued at this level. The key question at this level is: Given the analytical structure assumed, how does this situation work to produce outcomes?

Rules as relations

Let me return now to the point I made above that all rules can be represented as relations. I can now be more specific. From sets of physically possible actions, outcomes, decision functions, information, positions, payoffs, and participants, rules select the feasible sets of the values of these variables. The action situation is the intersection of these feasible sets. In regard to driving a car for example, it is physically possible for a 13 year old to drive a car at 120 miles per hour on a freeway. If one were to model the action situation of a freeway in a state with well enforced traffic laws, one would posit the position of licensed drivers traveling an average of 60 to 65 miles per hour (depending on the enforcement patterns of the state). The values of the variables in the action situation are constrained by physical and behavior laws, and then, further contained by the rules in use. Most of formal analyses, to date, are of action situations; this is the surface structure that our representations model. The rules are part of the underlying structure that shapes the representations we use.

But, how do we overtly examine this part of the underlying structure? What rules should be examined when we conduct analysis at a deeper level? The approach I recommend is that we focus on those rules that can directly affect the structure of an action situation. This strategy helps us identify seven broad types of rules that operate configurationally to affect the structure of an action situation.

---

a convener, is added to the situation, and the action set of the convener includes actions not available to the other members (e.g. Isaac and Plott 1978; Eavey and Miller 1982). *See* also Gardner (1983) for an analysis of purges of recruitment to committees. Gardner's approach is very similar to the general strategy I am recommending.

These rules include:

1. *Position rules* that specify a set of positions and how many participants hold each position.

2. *Boundary rules* that specify how participants are chosen to hold these positions and how participants leave these positions.

3. *Scope rules* that specify the set of outcomes that may be affected and the external inducements and/or costs assigned to each of these outcomes.

4. *Authority rules* that specify the set of actions assigned to a position at a particular node.

5. *Aggregation rules* that specify the decision function to be used at a particular node to map actions into intermediate or final outcomes.

6. *Information rules* that authorize channels of communication among participants in positions and specify the language and form in which communication will take place.

7. *Payoff rules* prescribe how benefits and costs are to be distributed to participants in positions.

Given the wide diversity of rules that are found in everyday life, social rules could be classified in many ways. The method I am recommending has several advantages. First, rules are tied directly to the variables of an analytical entity familiar to all public choice theorists, economists, and game theorists. From this comes a strategy, or a heuristic, for identifying the rules affecting the structure of that situation. For each variable identified in the action situation, the theorist interested in rules needs to ask what rules produced the variable as specified in the situation. For example, in regard to the number of participants, the rule analyst would be led to ask: Why are there N participants? How did they enter? Under what conditions can they leave? Are there costs, incentives, or penalties associated with entering or exiting? Are some participants forced into entry because of their residence or occupation?

In regard to the actions that can be taken, the rule analyst would ask: Why these actions rather than others? Are all participants in positions assigned the same action set? Or, is some convener, or other position, assigned an action set containing options not available to the remaining participants? Are sets of actions time or path dependent?

In regard to the outcomes that can be affected, the rule analyst would ask: Why these outcomes rather than others? Are the participants all principals who can affect any state variable they are defined to own? Or, are the participants fiduciaries who are authorized to affect particular state variables within specified ranges but not beyond? Similar questions can be asked about each variable overtly placed in a model of an action situation.

Answers to these sets of questions can then be formalized as a set of relations that, combined with physical and behavioural laws, produce the particular values of the variables of the situation. I am not arguing that there is a unique set of relations that produce any particular model of a situation. Given the pervasiveness of situations with the structure of a Prisoners' Dilemma, one can expect that multiple sets of rules may produce action situations with the same structure. This is not problematic when one focuses exclusively on predicting behavior within the situation. It poses a serious problem when the question of how to change that structure. To change a situation, one must know which set of rules produce the situation.

Other factors also affect this structure. We know, for example, that rules which generate a competitive market produce relatively optimal equilibria when used to allocate homogeneous, divisible goods from which potential consumers can be excluded. The same rules generate less optimal situations when goods are jointly consumed and it is difficult to exclude consumers. But the theorist interested in how changes in rules affects behavior within situations must hold other factors constant while an analysis is conducted of changes in the rules.

Besides providing a general heuristic for identifying the relevant rules that affect the structure of a situation, a second advantage of this approach is that it leads to a relatively natural classification system for sets of rules. Classifying rules by what they affect enables us to identify sets of rules that all directly affect the same working part of the situation. This should enhance our capabilities for developing a formal language for representing rules themselves. Specific rules used in everyday life are named in a non-theoretical manner - frequently referring to the number of the rule in some written rule book or piece of legislation. Theorists studying rules tend to name the rule they are examining for some feature related to the particular type of situation in which the rule occurs.

For systematic cumulation to occur, we need to identify when rules, called by different names, are really the same rule. It is important that scholars understand, for example, that Romer and Rosenthal and Grether, Isaac and Plott all examined consequences of default conditions of aggregation rules. Proceeding to formalize the rules used by Grether, Isaac and Plott in their series of experiments would help other scholars identify which rules, called by other everyday terms, are similar to the 'grandfather' default condition, to the random default condition, or to 'taking from the large and giving to the small' default condition.

By paying as much care to the formalization of the rules affecting an action situation as we do to formalizing the action situation itself, we will eventually establish rigorous theoretical propositions concerning the completeness and consistency of rules themselves. From Romer and Rosenthal and from Grether, Isaac and Plott, we now know that any specification of a unanimity rule without an explicit default condition is incomplete. I am willing to speculate that any aggregation rule without a default condition is incomplete.

Some concluding thoughts

Given the multiple referents for the term 'institutions', our first need is for a consistent language if public choice scholars are going to return to a major study of institutions. To begin this task, I have focused on one term - that of rules - used by some theorists as a referent for the term institutions. My effort is intended to clarify what we mean by rules, how rules differ from physical or behavioural laws, how we can classify rules in a theoretically interesting manner, and how we can begin to formalize rule configurations. I have not answered the question, 'What are institutions?' This involves an argument over which referent is 'the' right or preferred referent. Rather, I try to clarify one referent and leave the clarification of other referents to other scholars.

Secondly, I provided several examples of how public choice analysts have studied rules. These examples illustrate two points. First, rules operate configurationally rather than separably. Second, the study of rules involves multiple levels of analysis rather than a single level of analysis. The configurational character of rules significantly affects the strategies we use to analyse rules. One approach has been to posit a single rule and examine the type of equilibria, or absence of equilibria, likely to result from the operation of this single rule. Scholars have concluded that stable equilibria do not exist in situations in which individuals use majority rule aggregation procedures. This is not consistent with empirical observation. Further, when scholars introduce rules constraining actions and outcomes into majority rule models, it is then possible to predict stable equilibria. The methodological consequence of the configurational character of rules is that theorists need to specify a set of rules, rather than a single rule, when attempting to ask what consequences are produced by changes in a particular rule.

Once this conclusion is accepted, a method to identify sets of rules is essential if we hope to develop any cumulative knowledge about the effects of rules. If more than one rule need be specified, the key question is how many different rules must be specified to know that we have identified a rule configuration. My preliminary answer is that we need to identify seven types of rules that directly affect the seven types of variables we use to construct most of the action situations we analyse. When we analyse changes in one of these rules, we should identify the specific setting of the other variables that condition how the changes in the first rule affects outcomes.

The analysis of rules needs at least two levels. We can represent these levels by reformulating Plott's fundamental equation into two equations:

$$\begin{array}{lll} \text{Structure of an} & & \text{Model of a} \\ \text{Action Situation} & \oplus & \text{Decision Maker} \end{array} = \text{Outcomes} \qquad (6)$$

$$\begin{array}{lll} \text{Rules + Physical} & & \\ \text{Law} & \oplus & \text{Behavioural Laws} \end{array} = \begin{array}{l} \text{Structure of an} \\ \text{Action Situation} \end{array} \qquad (7)$$

Equation (6) is the one most public choice theorists use in their work. As we delve somewhat deeper into the analysis of rules themselves, previous work that has focused on action situations themselves can be integrated into a broader framework. Equation (7) involves the specification of the rules, as well as the physical and behavioural laws, that affect the values of the variables in an action situation. The seventh equation is the one we must use when we want to analyse how rules change the structure of a situation leading, in turn, to a change in outcomes (*see* V. Ostrom 1982; 1984). The seventh equation makes apparent the need to study the effects of rules where physical and behavioural laws are invariant.

In light of these characteristics, much future work needs to be done. We need a formal language for the representation of rules as functions affecting the variables in an action situation. We also need to address questions concerning the origin and change of rule configurations in use. How do individuals evolve a particular rule configuration? What factors affect the likelihood of their following a set of rules? What affects the enforcement of rules? How is the level of enforcement related to rule conformance? What factors affect the reproducibility and reliability of a rule system? When is it possible to develop new rules through self-conscious choice? And, when are new rules bound to fail?

References

Advisory Commission on Intergovernmental Relations (1974). Governmental functions and processes: Local and area wide. Volume IV of substate regionalism and the federal system. Washington, D.C.: U.S. Government Printing Office.

Arrow, K. (1966) *Social Choice and Individual Values*, 2nd edition, New York: Wiley.

Becker, G. S. (1976) *The Economic Approach to Human Behavior*, Chicago: University of Chicago Press.

Buchanan, J. M. and Tullock, G. (1962) *The Calculus of Consent,* Ann Arbor: University of Michigan Press.

Commons, J. R. (1957) *Legal Foundations of Capitalism*, Madison: University of Wisconsin Press.

Dahl, R. A. and Tufte, E. R. (1973) *Size and Democracy*, Stanford, Calif.: Stanford University Press.

Dawson, R. E. and Robinson, J. A. (1963) 'Interparty competition, economic variables and welfare policies in the American states', *Journal of Politics* 25:265–289.

Downs, A. (1957) *An Economic Theory of Democracy,* New York: Harper and Row.

Dye, T. R. (1966) *Politics, Economics, and the Public*, Chicago: Rand McNally.

Eavey, C. L. and Miller, G. J. (1982) *Committee Leadership and the Chairman's Power*, Paper delivered at the Annual Meetings of the American Political Science Association, Denver, Colo., September 2–5.

Fiorina, M. P. (1980) 'Legislative facilitation of government growth: Universalism and reciprocity practices in majority rule institutions', *Research in Public Policy Analysis and Management* 1:197–221.

Ganz, J. S. (1971) *Rules: A systematic study,* The Hague: Mouton.

Gardner, R. (1983) 'Variation of the electorate: Veto and purge', *Public Choice* 40(3): 237–247.

Grether, D. M., Isaac, R. M. and Plott, C. R. (1979) *Alternative methods of allocating airport slots: Performance and evaluation*, A report prepared for the Civil Aeronautics Board.

Harré, R. (1974) 'Some remarks on "rule" as a scientific concept', in T. Mischel (ed.) *Understanding Other Persons*, Oxford: Basil-Blackwell, pp. 143–183.

Hayek, F. A. (1976) *The Mirage of Social Justice,* Chicago: University of Chicago Press.

Hayek, F. A. (1978) *New Studies in Philosophy, Politics, Economics, and the History of Ideas,* Chicago: University of Chicago Press.

Heiner, R. A. (1983) 'The origin of predictable behavior', *American Economic Review* 83 (4): 560–597.

Isaac, R. M. and Plott, C. R. (1978) 'Comparative game models of the influence of the closed rule in three person, majority rule committees: Theory and experiment', in P. C. Ordeshook (ed.) *Game Theory and Political Science*, New York: New York University Press pp. 283–322.

Kiser, L. and Ostrom, E. (1982) 'The three worlds of action: A meta-theoretical synthesis of institutional approaches', in E. Ostrom (ed.) *Strategies of Political Inquiry*, Beverly Hills: Sage Publications, pp. 179–222.

Mackay, R. J. and Weaver, C. (1979) 'Monopoly bureaus and fiscal outcomes: Deductive models and implications for reform', in G. Tullock and R.E. Wagner (eds) *Policy Analysis and Deductive Reasoning*, Lexington, Mass.: Lexington Books, 141–165.

McGuire, T., Coiner, M. and Spancake, L. (1979) 'Budget maximizing agencies and efficiency in government', *Public Choice* 34 (3/4): 333–359.

McKelvey, R. D. (1979) 'General conditions for global intransitivities', *Econometrica* 47: 1085–1111.

McKelvey, R. D. and Ordeshook, P. C. (1984) 'An experimental study of the effects of procedural rules on committee behavior', *Journal of Politics* 46 (1): 185–205.

Menger, K. (1963) *Problems in Economics and Sociology* (Originally published in 1883 and translated by Francis J. Nock), Urbana: University of Illinois Press.

Niskanen, W. A. (1971) *Bureaucracy and Representative Government*, Chicago: Aldine-Atherton.

Nozick, R. (1975) *Anarchy, State, and Utopia,* New York: Basic Books.

Ostrom, E. (1985) 'A method of institutional analysis', in F. X. Kaufmann, G. Majone and V. Ostrom (eds) *Guidance, Control and Performance Evaluation in the Public Sector*, Berlin, New York: de Gruyter.

Ostrom, V. (1980) 'Artisanship and artifact', *Public Administration Review* 40 (4): 309–317.

— (1982) 'A forgotten tradition: The constitutional level of analysis', in J. A. Gillespie.

— (1986) 'Constitutional considerations with particular reference to federal systems', in F. X. Kaufmann, G. Majone and V. Ostrom (eds), *Guidance, Control, and Performance Evaluation in the Public Sector*, Berlin, New York: de Gruyter, pp. 111–25.

Ostrom, V. and D. A. Zinnes (eds) *Missing Elements in Political Inquiry: Logic and Levels of Analysis*, Beverly Hills: Sage Publications, pp. 237–252.

Parks, R. B. and Ostrom, E. (1981) 'Complex models of urban service systems', in T. N. Clark (ed.) *Urban Policy Analysis: Directions for Future Research. Urban Affaire Annual Reviews* 21:171–199.

Plott, C. R. (1967) 'A notion of equilibrium and its possibility under majority rule', *American Economic Review* 57 (4): 787–807.

— (1979) 'The application of laboratory experimental methods to public choice', in C.S. Russell (ed.) *Collective Decision Making: Applications from Public Choice Theory*, Baltimore, Md.: Johns Hopkins University Press, pp. 137–160.

Plott, C. R. and Levine, M. E. (1978) 'A model for agenda influence on committee decisions', *American Economic Review,* 68:146–160.

Popper, K. R. (1967) 'La rationalité et le statut du principle de rationalité', in E. M. Classen (ed.) *Les foundements philosophiques des systemes economiques: Textes de Jacques Rueff et essais rediges en son honneur 23 aout 1966*, Paris, France: Payot, pp. 145–50.

Rawls, J. (1968) 'Two concepts of rules', in N. S. Care and C. Landesman (eds), *Readings in the Theory of Action*, Bloomington, Ind.: Indiana University Press, pp. 306–340. Originally printed in *the Philosophical Review* 4 (1955).

Riker, W. H. (1982) 'Implications from the disequilibrium of majority rule for the study of institutions', in P. C. Ordeshook and K. A. Shepsle (eds) *Political equilibrium*, Boston: Kluwer-Nijhoff, pp. 3–24. Originally published in *The American Political Science Review* 74 (June 1980): 432–447.

Romer, T. and Rosenthal, H. (1978) 'Political resource allocation, controlled agendas, and the status quo', *Public Choice* 33 (4): 27–43.

Schotter, A. (1981) *The Economic Theory of Social Institutions*, Cambridge: Cambridge University Press.

Selten, R. (1975) 'Reexamination of the perfectness concept for equilibrium points in extensive games', *International Journal of Game Theory* 4:25–55.

Shepsle, K. A. (1979a) 'Institutional arrangements and equilibrium in multidimensional voting models', *American Journal of Political Science*, 23 (1): 27–59.

—— (1979b) 'The role of institutional structure in the creation of policy equilibrium', in D. W. Rae and T. J. Eismeier (eds) *Public Policy and Public Choice*, Sage Yearbooks in Politics and Public Policy 6, Beverly Hills: Sage Publications, pp. 249–283.

Shepsle, K. A. and Weingast, B. R. (1981) 'Structure-induced equilibrium and legislative choice', *Public Choice* 37 (3): 503–520.

Shimanoff, S. B. (1980) *Communication Rules: Theory and Research*, Beverly Hills: Sage Publications.

Shubik, M. (1982) *Game Theory in the Social Sciences: Concepts and Solutions*, Cambridge, Mass.: The MIT Press.

Taylor, M. (1976) *Anarchy and Cooperation*, New York: Wiley.

Toulmin, S. (197) 'Rules and their relevance for understanding human behavior', in T. Mischel (ed.), *Understanding Other Persons*, Oxford: Basil-Blackwell, pp. 185–215.

Tullock, G. (1981) 'Why so much stability?', *Public Choice* 37 (2): 189–205.

Ullman-Margalit, E. (1978) *The Emergence of Norms*, New York: Oxford University Press.

von Wright, G. H. (1968) 'The logic of practical discourse' in R. Klibansky (ed.) *Contemporary Philosophy*, Florence: La Nuova Italia Editrice, pp. 141–167.

Wilson, R. and Herzberg, R. (1984) 'Voting is only a block away: Theory and experiments on blocking coalitions', Paper presented at the Public Choice Society meetings, Phoenix, Ariz., March 29–31.

Chapter Five

A Behavioral Approach to the Rational Choice Theory of Collective Action[1]

Elinor Ostrom[2]

Let me start with a provocative statement. You would not be reading this article if it were not for some of our ancestors learning how to undertake collective action to solve social dilemmas. Successive generations have added to the stock of everyday knowledge about how to instil productive norms of behavior in their children and to craft rules to support collective action that produces public goods and avoids 'tragedies of the commons'.[3] What our ancestors and contemporaries have learned about engaging in collective action for mutual defense, child rearing, and survival is not, however, understood or explained by the extant theory of collective action.

Yet, the theory of collective action is *the* central subject of political science. It is the core of the justification for the state. Collective-action problems pervade international relations, face legislators when devising public budgets, permeate public bureaucracies, and are at the core of explanations of voting, interest group formation, and citizen control of governments in a democracy. If political scientists do not have an empirically grounded theory of collective action, then we are hand-waving at our central questions. I am afraid that we do a lot of hand-waving.

The lessons of effective collective action are not simple – as is obvious from human history and the immense tragedies that humans have endured, as well as the successes we have realized. As global relationships become even more intricately intertwined and complex, however, our survival becomes more dependent on empirically grounded scientific understanding. We have not yet developed a *behavioural theory of collective action* based on models of the individual consistent

1. Presidential Address, American Political Science Association, 1997 published initially in *American Political Science Review*, vol. 92, 1998, pp. 1–22.

2. The author gratefully acknowledges the support of the National Science Foundation (Grant #SBR-9319835 and SBR-9521918), the Ford Foundation, the Bradley Foundation, and the MacArthur Foundation. My heartiest thanks go to James Alt, Jose Apesteguia, Patrick Brandt, Kathryn Firmin-Sellers, Roy Gardner, Derek Kauneckis, Fabrice Lehoucq, Margaret Levi, Thomas Lyon, Tony Matejczyk, Mike McGinnis, Trudi Miller, John Orbell, Vincent Ostrom, Eric Rasmusen, David Schmidt, Sujai Shivakumar, Vernon Smith, Catherine Tucker, George Varughese, Jimmy Walker, John Williams, Rick Wilson, Toshio Yamagishi, and Xin Zhang for their comments on earlier drafts and to Patty Dalecki for all her excellent editorial and moral support.

3. The term 'tragedy of the commons' refers to the problem that common-pool resources, such as oceans, lakes, forests, irrigation systems, and grazing lands, can easily be overused or destroyed if property rights to these resources are not well defined (*see* Hardin 1968).

with empirical evidence about how individuals make decisions in social-dilemma situations. A behavioural commitment to theory grounded in empirical inquiry is essential if we are to understand such basic questions as why face-to-face communication so consistently enhances cooperation in social dilemmas or how structural variables facilitate or impede effective collective action.

Social dilemmas occur whenever individuals in interdependent situations face choices in which the maximization of short-term self-interest yields outcomes leaving all participants worse off than feasible alternatives. In a public-good dilemma, for example, all those who would benefit from the provision of a public good – such as pollution control, radio broadcasts, or weather forecasting – find it costly to contribute and would prefer others to pay for the good instead. If everyone follows the equilibrium strategy, then the good is not provided or is underprovided.

Yet, everyone would be better off if everyone were to contribute.

Social dilemmas are found in all aspects of life, leading to momentous decisions affecting war and peace as well as the mundane relationships of keeping promises in everyday life. Social dilemmas are called by many names, including the public-good or collective-good problem (Olson 1965; P. Samuelson 1954), shirking (Alchian and Demsetz 1972), the free-rider problem (Edney 1979; Grossman and Hart 1980), moral hazard (Holmstrom 1982), the credible commitment dilemma (Williams, Collins and Lichbach 1997), generalized social exchange (Ekeh 1974; Emerson 1972a, 1972b; Yamagishi and Cook 1993), the tragedy of the commons (G. Hardin 1968) and exchanges of threats and violent confrontations (Boulding 1963). The prisoners' dilemma has become the best-known social dilemma in contemporary scholarship. Among the types of individuals who are posited to face these kinds of situations are politicians (Geddes 1994), international negotiators (Sandler 1992; Snidal 1985), legislators (Shepsle and Weingast 1984), managers (Miller 1992), workers (Leibenstein 1976), long-distance traders (Greif, Milgrom and Weingast 1994), ministers (Bullock and Baden 1977), oligopolists (Cornes, Mason and Sandler 1986), labour union organisers (Messick 1973), revolutionaries (Lichbach 1995), homeowners (Boudreaux and Holcombe 1989), even cheerleaders (Hardy and Latané 1988) and, of course, all of us – whenever we consider trusting others to cooperate with us on long-term joint endeavours.

In prehistoric times, simple survival was dependent both on the aggressive pursuit of self-interest and on collective action to achieve cooperation in defence, food acquisition, and child rearing. Reciprocity among close kin was used to solve social dilemmas, leading to a higher survival rate for those individuals who lived in families and used reciprocity within the family (Hamilton 1964). As human beings began to settle in communities and engage in agriculture and long-distance trade, forms of reciprocity with individuals other than close kin were essential to achieve mutual protection, to gain the benefits of long-distance trading, and to build common facilities and preserve common-pool resources.[4] Evolutionary

4. The term 'reciprocal altruism' is used by biologists and evolutionary theorists to refer to strategies of conditional cooperation with non kin that produce higher benefits for the individuals

psychologists have produced substantial evidence that human beings have evolved the capacity – similar to that of learning a language – to learn reciprocity norms and general social rules that enhance returns from collective action (Cosmides and Tooby 1992). At the same time, cognitive scientists have also shown that our genetic inheritance does not give us the capabilities to do unbiased, complex, and full analyses without substantial acquired knowledge and practice as well as reliable feedback from the relevant environment. Trial-and-error methods are used to learn individual skills as well as rules and procedures that increase the joint returns individuals may obtain through specialization, coordination, and exchange. All long-enduring political philosophies have recognized human nature to be complex mixtures of the pursuit of self-interest combined with the capability of acquiring internal norms of behavior and following enforced rules when understood and perceived to be legitimate. Our evolutionary heritage has hardwired us to be boundedly self-seeking at the same time that we are capable of learning heuristics and norms, such as reciprocity, that help achieve successful collective action.

One of the most powerful theories used in contemporary social sciences – rational choice theory – helps us understand humans as self-interested, short-term maximisers. Models of complete rationality have been highly successful in predicting marginal behavior in competitive situations in which selective pressures screen out those who do not maximize external values, such as profits in a competitive market or the probability of electoral success in party competition. Thin models of rational choice have been unsuccessful in explaining or predicting behavior in one-shot or finitely repeated social dilemmas in which the theoretical prediction is that no one will cooperate. In indefinitely (or infinitely) repeated social dilemmas, standard rational choice models predict a multitude of equilibria ranging from the very best to the very worst of available outcomes without any hypothesized process for how individuals might achieve more productive outcomes and avert disasters.[5] Substantial evidence from experiments demonstrates that cooperation levels for most one-shot or finitely repeated social dilemmas far exceed the predicted levels and are systematically affected by variables that play no theoretical role in affecting outcomes. Field research also shows that individuals systematically engage in collective action to provide local public goods or manage common-pool resources without an external authority to offer inducements or impose sanctions. Simply assuming that individuals use long-range thinking 'to achieve the goal of establishing and/or maintaining continued mutual cooperation' (Pruitt and Kimmel 1977: 375) is not a sufficient theory either. It does not explain why some groups fail to obtain joint outcomes easily available to them or why initial cooperation can break down.

who follow these strategies if they interact primarily with others who are reciprocators (Trivers 1971). Since these strategies benefit the individual using them in the long term, I prefer the term 'reciprocity'.

5. *See* Farrell and Maskin (1989) for a different approach to this problem.

We now have enough scholarship from multiple disciplines to expand the range of rational choice models we use. For at least five reasons, we need to formulate a behavioural theory of boundedly rational and moral behavior.

First, behavior in social dilemmas is affected by many structural variables, including size of group, heterogeneity of participants, their dependence on the benefits received, their discount rates, the type and predictability of transformation processes involved, the nesting of organisational levels, monitoring techniques, and the information available to participants.[6] In theories that predict either zero or 100 percent cooperation in one-shot or finitely repeated dilemmas, structural variables do not affect levels of cooperation at all. A coherent explanation of the relationship among structural variables and the likelihood of individuals solving social dilemmas depends on developing a behavioural theory of rational choice. This will allow scholars who stress structural explanations of human behavior and those who stress individual choice to find common ground, rather than continue the futile debate over whether structural variables or individual attributes are the most important.

Second, scholars in all the social and some biological sciences have active research programs focusing on how groups of individuals achieve collective action. An empirically supported theoretical framework for the analysis of social dilemmas would integrate and link their efforts. Essential to the development of such a framework is a conception of human behavior that views complete rationality as one member of a family of rationality models rather than the only way to model human behavior. Competitive institutions operate as a scaffolding structure so that individuals who fail to learn how to maximize some external value are no longer in the competitive game (Alchian 1950; Clark 1995; Satz and Ferejohn 1994). If all institutions involved strong competition, then the thin model of rationality used to explain behavior in competitive markets would be more useful. Models of human behavior based on theories consistent with our evolutionary and adaptive heritage need to join the ranks of theoretical tools used in the social and biological sciences.

Third, sufficient work by cognitive scientists, evolutionary theorists, game theorists, and social scientists in all disciplines (Axelrod 1984; Boyd and Richerson 1988, 1992; Cook and Levi 1990; Guth and Kliemt 1995; Sethi and Somanathan 1996; Simon 1985, 1997) on the use of heuristics and norms of behavior, such as reciprocity, has already been undertaken. It is now possible to continue this development toward a firmer behavioural foundation for the study of collective action to overcome social dilemmas.

Fourth, much of our current public policy analysis – particularly since Garrett Hardin's (1968) evocative paper, 'The Tragedy of the Commons' – is based on an

---

6. This is only a short list of the more important variables found to affect behavior within social dilemmas (for summary overviews of this literature, *see* Goetze and Orbell 1988; Ledyard 1995; Lichbach 1996; E. Ostrom 1990, 1998; E. Ostrom, Gardner, and Walker 1994; Sally 1995; Schroeder 1995).

Figure 5.1: N-person Social Dilemma

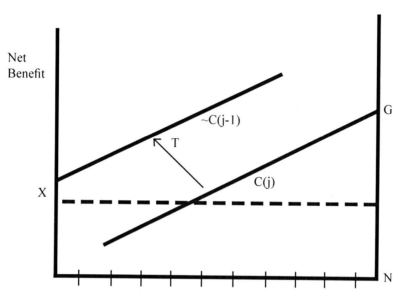

Number of cooperating players

Note: N players choose between cooperating (C) or not cooperating (~C). When j individuals cooperate, their payoffs are always lower than the j-1 individuals who do not cooperate. The predicted outcome is that no one will cooperate and all players will receive X benefits. The temptation (*T*) not to cooperate is the increase in benefit any co-operator would receive for switching to not cooperating. If all cooperate, they all receive G-X more benefits than if all do not cooperate.

assumption that rational individuals are helplessly trapped in social dilemmas from which they cannot extract themselves without inducement or sanctions applied from the outside. Many policies based on this assumption have been subject to major failure and have exacerbated the very problems they were intended to ameliorate (Arnold and Campbell 1986; Baland and Platteau 1996; Morrow and Hull 1996). Policies based on the assumptions that individuals can learn how to devise well-tailored rules and cooperate conditionally when they participate in the design of institutions affecting them are more successful in the field (Berkes 1989; Bromley *et al.* 1992; Ellickson 1991; Feeny *et al.* 1990; McCay and Acheson 1987; McKean and Ostrom 1995; Pinkerton 1989; Yoder 1994).

Fifth, the image of citizens we provide in our textbooks affects the long-term viability of democratic regimes. Introductory textbooks that presume rational citizens will be passive consumers of political life – the masses – and focus primarily on the role of politicians and officials at a national level – the elite – do not inform future citizens of a democratic polity of the actions they need to know and can undertake. While many political scientists claim to eschew teaching the normative foundations of a democratic polity, they actually introduce a norm of cynicism and distrust without providing a vision of how citizens could do anything to challenge corruption, rent seeking,[7] or poorly designed policies.

The remainder of this article is divided into six sections. In the first I briefly review the theoretical predictions of currently accepted rational choice theory related to social dilemmas. The next will summarize the challenge to the sole reliance on a complete model of rationality presented by extensive experimental research. Then I examine two major empirical findings that begin to show how individuals achieve results that are 'better than rational' (Cosmides and Tooby 1994) by building conditions in which reciprocity, reputation, and trust can help to overcome the strong temptations of short-run self-interest. The following section raises the possibility of developing second-generation models of rationality, and the next develops an initial theoretical scenario. I conclude by examining the implications of placing reciprocity, reputation, and trust at the core of an empirically tested, behavioural theory of collective action.

Theoretical predictions for social dilemmas

The term 'social dilemma' refers to a large number of situations in which individuals make independent choices in an interdependent situation (Dawes 1975: 1980; R. Hardin 1971). In all N-person social dilemmas, a set of participants has a choice of contributing (C) or not contributing ($-C$) to a joint benefit. While I represent this as an either-or choice in Figure 5.1, it frequently is a choice of how much to contribute rather than whether to contribute or not.

If everyone contributes, they get a net positive benefit (G). Everyone faces a temptation (T) to shift from the set of contributors to the set of those who do not contribute. The theoretical prediction is that everyone will shift and that no one will contribute. If this happens, then the outcome will be at the intercept. The difference between the predicted outcome and everyone contributing is $G - X$. Since the less-valued payoff is at a Nash equilibrium, no one is independently motivated to change his or her choice, given the choices of other participants. These situations are dilemmas because at least one outcome exists that yields greater advantage for *all* participants. Thus, a Pareto-superior alternative exists, but rational participants making isolated choices are not predicted to realize this outcome. A conflict is posed between individual and group rationality. The problem of collective action raised by social dilemmas is to find a way to avoid Pareto-inferior equilibria and to move closer to the optimum. Those who find ways to coordinate strategies in some fashion receive a 'cooperators' dividend' equal to the difference between the predicted outcome and the outcome achieved.

Many models of social dilemmas exist in the literature (*see* Schelling 1978 and Lichbach 1996 for reviews of alternative formalizations). In all models, a

---

7. The term 'rent seeking' refers to nonproductive activities directed toward creating opportunities for profits higher than would be obtained in an open, competitive market.

set of individuals is involved in a game in which a strategy leading to a Nash equilibrium for a single iteration of the game yields less than an optimal outcome for all involved. The equilibrium is thus Pareto inferior. The optimal outcome could be achieved if those involved 'cooperated' by selecting strategies other than those prescribed by an equilibrium solution to a noncooperative game (Harsanyi and Selten 1988). Besides these assumptions regarding the structure of payoffs in the one-shot version of the game, other assumptions are made in almost all formal models of social dilemmas. (1) All participants have common knowledge of the exogenously fixed structure of the situation and of the payoffs to be received by all individuals under all combinations of strategies. (2) Decisions about strategies are made independently, often simultaneously. (3) In a symmetric game, all participants have available the same strategies. (4) No external actor (or central authority) is present to enforce agreements among participants about their choices.

When such a game is finitely repeated, participants are assumed to solve the game through backward induction. Assumptions about the particular payoff functions differ. Rather than describe the Nash equilibrium and Pareto-efficient outcome for all models considered in this article, aggregate behavior consistent with the Nash equilibrium will be described as zero cooperation, while behavior consistent with the efficient outcome will be described as 100 percent cooperation.

The grim predictions evoked considerable empirical challenges as well as important theoretical breakthroughs. The predictions ran counter to so many everyday experiences that some scholars turned to survey and field studies to examine the level of voluntary contributions to public goods (see Lichbach 1995 for a summary). Others turned to the experimental lab and confirmed much higher than predicted levels of cooperation in one-shot experiments. Game theorists were challenged to rethink their own firm conclusions and to pose new models of when cooperation might emerge (see Benoit and Krishna 1985).

The introduction of two kinds of uncertainty into repeated games – about the number of repetitions and about the types of players participating in a social dilemma – has led to more optimistic predictions. When individuals, modelled as fully rational actors with low discount rates, interact in a repeated social dilemma whose end point is determined stochastically, it is now theoretically well established that it is *possible* for them to achieve optimal or near optimal outcomes and avoid the dominant strategies of one-shot and finitely repeated games that yield suboptimal outcomes (Fudenberg and Maskin 1986). This is possible when players achieve self-enforcing equilibria by committing themselves to punish noncooperators sufficiently to deter noncooperation. Kreps et al. (1982) introduced a second kind of uncertainty related to whether all the players use complete rationality as their guide to action. The probability of the presence of an 'irrational' player, who reciprocates cooperation with cooperation, is used as the grounds for a completely rational player to adopt the strategy of cooperating early in a sequence of games and switching to noncooperation at the end. Once either of these two forms of uncertainty is introduced, the number of possible equilibria explode in number (Abreau 1988). Everything is predicted: optimal outcomes, the Pareto-inferior Nash equilibria, and everything in between.

To generate predictions other than noncooperation, theorists using standard rational choice theory have found it necessary to assume real uncertainty about the duration of a situation or to assume that some players are 'irrational' in their willingness to reciprocate cooperation with cooperation. To assume that if some players *irrationally* choose reciprocity, then others can *rationally* choose reciprocity is a convoluted explanation – to say the least – of the growing evidence that reciprocity is a core norm used by many individuals in social dilemma situations.

The lack of a general fit

In all the social sciences, experiments have been conducted on various types of social dilemmas for several decades. While some scholars question the value of laboratory experiments for testing the predictions of major theories in the social sciences, this method has many advantages. First, one can design experiments that test multiple predictions from the same theory under controlled conditions. Second, replication is feasible. Third, researchers can challenge whether a particular design adequately captures the theoretically posited variables and conduct further experiments to ascertain how changes in a design affect outcomes. The evidence discussed below is based on multiple studies by diverse research teams. Fourth, experimental methods are particularly relevant for studying human choice under diverse institutional arrangements. Subjects in experimental studies draw on the modes of analysis and values they have learned throughout their lives to respond to diverse incentive structures. Experiments thus allow one to test precisely whether individuals behave within a variety of institutional settings as predicted by theory (Plott 1979; Smith 1982).

In this section, I will summarize four consistently replicated findings that directly challenge the general fit between behavior observed in social-dilemma experiments and the predictions of noncooperative game theory using complete rationality and complete information for one-shot and finitely repeated social dilemmas. I focus first on the fit between theory and behavior, because the theoretical predictions are unambiguous and have influenced so much thinking across the social sciences. Experiments on market behavior do fit the predictions closely (*see* Davis and Holt 1993 for an overview). If one-shot and finitely repeated social-dilemma experiments were to support strongly the predictions of noncooperative game theory, then we would have a grounded theory with close affinities to a vast body of economic theory for which there is strong empirical support. We would need to turn immediately to the problem of indefinitely repeated situations for which noncooperative game theory faces an embarrassment of too many equilibria. As it turns out, we have a different story to tell. The four general findings are as follows:

1. High levels of initial cooperation are found in most types of social dilemmas, but the levels are consistently less than optimal.

2. Behavior is not consistent with backward induction in finitely repeated social dilemmas.

3. Nash equilibrium strategies are not good predictors at the individual level.

4. Individuals do not learn Nash equilibrium strategies in repeated social dilemmas.

High but suboptimal levels of initial cooperation

Most experimental studies of social dilemmas with the structure of a public-goods provision problem have found levels of cooperative actions in one-shot games, or in the first rounds of a repeated game, that are significantly above the predicted level of zero.[8] 'In a wide variety of treatment conditions, participants rather persistently contributed 40 to 60 percent of their token endowments to the [public good], far in excess of the 0 percent contribution rate consistent with a Nash equilibrium' (Davis and Holt 1993: 325). Yet, once an experiment is repeated, cooperation levels in public-good experiments tend to decline. The individual variation across experiment sessions can be very great.[9] While many have focused on the unexpectedly high rates of cooperation, it is important to note that in sparse institutional settings with no feedback about individual contributions, cooperation levels never reach the optimum. Thus, the prediction of zero levels of cooperation can be rejected, but cooperation at a suboptimal level is consistently observed in sparse institutional settings.

Behavior in social dilemmas inconsistent with backward induction

In all finitely repeated experiments, players are predicted to look ahead to the last period and determine what they would do in that period. In the last period, there is no future interaction; the prediction is that they will not cooperate in that round. Since that choice would be determined at the beginning of an experiment, the players are presumed to look at the second to-last period and ask themselves what they would do there. Given that they definitely would not cooperate in the

---

8. *See* Isaac, McCue, and Plott 1985; Kim and Walker 1984; Marwell and Ames 1979, 1980, 1981; Orbell and Dawes 1991, 1993; Schneider and Pommerehne 1981. An important exception to this general finding is that when subjects are presented with an experimental protocol with an opportunity to invest tokens in a common-pool resource (the equivalent of harvesting from a common pool), they tend to overinvest substantially in the initial rounds (*see* E. Ostrom, Gardner and Walker 1994 and comparison of public goods and common-pool resource experiments in Goetze 1994 and E. Ostrom and Walker 1997). Ledyard (1995) considers common-pool resource dilemmas to have the same underlying structure as public good dilemmas, but behavior in common-pool resource experiments without communication is consistently different from public good experiments without communication. With repetition, outcomes in common-pool resource experiments approach the Nash equilibrium from below rather than from above, as is typical in public good experiments.

9. In a series of eight experiments with different treatments conducted by Isaac, Walker and Thomas (1984), in which the uniform theoretical prediction was zero contributions, contribution rates varied from nearly 0 percent to around 75 percent of the resources available to participants.

last period, it is assumed that they also would not cooperate in the second-to-last period. This logic would then extend backward to the first round (Luce and Raiffa 1957: 98–9).

While backward induction is still the dominant method used in solving finitely repeated games, it has been challenged on theoretical grounds (Binmore 1997: R. Hardin 1997). Furthermore, as discussed above, uncertainty about whether others use norms like tit-for-tat rather than follow the recommendations of a Nash equilibrium may make it rational for a player to signal a willingness to cooperate in the early rounds of an iterated game and then defect at the end (Kreps *et al.* 1982). What is clearly the case from experimental evidence is that players do not use backward induction in their decision-making plans in an experimental laboratory Amnon Rapoport (1997: 122) concludes from a review of several experiments focusing on resource dilemmas that 'subjects are not involved in or capable of backward induction'.[10]

Nash equilibrium strategies do not predict individual behavior in social dilemmas

From the above discussion, it is obvious that individuals in social dilemmas tend not to use the predicted Nash equilibrium strategy, even though this is a good predictor at both an individual and group level in other types of situations. While outcomes frequently approach Nash equilibria at an aggregate level, the variance of individual actions around the mean is extremely large. When groups of eight subjects made appropriation decisions in repeated common-pool resource experiments of 20 to 30 rounds, the unique symmetric Nash equilibrium strategy was never played (Walker, Gardner and Ostrom 1990). Nor did individuals use Nash equilibrium strategies in repeated public good experiments (Dudley 1993; Isaac and Walker 1991, 1993). In a recent set of thirteen experiments involving seven players making ten rounds of decisions without communication or any other institutional structure, Walker *et al.* (1997) did not observe a single individual choice of a symmetric Nash equilibrium strategy in the 910 opportunities available to subjects. Chan *et al.* (1996: 58) also found little evidence to support the use of Nash equilibria when they examined the effect of heterogeneity of income on outcomes: 'It is clear that the outcomes of the laboratory sessions reported here cannot be characterized as Nash equilibria outcomes'.

Individuals do not learn Nash equilibrium strategies in social dilemmas

In repeated experiments without communication or other facilitating institutional conditions, levels of cooperation fall (rise) toward the Nash equilibrium in public-good (common-pool resource) experiments. Some scholars have speculated that

---

10. Subjects in Centipede games also do not use backward induction (*see* McKelvey and Palfrey 1992).

it just takes some time and experience for individuals to learn Nash equilibrium strategies (Ledyard 1995). But this does not appear to be the case. In all repeated experiments, there is considerable pulsing as subjects obtain outcomes that vary substantially with short spurts of increasing and decreasing levels of cooperation, while the general trend is toward an aggregate that is consistent with a Nash equilibrium (Isaac, McCue and Plott 1985; E. Ostrom, Gardner and Walker 1994).[11] Furthermore, there is substantial variation in the strategies followed by diverse participants within the same game (Dudley 1993; Isaac and Walker 1988b; E. Ostrom, Gardner and Walker 1994).

It appears that subjects learn something other than Nash strategies in finitely repeated experiments. Isaac, Walker and Williams (1994) compare the rate of decay when experienced subjects are explicitly told that an experiment will last 10, 40, or 60 rounds. The rate of decay of cooperative actions is inversely related to the number of decision rounds. Instead of learning the noncooperative strategy, subjects appear to be learning how to cooperate at a moderate level for even longer periods. Cooperation rates approach zero only in the last few periods, whenever these occur.

Two internal ways out of the social dilemmas

The combined effect of these four frequently replicated, general findings represents a strong rejection of the predictions derived from a complete model of rationality. Two more general findings are also contrary to the predictions of currently accepted models. At the same time, they also begin to show how individuals are able to obtain results that are substantially 'better than rational' (Cosmides and Tooby 1994), at least as *rational* has been defined in currently accepted models. The first is that simple, cheap talk allows individuals an opportunity to make conditional promises to one another and potentially to build trust that others will reciprocate. The second is the capacity to solve second-order social dilemmas that change the structure of the first-order dilemma.

Communication and collective action

In noncooperative game theory, players are assumed to be unable to make enforceable agreements.[12] Thus, communication is viewed as cheap talk (Farrell 1987). In a social dilemma, self-interested players are expected to use communication to try to convince others to cooperate and promise cooperative action, but then to choose the Nash equilibrium strategy when they make their

---

11. The pulsing cannot be explained using a complete model of rationality, but it can be explained as the result of a heuristic used by subjects to raise or lower their investments depending upon the average return achieved on the most recent round (*see* E. Ostrom, Gardner and Walker 1994).

12. In cooperative game theory, in contrast, it is assumed that players can communicate and make enforceable agreements (Harsanyi and Selten 1988: 3).

private decision (Barry and Hardin 1982: 381; Farrell and Rabin 1996: 113).[13] Or, as Gary Miller (1992: 25) expresses it: 'It is obvious that simple communication is not sufficient to escape the dilemma'.[14]

From this theoretical perspective, face-to-face communication should make no difference in the outcomes achieved in social dilemmas. Yet, consistent, strong, and replicable findings are that substantial increases in the levels of cooperation are achieved when individuals are allowed to communicate face to face.[15] This holds true across all types of social dilemmas studied in laboratory settings and in both one-shot and finitely repeated experiments. In a meta-analysis of more than 100 experiments involving more than 5,000 subjects conducted by economists, political scientists, sociologists, and social psychologists, Sally (1995) finds that opportunities for face-to-face communication in one-shot experiments significantly raise the cooperation rate, on average, by more than 45 percentage points. When subjects are allowed to talk before each decision round in repeated experiments, they achieve 40 percentage points more on average than in repeated games without communication. No other variable has as strong and consistent an effect on results as face-to-face communication. Communication even has a robust and positive effect on cooperation levels when individuals are not provided with feedback on group decisions after every round (Cason and Khan 1996).

The efficacy of communication is related to the capability to talk face to face. Sell and Wilson (1991, 1992), for example, developed a public-good experiment in which subjects could signal promises to cooperate via their computer terminal. There was much less cooperation than in the face-to-face experiments using the same design (Isaac and Walker 1988a, 1991). Rocco and Warglien (1995) replicated all aspects of prior common-pool resource experiments, including the efficacy of face-to-face communication.[16] They found, however, that subjects who had to rely on computerized communication did not achieve the same increase in efficiency as did those who were able to communicate face to face.[17] Palfrey and Rosenthal (1988) report that no significant difference occurred in a provision point public-good experiment in which subjects could send a computerized message stating whether they intended to contribute.

---

13. In social-dilemma experiments, subjects make anonymous decisions and are paid privately. The role of cheap talk in coordination experiments is different since there is no dominant strategy. In this case, preplay communication may help players coordinate on one of the possible equilibria (*see* Cooper, DeJong and Forsythe 1992).

14. As Aumann (1974) cogently points out, the players are faced with the problem that whatever they agree upon has to be self-enforcing. That has led Aumann and most game theorists to focus entirely on Nash equilibria which, once reached, are self-enforcing. In coordination games, cheap talk can be highly efficacious.

15. *See* E. Ostrom, Gardner and Walker 1994 for extensive citations to studies showing a positive effect of the capacity to communicate. Dawes, McTavish and Shaklee 1977; Frey and Bohnet 1996; Hackett, Schlager and Walker 1994; Isaac and Walker 1988a, 1991; Orbell, Dawes and van de Kragt 1990; Orbell, van de Kragt and Dawes 1988, 1991; E. Ostrom, Gardner and Walker 1994; Sally 1995.

16. Moir (1995) also replicated these findings with face-to-face communication.

17. Social psychologists have found that groups who perform tasks using electronic media do much better if they have had an opportunity to work face to face prior to the use of electronic communication only (Hollingshead, McGrath and O'Connor 1993).

The reasons offered by those doing experimental research for why communication facilitates cooperation include (1) transferring information from those who can figure out an optimal strategy to those who do not fully understand what strategy would be optimal, (2) exchanging mutual commitment, (3) increasing trust and thus affecting expectations of others' behavior, (4) adding additional values to the subjective payoff structure, (5) reinforcement of prior normative values, and (6) developing a group identity (Davis and Holt 1993; Orbell, Dawes and van de Kragt 1990; Orbell, van de Kragt and Dawes 1988; E. Ostrom and Walker 1997). Carefully crafted experiments demonstrate that the effect of communication is not primarily due to the first reason. When information about the individual strategy that produces an optimal joint outcome is clearly presented to subjects who are not able to communicate, the information makes little difference in outcomes achieved (Isaac, McCue and Plott 1985; Moir 1995).

Consequently, exchanging mutual commitment, increasing trust, creating and reinforcing norms, and developing a group identity appear to be the most important processes that make communication efficacious. Subjects in experiments do try to extract mutual commitment from one another to follow the strategy they have identified as leading to their best joint outcomes. They frequently go around the group and ask each person to promise the others that they will follow the joint strategy. Discussion sessions frequently end with such comments as: 'Now remember everyone that we all do much better if we all follow X strategy' (*see* transcripts in E. Ostrom, Gardner and Walker 1994). In repeated experiments, subjects use communication opportunities to lash out verbally at unknown individuals who did not follow mutually agreed strategies, using such evocative terms as scumbuckets and finks. Orbell, van de Kragt and Dawes (1988) summarize the findings from ten years of research on one-shot public-good experiments by stressing how many mutually reinforcing processes are evoked when communication is allowed.[18] Without increasing mutual trust in the promises that are exchanged, however, expectations of the behavior of others will not change. Given the very substantial difference in outcomes, communication is most likely to affect individual trust that others will keep to their commitments. As discussed below, the relationships among trust, conditional commitments, and a reputation for being trustworthy are key links in a second-generation theory of boundedly rational and moral behavior.

As stakes increase and it is difficult to monitor individual contributions, communication becomes less efficacious, however. E. Ostrom, Gardner and Walker (1994) found that subjects achieved close to fully optimal results when each subject had relatively low endowments and was allowed opportunities for face-to-face communication. When endowments were substantially increased – increasing the temptation to cheat on prior agreements – subjects achieved far more in communication experiments as contrasted to non-communication experiments but less than in small-stake situations. Failures to achieve collective action in field settings in which communication has been feasible point out that communication alone is not a sufficient mechanism to assure successful collective action under all conditions.

---

18. *See* also Banks and Calvert (1992a, 1992b) for a discussion of communication in incomplete information games.

Innovation and collective action

Changing the rules of a game or using scarce resources to punish those who do not cooperate or keep agreements are usually not considered viable options for participants in social dilemmas, since these actions create public goods. Participants face a second-order social dilemma (of equal or greater difficulty) in any effort to use costly sanctions or change the structure of a game (Oliver 1980). The predicted outcome of any effort to solve a second-order dilemma is failure.

Yet, participants in many field settings and experiments do exactly this. Extensive research on how individuals have governed and managed common-pool resources has documented the incredible diversity of rules designed and enforced by participants themselves to change the structure of underlying social-dilemma situations (Blomquist 1992; Bromley *et al.* 1992; Lam 1998; McKean 1992; E. Ostrom 1990; Schlager 1990; Schlager and Ostrom 1993; Tang 1992). The particular rules adopted by participants vary radically to reflect local circumstances and the cultural repertoire of acceptable and known rules used generally in a region. Nevertheless, general design principles characterize successfully self-organised, sustainable, local, regional, and international regimes (E. Ostrom 1990). Most robust and long-lasting common-pool regimes involve clear mechanisms for monitoring rule conformance and graduated sanctions for enforcing compliance. Thus, few self-organised regimes rely entirely on communication alone to sustain cooperation in situations that generate strong temptations to break mutual commitments. Monitors – who may be participants themselves – do not use strong sanctions for individuals who rarely break rules. Modest sanctions indicate to rule breakers that their lack of conformance has been observed by others. By paying a modest fine, they rejoin the community in good standing and learn that rule infractions are observed and sanctioned. Repeated rule breakers are severely sanctioned and eventually excluded from the group. Rules meeting these design principles reinforce contingent commitments and enhance the trust participants have that others are also keeping their commitments.

In field settings, innovation in rules usually occurs in a continuous trial-and-error process until a rule system is evolved that participants consider yields substantial net benefits. Given the complexity of the physical world that individuals frequently confront, they are rarely ever able to 'get the rules right' on the first or second try (E. Ostrom 1990). In highly unpredictable environments, a long period of trial and error is needed before individuals can find rules that generate substantial positive net returns over a sufficiently long time horizon. Nonviolent conflict may be a regular feature of successful institutions when arenas exist to process conflict cases regularly and, at times, to innovate new rules to cope with conflict more effectively (V. Ostrom 1987; V. Ostrom, Feeny, and Picht 1993).

In addition to the extensive field research on changes that participants make in the structure of situations they face, subjects in a large number of experiments have also solved second-order social dilemmas and consequently moved the outcomes in their first-order dilemmas closer to optimal levels (Dawes, Orbell, and van de Kragt 1986; Messick and Brewer 1983; Rutte and Wilke 1984; Sato 1987; van de Kragt,

Orbell and Dawes 1983; Yamagishi 1992). Toshio Yamagishi (1986), for example, conducted experiments with subjects who had earlier completed a questionnaire including items from a scale measuring trust. Subjects who ranked higher on the trust scale consistently contributed about 20 percent more to collective goods than those who ranked lower. When given an opportunity to contribute to a substantial 'punishment fund' to be used to fine the individual who contributed the least to their joint outcomes, however, low-trusting individuals contributed significantly more to the punishment fund and also achieved the highest level of cooperation. In the last rounds of this experiment, they were contributing 90 percent of their resources to the joint fund. These results, which have now been replicated with North American subjects (Yamagishi 1988a, 1988b), show that individuals who are initially the least trusting are willing to contribute to sanctioning systems and then respond more to a change in the structure of the game than those who are initially more trusting.

E. Ostrom, Walker and Gardner (1992) also examined the willingness of subjects to pay a 'fee' in order to 'fine' another subject. Instead of the predicted zero use of sanctions, individuals paid fees to fine others at a level significantly above zero.[19] When sanctioning was combined with a single opportunity to communicate or a chance to discuss and vote on the creation of their own sanctioning system, outcomes improved dramatically. With only a single opportunity to communicate, subjects were able to obtain an average of 85 percent of the optimal level of investments (67 percent with the costs of sanctioning subtracted). Those subjects who met face to face and agreed by majority vote on their own sanctioning system achieved 93 percent of optimal yield. The level of defections was only 4 percent, so that the costs of the sanctioning system were low, and net benefits were at a 90 percent level (E. Ostrom, Walker and Gardner 1992).

Messick and his colleagues have undertaken a series of experiments designed to examine the willingness of subjects to act collectively to change institutional structures when facing common-pool resource dilemmas (see Messick *et al.* 1983; Samuelson *et al.* 1984; C. Samuelson and Messick 1986). In particular, they have repeatedly given subjects the opportunity to relinquish their individual decisions concerning withdrawals from the common resource to a leader who is given the authority to decide for the group. They have found that 'people want to change the rules and bring about structural change when they observe that the common resource is being depleted' (C. Samuelson and Messick 1995; 147). Yet, simply having an unequal distribution of outcomes is not a sufficient inducement to affect the decision whether to change institutional structure.

What do these experiments tell us? They complement the evidence from field settings and show that individuals temporarily caught in a social-dilemma

---

19. Furthermore, they invested more when the fine was lower or when it was more efficacious, and they tended to direct their fines to those who had invested the most on prior rounds. Given the cost of the sanctioning mechanism, subjects tended to overuse it and to end up with a less efficient outcome after sanctioning costs were subtracted from their earnings. This finding is consistent with the Boyd and Richerson (1992) result that moralistic strategies may result in negative net outcomes.

structure are likely to invest resources to innovate and change the structure itself in order to improve joint outcomes. They also strengthen the earlier evidence that the currently accepted, noncooperative gametheoretical explanation relying on a particular model of the individual does not adequately predict behavior in one-shot and finitely repeated social dilemmas. Cooperative game theory does not provide a better explanation. Since both cooperative and noncooperative game theory predict extreme values, neither provides explanations for the conditions that tend to enhance or detract from cooperation levels.

The really big puzzle in the social sciences is the development of a consistent theory to explain why cooperation levels vary so much and why specific configurations of situational conditions increase or decrease cooperation in first- or second-level dilemmas. This question is important not only for our scientific understanding but also for the design of institutions to facilitate individuals' achieving higher levels of productive outcomes in social dilemmas. Many structural variables affect the particular innovations chosen and the sustainability and distributional consequences of these institutional changes (Knight 1992). A coherent theory of institutional change is not within reach, however, with a theory of individual choice that predicts no innovation will occur. We need a second-generation theory of boundedly rational, innovative, and normative behavior.

Toward second-generation models of rationality

First-generation models of rational choice are powerful engines of prediction when strong competition eliminates players who do not aggressively maximize immediate external values. While incorrectly confused with a general theory of human behavior, complete rationality models will continue to be used productively by social scientists, including the author. But the thin model of rationality needs to be viewed, as Selten (1975) points out, as the limiting case of bounded or incomplete rationality. Consistent with all models of rational choice is a general theory of human behavior that views all humans as complex, fallible learners who seek to do as well as they can given the constraints that they face and who are able to learn heuristics, norms, rules, and how to craft rules to improve achieved outcomes.

Learning heuristics, norms, and rules

Because individuals are boundedly rational, they do not calculate a complete set of strategies for every situation they face. Few situations in life generate information about all potential actions that one can take, all outcomes that can be obtained, and all strategies that others can take. In a model of complete rationality, one simply assumes this level of information. In field situations, individuals tend to use heuristics – rules of thumb – that they have learned over time regarding responses that tend to give them good outcomes in particular kinds of situations. They bring these heuristics with them when they participate in laboratory experiments. In frequently encountered, repetitive situations, individuals learn better and better heuristics that are tailored to particular situations.

With repetition, sufficiently large stakes, and strong competition, individuals may learn heuristics that approach best-response strategies.

In addition to learning instrumental heuristics, individuals also learn to adopt and use norms and rules. By *norms* I mean that the individual attaches an internal valuation – positive or negative – to taking particular types of action. Crawford and Ostrom (1995) refer to this internal valuation as a delta parameter that is added to or subtracted from the objective costs of an action.[20] Andreoni (1989) models individuals who gain a 'warm glow' when they contribute resources that help others more than they help themselves in the short term. Knack (1992) refers to negative internal valuations as 'duty'.[21] Many norms are learned from interactions with others in diverse communities about the behavior that is expected in particular types of situations (Coleman 1987). The change in preferences represents the internalization of particular moral lessons from life (or from the training provided by one's elders and peers).[22] The strength of the commitment (Sen 1977) made by an individual to take particular types of future actions (telling the truth, keeping promises) is reflected in the size of the delta parameter. After experiencing repeated benefits from other people's cooperative actions, an individual may resolve that s/he should always initiate cooperative actions in the future.[23] Or, after many experiences of being the 'sucker' in such experiences, an individual may resolve never to be the first to cooperate.

Since norms are learned in a social milieu, they vary substantially across cultures, across individuals within any one culture, within individuals across different types of situations they face, and across time within any particular situation. The behavioural implications of assuming that individuals acquire norms do not vary substantially from the assumption that individuals learn to use heuristics. One may think of norms as heuristics that individuals adopt from a moral perspective, in that these are the kinds of actions they wish to follow in living their life. Once some members of a population acquire norms of behavior, they affect the expectations of others.

By *rules* I mean that a group of individuals has developed shared understandings that certain actions in particular situations must, must not, or may be undertaken and that sanctions will be taken against those who do not conform. The distinction

---

20. When constructing formal models, one can include overt delta parameters in the model (*see* Crawford and Ostrom 1995; Palfrey and Rosenthal 1988). Alternatively, one can assume that these internal delta parameters lead individuals to enter new situations with differing probabilities that they will follow norms such as reciprocity. These probabilities not only vary across individuals but also increase or decrease as a function of the specific structural parameters of the situation and, in repeated experiments, the patterns of behavior and outcomes achieved in that situation over time.

21. The change in valuations that an individual may attach to an action-outcome linkage may be generated strictly internally or may be triggered by external observation and, thus, a concern with how others will evaluate the normative appropriateness of actions.

22. Gouldner (1960; 171) considers norms of reciprocity to be universal and as important in most cultures as incest taboos, even though the 'concrete formulations may vary with time and place'.

23. *See* Selten (1986) for a discussion of his own and John Harsanyi's (1977) conception of 'rule utilitarianism' as contrasted to 'act utilitarianism'.

between internalized but widely shared norms for what are appropriate actions in broad types of situations and rules that are self-consciously adopted for use in particular situations is at times difficult to draw when doing fieldwork. Analytically, individuals can be thought of as learning norms of behavior that are general and fit a wide diversity of particular situations. Rules are artifacts related to particular actions in specific situations (V. Ostrom 1980, 1997). Rules are created in private associations as well as in more formalized public institutions, where they carry the additional legal weight of being enforced legal enactments.[24] Rules can enhance reciprocity by making mutual commitments clear and overt. Alternatively, rules can assign authority to act so that benefits and costs are distributed inequitably and thereby destroy reliance on positive norms.

Reciprocity: An especially important class of norms

That humans rapidly learn and effectively use heuristics, norms, and rules is consistent with the lessons learned from evolutionary psychology (*see* Barkow, Cosmides and Tooby 1992), evolutionary game theory (*see* Guth and Kliemt 1996; Hirshleifer and Rasmusen 1989),[25] biology (Trivers 1971) and bounded rationality (Selten 1990, 1991; Selten, Mitzkewitz and Uhlich 1997; Simon 1985). Humans appear to have evolved specialized cognitive modules for diverse tasks, including making sense out of what is seen (Marr 1982), inferring rules of grammar by being exposed to adult speakers of a particular language (Pinker 1994) and increasing their long-term returns from interactions in social dilemmas (Cosmides and Tooby 1992). Humans dealt with social dilemmas related to rearing and protecting offspring, acquiring food, and trusting one another to perform future promised action millennia before such oral commitments could be enforced by external authorities (de Waal 1996). Substantial evidence has been accumulated (and reviewed in Cosmides and Tooby 1992) that humans inherit a strong capacity to learn reciprocity norms and social rules that enhance the opportunities to gain benefits from coping with a multitude of social dilemmas.

Reciprocity refers to a family of strategies that can be used in social dilemmas involving (1) an effort to identify who else is involved, (2) an assessment of the likelihood that others are conditional cooperators, (3) a decision to cooperate initially with others if others are trusted to be conditional cooperators, (4) a refusal to cooperate with those who do not reciprocate, and punishment of those who betray trust. All reciprocity norms share the common ingredients that individuals tend to react to the positive actions of others with positive responses and the negative actions of others with negative responses. Reciprocity is a basic norm taught in all societies (*see* Becker 1990; Blau 1964; Gouldner 1960; Homans 1961; Oakerson 1993; V. Ostrom 1997; Thibaut and Kelley 1959).

---

24. Crawford and Ostrom (1995) discuss these issues in greater depth. *See* also Piaget ([1932] 1969).

25. The evolutionary approach has been strongly influenced by the work of Robert Axelrod (*see*, in particular, Axelrod 1984, 1986; Axelrod and Hamilton 1981; and Axelrod and Keohane 1985).

By far the most famous reciprocal strategy – tit-for-tat – has been the subject of considerable study from an evolutionary perspective. In simulations, pairs of individuals are sampled from a population, and they then interact with one another repeatedly in a prisoners' dilemma game. Individuals are each modeled as if they had inherited a strategy that included the fixed maxims of always cooperate, always defect, or the reciprocating strategy of tit-for-tat (cooperate first, and then do whatever the others did in the last round). Axelrod and Hamilton (1981) and Axelrod (1984) have shown that when individuals are grouped so that they are more likely to interact with one another than with the general population, and when the expected number of repetitions is sufficiently large, reciprocating strategies such as tit-for-tat can successfully invade populations composed of individuals following an all-defect strategy. The size of the population in which interactions are occurring may need to be relatively small for reciprocating strategies to survive potential errors of players (Bendor and Mookherjee 1987; but *see* Boyd and Richerson 1988, 1992; Hirshleifer and Rasmusen 1989; Yamagishi and Takahashi 1994).

The reciprocity norms posited to help individuals gain larger cooperators' dividends depend upon the willingness of participants to use retribution to some degree. In tit-for-tat, for example, an individual must be willing to 'punish' a player who defected in the last round by defecting in the current round. In grim trigger, an individual must be willing to cooperate initially but then 'punish' everyone for the rest of the game if any defection is noticed in the current round.[26]

Human beings do not inherit particular reciprocity norms via a biological process. The argument is more subtle. Individuals inherit an acute sensitivity for learning norms that increase their own long-term benefits when confronting social dilemmas with others who have learned and value similar norms. The process of growing up in any culture provides thousands of incidents (learning trials) whereby parents, siblings, friends, and teachers provide the specific content of the type of mutual expectations prevalent in that culture. As Mueller (1986) points out, the first dilemmas that humans encounter are as children. Parents reward and punish them until cooperation is a learned response. In the contemporary setting, corporate managers strive for a trustworthy corporate reputation by continuously reiterating and rewarding the use of key principles or norms by corporate employees (Kreps 1990).

Since particular reciprocity norms are *learned*, not everyone learns to use the same norms in all situations. Some individuals learn norms of behavior that are not so 'nice'. Clever and unscrupulous individuals may learn how to lure others into dilemma situations and then defect on them. It is possible to gain substantial

---

26. The grim trigger has been used repeatedly as a support for cooperative outcomes in infinitely (or indefinitely) repeated games (Fudenberg and Maskin 1986). In games in which substantial joint benefits are to be gained over the long term from mutual cooperation, the threat of the grim trigger is thought to be sufficient to encourage everyone to cooperate. A small error on the part of one player or exogenous noise in the payoff function, however, makes this strategy a dangerous one to use in larger groups, where the cooperators' dividend may also be substantial.

resources by such means, but one has to hide intentions and actions, to keep moving, or to gain access to power over others. In any group composed only of individuals who follow reciprocity norms, skills in detecting and punishing cheaters could be lost. If this happens, it will be subject to invasion and substantial initial losses by clever outsiders or local deviants who can take advantage of the situation. Being too trusting can be dangerous. The presence of some untrustworthy participants hones the skills of those who follow reciprocity norms.

Thus, individuals vary substantially in the probability that they will use particular norms, in how structural variables affect their level of trust and willingness to reciprocate cooperation in a particular situation, and in how they develop their own reputation. Some individuals use reciprocity only in situations in which there is close monitoring and strong retribution is likely. Others will only cooperate in dilemmas when they have publicly committed themselves to an agreement and have assurances from others that their trust will be returned. Others find it easier to build an external reputation by building their own personal identity as someone who always trusts others until proven wrong. If this trust proves to be misplaced, then they stop cooperating and either exit the situation or enter a punishment phase. As Hoffman, McCabe and Smith (1996a; 23–4) express it:

> A one-shot game in the laboratory is part of a life-long sequence, not an isolated experience that calls for behavior that deviates sharply from one's reputational norm. Thus we should expect subjects to rely upon reciprocity norms in experimental settings unless they discover in the process of participating in a particular experiment that reciprocity is punished and other behaviours are rewarded. In such cases they abandon their instincts and attempt other strategies that better serve their interests.

In any population of individuals, one is likely to find some who use one of three reciprocity norms when they confront a repeated social dilemma:[27]

1. Always cooperate first; stop cooperating if others do not reciprocate; punish noncooperators if feasible.

2. Cooperate immediately only if one judges others to be trustworthy; stop cooperating if others do not reciprocate; punish noncooperators if feasible.

3. Once cooperation is established by others, cooperate oneself; stop cooperating if others do not reciprocate; punish noncooperators if feasible.

In addition, one may find at least three other norms:

---

27. This is not the complete list of all types of reciprocity norms, but it captures the vast majority.

1. Never cooperate.

2. Mimic (1) or (2), but stop cooperating if one can successfully free ride on others.

3. Always cooperate (an extremely rare norm in all cultures).

The proportion of individuals who follow each type of norm will vary from one subpopulation to another and from one situation to another.[28] Whether reciprocity is advantageous to individuals depends sensitively on the proportion of other individuals who use reciprocity and on an individual's capacity to judge the likely frequency of reciprocators in any particular situation and over time. When there are many others who use a form of reciprocity that always cooperates first, then even in one-shot situations cooperation may lead to higher returns when diverse situations are evaluated together. Boundedly rational individuals would expect other boundedly rational individuals to follow a *diversity* of heuristics, norms, and strategies rather than expect to find others who adopt a single strategy – except in those repeated situations in which institutional selection processes sort out those who do not search out optimal strategies. Investment in detection of other individuals' intentions and actions improves one's own outcomes. One does not have to assume that others are 'irrational' in order for it to be rational to use reciprocity (Kreps *et al.* 1982).

Evidence of the use of reciprocity in experimental settings

Laboratory experiments provide evidence that a substantial proportion of individuals use reciprocity norms even in the very short-term environments of an experiment (McCabe, Rassenti and Smith 1996). Some evidence comes from experiments on ultimatum games. In such games, two players are asked to divide a fixed sum of money. The first player suggests a division to the second, who then decides to accept or reject the offer. If the offer is accepted, then the funds are divided as proposed. If it is rejected, then both players receive zero. The predicted equilibrium is that the first player will offer a minimal unit to the second player, who will then accept anything more than zero. This prediction has repeatedly been falsified, starting with the work of Guth, Schmittberger and Schwarze (1982; *see* Frey and Bohnet 1996; Guth and Tietz 1990; Roth 1995; Samuelson, Gale, and Binmore 1995).[29] Subjects assigned to the first position tend to offer substantially

---

28. The proportion of individuals who follow the sixth norm – cooperate always – will be minuscule or nonexistent. Individuals following the first norm will be those, along with those following the sixth norm, who cooperate in the first few rounds of a finitely repeated experimental social dilemma without prior communication. Individuals following the second norm will cooperate (immediately) in experiments if they have an opportunity to judge the intentions and trustworthiness of the other participants and expect most of the others to be trustworthy. Those following the third norm will cooperate (after one or a few rounds) in experiments in which others cooperate.

29. The results obtained by Hoffman, McCabe and Smith (1996b) related to dictator games under varying conditions of social distance are also quite consistent with the behavioural approach of this chapter.

more than the minimum unit. They frequently offer the 'fair' division of splitting the sum. Second movers tend to reject offers that are quite small. The acceptance level for offers tends to cluster around different values in diverse cultures (Roth *et al.* 1991). Given that the refusal to accept the funds offered contradicts a basic tenet in the complete model of rationality, these findings have represented a major challenge to the model's empirical validity in this setting.

Several hypotheses have been offered to explain these findings, including a 'punishment hypothesis' and a 'learning hypothesis'.

The punishment hypothesis is in essence a reciprocity argument. In contrast to adaptive learning, punishment attributes a motive to the second mover's rejection of an unequal division asserting that it is done to punish the first mover for unfair treatment. This propensity toward negative reciprocity is the linchpin of the argument. Given this propensity, first movers should tend to shy away from the perfect equilibrium offer out of fear of winding up with nothing (Abbink *et al.* 1996; 6).

Abbink and his colleagues designed an experiment in which the prediction of the learning and punishment hypotheses is clearly different and found strong support for the punishment hypothesis. 'We found that second movers were three times more likely to reject the unequal split when doing so punished the first mover [...] than when doing so rewarded the first mover' (Abbink *et al.* 1996; 15–6). Consequently, second movers do appear to punish first movers who propose unfair divisions.

Two additional findings from one-shot social dilemmas provide further evidence of the behavioural propensities of subjects. First, those who intend to cooperate in a particular one-shot social dilemma also expect cooperation to be returned by others at a much higher rate than those who intend to defect (Dawes, McTavish and Shaklee 1977; Dawes, Orbell and van de Kragt 1986). As Orbell and Dawes (1991; 519) summarize their own work: 'One of our most consistent findings throughout these studies – a finding replicated by others' work – is that cooperators expect significantly more cooperation than do defectors'. Second, when there is a choice whether to participate in a social dilemma, those who intend to cooperate exhibit a greater willingness to enter such transactions (Orbell and Dawes 1993). Given these two tendencies, reciprocators are likely to be more optimistic about finding others following the same norm and disproportionately enter more voluntary social dilemmas than nonreciprocators. Given both propensities, the feedback from such voluntary activities will generate confirmatory evidence that they have adopted a norm which serves them well over the long run.

Thus, while individuals vary in their propensity to use reciprocity, the evidence from experiments shows that a substantial proportion of the population drawn on by social science experiments has sufficient trust that others are reciprocators to cooperate with them even in one-shot, no-communication experiments. Furthermore, a substantial proportion of the population is also willing to punish noncooperators (or individuals who do not make fair offers) at a cost to themselves. Norms are learned from prior experience (socialization) and are affected by situational variables yielding systematic differences among experimental designs.

The level of trust and resulting levels of cooperation can be increased by (1) providing subjects with an opportunity to see one another (Frey and Bohnet 1996; Orbell and Dawes 1991), (2) allowing subjects to choose whether to enter or exit a social-dilemma game (Orbell and Dawes 1991, 1993; Orbell, Schwartz-Shea, and Simmons 1984; Schuessler 1989; Yamagishi 1988c; Yamagishi and Hayashi 1996), (3) sharing the costs equally if a minimal set voluntarily contributes to a public good (Dawes, Orbell, and van de Kragt 1986), (4) providing opportunities for distinct punishments of those who are not reciprocators (Abbink *et al.* 1996; McCabe, Rassenti and Smith 1996) and, as discussed above, (5) providing opportunities for face-to-face communication.

The core relationships: reciprocity, reputation, and trust

When many individuals use reciprocity, there is an incentive to acquire a *reputation* for keeping promises and performing actions with short-term costs but longterm net benefits (Keohane 1984; Kreps 1990; Milgrom, North, and Weingast 1990; Miller 1992). Thus, trustworthy individuals who trust others with a reputation for being trustworthy (and try to avoid those who have a reputation for being untrustworthy) can engage in mutually productive social exchanges, even though they are dilemmas, so long as they can limit their interactions primarily to those with a reputation for keeping promises. A reputation for being trustworthy, or for using retribution against those who do not keep their agreements or keep up their fair share, becomes a valuable asset. In an evolutionary context, it increases fitness in an environment in which others use reciprocity norms. Similarly, developing *trust* in an environment in which others are trustworthy is also an asset (Braithwaite and Levi 1998; Fukuyama 1995; Gambetta 1988; Putnam 1993). Trust is the expectation of one person about the actions of others that affects the first person's choice, when an action must be taken before the actions of others are known (Dasgupta 1997: 5). In the context of a social dilemma, trust affects whether an individual is willing to initiate cooperation in the expectation that it will be reciprocated. Boundedly rational individuals enter situations with an initial probability of using reciprocity based on their own prior training and experience.

Thus, at the core of a behavioural explanation are the links between the trust that individuals have in others, the investment others make in trustworthy reputations, and the probability that participants will use reciprocity norms (*see* Figure 5.2). This mutually reinforcing core is affected by structural variables as well as the past experiences of participants. In the initial round of a repeated dilemma, individuals do or do not initiate cooperative behavior based on their own norms, how much trust they have that others are reciprocators (based on any information they glean about one another) and how structural variables affect their own and their expectation of others' behavior.

If initial levels of cooperation are moderately high, then individuals may learn to trust one another, and more may adopt reciprocity norms. When more individuals use reciprocity norms, gaining a reputation for being trustworthy is a better investment. Thus, levels of trust, reciprocity, and reputations for being

Figure 5.2: The Core Relationship

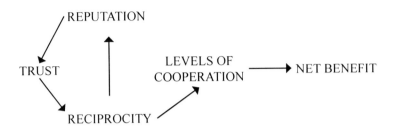

trustworthy are positively reinforcing. This also means that a decrease in any one of these can lead to a downward spiral. Instead of explaining levels of cooperation directly, this approach leads one to link structural variables to an inner triangle of trust, reciprocity, and reputation as these, in turn, affect levels of cooperation and net benefits.

Communication and the core relationships

With these core relationships, one can begin to explain why repeated face-to-face communication substantially changes the structure of a situation (*see* discussion in E. Ostrom, Gardner and Walker 1994: 199). With a repeated chance to see and talk with others, a participant can assess whether s/he trusts others sufficiently to try to reach a simple contingent agreement regarding the level of joint effort and its allocation. In a contingent agreement, individuals agree to contribute X resources to a common effort so long as at least Y others also contribute. Contingent agreements do not need to include all those who benefit. The benefit to be obtained from the contribution of Y proportion of those affected may be so substantial that some individuals are willing to contribute so long as Y proportion of others also agree and perform.

Communication allows individuals to increase (or decrease) their trust in the reliability of others.[30] When successful, individuals change their expectations from the initial probability that others use reciprocity norms to a higher probability that others will reciprocate trust and cooperation. When individuals are symmetric in assets and payoffs, the simplest agreement is to share a contribution level equally that closely approximates the optimum joint outcome. When individuals are not symmetric, finding an agreement is more difficult, but various fairness norms can be used to reduce the time and effort needed to achieve an agreement (*see* Hackett, Dudley and Walker 1995; Hackett, Schlager and Walker 1994).

---

30. Frank, Gilovich and Regan (1993) found, for example, that the capacity of subjects to predict whether others would play cooperatively was significantly better than chance after a face-to-face group discussion. Kikuchi, Watanabe and Yamagishi (1996) found that high trusters predicted other players' trustworthiness significantly better than did low trusters.

Contingent agreements may deal with punishment of those who do not cooperate (Levi 1988). How to punish noncooperative players, keep one's own reputation, and sustain any initial cooperation that has occurred in N-person settings is more difficult than in two-person settings.[31] In an N-person, uncertain situation, it is difficult to interpret from results that are less than expected whether one person cheated a lot, several people cheated a little, someone made a mistake, or everyone cooperated and an exogenous random variable reduced the expected outcome. If there is no communication, then the problem is even worse. Without communication and an agreement on a sharing formula, individuals can try to signal a willingness to cooperate through their actions, but no one has agreed to any particular contribution. Thus, no one's reputation (external or internal) is at stake.

Once a verbal agreement in an N-person setting is reached, that becomes the focal point for further action within the context of a particular ongoing group. If everyone keeps to the agreement, then no further reaction is needed by someone who is a reciprocator. If the agreement is not kept, however, then an individual following a reciprocity norm – without any prior agreement regarding selective sanctions for nonconformance – needs to punish those who did not keep their commitment. A frequently posited punishment is the grim trigger, whereby a participant plays the Nash equilibrium strategy forever upon detecting any cheating. Subjects in repeated experiments frequently discuss the use of a grim trigger to punish mild defections but reject the idea because it would punish everyone – not just the cheater(s) (E. Ostrom, Gardner and Walker 1994). A much less drastic punishment strategy is the measured reaction. 'In a measured reaction, a player reacts mildly (if at all) to a small deviation from an agreement. Defections trigger mild reactions instead of harsh punishments. If defections continue over time, the measured response slowly moves from the point of agreement toward the Nash equilibrium' (pp. 199–200).

For several reasons, this makes sense as the initial 'punishment' phase in an N-person setting with a minimal institutional structure and no feedback concerning individual contributions. If only a small deviation occurs, then the cooperation of most participants is already generating positive returns. By keeping one's own reaction close to the agreement, one keeps up one's own reputation for cooperation, keeps cooperation levels higher, and makes it easier to restore full conformance. Using something like a grim trigger immediately leads to the unravelling of the agreement and the loss of substantial benefits over time. To supplement the measured reaction, effort is expended on determining who is

---

31. In a two-person situation of complete certainty, individuals can easily follow the famous tit-for-tat (or tit-for-tat or exit) strategy even without communication. When a substantial proportion of individuals in a population follows this norm, and they can identify with whom they have interacted in the past (to either refuse future interactions or to punish prior uncooperative actions) and when discount rates are sufficiently low, tit-for-tat has been shown to be a highly successful strategy, yielding higher payoffs than are available to those using other strategies (Axelrod 1984, 1986). With communication, it is even easier.

breaking the agreement, on using verbal rebukes to try to get that individual back in line, and on avoiding future interactions with that individual.[32]

Thus, understanding how trust, reciprocity, and reputation feed one another (or their lack, which generates a cascade of negative effects) helps to explain why repeated, face-to-face communication has such a major effect. Coming to an initial agreement and making personal promises to one another places at risk an individual's own identity as one who keeps one's word, increases trust, and makes reciprocity an even more beneficial strategy. Tongue-lashing can be partially substituted in a small group for monetary losses and, when backed by measured responses, can keep many groups at high levels of cooperation. Meeting only once can greatly increase trust, but if some individuals do not cooperate immediately, the group never has a further opportunity to hash out these problems. Any evidence of lower levels of cooperation undermines the trust established in the first meeting, and there is no further opportunity to build trust or use verbal sanctioning. It is also clearer now why sending anonymous, computerized messages is not as effective as face-to-face communication. Individuals judge one another's trustworthiness by watching facial expressions and hearing the way something is said. It is hard to establish trust in a group of strangers who will make decisions independently and privately without seeing and talking with one another.

Illustrative theoretical scenarios

I have tried to show the need for the development of second-generation models of rationality in order to begin a coherent synthesis of what we know from empirical research on social dilemmas. Rather than try to develop a new formal model, I have stayed at the theoretical level to identify the attributes of human behavior that should be included in future formal models. The individual attributes that are particularly important in explaining behavior in social dilemmas include the expectations individuals have about others' behavior (trust), the norms individuals learn from socialization and life's experiences (reciprocity) and the identities individuals create that project their intentions and norms (reputation). Trust, reciprocity, and reputation can be included in formal models of individual behavior (*see* the works cited by Boyd and Richerson 1988; Guth and Yaari 1992; Nowak and Sigmund 1993).

In this section, I construct theoretical scenarios of how exogenous variables combine to affect endogenous structural variables that link to the core set of relationships shown in Figure 5.2. It is not possible to relate all structural variables

---

32. In a series of 18 common-pool resource experiments, each involving eight subjects in finitely repeated communication experiments, E. Ostrom, Gardner and Walker (1994; 215) found that subjects kept to their agreements or used measured responses in two-thirds of the experiments. In these experiments, joint yields averaged 89 percent of optimum. In the six experiments in which some players deviated substantially from agreements and measured responses did not bring them back to the agreement, cooperation levels were substantially less, and yields averaged 43 percent of optimum (which is still far above zero levels of cooperation).

in one large causal model, given the number of important variables and the fact that many depend for their effect on the values of other variables. It is possible, however, to produce coherent, cumulative, theoretical scenarios that start with relatively simple baseline models. One can then begin the systematic exploration of what happens as one variable is changed. Let me illustrate what I mean by theoretical scenarios.

Let us start with a scenario that should be conducive to cooperation – a small group of ten farmers who own farms of approximately the same size. These farmers share the use of a creek for irrigation that runs by their relatively flat properties. They face the problem each year of organising one collective workday to clear out the fallen trees and brush from the prior winter. All ten expect to continue farming into the indefinite future. Let us assume that the creek delivers a better water supply directly in response to how many days of work are completed. All farmers have productive opportunities for their labor that return more at the margin than the return they would receive from their own input into this effort. Thus, free riding and hoping that the others contribute labor is objectively attractive. The value to each farmer, however, of participation in a successful collective effort to clear the creek is greater than the costs of participating.

Now let us examine how some structural variables affect the likelihood of collective action (*see* Figure 5.3). As a small group, it would be easy for them to engage in face-to-face communication. Since their interests and resources are relatively symmetric, arriving at a fair, contingent agreement regarding how to share the work should not be too difficult. One simple agreement that is easy to monitor is that they all work on the same day, but each is responsible for clearing the part of the creek going through his or her property. Conformance to such an agreement would be easy to verify. While engaged in discussions, they can reinforce the importance of everyone participating in the workday. In face-to-face meetings, they can also gossip about anyone who failed to participate in the past, urge them to change their ways, and threaten to stop all labor contributions if they do not 'shape up'. Given the small size of the group, its symmetry, and the relatively low cost of providing the public good, combined with the relatively long time horizon, we can predict with some confidence that a large proportion of individuals facing such a situation will find a way to cooperate and overcome the dilemma. Not only does the evidence from experimental research support that prediction, but also substantial evidence from the field is consistent with this explanation (*see* E. Ostrom 1998).

This is a rough but coherent causal theory that uses structural variables (small size, symmetry of assets and resources, long time horizon, and a low-cost production function) to predict with high probability that participants can themselves solve this social dilemma. Changes in any of the structural variables of this relatively easy scenario affect that prediction. Even a small change may suffice to reverse the predicted outcome. For example, assume that another local farmer buys five parcels of land with the plan to farm them for a long time. Now there are only six farmers, but one of them holds half the relevant assets. If that farmer shares the norm that it is fair to share work allocated to a collective benefit in the same ratio as the benefits are allocated, then the increased heterogeneity will not be a difficult problem to overcome. They would agree – as farmers around the world have frequently agreed (*see* Lam 1998; Tang 1992) – to share the work in proportion to the amount of land they own. If the new farmer uses a different concept of fairness, then the smaller group may face a more challenging problem than the larger group due to its increased heterogeneity.

Now, assume that the five parcels of land are bought by a local developer to hold for future use as a suburban housing development. The time horizon of one of the six actors – the developer – is extremely short with regard to investments in irrigation. From the developer's perspective, he is not a 'free rider', as he sees no benefit to clearing out the creek. Thus, such a change actually produces several: A decrease in the N of the group, an introduction of an asymmetry of interests and resources, and the presence of one participant with half the resources but a short time horizon and no interest in the joint benefit. This illustrates how changes in one structural variable can lead to a cascade of changes in the others, and thus how difficult it is to make simple bivariate hypotheses about the effect of one variable on the level of cooperation. In particular, this smaller group is much less likely to cooperate than the larger group of ten symmetric farmers, exactly the reverse of the standard view of the effect of group size.

Figure 5.3: A Simple Scenario

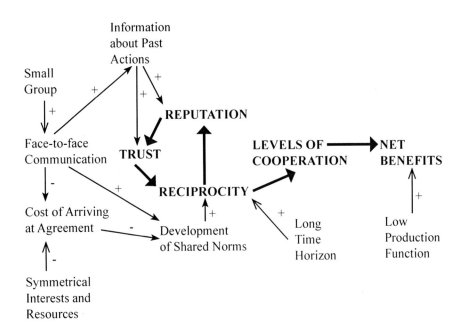

Implications

The implications of developing second-generation models of empirically grounded, boundedly rational, and moral decision making are substantial. Puzzling research questions can now be addressed more systematically. New research questions will open up. We need to expand the type of research methods regularly used in political science. We need to increase the level of understanding among those engaged in formal theory, experimental research, and field research across the social and biological sciences. The foundations of policy analysis need rethinking. And civic education can be based on empirically validated theories of collective action empowering citizens to use the 'science and art of association' (Tocqueville [1835 and 1840] 1945) to help sustain democratic polities in the twenty-first century.

Implications for research

What the research on social dilemmas demonstrates is a world of *possibility* rather than of *necessity*. We are neither trapped in inexorable tragedies nor free of moral responsibility for creating and sustaining incentives that facilitate our own achievement of mutually productive outcomes. We cannot adopt the smug presumption of those earlier group theorists who thought groups would always form whenever a joint benefit would be obtained. We can expect many groups to fail to achieve mutually productive benefits due to their lack of trust in one another or to the lack of arenas for low-cost communication, institutional innovation, and the creation of monitoring and sanctioning rules (V. Ostrom 1997). Nor can we simply rest assured that only one type of institution exists for all social dilemmas, such as a competitive market, in which individuals pursuing their own preferences are led to produce mutually productive outcomes. While new institutions often facilitate collective action, the key problems are to design new rules, motivate participants to conform to rules once they are devised, and find and appropriately punish those who cheat. Without individuals viewing rules as appropriate mechanisms to enhance reciprocal relationships, no police force and court system on earth can monitor and enforce all the needed rules on its own. Nor would most of us want to live in a society in which police were really the thin blue line enforcing all rules.

While I am proposing a further development of second-generation theories of rational choice, theories based on complete but thin rationality will continue to play an important role in our understanding of human behavior. The clear and unambiguous predictions stemming from complete rational choice theories will continue to serve as a critical benchmark in conducting empirical studies and for measuring the success or failure of any other explanation offered for observed behavior. A key research question will continue to be: What is the difference between the predicted equilibrium of a complete rationality theory and observed behavior? Furthermore, game theorists are already exploring ways of including reputation, reciprocity, and various norms of behavior in game-theoretic models (*see* Abbink *et al.* 1996; Girth 1995; Kreps 1990; Palfrey and Rosenthal 1988; Rabin 1994; Selten 1990, 1991). Thus, bounded and complete rationality models may become more complementary in the next decade than appears to be the case today.

For political scientists interested in diverse institutional arrangements, complete rational choice theories provide well-developed methods for analysing the vulnerability of institutions to the strategies devised by talented, analytically sophisticated, short-term hedonists (Brennan and Buchanan 1985). Any serious institutional analysis should include an effort to understand how institutions – including ways of organising legislative procedures, formulas used to calculate electoral weights and minimal winning coalitions, and international agreements on global environmental problems – are vulnerable to manipulation by calculating, amoral participants.[33] In addition to the individuals who have learned norms of reciprocity in any population, others exist who may try to subvert the process so as to obtain very substantial returns for themselves while ignoring the interests of others. One should always know the consequences of letting such individuals operate in any particular institutional setting.

The most immediate research questions that need to be addressed using second-generation models of human behavior relate to the effects of structural variables on the likelihood of organising for successful modes of collective action. It will not be possible to relate all structural variables in one large causal theory, given that they are so numerous and that many depend for their effect on the values of other variables. What is possible, however, is the development of coherent, cumulative, theoretical scenarios that start with relatively simple baseline models and then proceed to change one variable at a time, as briefly illustrated above. From such scenarios, one can proceed to formal models and empirical testing in field and laboratory settings. The kind of *theory* that emerges from such an enterprise does not lead to the global bivariate (or even multivariate) predictions that have been the ideal to which many scholars have aspired. Marwell and Oliver (1993) have constructed such a series of theoretical scenarios for social dilemmas involving large numbers of heterogeneous participants in collective action. They have come to a similar conclusion about the nature of the theoretical and empirical enterprise: 'This is not to say that general theoretical predictions are impossible using our perspective, only that they cannot be simple and global. Instead, the predictions that we can validly generate must be complex, interactive, and conditional' (p. 25).

As political scientists, we need to recognize that political systems are complexly organised and that we will rarely be able to state that one variable is always positively or negatively related to a dependent variable. One can do comparative statics, but one must know the value of the other variables and not simply assume that they vary around the average.

The effort to develop second-generation models of boundedly rational and moral behavior will open up a variety of *new* questions to be pursued that are of major importance to all social scientists and many biologists interested in

---

33. Consequently, research on the effect of institutional arrangements on strategies and outcomes continues to be crucial to future developments. *See* Agrawal 1998; Alt and Shepsle 1990; Bates 1989; Dasgupta 1993; Eggertsson 1990; Gibson 1999; Levi 1997; V. Ostrom 1997; V. Ostrom, Feeny, and Picht 1993; Scharpf 1997.

human behavior. Among these questions are: How do individuals gain trust in other individuals? How is trust affected by diverse institutional arrangements? What verbal and visual clues are used in evaluating others' behavior? How do individuals gain common understanding so as to craft and follow self-organised arrangements (V. Ostrom 1990)? John Orbell (personal communication) posits a series of intriguing questions: 'Why do people join together in these games in the first place? How do we select partners in these games? How do our strategies for selecting individual partners differ from our strategies for adding or removing individuals from groups?'

An important set of questions is related to how institutions enhance or restrict the building of mutual trust, reciprocity, and reputations. A recent set of studies on tax compliance raises important questions about the trust heuristics used by citizens and their reactions to governmental efforts to monitor compliance (*see* Scholz 1998). Too much monitoring may have the counterintuitive result that individuals feel they are *not* trusted and thus become less trustworthy (Frey 1993). Bruno Frey (1997) questions whether some formal institutional arrangements, such as social insurance and paying people to contribute effort, reduce the likelihood that individuals continue to place a positive intrinsic value on actions taken mainly because of internal norms. Rather, they may assume that formal organisations are charged with the responsibility of taking care of joint needs and that reciprocity is no longer needed (*see also* Taylor 1987).

Since all rules legitimate the use of sanctions against those who do not comply, rules can be used to assign benefits primarily to a dominant coalition. Those who are, thus, excluded have no motivation to cooperate except in order to avoid sanctions. Using first-generation models, that is what one expects in any case. Using second-generation models, one is concerned with how constitutional and collective-choice rules affect the distribution of benefits and the likelihood of reciprocal cooperation. While much research has been conducted on long-term successful self-organised institutions, less has been documented about institutions that never quite got going or failed after years of success. More effort needs to be made to find reliable archival information concerning these failed attempts and why they failed.

It may be surprising that I have relied so extensively on experimental research. I do so for several reasons. As theory becomes an ever more important core of our discipline, experimental studies will join the ranks of basic empirical research methods for political scientists. As an avid field researcher for the past 35 years, I know the importance and difficulty of testing theory in field settings – particularly when variables function interactively. Large-scale field studies will continue to be an important source of empirical data, but frequently they are a very expensive and inefficient method for addressing how institutional incentives combine to affect individual behavior and outcomes. We can advance much faster and more coherently when we examine hypotheses about contested elements among diverse models or theories of a coherent framework. Careful experimental research designs frequently help sort out competing hypotheses more effectively than does trying to find the precise combination of variables in the field. By adding experimental methods to the battery of field methods already used extensively, the political science of the twenty-first century will advance more rapidly in acquiring well-grounded theories of human behavior and of the effect of diverse institutional arrangements on behavior. Laboratory research will still need to be complemented by sound field studies to meet the criteria of external validity.

Implications for policy

Using a broader theory of rationality leads to potentially different views of the state. If one sees individuals as helpless, then the state is the essential external authority that must solve social dilemmas for everyone. If, however, one assumes individuals can draw on heuristics and norms to solve some problems and create new structural arrangements to solve others, then the image of what a national government might do is somewhat different. There is a very considerable role for large-scale governments, including national defence, monetary policy, foreign policy, global trade policy, moderate redistribution, keeping internal peace when some groups organise to prey on others, provision of accurate information and of arenas for resolving conflicts with national implications, and other large-scale activities. But national governments are too small to govern the global commons and too big to handle smaller scale problems.

To achieve a complex, multitiered governance system is quite difficult. Many types of questions are raised. How do different kinds of institutions support or undermine norms of reciprocity both within hierarchies (Miller 1992) and among members of groups facing collective action problems (Frohlich and Oppenheimer 1970; Galjart 1992)? Field studies find that monitoring and graduated sanctions are close to universal in all robust common-pool resource institutions (E. Ostrom 1990). This tells us that without some external support of such institutions, it is unlikely that reciprocity *alone* completely solves the more challenging common-pool resource problems. Note that sanctions are graduated rather than initially severe. Our current theory of crime – based on a strict expected value theory – does not explain this. If people can learn reciprocity as the fundamental norm for organising their lives, and if they agree to a set of rules contingent upon others following these rules, then graduated sanctions do something more than deter rule infractions.

Reciprocity norms can have a dark side. If punishment consists of escalating retribution, then groups who overcome social dilemmas may be limited to very tight circles of kin and friends, who cooperate only with one another, embedded in a matrix of hostile relationships with outsiders (R. Hardin 1995). This pattern can escalate into feuds, raids, and overt warfare (Boyd and Richerson 1992; Chagnon 1988; Elster 1985; Kollock 1993). Or tight circles of individuals who trust one another may discriminate against anyone of a different colour, religion, or ethnicity. A focus on the return of favours for favours can also be the foundation for corruption. It is in everyone else's interest that some social dilemmas are *not* resolved, such as those involved in monopolies and cartel formation, those that countervene basic moral standards and legal relationships, and those that restrict the opportunities of an open society and an expanding economy. Policies that provide alternative opportunities for those caught in dysfunctional networks are as important as those that stimulate and encourage positive networks (Dasgupta 1997).

Implications for civic education

Human history teaches us that autocratic governments often wage war on their own citizens as well as on those of other jurisdictions. Democracies are characterized by the processing of conflict among individuals and groups without resort to massive killings. Democracies are, however, themselves fragile institutions that are vulnerable to manipulation if citizens and officials are not vigilant (V. Ostrom 1997). For those who wish the twenty-first century to be one of peace, we need to translate our research findings on collective action into materials written for high school and undergraduate students. All too many of our textbooks focus exclusively on leaders and, worse, only national-level leaders. Students completing an introductory course on American government, or political science more generally, will not learn that they play an essential role in sustaining democracy. Citizen participation is presented as contacting leaders, organising interest groups and parties, and voting. That citizens need additional skills and knowledge to resolve the social dilemmas they face is left unaddressed. Their moral decisions are not discussed. We are producing generations of cynical citizens with little trust in one another, much less in their governments. Given the central role of trust in solving social dilemmas, we may be creating the very conditions that undermine our own democratic ways of life. It is ordinary persons and citizens who craft and sustain the workability of the institutions of everyday life. We owe an obligation to the next generation to carry forward the best of our knowledge about how individuals solve the multiplicity of social dilemmas – large and small – that they face.

References

Abbink, K., Bolton, G. E., Sadrieh, A. and Tang, F. F. (1996) 'Adaptive Learning versus Punishment in Ultimatum Bargaining', *Discussion paper no. B-381*, Rheinische FriedrichWilhelms-Universitat Bonn.

Abreau, D. (1988) 'On the Theory of Infinitely Repeated Games with Discounting', *Econometrica* 80 (4): 383–96.

Agrawal, A. (1998) *Greener Pastures: Exchange, Politics and Community among a Mobile Pastoral People*, Durham, NC: Duke University Press.

Alchian, A. A. (1950) 'Uncertainty, Evolution, and Economic Theory', *Journal of Political Economy* 58 (3): 211–21.

Alchian, A. A. and Demsetz, H. (1972) 'Production, Information Costs, and Economic Organisation', *American Economic Review* 62(December): 777–95.

Alt, James E. and Shepsle, K. A. (eds) (1990) *Perspectives on Positive Political Economy*, New York: Cambridge University Press.

Andreoni, J. (1989) 'Giving with Impure Altruism: Applications to Charity and Ricardian Equivalence', *Journal of Political Economy* 97 (December): 1, 447–51, 458.

Arnold, J. E. M. and Campbell, J. G. (1986) 'Collective Management of Hill Forests in Nepal: The Community Forestry Development Project', in *Proceedings of the Conference on Common Property Resource Management*, National Research Council. Washington, DC: National Academy Press, pp. 425–54.

Aumann, R. J. (1974) 'Subjectivity and Correlation in Randomized Strategies', *Journal of Mathematical Economics* 1(March): 67–96.

Axelrod, Robert (1984) *The Evolution of Cooperation*, New York: Basic Books.

— (1986) 'An Evolutionary Approach to Norms', *American Political Science Review* 80 (December): 1095–111.

Axelrod, R. and Hamilton, W. D. (1981) 'The Evolution of Cooperation', *Science* 211 (March): 1390–6.

Axelrod, R. and Keohane, R. O. (1985) 'Achieving Cooperation under Anarchy: Strategies and Institutions', *World Politics* 38 (October): 226–54.

Baland, J.-M. and Platteau, J.-P. (1996) *Halting Degradation of Natural Resources: Is There a Role for Rural Communities*, Oxford: Clarendon Press.

Banks, Jeffrey S. and Calvert, Randall L. (1992a) 'A Battle-of-the-Sexes Game with Incomplete Information', *Games and Economic Behavior* 4 (July): 347–72.

— (1992b) 'Communication and Efficiency in Coordination Games', Working paper, Department of Economics and Department of Political Science, University of Rochester, New York.

Barkow, J. H., Cosmides, L. and Tooby, J. (eds) (1992) *The Adapted Mind. Evolutionary Psychology and the Generation of Culture*, Oxford: Oxford University Press.

Barry, B. and Hardin, R. (1982) *Rational Man and Irrational Society? An Introduction and Source Book*, Beverly Hills, CA: Sage.

Bates, R. H. (1989) *Beyond the Miracle of the Market: The Political Economy of Agrarian Development in Kenya*, New York: Cambridge University Press.

Becker, L. C. (1990) *Reciprocity*, Chicago: University of Chicago Press.

Bendor, J. and Dilip, M. (1987) 'Institutional Structure and the Logic of Ongoing Collective Action', *American Political Science Review* 81 (March): 129–54.

Benoit, J.-P. and Krishna, V. (1985) 'Finitely Repeated Games', *Econometrica* 53 (July): 905–22.

Berkes, F. (ed.) (1989) *Common Property Resources: Ecology and Community-Based Sustainable Development*, London: Belhaven.

Binmore, K. (1997) 'Rationality and Backward Induction', *Journal of Economic Methodology* 4:23–41.

Blau, P. M. (1964) *Exchange of Power in Social Life*, New York: Wiley.

Blomquist, W. (1992) *Dividing the Waters: Governing Groundwater in Southern California*, San Francisco, CA: Institute for Contemporary Studies Press.

Boudreaux, D. J. and Holcombe, R. G. (1989) 'Government by Contract', *Public Finance Quarterly* 17 (July): 264–80.

Boulding, K. E. (1963) 'Towards a Pure Theory of Threat Systems', *American Economic Review* 53 (May): 424–34.

Boyd, R. and Richerson, P. J. (1988) 'The Evolution of Reciprocity in Sizable Groups', *Journal of Theoretical Biology* 132 (June): 337–56.

—— (1992) 'Punishment Allows the Evolution of Cooperation (or Anything Else) in Sizable Groups', *Ethology and Sociobiology* 13 (May): 171–95.

Braithwaite, V. and Levi, M. (eds) (1998) *Trust and Governance*, New York: Russell Sage Foundation.

Brennan, G. and Buchanan, J. (1985) *The Reason of Rules*, Cambridge: Cambridge University Press.

Bromley, D. W., Feeny, D., McKean, M., Peters, P., Gilles, J., Oakerson, R. C., Runge, F. and Thomson, J. (eds) (1992) *Making the Commons Work: Theory, Practice, and Policy*, San Francisco, CA: Institute for Contemporary Studies Press.

Bullock, K. and Baden, J. (1977) 'Communes and the Logic of the Commons', in G. Hardin and J. Baden (eds), *Managing the Commons*, San Francisco, CA: Freeman, pp. 182–99.

Cason, T. N. and Khan, F. U. (1996) 'A Laboratory Study of Voluntary Public Goods Provision with Imperfect Monitoring and Communication', Working paper, Department of Economics, University of Southern California, Los Angeles.

Chagnon, N. A. (1988) 'Life Histories, Blood Revenge, and Warfare in a Tribal Population', *Science* 239 (February): 985–92.

Chan, K., Mestelman, S., Moir, R. and Muller, A. (1996) 'The Voluntary Provision of Public Goods under Varying Endowments', *Canadian Journal of Economics* 29 (1): 54–69.

Clark, A. (1995) 'Economic Reason: The Interplay of Individual Learning and External Structure', Working paper. Department of Philosophy, Washington University in St. Louis.

Coleman, J. S. (1987) 'Norms as Social Capital', in G. Radnitzky and P. Bernholz (eds) *Economic Imperialism: The Economic Approach Applied Outside the Field of Economics,* New York: Paragon House pp. 133–55.

Cook, K. S. and Levi, M. (1990) *The Limits of Rationality,* Chicago: University of Chicago Press.

Cooper, R., DeJong, D. V. and Forsythe, R. (1992) 'Communication in Coordination Games', *Quarterly Journal of Economics* 107 (2): 739–71.

Comes, R., Mason, C. F. and Sandler, T. (1986) 'The Commons and the Optimal Number of Firms', *Quarterly Journal of Economics* 101(August): 641–6.

Cosmides, L. and Tooby, J. (1992) 'Cognitive Adaptations for Social Exchange', in Jerome H. Barkow, L. Cosmides, and J. Tooby (eds) *The Adapted Mind, Evolutionary Psychology and the Generation of Culture,* New York: Oxford University Press, pp. 163–228.

— (1994) 'Better than Rational: Evolutionary Psychology and the Invisible Hand', *American Economic Review* 84 (May): 327–32.

Crawford, S. E. S. and Ostrom, E. (1995) 'A Grammar of Institutions', *American Political Science Review* 89 (September): 582–600.

Dasgupta, P. S. (1993) *An Inquiry into Well-Being and Destitution,* Oxford: Clarendon Press.

— (1997) 'Economic Development and the Idea of Social Capital', Working paper, Faculty of Economics, University of Cambridge.

Davis, D. D. and Holt, C. A. (1993) *Experimental Economics,* Princeton, NJ: Princeton University Press.

Dawes, R. M. (1975) 'Formal Models of Dilemmas in Social Decision Making', in M. F. Kaplan and S. Schwartz (eds) *Human Judgment and Decision Processes: Formal and Mathematical Approaches,* New York: Academic Press, pp. 87–108.

— (1980) 'Social Dilemmas', *Annual Review of Psychology* 31: 169–93.

Dawes, R. M., McTavish, J. and Shaklee, H. (1977) 'Behavior, Communication, and Assumptions about Other People's Behavior in a Commons Dilemma Situation', *Journal of Personality and Social Psychology* 35(1): 1–11.

Dawes, R. M., Orbell, J. M. and van de Kragt, A. (1986) 'Organising Groups for Collective Action', *American Political Science Review* 80 (December): 1171–85.

de Waal, F. (1996) *Good Natured: The Origins of Right and Wrong in Humans and Other Animals,* Cambridge, MA: Harvard University Press.

Dudley, D. (1993) 'Essays on Individual Behavior in Social Dilemma Environments: An Experimental Analysis', PhD diss., Indiana University.

Edney, J. (1979) 'Freeriders en Route to Disaster', *Psychology Today* 13 (December): 80–102.

Eggertsson, T. (1990) *Economic Behavior and Institutions,* New York: Cambridge University Press.

Ekeh, P. P. (1974) *Social Exchange Theory: The Two Traditions,* Cambridge, MA: Harvard University Press.

Ellickson, R. C. (1991) *Order without Law: How Neighbours Settle Disputes,* Cambridge, MA: Harvard University Press.

Elster, J. (1985) *Sour Grapes: Studies in the Subversion of Rationality,* Cambridge: Cambridge University Press.

Emerson, R. (1972a) 'Exchange Theory, Part I: A Psychological Basis for Social Exchange', in J. Berger, M. Zelditch and B. Anderson (eds) *Sociological Theories in Progress,* Vol. 2. Boston: Houghton Mifflin, pp. 38–57.

— (1972b) 'Exchange Theory, Part II: Exchange Relations and Networks', in J. Berger, M. Zelditch and B. Anderson (eds) *Sociological Theories in Progress,* Vol. 2. Boston: Houghton Mifflin, pp. 58–87.

Farrell, J. (1987) 'Cheap Talk, Coordination, and Entry', *Rand Journal of Economics,* 18 (Spring): 34–9.

Farrell, J. and Maskin, E. (1989) 'Renegotiation in Repeated Games', *Games and Economic Behavior* 1 (December): 327–60.

Farrell, J. and Rabin, M. (1996) 'Cheap Talk', *Journal of Economic Perspectives* 10 (Summer): 103–18.

Feeny, D., Berkes, F., McCay, B. J. and Acheson, J. M. (1990) 'The Tragedy of the Commons: Twenty-Two Years Later', *Human Ecology* 18 (1) :1–19.

Frank, R. H., Gilovich, T. and Regan, D. T. (1993) 'The Evolution of One-Shot Cooperation: An Experiment', *Ethology and Sociobiology* 14 (July): 247–56.

Frey, B. S. (1993) 'Does Monitoring Increase Work Effort? The Rivalry with Trust and Loyalty', *Economic Inquiry* 31 (October): 663–70.

— (1997) *Not Just for the Money: An Economic Theory of Personal Motivation,* Cheltenham, UK: Edward Elgar.

Frey, B. S. and Bohnet, I. (1996) 'Cooperation, Communication and Communitarianism: An Experimental Approach', *Journal of Political Philosophy* 4 (4): 322–36.

Frohlich, N. and Oppenheimer, J. (1970) 'I Get By with a Little Help from My Friends', *World Politics* 23(October): 104–20.

Fudenberg, D. and Maskin, E. (1986) 'The Folk Theorem in Repeated Games with Discounting or with Incomplete Information', *Econometrica* 54 (3): 533–54.

Fukuyama, F. (1995) *Trust: The Social Virtues and the Creation of Prosperity,* New York: Free Press.

Galjart, B. (1992) 'Cooperation as Pooling: A Rational Choice Perspective', *Sociologia Ruralis* 32 (4): 389–407.

Gambetta, D. (ed.) (1988) *Trust: Making and Breaking Cooperative Relations,* Oxford: Basil Blackwell.

Geddes, B. (1994) *Politician's Dilemma: Building State Capacity in Latin America,* Berkeley: University of California Press.

Gibson, C. (1999) *Politicians, Peasants and Poachers: The Political Economy of Wildlife in Africa,* Cambridge: Cambridge University Press.

Goetze, D. (1994) 'Comparing Prisoner's Dilemma, Commons Dilemma, and Public Goods Provision Designs in Laboratory Experiments', *Journal of Conflict Resolution* 38 (March): 56–86.

Goetze, D. and Orbell, J. (1988) 'Understanding and Cooperation in Social Dilemmas', *Public Choice* 57 (June): 275–9.

Gouldner, A. W. (1960) 'The Norm of Reciprocity: A Preliminary Statement', *American Sociological Review* 25 (April): 161–78.

Greif, A., Milgrom, P. and Weingast, B. R. (1994) 'Coordination, Commitment, and Enforcement: The Case of the Merchant Guild', *Journal of Political Economy* 102 (August): 745–76.

Grossman, S. J. and Hart, O. D. (1980) 'Takeover Bids, the Free-Rider Problem, and the Theory of the Corporation', *Bell Journal of Economics* 11 (Spring): 42–64.

Guth, W. (1995) 'An Evolutionary Approach to Explaining Cooperative Behavior by Reciprocal Incentives', *International Journal of Game Theory* 24 (4): 323–44.

Guth, W. and Kliemt, H. (1995) 'Competition or Cooperation. On the Evolutionary Economics of Trust, Exploitation and Moral Attitudes', Working paper, Humboldt University, Berlin.

— (1996) 'Towards a Completely Indirect Evolutionary Approach-a Note', *Discussion Paper* 82, Economics Faculty, Humboldt University, Berlin.

Guth, W., Schmittberger, R. and Schwarze, B. (1982) 'An Experimental Analysis of Ultimatum Bargaining', *Journal of Economic Behavior and Organisation* 3 (December): 367–88.

Guth, W. and Tietz, R. (1990) 'Ultimatum Bargaining Behavior. A Survey and Comparison of Experimental Results', *Journal of Economic Psychology* 11 (September): 417–49.

Guth, W. and Yaari, M. (1992) 'An Evolutionary Approach to Explaining Reciprocal Behavior in a Simple Strategic Game', in U. Witt (ed.) *Explaining Process and Change: Approaches to Evolutionary Economics,* Ann Arbor: University of Michigan Press, pp. 23–34.

Hackett, S., Dudley, D. and Walker, J. (1995) 'Heterogeneities, Information and Conflict Resolution: Experimental Evidence on Sharing Contracts', in R. O. Keohane and E. Ostrom (eds) *Local Commons and Global Interdependence: Heterogeneity and Cooperation in Two Domains,* London: Sage, pp. 93–124.

Hackett, S., Schlager, E. and Walker, J. (1994) 'The Role of Communication in Resolving Commons Dilemmas: Experimental Evidence with Heterogeneous Appropriators', *Journal of Environmental Economics and Management* 27 (September): 99–126.

Hamilton, W. D. (1964) 'The Genetical Evolution of Social Behavior', *Journal of Theoretical Biology* 7(July): 1–52.

Hardin, G. (1968) 'The Tragedy of the Commons', *Science* 162 (December): 1243–8.

Hardin, R. (1971) 'Collective Action as an Agreeable n-Prisoners' Dilemma', *Science* 16 (September-October): 472–81.

— (1995) *One for All: The Logic of Group Conflict*, Princeton, NJ: Princeton University Press.

— (1997) 'Economic Theories of the State', in D. C. Mueller (ed.) *Perspectives on Public Choice: A Handbook,* Cambridge: Cambridge University Press, pp. 21–34.

Hardy, C. J. and Latane, B. (1988) 'Social Loafing in Cheerleaders: Effects of Team Membership and Competition', *Journal of Sport and Exercise Psychology* 10 (March): 109–14.

Harsanyi, J. (1977) 'Rule Utilitarianism and Decision Theory', *Erkenntnis* 11 (May): 25–53.

Harsanyi, J. C. and Selten, R. (1988) *A General Theory of Equilibrium Selection in Games,* Cambridge, MA: MIT Press.

Hirshleifer, D. and Rasmusen, E. (1989) 'Cooperation in a Repeated Prisoner's Dilemma with Ostracism', *Journal of Economic Behavior and Organisation* 12 (August): 87–106.

Hoffman, E., McCabe, K. and Smith, V. (1996a) 'Behavioural Foundations of Reciprocity: Experimental Economics and Evolutionary Psychology', Working paper, Department of Economics, University of Arizona, Tucson.

— (1996b) 'Social Distance and Other-Regarding Behavior in Dictator Games', *American Economic Review* 86 (June): 653–60.

Hollingshead, A. B., McGrath, J. E. and O'Connor, K. M. (1993) 'Group Task Performance and Communication Technology: A Longitudinal Study of Computer-Mediated versus Face-to-Face Work Groups', *Small Group Research* 24 (August): 307–33.

Holmstrom, B. (1982) 'Moral Hazard in Teams', *Bell Journal of Economics* 13 (Autumn): 324–40.

Homans, G. C. (1961) *Social Behavior: Its Elementary Forms,* New York: Harcourt, Brace, & World.

Isaac, R. M., McCue, K. and Plott, C. S. R. (1985) 'Public Goods Provision in an Experimental Environment', *Journal of Public Economics* 26 (February): 51–74.

Isaac, R. M. and Walker, J. (1988a) 'Communication and Free-Riding Behavior: The Voluntary Contribution Mechanism', *Economic Inquiry* 26 (October): 585–608.

— (1988b) 'Group Size Effects in Public Goods Provision: The Voluntary Contributions Mechanism', *Quarterly Journal of Economics* 103 (February) :179–99.

— (1991) 'Costly Communication: An Experiment in a Nested Public Goods Problem', in Thomas R. Palfrey (ed.) *Laboratory Research in Political Economy,* Ann Arbor: University of Michigan Press, pp. 269–86.

— (1993) 'Nash as an Organising Principle in the Voluntary Provision of Public Goods: Experimental Evidence', Working paper, Indiana University, Bloomington.

Isaac, R. M., Walker, J. and Thomas, S. (1984) 'Divergent Evidence on Free Riding: An Experimental Examination of Some Possible Explanations', *Public Choice* 43 (2): 113–49.

Isaac, R. M., Walker, J. and Williams, A. W. (1994) 'Group Size and the Voluntary Provision of Public Goods: Experimental Evidence Utilizing Large Groups', *Journal of Public Economics* 54 (May): 1–36.

Keohane, R. O. (1984) *After Hegemony*, Princeton, NJ: Princeton University Press.

Kikuchi, M., Watanabe, Y. and Yamagishi, T. (1996) 'Accuracy in the Prediction of Others' Trustworthiness and General Trust: An Experimental Study', *Japanese Journal of Experimental Social Psychology* 37 (1): 23–36.

Kim, O. and Walker, M. (1984) 'The Free Rider Problem: Experimental Evidence', *Public Choice* 43 (1): 3–24.

Knack, S. (1992) 'Civic Norms, Social Sanctions, and Voter Turnout', *Rationality and Society* 4 (April) :133–56.

Knight, J. (1992) *Institutions and Social Conflict,* Cambridge: Cambridge University Press.

Kollock, P.(1993) 'An Eye for an Eye Leaves Everyone Blind: Cooperation and Accounting Systems', *American Sociological Review* 58 (6): 768–86.

Kreps, D. M. (1990) 'Corporate Culture and Economic Theory', in J. E. Alt and K. A. Shepsle (eds) *Perspectives on Positive Political Economy,* New York: Cambridge University Press, pp. 90–143.

Kreps, D. M., Milgrom, P., Roberts, J. and Wilson, R. (19820 'Rational Cooperation in the Finitely Repeated Prisoner's Dilemma', *Journal of Economic Theory* 27 (August): 245–52.

Lam, W. F. (1998) *Institutions, Infrastructure, and Performance in the Governance and Management of Irrigation Systems: The Case of Nepal,* San Francisco, CA: Institute for Contemporary Studies Press. Forthcoming.

Ledyard, J. (1995) 'Public Goods: A Survey of Experimental Research', in J. Kagel and A. Roth (eds) *The Handbook of Experimental Economics,* Princeton, NJ: Princeton University Press, pp. 111–94.

Leibenstein, H. (1976) *Beyond Economic Man,* Cambridge, MA: Harvard University Press.

Levi, M. (1988) *Of Rule and Revenue,* Berkeley: University of California Press.

— (1997) *Consent, Dissent, and Patriotism,* New York: Cambridge University Press.

Lichbach, M. I. (1995) *The Rebel's Dilemma,* Ann Arbor: University of Michigan Press.

— (1996) *The Cooperator's Dilemma,* Ann Arbor: University of Michigan Press.

Luce, R. D. and Raiffa, H. (1957) *Games and Decisions: Introduction and Critical Survey,* New York: Wiley.

Marr, D. (1982) *Vision: A Computational Investigation into the Human Representation and Processing of Visual Information,* San Francisco, CA: W. H. Freeman.

Marwell, G. and Ames, R. E. (1979) 'Experiments on the Provision of Public Goods I: Resources, Interest, Group Size, and the Free Rider Problem', *American Journal of Sociology* 84 (May): 1335–60.

— (1980) 'Experiments on the Provision of Public Goods II: Provision Points, Stakes, Experience and the Free Rider Problem', *American Journal of Sociology* 85 (January): 926–37.

— (1981) 'Economists Free Ride: Does Anyone Else?', *Journal of Public Economics* 15 (November): 295–310.

Marwell, G. and Oliver, P. (1993) *The Critical Mass in Collective Action: A Micro-Social Theory*, New York: Cambridge University Press.

McCabe, K., Rassenti, S. and Smith, V. (1996) 'Game Theory and Reciprocity in Some Extensive Form Bargaining Games', Working paper, Economic Science Laboratory, University of Arizona, Tucson.

McCay, B. J. and Acheson, J. M. (1987) *The Question of the Commons: The Culture and Ecology of Communal Resources*, Tucson: University of Arizona Press.

McKean, M. (1992) 'Success on the Commons: A Comparative Examination of Institutions for Common Property Resource Management', *Journal of Theoretical Politics* 4 (July): 247–82.

McKean, M. and Ostrom, E. (1995) 'Common Property Regimes in the Forest: Just a Relic from the Past?', *Unasylva* 46 (January): 3–15.

McKelvey, R. D. and Thomas P. (1992) 'An Experimental Study of the Centipede Game', *Econometrica* 60 (July): 803–36.

Messick, D. M. (1973) 'To Join or Not to Join: An Approach to the Unionization Decision', *Organisational Behavior and Human Performance* 10 (August): 146–56.

Messick, D. M. and Brewer, M. B. (1983) 'Solving Social Dilemmas: A Review', in L. Wheeler and P. Shaver (eds) *Annual Review of Personality and Social Psychology*, Beverly Hills, CA: Sage, pp. 11–44.

Messick, D. M., Wilke, H. A. M., Brewer, M. B., Kramer, R. M., Zemke, P. E. and Lui, L. (1983) 'Individual Adaptations and Structural Change as Solutions to Social Dilemmas', *Journal of Personality and Social Psychology* 44 (February): 294–309.

Milgrom, P. R., North, D. C. and Weingast, B. R. (1990) 'The Role of Institutions in the Revival of Trade: The Law Merchant, Private Judges, and the Champagne Fairs', *Economics and Politics* 2 (March): 1–23.

Miller, G. (1992) *Managerial Dilemmas: The Political Economy of Hierarchy*, New York: Cambridge University Press.

Moir, R. (1995) 'The Effects of Costly Monitoring and Sanctioning upon Common Property Resource Appropriation', Working paper, Department of Economics, University of New Brunswick, Saint John.

Morrow, C. E. and Hull, R. W. (1996) 'Donor-Initiated Common Pool Resource Institutions: The Case of the Yanesha Forestry Cooperative', *World Development* 24 (10): 164157.

Mueller, D. (1986) 'Rational Egoism versus Adaptive Egoism as Fundamental Postulate for a Descriptive Theory of Human Behavior', *Public Choice* 51 (1): 3–23.

Nowak, M. A. and Sigmund, K. (1993) 'A Strategy of Win-Stay, Lose-Shift that Outperforms Tit-for-Tat in the Prisoner's Dilemma Game', *Nature* 364 (July): 56–8.

Oakerson, R. J. (1993) 'Reciprocity: A Bottom-Up View of Political Development', in V. Ostrom, D. Feeny and H. Picht (eds) *Rethinking Institutional Analysis and Development: Issues, Alternatives, and Choices,* San Francisco, CA: Institute for Contemporary Studies Press, pp. 141–58.

Oliver, P. (1980) 'Rewards and Punishments as Selective Incentives for Collective Action: Theoretical Investigations', *American Journal of Sociology* 85 (May): 1356–75.

Olson, M. (1965) *The Logic of Collective Action: Public Goods and the Theory of Groups,* Cambridge, MA: Harvard University Press.

Orbell, J. M. and Dawes, R. M. (1991) 'A 'Cognitive Miser' Theory of Cooperators' Advantage', *American Political Science Review* 85 (June): 515–28.

—— (1993) 'Social Welfare, Cooperators' Advantage, and the Option of Not Playing the Game', *American Sociological Review* 58 (December): 787–800.

Orbell, J. M., Dawes, R. M. and van de Kragt, A. (1990) 'The Limits of Multilateral Promising', *Ethics* 100 (April): 616–27.

Orbell, J. M., Schwartz-Shea, P. and Simmons, R. (1984) 'Do Cooperators Exit More Readily than Defectors?', *American Political Science Review* 78 (March): 147–62.

Orbell, J. M., van de Kragt, A. and Dawes, R. M. (1988) 'Explaining Discussion-Induced Cooperation', *Journal of Personality and Social Psychology* 54 (5): 811–9.

Ostrom, E. (1990) *Governing the Commons: The Evolution of Institutions for Collective Action,* New York: Cambridge University Press.

—— (1998) 'Self-Governance of Common-Pool Resources', in P. Newman (ed.) *The New Palgrave Dictionary of Economics and the Law,* London: Macmillan.

Ostrom, E., Gardner, R. and Walker, J. (1992) 'Covenants with and without a Sword: Self-Governance Is Possible', *American Political Science Review* 86 (June): 404–17.

—— (1994) *Rules, Games, and Common-Pool Resources,* A. Arbor: University of Michigan Press.

—— (1997) 'Neither Markets Nor States: Linking Transformation Processes in Collective Action Arenas', in D. C. Mueller (ed.) *Perspectives on Public Choice: A Handbook,* Cambridge: Cambridge University Press, pp. 35–72.

Ostrom, V. (1980) 'Artisanship and Artifact', *Public Administration Review* 40 (July-August): 309–17.

—— (1987) *The Political Theory of a Compound Republic: Designing the American Experiment,* 2nd rev. edn. San Francisco, CA: Institute for Contemporary Studies Press.

—— (1990) 'Problems of Cognition as a Challenge to Policy Analysts and Democratic Societies', *Journal of Theoretical Politics* 2 (3): 243–62.

—— (1997) *The Meaning of Democracy and the Vulnerability of Democracies:*

A Response to Tocqueville's Challenge, Ann Arbor: University of Michigan Press.

Ostrom, V., Feeny, D. and Picht, H. (eds) (1993) *Rethinking Institutional Analysis and Development: Issues, Alternatives, and Choices,* San Francisco, CA: Institute for Contemporary Studies Press.

Palfrey, T. R. and Rosenthal, H. (1988) 'Private Incentives in Social Dilemmas', *Journal of Public Economics* 35 (April): 309–32.

Piaget, J. [1932] (1969) *The Moral Judgment of the Child,* New York: Free Press.

Pinker, S. (1994) *The Language Instinct,* New York: W. Morrow.

Pinkerton, E. (ed.) (1989) *Co-operative Management of Local Fisheries: New Directions for Improved Management and Community Development,* Vancouver: University of British Columbia Press.

Plott, C. R. (1979) 'The Application of Laboratory Experimental Methods to Public Choice', in C. S. Russell (ed.) *Collective Decision Making: Applications from Public Choice Theory,* Baltimore, MD: Johns Hopkins University Press, pp. 137–60.

Pruitt, D. G. and Kimmel, M. J. (1977) 'Twenty Years of Experimental Gaming: Critique, Synthesis, and Suggestions for the Future', *Annual Review of Psychology* 28:363–92.

Putnam, R. D., with R. Leonardi and R. Nanetti (1993) *Making Democracy Work: Civic Traditions in Modern Italy,* Princeton, NJ: Princeton University Press.

Rabin, M. (1994) 'Incorporating Behavioural Assumptions into Game Theory', in J. Friedman, *Problems of Coordination in Economic Activity,* Norwell, MA: Kluwer Academic Press.

Rapoport, A. (1997) 'Order of Play in Strategically Equivalent Games in Extensive Form', *International Journal of Game Theory* 26 (1): 113–36.

Rocco, E. and Warglien, M. (1995) 'Computer Mediated Communication and the Emergence of 'Electronic Opportunism', Working paper RCC#13659, Universita degli Studi di Venezia.

Roth, A. E. (1995) 'Bargaining Experiments', in *Handbook of Experimental Economics,* J. Kagel and A. E. Roth (eds) Princeton, NJ: Princeton University Press.

Roth, A. E., Prasnikar, V., Okuno-Fujiwara, M. and Zamir, S. (1991) 'Bargaining and Market Behavior in Jerusalem, Ljubljana, Pittsburgh, and Tokyo: An Experimental Study', *American Economic Review,* 81 (December): 1068–95.

Rutte, C. G. and Wilke, H. A. M. (1984) 'Social Dilemmas and Leadership', *European Journal of Social Psychology* 14(January/March) :105–21.

Sally, D. (1995) 'Conservation and Cooperation in Social Dilemmas. A Meta-Analysis of Experiments from 1958 to 1992', *Rationality and Society* 7 (January): 58–92.

Samuelson, C. D. and Messick, D. M. (1986) 'Alternative Structural Solutions to Resource Dilemmas', *Organisational Behavior and Human Decision Processes* 37 (February): 139–55.

— (1995) 'When Do People Want to Change the Rules for Allocating Shared Resources', in D. A. Schroeder (ed.) *Social Dilemmas: Perspectives on Individuals and Groups,* Westport, CT: Praeger, pp. 143–62.

Samuelson, C. D., Messick, D. M., Rutte, C. G. and Wilke, H. A. M. (1984) 'Individual and Structural Solutions to Resource Dilemmas in Two Cultures', *Journal of Personality and Social Psychology* 47 (July): 94–104.

Samuelson, L., Gale, J. and Binmore, K. (1995) 'Learning to be Imperfect: The Ultimatum Game', *Games and Economic Behavior* 8 (January): 56–90.

Samuelson, P. A. (1954) 'The Pure Theory of Public Expenditure', *Review of Economics and Statistics* 36 (November): 387–9.

Sandler, T. (1992) *Collective Action: Theory and Applications,* Ann Arbor: University of Michigan Press.

Sato, K. (1987) 'Distribution of the Cost of Maintaining Common Property Resources', *Journal of Experimental Social Psychology* 23 (January): 19–31.

Satz, D. and Ferejohn, J. (1994) 'Rational Choice and Social Theory', *Journal of Philosophy* 91 (February): 71–82.

Scharpf, F. W. (1997) *Games Real Actors Play: Actor Centred Institutionalism in Policy Research,* Boulder, CO: Westview Press.

Schelling, T. C. (1978) *Micromotives & Macrobehaviour,* New York: W. W. Norton.

Schlager, E. (1990) 'Model Specification and Policy Analysis: The Governance of Coastal Fisheries', PhD diss., Indiana University.

Schlager, E. and Ostrom, E. (1993) 'Property-Rights Regimes and Coastal Fisheries: An Empirical Analysis', in R. Simmons and T. Anderson (eds) *The Political Economy of Customs and Culture: Informal Solutions to the Commons Problem,* Lanham, MD: Rowman & Littlefield, pp. 13–41.

Schneider, F. and Pommerehne, W. W. (1981) 'Free Riding and Collective Action: An Experiment in Public Microeconomics', *Quarterly Journal of Economics* 96 (November): 689–704.

Scholz, J. T. (1998) 'Trust, Taxes, and Compliance', in V. Braithwaite and M. Levi (eds) *Trust and Governance,* New York: Russell Sage Foundation.

Schroeder, D. A. (ed.) (1995) *Social Dilemmas: Perspectives on Individuals and Groups,* Westport, CT: Praeger.

Schuessler, R. (1989) 'Exit Threats and Cooperation Under Anonymity', *Journal of Conflict Resolution* 33 (December): 728–49.

Sell, J. and Wilson, R. (1991) 'Levels of Information and Contributions to Public Goods', *Social Forces* 70 (September): 107–24.

— (1992) 'Liar, Liar, Pants on Fire: Cheap Talk and Signalling in Repeated Public Goods Settings', Working paper, Department of Political Science, Rice University.

Selten, R. (1975) 'Reexamination of the Perfectness Concept for Equilibrium Points in Extensive Games', *International Journal of Game Theory* 4 (1): 25–55.

—   (1986) 'Institutional Utilitarianism', in F.-X. Kaufmann, G. Majone, and
V. Ostrom (eds) *Guidance, Control, and Evaluation in the Public Sector,*
New York: de Gruyter, pp. 251–63.

—   (1990) 'Bounded Rationality', *Journal of Institutional and Theoretical
Economics* 146 (December) :649–58.

—   (1991) 'Evolution, Learning, and Economic Behavior', *Games and
Economic Behavior.* 3 (February): 3–24.

Selten, R., Mitzkewitz, M. and Uhlich, G. R. (1997) 'Duopoly Strategies
Programmed by Experienced Players', *Econometrica* 65 (May) :517–55.

Sen, A. K. (1977) 'Rational Fools: A Critique of the Behavioural Foundations of
Economic Theory', *Philosophy & Public Affairs* 6 (Summer): 317–44.

Sethi, R. and Somanathan, E. (1996) 'The Evolution of Social Norms in Common
Property Resource Use', *American Economic Review* 86 (September):
766–88.

Shepsle, K. A. and Weingast, Barry R. (1984) 'Legislative Politics and Budget
Outcomes', in G. Mills and J. Palmer (eds) *Federal Budget Policy in the
1980s,* Washington, DC: Urban Institute Press, pp. 343–67.

Simon, H. A. (1985) 'Human Nature in Politics: The Dialogue of Psychology
with Political Science', *American Political Science Review* 79 (June):
293–304.

—   (1997) *Models of Bounded Rationality: Empirically Grounded Economic
Reason,* Cambridge, MA: MIT Press.

Smith, V. (1982) 'Microeconomic Systems as an Experimental Science', *American
Economic Review* 72 (December): 923–55.

Snidal, D. (1985) 'Coordination versus Prisoner's Dilemma: Implications for
International Cooperation and Regimes', *American Political Science
Review* 79 (December): 923–42.

Tang, S. Y. (1992) *Institutions and Collective Action: Self-Governance in
Irrigation,* San Francisco, CA: Institute for Contemporary Studies Press.

Taylor, M. (1987) *The Possibility of Cooperation,* New York: Cambridge
University Press.

Thibaut, J. W. and Kelley, H. H. (1959) *The Social Psychology of Groups,* New
York: Wiley.

Tocqueville, A. de [1835 and 1840] (1945) *Democracy in America,* 2 vols. New
York: Alfred A. Knopf.

Trivers, R. L. (1971) 'The Evolution of Reciprocal Altruism', *Quarterly Review of
Biology* 46 (March): 35–57.

van de Kragt, A., Orbell, J. M. and Dawes, R. M. (1983) 'The Minimal Contributing
Set as a Solution to Public Goods Problems', *American Political Science
Review* 77 (March): 112–22.

Walker, J., Gardner, R., Herr, A. and Ostrom, E. (1997) 'Voting on Allocation
Rules in a Commons: Predictive Theories and Experimental Results',
Presented at the 1997 annual meeting of the Western Political Science
Association, Tucson, Arizona, March 13–15.

Walker, J., Gardner, R. and Ostrom, E. (1990) 'Rent Dissipation in a Limited-
Access Common-Pool Resource: Experimental Evidence', *Journal of
Environmental Economics and Management* 19 (November): 203–11.

Williams, J. T., Collins, B. and Lichbach, M. I. (1997) 'The Origins of Credible Commitment to the Market', presented at the 1995 annual meeting of the American Political Science Association, Chicago, Illinois.

Yamagishi, T. (1986) 'The Provision of a Sanctioning System as a Public Good', *Journal of Personality and Social Psychology* 51 (1): 110–6.

—   (1988a) 'Exit from the Group as an Individualistic Solution to the Free Rider Problem in the United States and Japan', *Journal of Experimental Social Psychology* 24 (6): 530–42.

—   (1988b) 'The Provision of a Sanctioning System in the United States and Japan', *Social Psychology Quarterly* 51 (3): 265–71.

—   (1988c) 'Seriousness of Social Dilemmas and the Provision of a Sanctioning System', *Social Psychology Quarterly* 51 (1): 32–42.

—   (1992) 'Group Size and the Provision of a Sanctioning System in a Social Dilemma', in W. B. G. Liebrand, D. M. Messick, and H. A. M. Wilke (eds) *Social Dilemmas: Theoretical Issues and Research Findings*, Oxford, England: Pergamon Press, pp. 267–87.

Yamagishi, T. and Cook, K. S. (1993) 'Generalized Exchange and Social Dilemmas', *Social Psychological Quarterly* 56 (4): 235–48.

Yamagishi, T. and Hayashi, N. (1996) 'Selective Play: Social Embeddedness of Social Dilemmas', in W. B. G. Liebrand and D. M. Messick (eds) *Frontiers in Social Dilemmas Research*, Berlin: Springer-Verlag.

Yamagishi, T. and Takahashi, N. (1994) 'Evolution of Norms without Metanorms', in U. Schulz, W. Albers and U. Mueller (eds) *Social Dilemmas and Cooperation*, Berlin: Springer-Verlag, pp. 311–26.

Yoder, R. (1994) *Locally Managed Irrigation Systems*, Colombo, Sri Lanka: International Irrigation Management Institute.

Chapter Six

Beyond Markets and States: Polycentric Governance of Complex Economic Systems[1]

Elinor Ostrom[2]

Contemporary research on the outcomes of diverse institutional arrangements for governing common-pool resources (CPRs) and public goods at multiple scales builds on classical economic theory while developing new theory to explain phenomena that do not fit in a dichotomous world of 'the market' and 'the state'. Scholars are slowly shifting from positing simple systems to using more complex frameworks, theories, and models to understand the diversity of puzzles and problems facing humans interacting in contemporary societies. The humans we study have complex motivational structures and establish diverse private-for-profit, governmental, and community institutional arrangements that operate at multiple scales to generate productive and innovative as well as destructive and perverse outcomes (North 1990, 2005).

In this chapter, I will describe the intellectual journey that I have taken the last half century from when I began graduate studies in the late 1950s. The early efforts to understand the poly-centric water industry in California were formative for me. In addition to working with Vincent Ostrom and Charles M. Tiebout as they formulated the concept of polycentric systems for governing metropolitan areas, I studied the efforts of a large group of private and public water producers facing the problem of an overdrafted groundwater basin on the coast and watching saltwater intrusion threaten the possibility of long term use. Then, in the 1970s, I participated with colleagues in the study of polycentric police industries serving US metropolitan areas to find that the dominant theory underlying massive reform

1. This chapter is a revised version of the lecture Elinor Ostrom delivered in Stockholm, Sweden, on December 8, 2009, when she received the Bank of Sweden Prize in Economic Sciences in Memory of Alfred Nobel. This article is copyright © The Nobel Foundation 2009 and is published with the permission of the Nobel Foundation. Published initially in *The American Economic Review*, 100(3), 2010, pp. 641–672.

2. I wish to thank Vincent Ostrom and my many colleagues at the Workshop who have worked with me throughout the years to develop the research program that is briefly discussed herein. I appreciate the helpful suggestions given me by Arun Agrawal, Andreas Leibbrandt, Mike McGinnis, Jimmy Walker, Tom Wisdom, and by the Applied Theory Working Group and the Experimental Reading Group, and the excellent editing skills of Patty Lezotte. Essential support received over the years from the Ford Foundation, the MacArthur Foundation, and the National Science Foundation is gratefully acknowledged.

proposals was incorrect. Metropolitan areas served by a combination of large and small producers could achieve economies of scale in the production of some police services and avoid diseconomies of scale in the production of others.

These early empirical studies led over time to the development of the Institutional Analysis and Development (IAD) framework. A common framework consistent with game theory enabled us to undertake a variety of empirical studies including a meta-analysis of a large number of existing case studies on common-pool resource systems around the world. Carefully designed experimental studies in the lab have enabled us to test precise combinations of structural variables to find that isolated, anonymous individuals overharvest from common-pool resources. Simply allowing communication, or 'cheap talk', enables participants to reduce overharvesting and increase joint payoffs contrary to game theoretical predictions. Large studies of irrigation systems in Nepal and forests around the world challenge the presumption that governments always do a better job than users in organizing and protecting important resources.

Currently, many scholars are undertaking new theoretical efforts. A core effort is developing a more general theory of individual choice that recognizes the central role of trust in coping with social dilemmas. Over time, a clear set of findings from the microsituational level have emerged regarding structural factors affecting the likelihood of increased cooperation. Due to the complexity of broader field settings, one needs to develop more configural approaches to the study of factors that enhance or detract from the emergence and robustness of self-organized efforts within multilevel, polycentric systems. Further, the application of empirical studies to the policy world leads one to stress the importance of fitting institutional rules to a specific social-ecological setting. 'One size fits all' policies are not effective. The frameworks and empirical work that many scholars have undertaken in recent decades provide a better foundation for policy analysis. With this brief overview, let us now discuss the journey itself.

The earlier world view of simple systems

In the mid-twentieth century, the dominant scholarly effort was to try to fit the world into simple models and to criticize institutional arrangements that did not fit. I will briefly review the basic assumptions that were made at that time but have been challenged by scholars around the world, including the work of Simon (1955) and V. Ostrom (2008).

A. Two optimal organizational forms

The market was seen as the optimal institution for the production and exchange of private goods. For non-private goods, on the other hand, one needed 'the' government to impose rules and taxes to force self-interested individuals to contribute necessary resources and refrain from self-seeking activities. Without a hierarchical government to induce compliance, self-seeking citizens and officials would fail to generate efficient levels of public goods, such as peace and security, at multiple scales (Hobbes [1651] 1960; Woodrow Wilson 1885). A single governmental unit, for example, was strongly recommended to reduce the 'chaotic' structure of metropolitan governance, increase efficiency, limit conflict among governmental units, and best serve a homogeneous view of the public (Anderson and Weidner 1950; Gulick 1957; Friesema 1966). This dichotomous view of the world explained patterns of interaction and outcomes related to markets for the production and exchange of strictly private goods (Alchian 1950), but it has not adequately accounted for internal dynamics within private firms (Williamson 1975, 1986). Nor does it adequately deal with the wide diversity of institutional arrangements that humans craft to govern, provide, and manage public goods and common-pool resources.

B. Two types of goods

In his classic definitional essay, Samuelson (1954) divided goods into two types. Pure private goods are both excludable (individual A can be excluded from consuming private goods unless paid for) and rivalrous (whatever individual A consumes, no one else can consume). Public goods are both non-excludable (impossible to keep those who have not paid for a good from consuming it) and non-rivalrous (whatever individual A consumes does not limit the consumption by others). This basic division was consistent with the dichotomy of the institutional world into private property exchanges in a market setting and government-owned property organized by a public hierarchy. The people of the world were viewed primarily as consumers or voter.

C. One model of the individual

The assumption that all individuals are fully rational was generally accepted in mainstream economics and game theory. Fully rational individuals are presumed to know (i) all possible strategies available in a particular situation, (ii) which outcomes are linked to each strategy given the likely behavior of others in a situation, and (iii) a rank order for each of these outcomes in terms of the individual's own preferences as measured by utility. The rational strategy for such an individual in every situation is to maximize expected utility. While utility was originally conceived of as a way of combining a diversity of external values on a single internal scale, in practice it has come to be equated with one externalized unit of measure – such as expected profits. This model of the individual has fruitfully generated useful and empirically validated predictions about the results of exchange transactions related to goods with specific attributes in a competitive market but not in a diversity of social dilemmas. I will return to a discussion of the theory of individual behavior in the section 'Developing a More General Theory of The Individual'.

Early efforts to develop a fuller understanding of complex human systems

The mid-twentieth-century worldviews of simple systems have slowly been transformed as a result of extensive empirical research and the development of a framework consistent with game theoretical models for the analysis of a broad array of questions.

A. Studying polycentric public industries

Undertaking empirical studies of how citizens, local public entrepreneurs, and public officials engage in diverse ways of providing, producing, and managing public service industries and common property regimes at multiple scales has generated substantial knowledge that is not explained by two models of optimal organizational forms. V. Ostrom, Tiebout and Warren (1961) introduced the concept of polycentricity in their effort to understand whether the activities of a diverse array of public and private agencies engaged in providing and producing of public services in metropolitan areas were chaotic, as charged by other scholars – or potentially a productive arrangement.

> 'Polycentric' connotes many centres of decision making that are formally independent of each other. Whether they actually function independently, or instead constitute an interdependent system of relations, is an empirical question in particular cases. To the extent that they take each other into account in competitive relationships, enter into various contractual and cooperative undertakings or have recourse to central mechanisms to resolve conflicts, the various political jurisdictions in a metropolitan area may function in a coherent manner with consistent and predictable patterns of interacting behavior. To the extent that this is so, they may be said to function as a 'system'. (V. Ostrom, Tiebout and Warren 1961: 831–32)

Drawing on the concept of a public service industry (Bain 1959; Caves 1964; V. Ostrom and E. Ostrom 1965), several studies of water industry performance were carried out in diverse regions of California during the 1960s (V. Ostrom 1962; Weschler 1968; Warren 1966; E. Ostrom 1965). Substantial evidence was found that multiple public and private agencies had searched out productive ways of organizing water resources at multiple scales contrary to the view that the presence of multiple governmental units without a clear hierarchy was chaotic. Further, evidence pointed out three mechanisms that increase productivity in polycentric metropolitan areas: (i) small to medium sized cities are more effective than large cities in monitoring performance of their citizens and relevant costs, (ii) citizens who are dissatisfied with service provision can 'vote with their feet' and move to jurisdictions that come closer to their preferred mix and costs of public services, and (iii) local incorporated communities can contract with larger producers and change contracts if not satisfied with the services provided, while neighbourhoods inside a large city have no voice.

In the 1970s, the earlier work on effects of diverse ways of organizing the provision of water in metropolitan areas was extended to policing and public safety. These studies directly addressed whether substantial economies of scale existed in the production of police services for urban neighbourhoods as asserted in calls for reform (Skoler and Hetler 1970). Not a single case was found where a large centralized police department outperformed smaller departments serving similar neighbourhoods in regard to multiple indicators. A series of studies was conducted in Indianapolis (E. Ostrom *et al.* 1973), Chicago (E. Ostrom and Whitaker 1974) and St. Louis (E. Ostrom and Parks 1973; E. Ostrom 1976) and then replicated in Grand Rapids, Michigan (IsHak 1972) and Nashville, Tennessee (Rogers and McCurdy Lipsey 1974).

We found that while many police departments served the 80 metropolitan areas that we also studied, duplication of services by more than one department to the same set of citizens rarely occurred (E. Ostrom, Parks and Whitaker 1978). Further, the widely held belief that a multiplicity of departments in a metropolitan area was less efficient was not found. In fact, the 'most efficient producers supply more output for given inputs in high multiplicity metropolitan areas than do the efficient producers in metropolitan areas with fewer producers' (E. Ostrom and Parks 1999: 287). Metropolitan areas with large numbers of autonomous direct service producers achieved higher levels of technical efficiency (*Ibid.*: 290). Technical efficiency was also enhanced in those metropolitan areas with a small number of producers providing indirect services such as radio communication and criminal laboratory analyses. We were able to reject the theory underlying the proposals of the metropolitan reform approach. We demonstrated that complexity is not the same as chaos in regard to metropolitan governance. That lesson has carried forth as we have undertaken further empirical studies of polycentric governance of resource and infrastructure systems across the world (Andersson and E. Ostrom 2008; E. Ostrom, Schroeder and Wynne 1993).

B. Doubling the types of goods

Studying how individuals cope with diverse public problems in the world led us to reject Samuelson's twofold classification of goods. Buchanan (1965) had already added a third type of good, which he called 'club goods'. In relation to these kinds of goods, it was feasible for groups of individuals to create private associations (clubs) to provide themselves with nonrivalrous but small-scale goods and services that they could enjoy while excluding nonmembers from participation and consumption of benefits.

In light of further empirical and theoretical research, we proposed additional modifications to the classification of goods to identify fundamental differences that affect the incentives facing individuals (V. Ostrom and E. Ostrom 1977).

Figure 6.1: Four Types of Goods

		Subtractability of use	
		High	Low
Difficulty of excluding potential beneficiaries	High	*Common-pool resources*: groundwater basins, lakes, irrigation systems, fisheries, forests, etc.	*Public goods*: peace and security of a community, national defence, knowledge, fire protection, weather forecasts, etc.
	Low	*Private goods*: food, clothing, automobiles, etc.	*Toll goods*: theatres, private clubs, daycare centres

Source: Adapted from E. Ostrom 2005: 24.

i.   Replacing the term 'rivalry of consumption' with 'subtractability of use'.

ii. Conceptualizing subtractability of use and excludability to vary from low to high rather than characterizing them as either present or absent.

iii. Overtly adding a very important fourth type of good – common-pool resources – that shares the attribute of subtractability with private goods and difficulty of exclusion with public goods (V. Ostrom and E. Ostrom 1977). Forests, water systems, fisheries, and the global atmosphere are all common-pool resources of immense importance for the survival of humans on this earth.

iv. Changing the name of a 'club' good to a 'toll' good since many goods that share these characteristics are provided by small scale public as well as private associations.

Figure 6.1 provides an overview of four broad types of goods that differentially affect the problems individuals face in devising institutions to enable them to provide, produce, and consume diverse goods. These four broad types of goods contain many subtypes of goods that vary substantially in regard to many attributes. For example, a river and a forest are both common-pool resources. They differ substantially, however, in regard to the mobility of the resource units produced, the ease of measurement, the time scale for regeneration, and other attributes. Specific common-pool resources also differ in regard to spatial extent, number of users, and many other factors.

When one engages in substantial fieldwork, one confronts an immense diversity of situations in which humans interact. Riding as an observer in a patrol car in the central district of a large American city at midnight on a Saturday evening, one sees different patterns of human interaction than in a suburb on a weekday afternoon when school is letting out. In both cases, one observes the production of a public good – local safety – by an official of a local government. Others, who are involved in each situation, differ in regard to age, sobriety, why they are there, and what they are trying to accomplish. And this context affects the strategies of the police officer one is observing.

Contrast observing the production of a public good to watching private water companies, city utilities, private oil companies, and local citizens meeting in diverse settings to assess who is to blame for overdrafting their groundwater basin causing massive saltwater intrusion, and what to do next. These individuals all face the same problem – the overdraft of a common-pool resource – but their behavior differs substantially when they meet monthly in a private water association, when they face each other in a courtroom, and when they go to the legislature and eventually to the citizens to sponsor a Special Replenishment District. These and many other situations observed in irrigation systems and forests in multiple countries do not closely resemble the standard models of a market or a hierarchy.

Developing a framework for analysing the diversity of human situations

The complexity and diversity of the field settings we have studied has generated an extended effort by colleagues associated with the Workshop in Political Theory and Policy Analysis (the Workshop) to develop the IAD framework (V. Ostrom 1975; Kiser and E. Ostrom 1982; McGinnis 1999a, b, 2000; E. Ostrom 1986, 2005). The framework contains a nested set of building blocks that social scientists can use in efforts to understand human interactions and outcomes across diverse settings. The IAD builds on earlier work on transactions (Commons [1924] 1968), logic of the situation (Popper 1961), collective structures (Allport 1962), frames (Goffman 1974) and scripts (Schank and Abelson 1977). The approach also draws inspiration from the work of Koestler (1973) and Simon (1981, 1995) who both challenged the assumption that human behavior and outcomes are entirely based on a small set of irreducible building blocks.

While the terms frameworks, theories, and models are used interchangeably by many scholars, we use these concepts in a nested manner to range from the most general to the most precise set of assumptions made by a scholar. The IAD framework is intended to contain the most general set of variables that an institutional analyst may want to use to examine a diversity of institutional settings including human interactions within markets, private firms, families, community organizations, legislatures, and government agencies. It provides a metatheoretical language to enable scholars to discuss any particular theory or to compare theories.

A specific theory is used by an analyst to specify which working parts of a framework are considered useful to explain diverse outcomes and how they relate to one another. Microlevel theories including game theory, microeconomic theory, transaction cost theory, and public goods/common-pool resource theories are examples of specific theories compatible with the IAD framework. Models make precise assumptions about a limited number of variables in a theory that scholars use to examine the formal consequences of these specific assumptions about the motivation of actors and the structure of the situation they face.

Figure 6.2: A Framework for Institutional Analysis

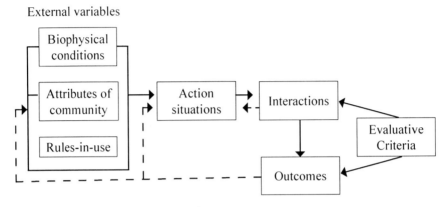

Source: Adapted from E. Ostrom 2005: 15.

The IAD framework is designed to enable scholars to analyse systems that are composed of a cluster of variables, each of which can then be unpacked multiple times depending on the question of immediate interest. At the core of the IAD framework is the concept of an action situation affected by external variables (*see* Figure 6.2). The broadest categories of external factors affecting an action situation at a particular time include:

i.   Biophysical conditions, which may be simplified in some analyses to be one of the four types of goods defined in Figure 6.1.

ii.   Attributes of a community, which may include the history of prior interactions, internal homogeneity or heterogeneity of key attributes, and the knowledge and social capital of those who may participate or be affected by others.

iii.   Rules-in-use, which specify common understanding of those involved related to who must, must not, or may take which actions affecting others subject to sanctions (Crawford and E. Ostrom 2005). The rules-in-use may evolve over time as those involved in one action situation interact with others in a variety of settings (E. Ostrom 2008; E. Ostrom and Basurto (2011); Boyd and Richerson 1985) or self-consciously change the rules in a collective choice or constitutional-choice setting.

The set of external variables impacts an action situation to generate patterns of interactions and outcomes that are evaluated by participants in the action situation (and potentially by scholars) and feed back on both the external variables and the action situation.

The internal working parts of an action situation are overtly consistent with the variables that a theorist uses to analyse a formal game.[3] This has meant that colleagues have been able to use formal game theory models consistent with the IAD framework to analyse simplified but interesting combinations of theoretical variables and derive testable conclusions from them (*see* Acheson and Gardner 2005; Gardner *et al.* 2000; Weissing and E. Ostrom 1993) as well as agent-based models (ABMs) (Jager and Janssen 2002; Janssen 2008). It is not feasible to develop a formal game (or even an ABM) to analyse the more complex empirical settings with many variables of relevance affecting outcomes and of importance for institutional analysis. It is possible, however, to use a common set of structural elements to develop structured coding forms for data collection and analysis. And one can design experiments using a common set of variables for many situations of interest to political economists and then examine why particular behavior and outcomes occur in some situations and not in others.

To specify the structure of a game and predict outcomes, the theorist needs to posit the:

i.   characteristics of the actors involved (including the model of human choice adopted by the theorist);

ii.   positions they hold (e.g. first mover or row player);

iii.   set of actions that actors can take at specific nodes in a decision tree;

iv.   amount of information available at a decision node;

v.   outcomes that actors jointly affect;

vi.   set of functions that map actors and actions at decision nodes into intermediate or final outcomes; and

vii.   benefits and costs assigned to the linkage of actions chosen and outcomes obtained.

These are also the internal working parts of an action situation as shown in Figure 6.3. As discussed below, using a common framework across a wide diversity of studies has enabled a greater cumulation of understanding of interactions and outcomes in very complex environments. The IAD framework overtly embeds a particular situation of interest in a broader setting of external variables, some of which can be self-consciously revised over time.

---

3.   I am much appreciative of the many hours of productive discussions that I had with Reinhard Selten in the early 1980s as we started to develop the IAD framework about the internal working parts of a formal game that could be used in the framework.

Figure 6.3: The Internal Structure of an Action Situation

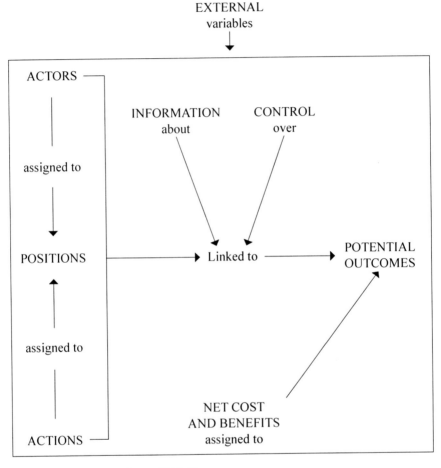

Source: Adapted from E. Ostrom 2005: 33.

Are rational individuals helplessly trapped in social dilemmas?

The classic assumptions about rational individuals facing a dichotomy of organizational forms and of goods hide the potentially productive efforts of individuals and groups to organize and solve social dilemmas such as the overharvesting of common-pool resources and the underprovision of local public goods. The classic models have been used to view those who are involved in a prisoner's dilemma game or other social dilemmas as always trapped in the situation without capabilities to change the structure themselves. This analytical step was a retrogressive step in the theories used to analyse the human condition. Whether or not the individuals, who are in a situation, have capacities to transform the external variables affecting their own situation varies dramatically from one situation to the next. It is an empirical condition that varies from situation to situation rather than a logical universality. Public investigators purposely keep prisoners separated so they cannot communicate. The users of a common-pool resource are not so limited.

When analysts perceive the human beings they model as being trapped inside perverse situations, they then assume that other human beings external to those involved – scholars and public officials – are able to analyse the situation, ascertain why counterproductive outcomes are reached, and posit what changes in the rules-in-use will enable participants to improve outcomes. Then, external officials are expected to impose an optimal set of rules on those individuals involved. It is assumed that the momentum for change must come from outside the situation rather than from the self-reflection and creativity of those within a situation to restructure their own patterns of interaction. As Sugden has described this approach:

> Most modern economic theory describes a world presided over by a *government* (not, significantly, by governments) and sees this world through the government's eyes. The government is supposed to have the responsibility, the will and the power to restructure society in whatever way maximizes social welfare; like the US Cavalry in a good Western, the government stands ready to rush to the rescue whenever the market 'fails', and the economist's job is to advise it on when and how to do so. Private individuals, in contrast, are credited with little or no ability to solve collective problems among themselves. This makes for a distorted view of some important economic and political issues. (Sugden 1986: 3; *emphasis* in original)

Hardin's (1968) portrayal of the users of a common-pool resource – a pasture open to all – being trapped in an inexorable tragedy of overuse and destruction has been widely accepted since it was consistent with the prediction of no cooperation in a prisoner's dilemma or other social dilemma games. It captured the attention of scholars and policymakers across the world. Many presumed that all common-pool resources were owned by no one. Thus, it was thought that government officials had to impose new external variables (e.g. new policies) to prevent destruction by users who could not do anything other than destroy the resources on which their own future (as well as the rest of our futures) depended.

A. Scholars from diverse disciplines examine whether resource users are always trapped

Dramatic incidents of overharvested resources had captured widespread attention, while studies by anthropologists, economic historians, engineers, historians, philosophers, and political scientists of local governance of smaller to medium scale common-pool resources over long periods of time were not noticed by many theorists and public officials (*see* Netting 1972; McCay and Acheson 1987; Coward 1980). Cumulation of the knowledge contained in these studies did not occur, due to the fact that the studies were written by scholars in diverse disciplines focusing on different types of resources located in many countries.

Fortunately, the National Research Council (NRC) established a committee in the mid-1980s to assess diverse institutional arrangements for effective conservation and utilization of jointly managed resources. The NRC committee brought scholars from multiple disciplines together and used the IAD framework in an effort to begin to identify common variables in cases where users had organized or failed to organize (Oakerson 1986: 178, 204; NRC 1986). Finding multiple cases where resource users were successful in organizing themselves challenged the presumption that it was impossible for resource users to solve their own problems of overuse. The NRC report opened up the possibility of a diversity of studies using multiple methods. The NRC effort also stimulated an extended research program at the Workshop that involved coding and analysing case studies of common-pool resources written by other scholars.

B. Meta-analyses of common-pool resource cases

In an effort to learn more than just the existence of multiple cases where resource users had self-organized, colleagues at the Workshop undertook a meta-analysis of existing case studies that were identified as a result of the activities of the NRC panel.[4] Because of our prior studies of complex urban systems and the development of a framework and common language for linking the parts of complex systems, we could use the framework to help organize our efforts. The IAD framework became the foundation for designing a coding manual that was used to record a consistent set of variables for each common-pool resource study.

This was an immense effort. More than two years was devoted to developing the final coding manual (E. Ostrom *et al.* 1989). A key problem was the minimal overlap of variables identified by case study authors from diverse disciplines. The team had to read and screen over 500 case studies in order to identify a small set of cases that recorded information about the actors, their strategies, the condition of the resource, and the rules-in-use.[5] A common set of variables was recorded for 44 subgroups of fishers who harvested from inshore fisheries (Schlager 1990, 1994) and 47 irrigation systems that were managed either by farmers or by a government (Tang 1992, 1994).

Of the 47 irrigation systems included in the analysis, 12 were managed by governmental agencies of which only 40 percent (n = 7) had high performance. Of the 25 farmer-managed, over 70 percent (n = 18) had high performance (Tang

---

4. This meta-analysis effort is described in Chapter Four of Poteete, Janssen, and E. Ostrom (2010).

5. Scholars across disciplines tend to use very different vocabularies and theoretical frameworks when they describe empirical settings. Other scholars, who have used meta-analysis, have also needed to screen many publications to obtain consistent data about human-used resource systems. Adcharaporn Pagdee, Yeon-Su Kim and P. J. Daugherty (2006) report screening over 100 articles in order to analyze 31 cases related to forest management. Thomas K. Rudel (2008) reported that he had screened nearly 1,200 studies for a meta-analysis of 268 cases of tropical forest cover change.

1994: 234). Rule conformance was a key variable affecting the adequacy of water over time (Tang 1994: 229). None of the inshore fishery groups analysed by Schlager were government managed and 11 (25 percent) were not organized in any way. The other 33 subgroups had a diversity of informal rules to define who was allowed to fish in a particular location and how harvesting was restricted (Schlager 1994: 179, 195, 260).

In addition to finding significant levels of cooperation, we found some support for earlier theoretical predictions of no cooperation in particular settings.

> In CPR dilemmas where individuals do not know one another, cannot communicate effectively, and thus cannot develop agreements, norms, and sanctions, aggregate predictions derived from models of rational individuals in a noncooperative game receive substantial support. These are sparse environments and full rationality appears to be a reasonable assumption in them. (E. Ostrom, Gardner and Walker 1994: 319)

On the other hand, the capacity to overcome dilemmas and create effective governance occurred far more frequently than expected and depended upon the structure of the resource itself and whether the rules-in-use developed by users were linked effectively to this structure (Blomquist *et al.* 1994). In all self-organized systems, we found that users had created boundary rules for determining who could use the resource, choice rules related to the allocation of the flow of resource units, and active forms of monitoring and local sanctioning of rule breakers (*Ibid.*: 301). On the other hand, we did not find a single case where harvesters used the 'grim trigger' strategy – a form of punishment that was posited in many theoretical arguments for how individuals could solve repeated dilemmas (Dutta 1990: 264).

C. The bundles of property rights related to common-pool resources

Resource economists have used the term 'common property resource' to refer to fisheries and water resources (H. Scott Gordon 1954; Anthony D. Scott 1955; Frederick W. Bell 1972). Combining the term 'property' with 'resource' introduced considerable confusion between the nature of a good and the absence or presence of a property regime (Ciriacy-Wantrup and Bishop 1975). A common-pool resource can be owned and managed as government property, private property, community property, or owned by no one (Bromley 1986). A further reason for the lack of awareness about property systems developed by local users was that many scholars presumed that unless users possessed alienation rights – the right to sell their property – they did not have any property rights (Alchian and Demsetz 1973; Anderson and Hill 1990; Posner 1975).

Schlager and E. Ostrom (1992) drew on the earlier work of Commons ([1924] 1968) to conceptualize property rights systems as containing bundles of rights rather than a single right. The meta-analysis of existing field cases helped to identify five property rights that individuals using a common-pool resource might cumulatively

Figure 6.4: Rules as Exogenous Variables Directly Affecting the Elements of an Action Situation.

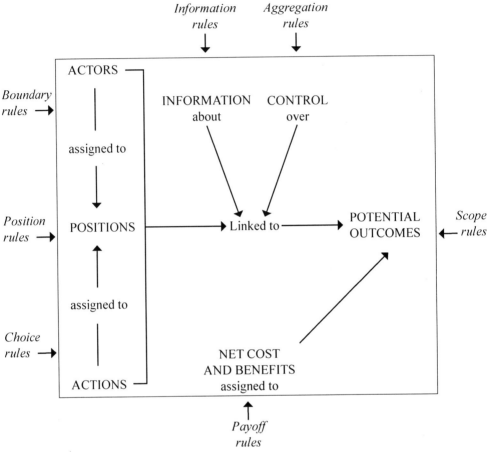

Source: Adapted from E. Ostrom 2005: 189.

have: (i) access – the right to enter a specified property,[6] (ii) withdrawal – the right to harvest specific products from a resource, (iii) management – the right to transform the resource and regulate internal use patterns, (iv) exclusion – the right to decide who will have access, withdrawal, or management rights, and (v) alienation – the right to lease or sell any of the other four rights. Conceiving of property rights bundles is now widely accepted by scholars who have studied diverse property rights systems around the world (Brunckhorst 2000; Degnbol and McCay 2007; Paavola and Adger 2005; Trawick 2001; Wilson *et al.* 1994).

---

6. The concept of access rights has puzzled some scholars. An everyday example of an access right is the buying of a permit to enter a public park. This assigns the holder of a permit the right to enter and enjoy hiking and other nonharvesting activities for a defined period of time.

D. Linking the internal parts of an action situation to external rules

Actors who have specific property rights to a resource also face more fundamental rules that affect the structure of the action situations they are in. In our meta-analysis, we found an incredible array of specific rules used in different settings (e.g. who could withdraw how many resource units at what location and time, what information was required of all users, what costs and benefits were attached to which actions, etc.). As we attempted to find a consistent way of coding and analysing this rich diversity of specific rules described by case authors, we turned again to the IAD framework. Since we had identified seven working parts of a game or action situation itself, it seemed reasonable to think of seven broad types of rules operating as external variables affecting the individual working parts of action situations (*see* Figure 6.4). The seven types of rules are:

i.   Boundary rules that specify how actors were to be chosen to enter or leave these positions.

ii.   Position rules that specify a set of positions and how many actors hold each one.

iii. Choice rules that specify which actions are assigned to an actor in a position.

iv.   Information rules that specify channels of communication among actors and what information must, may, or must not be shared.

v.   Scope rules that specify the outcomes that could be affected.

vi.   Aggregation rules (such as majority or unanimity rules) that specify how the decisions of actors at a node were to be mapped to intermediate or final outcomes.

vii. Payoff rules that specify how benefits and costs were to be distributed to actors in positions (Crawford and E. Ostrom 2005).

A useful way of thinking about institutional rules is to conceptualize what part of an action situation is affected by a rule (*see* Figure 6.4).

Conceptualizing seven broad types of rules (rather than one or two) has been upsetting to scholars who wanted to rely on simple models of interactions among humans. In addition to finding seven broad types of rules, however, we also found multiple variants of each type. For example, we found 27 boundary rules described by case study authors as used in at least one common-pool resource setting (E. Ostrom 1999: 510). Some rules specified diverse forms of residence, organizational memberships, or personal attributes that are ascribed or acquired. Similarly, we found 112 different choice rules that were usually composed of two parts – an allocation formula specifying where, when, or how resource units could be harvested and a specific basis for the implementation of the formula (such as the amount of land held, historical use patterns, or assignment through lottery) (*Ibid.*: 512).

E. Long surviving resource institutions

After working for several years with colleagues to code cases of successful and failed systems, I thought my next task would be to undertake careful statistical analysis to identify which specific rules were associated with successful systems. I had not yet fully absorbed the incredible number and diversity of rules that the team had recorded. In 1988, I spent a sabbatical leave in a research group organized by Selten: 182 at the Center for Interdisciplinary Research at Bielefeld University. I struggled to find rules that worked across ecological, social, and economic environments, but the specific rules associated with success or failure varied extensively across sites. Finally, I had to give up the idea that specific rules might be associated with successful cases.

Moving up a level in generality, I tried to understand the broader institutional regularities among the systems that were sustained over a long period of time and were absent in the failed systems. I used the term 'design principle' to characterize these regularities. I did not mean that the fishers, irrigators, pastoralists, and others overtly had these principles in their minds when they developed systems that survived for long periods of time. My effort was to identify a set of core underlying lessons that characterized the long sustained regimes as contrasted to the cases of failure (E. Ostrom 1990).[7]

Since the design principles are described extensively in E. Ostrom (1990 2005), I will mention only a brief updated list as developed by Cox, Arnold and Villamayor-Tomás (2009):

1A. *User Boundaries*: Clear and locally understood boundaries between legitimate users and nonusers are present.

1B. *Resource Boundaries*: Clear boundaries that separate a specific common-pool resource from a larger social-ecological system are present.

2A. *Congruence with Local Conditions*: Appropriation and provision rules are congruent with local social and environmental conditions.

2B. *Appropriation and Provision*: Appropriation rules are congruent with provision rules; the distribution of costs is proportional to the distribution of benefits.

3. *Collective Choice Arrangements*: Most individuals affected by a resource regime are authorized to participate in making and modifying its rules.

4A. *Monitoring Users*: Individuals who are accountable to or are the users monitor the appropriation and provision levels of the users.

---

7. The term 'design principle' has confused many readers. Perhaps I should have used the term 'best practices' to describe the rules and structure of robust institutions.

4B. *Monitoring the Resource*: Individuals who are accountable to or are the users monitor the condition of the resource.

5. *Graduated Sanctions*: Sanctions for rule violations start very low but become stronger if a user repeatedly violates a rule.

6. *Conflict Resolution Mechanisms*: Rapid, low cost, local arenas exist for resolving conflicts among users or with officials.

7. *Minimal Recognition of Rights*: The rights of local users to make their own rules are recognized by the government.

8. *Nested Enterprises*: When a common-pool resource is closely connected to a larger social-ecological system, governance activities are organized in multiple nested layers.

The design principles appear to synthesize core factors that affect the probability of long term survival of an institution developed by the users of a resource. Cox, Arnold and Villamayor-Tomás (2009) analysed over 100 studies by scholars who assessed the relevance of the principles as an explanation of the success or failure of diverse common-pool resources. Two-thirds of these studies confirm that robust resource systems are characterized by most of the design principles and that failures are not. The authors of some studies that found the design principles inadequate tended to interpret them very rigidly and felt that successful systems were characterized by more flexibility. In three instances, the initial wording of the design principles was too general and did not distinguish between ecological and social conditions. Thus, I have adopted the improvements to principles 1, 2, and 4 suggested by Cox and coauthors.

Conducting experiments to study common-pool resource problems

The existence of a large number of cases where users had overcome social dilemmas in order to sustain long term use of common-pool resources successfully challenged the presumption that this was impossible. Many variables simultaneously affect these outcomes in the field. Developing game theoretical models of common-pool resource situations (Weissing and E. Ostrom 1993; E. Ostrom and Gardner 1993) has been one strategy we have used to assess the theoretical outcomes of a set of variables we have observed in the field. We have also thought it was important to examine the effect of precise combinations of variables in an experimental setting.

A. Common-pool resource experiments in university laboratories

Gardner and Walker joined me in an extended effort to build and test well specified, game theoretical models consistent with the IAD framework (*see* E. Ostrom, Walker and Gardner 1992; E. Ostrom, Gardner and Walker 1994). The initial CPR experiments started with a static, baseline situation that was as simple as could be specified without losing crucial aspects of the appropriation problems facing harvesters in the field. We used a quadratic payoff production function based on Gordon's (1954) classic model. The initial resource endowment w for each of eight subjects was a set of tokens that the subject could allocate between Market 1 (which had a fixed return) and Market 2 (which functioned as a common-pool resource with a return affected by the actions of all subjects in the experiment). Subjects received aggregated information so they did not know each individual's actions. Each subject $_i$ could invest a portion x_i of his/her endowment in the common resource (Market 2) and the remaining portion would then be invested in Market 1. The payoff function we used (E. Ostrom, Gardner and Walker 1994: 110) was:

(1) $u_i(x) = we$ if $x_i = 0$

(2) $w(e-x_i) + (x_i / \Sigma\, x_i) F(\Sigma\, x_i)$ if $x_i > 0$

The baseline experiment was a commons dilemma in which the game-theoretic outcome involved substantial overuse of a resource while a much better outcome could be reached if subjects were to reduce their joint allocation. The prediction from noncooperative game theory was that subjects would invest according to the Nash equilibrium – 8 tokens each for a total of 64 tokens. Subjects could earn considerably more if they reduced their allocation to a total of 36 tokens in the common-pool resource. Subjects in baseline experiments with multiple decision rounds substantially overinvested – they invested even more tokens than predicted, so the joint outcome was worse than the predicted Nash equilibrium.[8]

Building off prior public goods research (Isaac and Walker 1988), we then conducted a series of face-to-face communication experiments in which the same payoff function was retained. After an initial ten rounds without communication, subjects were told they could communicate with each other in a group setting before returning to their terminals to make their own private decisions. This provided an opportunity for 'cheap talk'. The same outcome was predicted in these experiments as in the baseline since a subject could promise to cooperate but no external 'third party' ensured that the promise was fulfilled.

Subjects used face-to-face communication to discuss strategies to gain the best outcomes and then to agree – if possible – on what each subject should invest. They learned about their aggregate investments after each round, but not the decision of individual subjects. This gave them information as to whether the total investments were greater than agreed upon. In many rounds, subjects kept

---

8.   In simple, repeated public goods experiments, subjects initially tended to contribute at a higher level than predicted by the Nash equilibrium (Isaac et al. 1984, 1985, 1994; Isaac and Walker 1988; Marwell and Ames 1979) and outcomes slowly approach the predicted Nash equilibrium from a higher level. In common-pool resource games, on the other hand, subjects initially achieved outcomes that were much worse than the Nash equilibrium that they then slowly approached from below (see also Casari and Plott 2003).

their promises to each other. In other rounds, some defections did occur. Subjects used information about the aggregate investment levels to scold their unknown fellow subjects if the total investment was higher than they had agreed upon. The opportunity for repeated face-to-face communication was extremely successful in increasing joint returns. Findings from communication experiments are consistent with a large number of studies of the impact of face-to-face communication on the capacity of subjects to solve a variety of social dilemma problems (*see* E. Ostrom and Walker 1991; Orbell, van de Kragt and Dawes 1988; Sally 1995; Balliet 2010).

In many field settings, resource users have devised a variety of formal or informal ways of sanctioning one another if rules are broken, even though this behavior is not consistent with the theory of norm-free, complete rationality (Elster 1989: 40–41). It was thus important to see if subjects in a controlled experimental setting would actually use their own assets to financially punish other subjects. After subjects played ten rounds of the baseline common-pool resource game, they were told that in the subsequent rounds they would have an opportunity to pay a fee in order to impose a fine on another subject. We found much more sanctioning occurred in this design than the zero level predicted.[9] Subjects did increase gross benefits through their sanctioning but substantially reduced net returns due to the overuse of costly sanctions.[10] Sanctioning was primarily directed at those who defected, but a few sanctions appeared to be directed at low contributors as a form of revenge by those who had fined themselves. In a further design, subjects were given a chance to communicate and decide whether or not to adopt a sanctioning system of their own. Subjects who decided to adopt their own sanctioning system achieved the highest returns achieved in any of the common-pool resource laboratory experiments – 90 percent of optimal after the fines related to the small number of defections were subtracted (E. Ostrom, Walker and Gardner 1992).

The predictions of noncooperative game theory are roughly supported only when participants in a laboratory experiment do not know the reputation of the others involved in a common-pool resource dilemma and cannot communicate with them. On the other hand, when subjects communicate face-to-face, they frequently agree on joint strategies and keep to their agreements substantially increasing their net returns. Further, communication to decide on and design a sanctioning system enables those choosing this option to achieve close to optimal returns.

---

9. *See* Henrich *et al.* (2006) in which field experiments were conducted in multiple countries testing whether a much broader set of participants would also use punishments in public goods experiments. See also Henrich *et al.* (2004) for the reports of earlier field experiments of social dilemmas in 15 small communities.

10. Similar findings exist for public goods experiments where punishers typically punish low contributors (Yamagishi 1986: 185; Fehr and Gächter 2002).

B. Studying common-pool resources in field experiments

A series of field experiments have now been conducted by colleagues in Colombia to assess whether experienced villagers who are dependent on resources make decisions about the 'time spent in a forest' in a design that is mathematically consistent with those reported on above. Cardenas (2000) conducted field experiments in rural schoolhouses with over 200 users of local forests. He modified the design of the common-pool resource experiments without, and with, face-to-face communication so that villagers were asked to make decisions regarding 'harvesting trees'. The outcomes of these experiments were broadly consistent with the findings obtained with university students.

In a different design, Cardenas, Stranlund and Willis (2000) ran ten rounds of baseline experiments with resource users from five villages who were then given a chance to communicate face-to-face for the next set of experiments. In five additional villages, participants were told after the baseline rounds that a new regulation would go into force that mandated them to spend no more than the optimal time in the forest each round. The probability of an inspection was 1/16 per round – a low but realistic probability for monitoring rule conformance in rural areas in developing countries. If the person was over the limit imposed, a penalty was subtracted from that person's payoff, but the penalty was not revealed to the others. Subjects in this experimental condition increased their withdrawal levels when compared to the outcomes obtained when face-to-face communication was allowed and no rule was imposed. Other scholars have also found that externally imposed regulation that would theoretically lead to higher joint returns 'crowded out' voluntary behavior to cooperate (*see* Frey and Oberholzer-Gee 1997; Reeson and Tisdell 2008).

Fehr and Leibbrandt (2008) conducted an interesting set of public goods experiments with fishers who harvest from an 'open access' inland lake in northeastern Brazil. They found that a high percentage (87 percent) of fishers contributed in the first period of the field experiment and that contributions levelled off in the remaining periods. Fehr and Leibbrandt examined the mesh size of the nets used by individual fishermen and found that those who contributed more in the public goods experiment used nets with bigger mesh sizes. Larger mesh sizes allow young fish to escape, grow larger, and reproduce at a higher level than if they are caught when they are still small. In other words, cooperation in the field experiment was consistent with observed cooperation related to a real CPR dilemma. They conclude that the 'fact that our laboratory measure for other-regarding preferences predicts field behavior increases our confidence about the behavioural relevance of other-regarding preferences gained from laboratory experiments' (*Ibid.*: 17).

In summary, experiments on CPRs and public goods have shown that many predictions of the conventional theory of collective action do not hold. More cooperation occurs than predicted, 'cheap talk' increases cooperation, and subjects invest in sanctioning free riders. Experiments also establish that motivational heterogeneity exists in harvesting or contribution decisions as well as decisions on sanctioning.

Studying common-pool resource problems in the field

Having conducted extensive meta-analyses of case studies and experiments, we also needed to undertake field studies where we could draw on the IAD framework to design questions to obtain consistent information about key theoretically important variables across sites.

A. Comparing farmer and government managed irrigation systems in nepal

An opportunity to visit Nepal in 1988 led to the discovery of a large number of written studies of farmer built and maintained irrigation systems as well as some government constructed and managed systems. Shivakoti, Benjamin and I were able to revise the CPR coding manual so as to include variables of specific relevance to understanding irrigation systems in a new coding manual for the Nepal Irrigation and Institutions (NIIS) project. We coded existing cases and again found numerous 'missing variables' not discussed by the original author. Colleagues made several trips to Nepal to visit previously described systems in written case studies to fill in missing data and verify the data in the original study. While in the field, we were able to add new cases to the data set (Benjamin *et al.* 1994).

In undertaking analysis of this large dataset, Lam (1998) developed three performance measures that could be applied to all systems: (i) the physical condition of irrigation systems, (ii) the quantity of water available to farmers at the tail end of a system at different seasons of the year, and (iii) the agricultural productivity of the systems. Controlling for environmental differences among systems, Lam found that irrigation systems governed by the farmers themselves perform significantly better on all three performance measures. On the farmer governed systems, farmers communicate with one another at annual meetings and informally on a regular basis, develop their own agreements, establish the positions of monitors, and sanction those who do not conform to their own rules. Consequently, farmer managed systems are likely to grow more rice, distribute water more equitably, and keep their systems in better repair than government systems. While farmer systems do vary in performance, few perform as poorly as government systems – holding other relevant variables constant.

Over time, colleagues have visited and coded still further irrigation systems in Nepal. The earlier findings regarding the higher level of performance of farmer managed systems was again confirmed using the expanded database containing 229 irrigation systems (Joshi *et al.* 2000; Shivakoti and E. Ostrom 2002). Our findings are not unique to Nepal. Scholars have carefully documented effective farmer designed and operated systems in many countries including Japan (Aoki 2001), India (Meinzen-Dick 2007; Bardhan 2000) and Sri Lanka (Uphoff 1991).

B. Studying forests around the world

In 1992, Dr. M. Hoskins, who headed the Forest, Trees and People Program at the Food and Agriculture Organization (FAO) of the United Nations, asked colleagues at the Workshop to draw on our experience in studying irrigation systems to develop methods for assessing the impact of diverse forest governance arrangements in multiple countries. Two years of intense development and review by ecologists and social scientists around the world led to the development of ten research protocols to obtain reliable information about users and forest governance as well as about the ecological conditions of sampled forests. A long term collaborative research network – the International Forestry Resources and Institutions (IFRI) research program – was established with centres now located in Bolivia, Colombia, Guatemala, India, Kenya, Mexico, Nepal, Tanzania, Thailand, Uganda, and the United States, with new centres being established in Ethiopia and China (*see* Gibson, McKean and E. Ostrom 2000; Poteete and E. Ostrom 2004; Wollenberg *et al.* 2007). IFRI is unique among efforts to study forests as it is the only interdisciplinary long term monitoring and research program studying forests in multiple countries owned by governments, private organizations, and communities.

Forests are a particularly important form of common-pool resource given their role in climate change-related emissions and carbon sequestration (Canadell and Raupach 2008), the biodiversity they contain, and their contribution to rural livelihoods in developing countries. A 'favourite' policy recommendation for protecting forests and biodiversity is government owned protected areas (Terborgh 1999). In an effort to examine whether government ownership of protected areas is a necessary condition for improving forest density, Tanya Hayes (2006) used IFRI data to compare the rating of forest density (on a five point scale) assigned to a forest by the forester or ecologist who had supervised the forest mensuration of trees, shrubs, and groundcover in a random sample of forest plots.[11] Of the 163 forests included in the analysis, 76 were government owned forests legally designated as protected forests and 87 were public, private, or communally owned forested lands used for a diversity of purposes. No statistical difference existed between the forest density in officially designated protected areas versus other forested areas. Gibson, Williams and E. Ostrom (2005) examined the monitoring behavior of 178 forest user groups and found a strong correlation between the level of monitoring and a forester's assessment of forest density even when controlling for whether users were formally organized, whether the users were heavily dependent on a forest, and the level of social capital within a group.

Chhatre and Agrawal (2008) have now examined the changes in the condition of 152 forests under diverse governance arrangements as affected by the size of the forest, collective action around forests related to improvement activities, size of the user group, and the dependence of local users on a forest. They found

---

11. Extensive forest mensuration is conducted at every IFRI site at the same time that information is obtained about forest users, their activities and organization, and about governance arrangements. Comparing forest measures across ecological zones is misleading since the average diameter at breast height in a forest is strongly affected by precipitation, soils, elevation, and other factors that vary dramatically across ecological zones. Thus, we ask the forester or ecologist who has just supervised the collection of forest data to rate the forest on a five point scale from very sparse to very abundant.

that 'forests with a higher probability of regeneration are likely to be small to medium in size with low levels of subsistence dependence, low commercial value, high levels of local enforcement, and strong collective action for improving the quality of the forest' (*Ibid.*: 1327). In a second major analysis, Chhatre and Agrawal (2009) focus on factors that affect trade-offs and synergies between the level of carbon storage in forests and their contributions to livelihoods. They find that larger forests are more effective in enhancing both carbon and livelihoods outcomes, particularly when local communities also have high levels of rule-making autonomy. Recent studies by Coleman (2009) and Coleman and Steed (2009) also find that a major variable affecting forest conditions is the investment by local users in monitoring. Further, when local users are given harvesting rights, they are more likely to monitor illegal uses themselves. Other focused studies also stress the relationship between local monitoring and better forest conditions (Ghate and Nagendra 2005; E. Ostrom and Nagendra 2006; Banana and Gombya-Ssembajjwe 2000; Webb and Shivakoti 2008).

The legal designation of a forest as a protected area is not by itself related to forest density. Detailed field studies of monitoring and enforcement as they are conducted on the ground, however, illustrate the challenge of achieving high levels of forest regrowth without active involvement of local forest users (*see* Batistella, Robeson and Moran 2003; Agrawal 2005; Andersson, Gibson and Lehoucq 2006; Tucker 2008). Our research shows that forests under different property regimes – government, private, communal – sometimes meet enhanced social goals such as biodiversity protection, carbon storage, or improved livelihoods. At other times, these property regimes fail to provide such goals. Indeed, when governments adopt top-down decentralization policies leaving local officials and users in the dark, stable forests may become subject to deforestation (Banana *et al.* 2007). Thus, it is not the general type of forest governance that is crucial in explaining forest conditions; rather, it is how a particular governance arrangement fits the local ecology, how specific rules are developed and adapted over time, and whether users consider the system to be legitimate and equitable (for a more detailed overview of the IFRI research program, *see* Poteete, Janssen, and E. Ostrom 2010: chap. 5).

Current theoretical developments

Given the half century of our own extensive empirical research and that of many distinguished scholars (e.g. Baland and Platteau 2005; Berkes 2007; Berkes, Colding, and Folke 2003; Clark 2006; Marshall 2008; Schelling 1960, 1978, 1984), where are we now? What have we learned? We now know that the earlier theories of rational, but helpless, individuals who are trapped in social dilemmas are not supported by a large number of studies using diverse methods (Faysse 2005; Poteete, Janssen and E. Ostrom 2010). On the other hand, we cannot be overly optimistic and presume that dilemmas will always be solved by those involved. Many groups have struggled and failed (Dietz, E. Ostrom and Stern 2003). Further, simple policy prescriptions to turn over resources to a government, to privatize, or more recently to decentralize, may also fail (Berkes 2007; Brock and Carpenter 2007; Meinzen-Dick 2007).

We thus face the tough task of further developing our theories to help understand and predict when those involved in a common-pool resource dilemma will be able to self-organize and how various aspects of the broad context they face affect their strategies, the short term success of their efforts, and the long term robustness of their initial achievements. We need to develop a better theoretical understanding of human behavior as well as of the impact of the diverse contexts that humans face.

A. Developing a more general theory of the individual

As discussed earlier in Section III, efforts to explain phenomena in the social world are organized at three levels of generality. Frameworks, such as the IAD that have been used to organize diverse efforts to study common-pool resources, are metatheoretical devices that help provide a general language for describing relationships at multiple levels and scales. Theories are efforts to build understanding by making core assumptions about specific working parts of frequently encountered phenomena and predicting general outcomes. Models are very specific working examples of a theory – and they are frequently confused with being theories themselves. As Alchian (1950) pointed out long ago, what is called 'rational choice theory' is not a broad theory of human behavior but rather a useful model to predict behavior in a particular situation – a highly competitive market for private goods. Predictions derived from the rational choice model are empirically supported in open markets for private goods and other competitive environments (Holt 2007; Smith and Walker 1993; Satz and Ferejohn 1994). Thus, it is a useful model to retain for predicting outcomes in competitive settings related to excludable and divisible outcomes.

While it is not possible yet to point to a single theory of human behavior that has been successfully formulated and tested in a variety of settings, scholars are currently positing and testing assumptions that are likely to be at the core of future developments (Smith 2003, 2010). These relate to (i) the capability of boundedly rational individuals to learn fuller and more reliable information in repeated situations when reliable feedback is present, (ii) the use of heuristics in making daily decisions, and (iii) the preferences that individuals have related to benefits for self as well as norms and preferences related to benefits for others (*see* Poteete, Janssen and E. Ostrom 2010: chap. 9; E. Ostrom 1998).

The assumption that individuals have complete information about all actions available to them, the likely strategies that others will adopt, and the probabilities of specific consequences that will result from their own choices must be rejected in any but the very simplest of repeated settings. When boundedly rational individuals do interact over time, it is reasonable to assume that they learn more accurate information about the actions they can take and the likely actions of other individuals (Selten 1990; Simon 1955, 1999). Some highly complex common-pool resource environments, however, approach mathematical chaos (J. Wilson *et al.* 1994) in which resource users cannot gain complete information about all likely combinations of future events.

Figure 6.5: Microsituational and Broader Contexts of Social Dilemmas Affect Levels of Trust and Cooperation

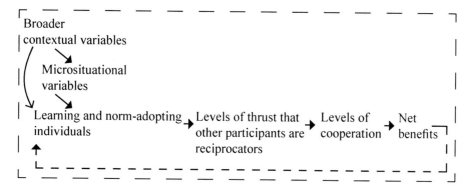

Source: Poteete, Janssen, and Ostrom 2010: 227.

In many situations, individuals use rules of thumb – heuristics – that they have learned over time that work relatively well in a particular setting. Fishers end up 'fishing for knowledge' (Wilson 1990) where using heuristics over time enables them to recognize diverse clues of environmental processes that they need to take into account when making their own decisions. When individuals do interact repeatedly, it is possible to learn heuristics that approach 'best response' strategies and achieve close to local optima (Gigerenzer and Selten 2001). In eras of rapid change or sudden shocks, however, heuristics may not enable individuals to achieve high payoffs.

Individuals also learn norms – internal valuations that are negative or positive related to specific actions such as lying or being brave in particular situations (Crawford and E. Ostrom 2005). The strength of an internal commitment (Sen 1977) may be represented in the size of the internal weight that an individual assigns to actions and outcomes in a particular setting. Among individual norms are those related to valuing outcomes achieved by others (Cox and Deck 2005; Cox, Sadiraj and Sadiraj 2008; Andreoni 1989; Bolton and Ockenfels 2000). Fehr and Schmidt (1999) propose that individuals dislike unequal outcomes of interactions and thus have an internal norm of 'inequity aversion'. Axelrod (1986) posits that individuals who adopt meta norms related to whether others follow the norms that have evolved in a group increase the probability that norms will be followed. Leibbrandt, Gneezy and List (2010) show that individuals who regularly work in teams are more likely to adopt norms and trust each other more than individuals working alone. Frohlich and Oppenheimer (1992) posit that many individuals adopt norms of fairness and justice. Not all individuals have the same norms or perceptions of a situation (Ones and Putterman 2007) and may differ substantially in whether they consider a way of sharing costs to be fair (Eckel and Grossman 1996).

Simply assuming that humans adopt norms, however, is not sufficient to predict behavior in a social dilemma, especially in very large groups with no arrangements for communication. Even with strong preferences to follow norms, 'observed behavior may vary by context because the perception of the "right thing" would change' (de Oliveira, Croson and Eckel 2009: 19). Various aspects of the context in which individuals interact affect how individuals learn about the situation they are in and about the others with whom they are interacting. Individual differences do make a difference, but the context of interactions also affects behavior over time (Walker and E. Ostrom 2009). Biologists recognize that an organism's appearance and behavior are affected by the environment in which it develops.

> For example, some plants produce large, thin leaves (which enhance photosynthetic photon harvest) in low light, and narrow, thicker leaves (which conserve water) in high light; certain insects develop wings only if they live in crowded conditions (and hence are likely to run out of adequate food in their current location). Such environmentally contingent development is so commonplace that it can be regarded as a universal property of living things. (Pfennig and Ledón-Rettig 2009: 268)

Social scientists also need to recognize that individual behavior is strongly affected by the context in which interactions take place rather than being simply a result of individual differences.

B. The central role of trust in coping with dilemmas

Even though Arrow (1974) long ago pointed to the crucial role of trust among participants as the most efficient mechanism to enhance transactional outcomes, collective action theory has paid more attention to payoff functions than to how individuals build trust that others are reciprocators of costly cooperative efforts. Empirical studies, however, confirm the important role of trust in overcoming social dilemmas (Rothstein 2005). As illustrated in Figure 6.5, the updated theoretical assumptions of learning and norm-adopting individuals can be used as the foundation for understanding how individuals may gain increased levels of trust in others, leading to more cooperation and higher benefits with feedback mechanisms that reinforce positive or negative learning. Thus, it is not only that individuals adopt norms but also that the structure of the situation generates sufficient information about the likely behavior of others to be trustworthy reciprocators who will bear their share of the costs of overcoming a dilemma. Thus, in some contexts, one can move beyond the presumption that rational individuals are helpless in overcoming social dilemma situations.

C. The microsituational level of analysis

Asserting that context makes a difference in building or destroying trust and reciprocity is not a sufficient theoretical answer to how and why individuals sometimes solve and sometimes fail to solve dilemmas. Individuals interacting in a dilemma situation face two contexts: (i) a microcontext related to the specific attributes of an action situation in which individuals are directly interacting and (ii) the broader context of the social-ecological system in which groups of individuals make decisions. A major advantage of studies conducted in an experimental lab or in field experiments is that the researcher designs the micro setting in which the experiment is conducted. Thus, empirical results are growing (and are summarized in Poteete, Janssen and E. Ostrom 2010) to establish that the following attributes of microsituations affect the level of cooperation that participants achieve in social dilemma settings (including both public goods and common-pool resource dilemmas).

i. Communication is feasible with the full set of participants. When face-to-face communication is possible, participants use facial expressions, physical actions, and the way that words are expressed to judge the trustworthiness of the others involved.

ii. Reputations of participants are known. Knowing the past history of other participants, who may not be personally known prior to interaction, increases the likelihood of cooperation.

iii. High marginal per capita return (MPCR). When MPCR is high, each participant can know that their own contributions make a bigger difference than with low MPCR, and that others are more likely to recognize this relationship.

iv. Entry or exit capabilities. If participants can exit a situation at low cost, this gives them an opportunity not to be a sucker, and others can recognize that cooperators may leave (and enter other situations) if their cooperation is not reciprocated.

v. Longer time horizon. Participants can anticipate that more could be earned through cooperation over a long time period versus a short time.

vi. Agreed-upon sanctioning capabilities. While external sanctions or imposed sanctioning systems may reduce cooperation, when participants themselves agree to a sanctioning system they frequently do not need to use sanctions at a high volume, and net benefits can be improved substantially.

Other microsituational variables are being tested in experiments around the world. The central core of the findings is that when individuals face a social dilemma in a microsetting, they are more likely to cooperate when situational variables increase the likelihood of gaining trust that others will reciprocate.

D. The broader context in the field

Individuals coping with common-pool resource dilemmas in the field are also affected by a broader set of contextual variables related to the attributes of the social-ecological system (SES) in which they are interacting. A group of scholars in Europe and the United States are currently working on the further development of a framework that links the IAD and its interactions and outcomes at a micro level with a broader set of variables observed in the field.[12] As illustrated in Figure 6.6, one can think of individuals interacting in an Action Situation generating Interactions and Outcomes that are affected by and affect a Resource System, Resource Units, Governance System, and Users who affect and are affected by Social, Economic, and Political Settings, and Related Ecosystems (*see* E. Ostrom 2007, 2009). Figure 6.6 provides an overview of the highest tier of variables that exist in all field settings. The highest tier can be unpacked several times when one is trying to analyse specific questions related to SESs in the field, but there is not enough time or space to undertake a thorough unpacking in this [chapter].

Experimental researchers have reached a higher level of agreement about the impact of microsituational variables on the incentives, levels of trust, and behavior of individuals in dilemma situations than exists among field researchers. Few SES variables have a fully independent impact on the action situations that participants face and their likely behavior. The SES variables that are most important differ depending on which interactions (such as monitoring, conflict, lobbying, self-organization) or longer term outcomes (such as overharvesting, regeneration of biodiversity, resilience of an ecological system to human and nature induced disturbances) one wishes to predict. A set of ten variables have been identified across many field studies as impacting the likelihood of users self-organizing in order to overcome a common-pool resource dilemma (E. Ostrom 2009; Basurto and E. Ostrom 2009). These include: the size, productivity, and predictability of the resource system, the extent of mobility of the resource units, the existence of collective choice rules that the users may adopt authoritatively in order to change their own operational rules, and four attributes of users (the number, the existence of leadership/entrepreneurship, knowledge about the SES, and the importance of the SES to the users). Linking the broader contextual variables and microcontextual variables is one of the major tasks facing scientists who work across disciplinary lines to understand how both social and ecological factors affect human behavior.[13]

---

12. Scholars at the Stockholm Environment Institute, the International Institute for Applied Systems Analysis, Delft University of Technology, the University of Zurich, the Nordland Research Institute of Bodø University College, the Potsdam Institute for Climate Impact Research (PIK), Humboldt University, Marburg University, and the EU NeWATER project located at the University of Osnabrück have had several meetings in Europe to begin plans for using a common framework (initially developed by E. Ostrom 2007) to study a variety of resource systems. Scholars at the Workshop in Bloomington and the Center for the Study of Institutional Diversity at Arizona State University will also participate in this effort. A core problem identified by these scholars is the lack of cumulation across studies on diverse natural resource systems as well as humanly engineered resources.

13. *See* Stewart (2009) for an important study that links size of group, acceptance of norms of cooperation, and support of property rights in 25 mining camps in the American Southwest.

Figure 6.6: Action Situations Embedded in Broader Social-Ecological Systems

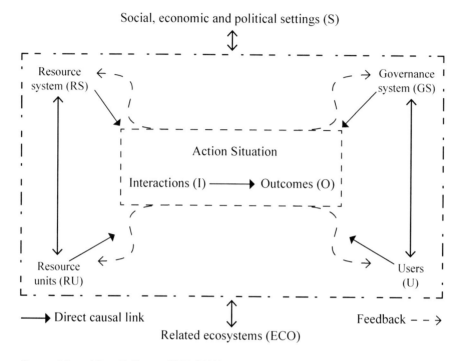

Source: Adapted from E. Ostrom 2007: 15182.

Complexity and reform

The economic and social sciences have significantly moved ahead over the past five decades since scholars posited two optimal organizational forms, two types of goods, and one model of the individual. Extensive empirical research documents the diversity of settings in which individuals solve common-pool resource problems on their own, when these solutions are sustainable over long periods of time, and how larger institutional arrangements enhance or detract from the capabilities of individuals at smaller scales to solve problems efficiently and sustainably (*see*, for example, Agrawal and Gibson 2001; Gibson *et al.* 2005; Schlager and Blomquist 2008). While there is not yet a single well developed theory that explains all of the diverse outcomes obtained in microsettings, such as the experimental lab, or broader contextual settings of fisheries, irrigation systems, forests, lakes, and other common-pool resources, considerable agreement does exist. Nor do we have a single normative theory of justice that can unambiguously be applied to all settings (Sen 2009).

Building trust in one another and developing institutional rules that are well matched to the ecological systems being used are of central importance for solving social dilemmas. The surprising but repeated finding that users of resources that are in relatively good condition – or even improving – do invest in various ways of monitoring one another relates to the core problem of building trust.

Unfortunately, policy analysts, public officials, and scholars who still apply simple mathematical models to the analysis of field settings have not yet absorbed the central lessons articulated here. All too often a single policy prescription – such as Individual Transferable Quotas (ITQs) is recommended for all resources of a particular type, such as all fisheries. While several ITQ systems are working successfully, the time and effort needed to tailor the broad theoretical concept of an ITQ system into an operational system in a particular location involves multiple years of hard work by the fishers involved as well as the government officials (*see* Clark 2006; Yandle 2007; Yandle and Dewees 2003; Eggertsson 1990).

Other scholars propose government-owned protected areas as the 'only' way to ensure that biodiversity is protected around the world (Terborgh 1999). Careful studies of protected areas have found, however, that the frequent eviction of indigenous peoples who had lived in a region for multiple centuries prior to the establishment of the park in their territory has not produced the positive results expected. Using remote sensing, Liu *et al.* (2001) assessed that the rate of loss and fragmentation of high quality habitat after the Wolong Nature Reserve was established in southwestern China was much higher than before the reserve was created. Brockington and Igoe (2006) reviewed 250 reports on protected areas and the level of evictions from them and conclude that 'forced relocation inflicts considerable material and psychological harm. But it is not just damaging for its material effects, rather for the reshaping of landscape and memory it imposes' (*Ibid.*: 246). Barton Bray and colleagues (2004) made a detailed study of another type of reform that created a forested landscape that was inhabited and productively used. Using Landsat images, they found a very 'low incidence of net deforestation, 0.01 percent for the 1984–2000 period, the lowest recorded deforestation rate for southeastern Mexico' (*Ibid.*: 333) based on a reform that created common property institutions.

A positive development of recent research is that more scholars are carefully assessing diverse policies adopted for the governance of common-pool resources (Copeland and Taylor 2009). In light of a comparative study of private, community, and state governed common-pool resources, Grafton (2000) found each to be successful when well matched to local settings and involving the active participation of local users.

> Each is capable of preventing resource degradation and ensuring the on-going flow of benefits to resource users. A comparison of the bundle of rights of the three regimes suggests that a common factor in ensuring successful governance of CPRs is the active participation of resource users in the management of the flow of benefits from the resources. (Grafton 2000: 515)

Brooks *et al.* (2006) reviewed data generated by 124 conservation projects and found that allowing local users to harvest and sell some products and involving communities in the design and administration of a project were all important factors for successful outcomes. Moving away from the presumption that the government must solve all common-pool resource problems while recognizing the important role of governments is a big step forward. Hopefully, in the future, more national officials will learn to work with local and regional officials, nongovernmental organizations, and local groups of citizens.

The most important lesson for public policy analysis derived from the intellectual journey I have outlined here is that humans have a more complex motivational structure and more capability to solve social dilemmas than posited in earlier rational-choice theory. Designing institutions to force (or nudge) entirely self-interested individuals to achieve better outcomes has been the major goal posited by policy analysts for governments to accomplish for much of the past half century. Extensive empirical research leads me to argue that instead, a core goal of public policy should be to facilitate the development of institutions that bring out the best in humans. We need to ask how diverse polycentric institutions help or hinder the innovativeness, learning, adapting, trustworthiness, levels of cooperation of participants, and the achievement of more effective, equitable, and sustainable outcomes at multiple scales (Toonen 2010).

To explain the world of interactions and outcomes occurring at multiple levels, we also have to be willing to deal with complexity instead of rejecting it. Some mathematical models are very useful for explaining outcomes in particular settings. We should continue to use simple models where they capture enough of the core underlying structure and incentives that they usefully predict outcomes. When the world we are trying to explain and improve, however, is not well described by a simple model, we must continue to improve our frameworks and theories so as to be able to understand complexity and not simply reject it.

References

Acheson, J. M. and Gardner, R. (2005) 'Spatial Strategies and Territoriality in the Maine Lobster Industry', *Rationality and Society*, 17 (3): 309–41.

Agrawal, A. (2005) *Environmentality: Technologies of Government and the Making of Subjects*, Durham, NC: Duke University Press.

Agrawal, A. and Gibson, C. (ed.) (2001) *Communities and the Environment: Ethnicity, Gender, and the State in Community-Based Conservation*, New Brunswick, NJ: Rutgers University Press.

Alchian, A. A. (1950) 'Uncertainty, Evolution, and Economic Theory', *Journal of Political Economy*, 58 (3): 211–21.

Alchian, A. A. and Demsetz, H. (1973) 'The Property Rights Paradigm', *Journal of Economic History*, 33 (1): 16–27.

Allport, F. H. (1962) 'A Structuronomic Conception of Behavior: Individual and Collective', *Journal of Abnormal and Social Psychology*, 64 (1): 3–30.

Anderson, T. L. and Hill, P. J. (1990) 'The Race for Property Rights', *Journal of Law and Economics*, 33 (1): 177–97.

Anderson, W. and Weidner, E. W. (1950) *American City Government*, New York: Henry Holt.

Andersson, K. P. and Ostrom, E. (2008) 'Analysing Decentralized Resource Regimes from a Polycentric Perspective', *Policy Sciences*, 41(1): 71–93.

Andersson, K. P., Gibson, C. C. and Fabrice L. (2006) 'Municipal Politics and Forest Governance: Comparative Analysis of Decentralization in Bolivia and Guatemala', *World Development*, 34 (3): 576–95.

Andreoni, J. (1989) 'Giving with Impure Altruism: Applications to Charity and Ricardian Equivalence', *Journal of Political Economy*, 97 (6): 1447–58.

Aoki, M. (2001) *Toward a Comparative Institutional Analysis*, Cambridge, MA: MIT Press.

Arrow, K. J. (1974) *The Limits of Organization*, New York: Norton.

Axelrod, R. (1986) 'An Evolutionary Approach to Norms', *American Political Science Review*, 80 (4): 1095–111.

Bain, J. S. (1959) *Industrial Organization*, New York: Wiley.

Baland, J.-M. and Platteau, J.-P. (2005) *Halting Degradation of Natural Resources: Is There a Role for Rural Communities?*, Oxford: Clarendon Press.

Balliet, D. (2010) 'Communication and Cooperation in Social Dilemmas: A Meta-Analytic Review', *Journal of Conflict Resolution*, 54 (1): 39–57.

Banana, A. Y. and Gombya-Ssembajjwe, W. (20000 'Successful Forest Management: The Importance of Security of Tenure and Rule Enforcement in Ugandan Forests', in C. C. Gibson, M. A. McKean and E. Ostrom (eds) *People and Forests: Communities, Institutions, and Governance*, Cambridge, MA: MIT Press, pp. 87–98.

Banana, A., Vogt, N. D. Bahati, J. and Gombya-Ssembajjwe, W. (2007) 'Decentralized Governance and Ecological Health: Why Local Institutions Fail to Moderate Deforestation in Mpigi District of Uganda', *Scientific Research and Essays*, 2 (10): 434–45.

Bardhan, P. (2000) 'Irrigation and Cooperation: An Empirical Analysis of 48 Irrigation Communities in South India', *Economic Development and Cultural Change*, 48 (4): 847–65.

Basurto, X. and Ostrom, E. (2009) 'Beyond the Tragedy of the Commons', *Economia delle fonti di energia e dell'ambiente*, 52 (1): 35–60.

Batistella, M., Robeson, S. and Moran, E. F. (2003) 'Settlement Design, Forest Fragmentation, and Landscape Change in Rondonia, Amazonia', *Photogrammetric Engineering and Remote Sensing*, 69 (7): 805–12.

Bell, F. W. (1972) 'Technological Externalities and Common-Property Resources: An Empirical Study of the U.S. Northern Lobster Fishery', *Journal of Political Economy*, 80 (1): 148–58.

Benjamin, P., Lam, W. F., Ostrom, E. and Shivakoti. G. (1994) *Institutions, Incentives, and Irrigation in Nepal*, Burlington, VT: Associates in Rural Development.

Berkes, F. (2007) 'Community-Based Conservation in a Globalized World', *Proceedings of the National Academy of Sciences*, 104 (39): 15188–93.

Berkes, F., Colding, J. and Folke, C. (2003) *Navigating Social-Ecological Systems: Building Resilience for Complexity and Change*, Cambridge, UK: Cambridge University Press.

Blomquist, W., Schlager, E., Tang, S. Y. and Ostrom. E. (1994) 'Regularities from the Field and Possible Explanations', in E. Ostrom, R. Gardner and J. Walker (eds) *Rules, Games, and Common-Pool Resources*, A. Arbor, MI: University of Michigan Press, pp. 301–318.

Bolton, G. E. and Ockenfels, A. (20000 'ERC: A Theory of Equity, Reciprocity, and Competition', *American Economic Review*, 90(1): 166–193.

Boyd, R. and Richerson, P. J. (1985) *Culture and the Evolutionary Process*, Chicago: University of Chicago Press.

Bray, D., Barton, Ellis, E. A., Armijo-Canto, N. and Beck, C. T. (2004) 'The Institutional Drivers of Sustainable Landscapes: A Case Study of the 'Mayan Zone' in Quintana Roo, Mexico', *Land Use Policy*, 21 (4): 333–46.

Brock, W. A. and Carpenter, S. R. (2007) 'Panaceas and Diversification of Environmental Policy', *Proceedings of the National Academy of Sciences*, 104 (39): 15206–11.

Brockington, D. and Igoe, J. (2006) 'Eviction for Conservation: A Global Overview', *Conservation and Society*, 4 (3): 424–70.

Bromley, D. W. (1986) 'Closing Comments at the Conference on Common Property Resource Management', *Proceedings of the Conference on Common Property Resource Management*, Washington, DC: National Academies Press, pp. 591–98.

Brooks, J. S., Franzen, M. A., Holmes, C. M., Grote, M. N. and Borgerhoff Mulder, M. (2006) 'Testing Hypotheses for the Success of Different Conservation Strategies', *Conservation Biology*, 20 (5): 1528–38.

Brunckhorst, D. J. (2000) *Bioregional Planning: Resource Management beyond the New Millennium*, Amsterdam: Harwood Academic.

Buchanan, J. M. (1965) 'An Economic Theory of Clubs', *Economica*, 32 (125): 1–14.

Canadell, J. G. and Raupach, M. R. (2008) 'Managing Forests for Climate Change Mitigation', *Science*, 320 (5882): 1456–57.

Cardenas, J -C. (2000) 'How Do Groups Solve Local Commons Dilemmas? Lessons from Experimental Economics in the Field', *Environment, Development and Sustainability*, 2 (3–4): 305–22.

Cardenas, J.-C., Stranlund, J. and Willis, C. (2000) 'Local Environmental Control and Institutional Crowding-Out', *World Development*, 28 (10): 1719–33.

Casari, M. and Plott, C. R. (2003) 'Decentralized Management of Common Property Resources: Experiments with a Centuries-Old Institution', *Journal of Economic Behavior and Organisation*, 51 (2): 217–47.

Caves, R. (1964) *American Industry: Structure, Conduct, Performance*, Englewood Cliffs, NJ: Prentice-Hall.

Chhatre, A. and Agrawal, A. (2008) 'Forest Commons and Local Enforcement', *Proceedings of the National Academy of Sciences*, 105(36): 13286–91.

—— (2009) 'Trade-offs and Synergies between Carbon Storage and Livelihood Benefits from Forest Commons', *Proceedings of the National Academy of Sciences*, 106 (42): 17667–70.

Ciriacy-Wantrup, S. V. and Bishop. R. C. (1975) 'Common Property' as a Concept in Natural Resources Policy', *Natural Resources Journal*, 15 (4) 713–27.

Clark, C. W. (2006) *The Worldwide Crisis in Fisheries: Economic Models and Human Behavior*, Cambridge, UK: Cambridge University Press.

Coleman, E. A. (2009) 'Institutional Factors Affecting Biophysical Outcomes in Forest Management', *Journal of Policy Analysis and Management*, 28 (1): 122–46.

Coleman, E. A. and Steed, B. C. (2009) 'Monitoring and Sanctioning in the Commons: An Application to Forestry', *Ecological Economics*, 68 (7): 2106–13.

Commons, J. R. (1968) *Legal Foundations of Capitalism*, Madison, WI: University of Wisconsin Press. (Orig. Pub. 1924).

Copeland, B. R. and Taylor, M. S. (2009) 'Trade, Tragedy, and the Commons', *American Economic Review*, 99 (3): 725–49.

Coward, E. W. (1980) *Irrigation and Agricultural Development in Asia*, Ithaca, NY: Cornell University Press.

Cox, J. C. and Deck, C. A. (2005) 'On the Nature of Reciprocal Motives', *Economic Inquiry*, 43 (3): 623–35.

Cox, J. C., Sadiraj, K. and Sadiraj, V. (2008) 'Implications of Trust, Fear, and Reciprocity for Modelling Economic Behavior', *Experimental Economics*, 11 (1): 1–24.

Cox, M., Arnold, G. and Villamayor-Tomás, S. (2009) *A Review and Reassessment of Design Principles for Community-Based Natural Resource Management,* Unpublished.

Crawford, S. E. S. and Ostrom, E. (2005) 'A Grammar of Institutions', *Understanding Institutional Diversity*, Princeton, NJ: Princeton University Press, pp. 137–74.

Degnbol, P. and McCay. B. J. (2007) 'Unintended and Perverse Consequences of Ignoring Linkages in Fisheries Systems', *ICES Journal of Marine Science*, 64 (4): 793–97.

de Oliveira, A. C. M., Croson, R. T. A. and Eckel, C. (2009) 'Are Preferences Stable across Domains? An Experimental Investigation of Social Preferences in the Field', *CBEES Working Paper*, 2008–3.

Dietz, T., Ostrom, E. and Stern, P. C. (2003) 'The Struggle to Govern the Commons', *Science*, 302 (5652): 1907–12.

Dutta, P. K. (1999) *Strategies and Games: Theory and Practice*, Cambridge, MA: MIT Press.

Eckel, C. C. and Grossman, P. J. (1996) 'The Relative Price of Fairness: Gender Differences in a Punishment Game', *Journal of Economic Behavior and Organization*, 30 (2): 143–58.

Eggertsson, T. (1990) *Economic Behavior and Institutions*, Cambridge, UK: Cambridge University Press.

Elster, J. (1989) *Solomonic Judgements: Studies in the Limitations of Rationality*, Cambridge, UK: Cambridge University Press.

Faysse, N. (2005) 'Coping with the Tragedy of the Commons: Game Structure and Design of Rules', *Journal of Economic Surveys*, 19 (2): 239–61.

Fehr, E. and Gächter, S. (2002) 'Altruistic Punishment in Humans', *Nature*, 415 (6868): 137–40.

Fehr, E. and Leibbrandt, A. (2008) 'Cooperativeness and Impatience in the Tragedy of the Commons', *IZA Discussion Paper*, 3625.

Fehr, E. and Schmidt, K. M. (1999) 'A Theory of Fairness, Competition, and Cooperation', *Quarterly Journal of Economics*, 114 (3): 817–68.

Frey, B. S. and Oberholzer-Gee, F. (1997) 'The Cost of Price Incentives: An Empirical Analysis of Motivation Crowding-Out', *American Economic Review*, 87 (4): 746–55.

Friesema, H. P. (1966) 'The Metropolis and the Maze of Local Government', *Urban Affairs Review*, 2 (2): 68–90.

Frohlich, N. and Oppenheimer, J. A. (1992) *Choosing Justice: An Experimental Approach to Ethical Theory*, Berkeley, CA: University of California Press.

Gardner, R., Herr, A., Ostrom, E. and Walker, J. A. (2000) 'The Power and Limitations of Proportional Cutbacks in Common-Pool Resources', *Journal of Development Economics*, 62 (2): 515–33.

Ghate, R. and Nagendra, H. (2005) 'Role of Monitoring in Institutional Performance: Forest Management in Maharashtra, India', *Conservation and Society*, 3 (2): 509–32.

Gibson, C. C., McKean, M. and Ostrom, E. (eds) (2000) *People and Forests: Communities, Institutions, and Governance*, Cambridge, MA: MIT Press.

Gibson, C. C., Williams, J. T. and Ostrom, E. (2005) 'Local Enforcement and Better Forests', *World Development*, 33 (2): 273–84.

Gibson, C. C., Andersson, K., Ostrom, E. and Shivakumar, S. (2005) *The Samaritan's Dilemma: The Political Economy of Development Aid*, Oxford: Oxford University Press.

Gigerenzer, G. and Selten, R. (eds) (2001) *Bounded Rationality: The Adaptive Toolbox,* Cambridge, MA: MIT Press.

Goffman, E. (1974) *Frame Analysis: An Essay on the Organization of Experience,* Cambridge, MA: Harvard University Press.

Gordon, H. S. (1954) 'The Economic Theory of a Common-Property Resource: The Fishery', *Journal of Political Economy,* 62 (2): 124–42.

Grafton, R. Q. (2000) 'Governance of the Commons: A Role for the State?', *Land Economics,* 76 (4): 504–17.

Gulick, L. (1957) 'Metropolitan Organization', *The Annals of the American Academy of Political and Social Science,* 314 (1): 57–65.

Hardin, G. (1968) 'The Tragedy of the Commons', *Science,* 162(3859): 1243–48.

Hayes, T. M. (2006) 'Parks, People, and Forest Protection: An Institutional Assessment of the Effectiveness of Protected Areas', *World Development,* 34 (12): 2064–75.

Henrich, J., Boyd, R., Bowles, S., Camerer, C., Ernst F. and Gintis, H. (eds) (2004) *Foundations of Human Sociality: Economic Experiments and Ethnographic Evidence from Fifteen Small-Scale Societies,* Oxford: Oxford University Press.

Henrich, J., McElreath, R., Barr, A., Ensminger, J., Barrett, C., Bolyanatz, A., Cardenas, J.-C. *et al.* (2006) 'Costly Punishment across Human Societies', *Science,* 312 (5781): 1767–70.

Hobbes, T. (1651 [1960]) *Leviathan or the Matter, Forme and Power of a Commonwealth Ecclesiasticall and Civil,* Oxford: Basil Blackwell.

Holt, C. A. (2007) *Markets, Games, and Strategic Behavior,* Boston: Pearson Addison Wesley.

Isaac, R. M. and Walker, J. M. (1988) 'Communication and Free-Riding Behavior: The Voluntary Contribution Mechanism', *Economic Inquiry,* 26 (4): 585–608.

Isaac, R. M., McCue, K. F. and Plott, C. R. (1985) 'Public Goods Provision in an Experimental Environment', *Journal of Public Economics,* 26 (1): 51–74.

Isaac, R. M., Walker, J. M. and Thomas, S. H. (1984) 'Divergent Evidence on Free Riding: An Experimental Examination of Possible Explanations', *Public Choice,* 43 (2): 113–49.

Isaac, R. M., Walker, J. M. and Williams, A. W. (1994) 'Group Size and the Voluntary Provision of Public Goods: Experimental Evidence Utilizing Large Groups', *Journal of Public Economics,* 54 (1): 1–36.

IsHak, S. (1972) 'Consumers' Perception of Police Performance: Consolidation *vs.* Deconcentration: The Case of Grand Rapids, Michigan', PhD diss., Indiana University.

Jager, W. and Janssen, M. A. (2002) 'Using Artificial Agents to Understand Laboratory Experiments of Common-Pool Resources with Real Agents', in M. A. Janssen (ed.) *Complexity and Ecosystem Management: The Theory and Practice of Multi-Agent Systems,* Cheltenham, UK: Elgar, pp. 75–102.

Janssen, M A. (2008) 'Evolution of Cooperation in a One-Shot Prisoner's Dilemma Based on Recognition of Trustworthy and Untrustworthy Agents', *Journal of Economic Behavior and Organisation*, 65 (3–4): 458–71.

Joshi, N N., Ostrom, E., Shivakoti, G. P. and Lam, W. F. (2000) 'Institutional Opportunities and Constraints in the Performance of Farmer-Managed Irrigation Systems in Nepal', *Asia-Pacific Journal of Rural Development*, 10 (2): 67–92.

Kiser, L. L. and Ostrom, E. (1982) 'The Three Worlds of Action: A Metatheoretical Synthesis of Institutional Approaches', in E. Osrom (ed.) *Strategies of Political Inquiry*, Beverly Hills, CA: Sage, pp. 179–222.

Koestler, A. (1973) 'The Tree and the Candle', in W. Gray and N. D. Rizzo (eds) *Unity through Diversity: A Festschrift for Ludwig von Bertalanffy*, New York: Gordon and Breach Science Publishers, pp. 287–314.

Lam, W. F. (1998) *Governing Irrigation Systems in Nepal: Institutions, Infrastructure, and Collective Action*, Oakland, CA: ICS Press.

Leibbrandt, A., Gneezy, U. and List, J. (2010) *Ode to the Sea: The Socio-Ecological Underpinnings of Social Norms*, Unpublished.

Liu, J., Linderman, M., Ouyang, Z., An, L., Yang, J. and Zhang, H. (2001) 'Ecological Degradation in Protected Areas: The Case of Wolong Nature Reserve for Giant Pandas', *Science*, 292 (5514): 98–101.

Marshall, G. R. (2008) 'Nesting, Subsidiarity, and Community-Based Environmental Governance beyond the Local Level', *International Journal of the Commons*, 2 (1): 75–97.

Marwell, G. and Ames, R. E. (1979) 'Experiments on the Provision of Public Goods I: Resources, Interest, Group Size, and the Free Rider Problem', *American Journal of Sociology*, 84 (6): 1335–60.

McCay, B. J. and Acheson, J. M. (1987) *The Question of the Commons: The Culture and Ecology of Communal Resources*, Tucson, AZ: University of Arizona Press.

McGinnis, M. D. (ed.) (1999a) *Polycentric Governance and Development: Readings from the Workshop in Political Theory and Policy Analysis*, A. Arbor, MI: University of Michigan Press.

— (ed.) (1999b) *Polycentricity and Local Public Economies: Readings from the Workshop in Political Theory and Policy Analysis*, A. Arbor, MI: University of Michigan Press.

— (2000) *Polycentric Games and Institutions: Readings from the Workshop in Political Theory and Policy Analysis*, A. Arbor, MI: University of Michigan Press.

Meinzen-Dick, R. (2007) 'Beyond Panaceas in Water Institutions', *Proceedings of the National Academy of Sciences*, 104 (39): 15200–05.

National Research Council (1986) *Proceedings of the Conference on Common Property Resource Management*, Washington, DC: National Academies Press.

Netting, R. McC. (1972) 'Of Men and Meadows: Strategies of Alpine Land Use', *Anthropological Quarterly*, 45 (3): 132–44.

North, D. C. (1990) *Institutions, Institutional Change and Economic Performance*, Cambridge, UK: Cambridge University Press.

—— (2005) *Understanding the Process of Economic Change*, Princeton, NJ: Princeton University Press.

Oakerson, R. J. (1986) 'A Model for the Analysis of Common Property Problems', *Proceedings of the Conference on Common Property Resource Management*, 13–30, Washington, DC: National Academies Press.

Ones, U. and Putterman, L. (2007) 'The Ecology of Collective Action: A Public Goods and Sanctions Experiment with Controlled Group Formation', *Journal of Economic Behavior and Organisation*, 62 (4): 495–521.

Orbell, J. M., van de Kragt, A. and Dawes, R. M. (1988) 'Explaining Discussion-Induced Cooperation', *Journal of Personality and Social Psychology*, 54 (5): 811–19.

Ostrom, E. (1965) 'Public Entrepreneurship: A Case Study in Ground Water Basin Management', PhD diss., University of California, Los Angeles.

—— (1976) 'Size and Performance in a Federal System', *Publius: The Journal of Federalism*, 6 (2): 33–73.

—— (1986) 'An Agenda for the Study of Institutions', *Public Choice*, 48 (1): 3–25.

—— (1990) *Governing the Commons: The Evolution of Institutions for Collective Action*, Cambridge, UK: Cambridge University Press.

—— (1998) 'A Behavioural Approach to the Rational Choice Theory of Collective Action', *American Political Science Review*, 92 (1): 1–22.

—— (1999) 'Coping with Tragedies of the Commons', *Annual Review of Political Science*, 2:493–535.

—— (2005) *Understanding Institutional Diversity*, Princeton, NJ: Princeton University Press.

—— (2007) 'A Diagnostic Approach for Going beyond Panaceas', *Proceedings of the National Academy of Sciences*, 104 (39): 15181–87.

—— (2008) 'Developing a Method for Analysing Institutional Change', in Sandra S. Batie and Nicholas Mercuro (eds) *Alternative Institutional Structures: Evolution and Impact*, New York: Routledge, pp. 48–76.

—— (2009) 'A General Framework for Analysing the Sustainability of Social-Ecological Systems', *Science*, 325 (5939): 419–22.

Ostrom, E. and Basurto, X. (2011) 'Crafting Analytical Tools to Study Institutional Change', *Journal of Institutional Economics*, 7 (3): 317–343.

Ostrom, E. and Gardner, R. (1993) 'Coping with Asymmetries in the Commons: Self-Governing Irrigation Systems Can Work', *Journal of Economic Perspectives*, 7 (4): 93–112.

Ostrom, E. and Nagendra, H. (2006) 'Insights on Linking Forests, Trees, and People from the Air, on the Ground, and in the Laboratory', *Proceedings of the National Academy of Sciences*, 103 (51): 19224–31.

Ostrom, E. and Parks, R. B. (1973) 'Suburban Police Departments: Too Many and Too Small?', in L. H. Masotti and J. K. Hadden (eds) *The Urbanization of the Suburbs*, Beverly Hills, CA: Sage, pp. 367–402.

— (1999) 'Neither Gargantua nor the Land of Lilliputs: Conjectures on Mixed Systems of Metropolitan Organization', in M. D. McGinnis (ed.) *Polycentricity and Local Public Economies: Readings from the Workshop in Political Theory and Policy Analysis*, Ann Arbor, MI: University of Michigan Press, pp. 284–305.

Ostrom, E. and Walker, J. (1991) 'Communication in a Commons: Cooperation without External Enforcement', in T. R. Palfrey (ed.) *Laboratory Research in Political Economy*, Ann Arbor, MI: University of Michigan Press, pp. 287–322.

Ostrom, E. and Whitaker, G. P. (1974) 'Community Control and Governmental Responsiveness: The Case of Police in Black Neighbourhoods', in W. Hawley and D. Rogers (eds) *Improving the Quality of Urban Management*, Beverly Hills, CA: Sage, pp. 303–34.

Ostrom, E., Gardner, R. and Walker, J. (1994) *Rules, Games, and Common-Pool Resources*, Ann Arbor, MI: University of Michigan Press.

Ostrom, E., Parks, R. B. and Whitaker, G. P. (1978) *Patterns of Metropolitan Policing*, Cambridge, MA: Ballinger.

Ostrom, E., Schroeder, L. and Wynne, S (1993) *Institutional Incentives and Sustainable Development: Infrastructure Policies in Perspective*, Boulder, CO: Westview Press.

Ostrom, E., Walker, J. and Gardner, R. (1992) 'Covenants with and without a Sword: Self-Governance Is Possible', *American Political Science Review*, 86 (2): 404–17.

Ostrom, E., Agrawal, A., Blomquist, W., Schlager, E. and Tang, S. Y. (1989) *CPR Coding Manual*, Bloomington, IN: Indiana University, Workshop in Political Theory and Policy Analysis.

Ostrom, E., Baugh, W., Guarasci, R., Parks, R. B. and Whitaker, G. P. (1973) *Community Organization and the Provision of Police Services,* Beverly Hills, CA: Sage.

Ostrom, E., Dietz, T., Dolšak, N., Stern, P. C., Stonich, S. and Weber, E. U. (eds) (2002) *The Drama of the Commons,* Washington, DC: National Academies Press.

Ostrom, V. (1962) 'The Political Economy of Water Development', *American Economic Review*, 52 (2): 450–58.

— (1975) 'Language, Theory and Empirical Research in Policy Analysis', *Policy Studies Journal*, 3 (3): 274–82.

— (2008) *The Intellectual Crisis in American Public Administration,* 3rd edn. Tuscaloosa, AL: University of Alabama Press.

Ostrom, V. and Ostrom, E. (1965) 'A Behavioural Approach to the Study of Intergovernmental Relations', *The Annals of the American Academy of Political and Social Science*, 359 (1): 137–46.

— (1977) 'Public Goods and Public Choices', in E. S. Savas (ed.) *Alternatives for Delivering Public Services: Toward Improved Performance*, Boulder, CO: West-view Press, pp. 7–49.

Ostrom, V., Tiebout, C. M. and Warren, R. (1961) 'The Organization of Government in Metropolitan Areas: A Theoretical Inquiry', *American Political Science Review*, 55 (4): 831–42.

Paavola, J. and Adger, W. N. (2005) 'Institutional Ecological Economics', *Ecological Economics*, 53 (3): 353–68.

Pagdee, A., Kim, Y.-S. and Daugherty, P. J. (2006) 'What Makes Community Forest Management Successful: A Meta-Study from Community Forests throughout the World', *Society & Natural Resources*, 19 (1): 33–52.

Pfennig, D. W. and Ledón-Rettig, C. (2009) 'The Flexible Organism', *Science*, 325 (5938): 268–69.

Popper, K. R. (1961) *The Poverty of Historicism*, New York: Harper & Row.

Posner, R. (1975) 'Economic Analysis of Law', in B. A. Ackerman (eds) *Economic Foundation of Property Law*, Boston, MA: Little, Brown and Co.

Poteete, A. R. and Ostrom, E. (2004) 'In Pursuit of Comparable Concepts and Data about Collective Action', *Agricultural Systems*, 82 (3): 215–32.

Poteete, A. R., Janssen, M. and Ostrom, E. (2010) *Working Together: Collective Action, the Commons, and Multiple Methods in Practice*, Princeton, NJ: Princeton University Press.

Reeson, A. F. and Tisdell, J. G. (2008) 'Institutions, Motivations and Public Goods: An Experimental Test of Motivational Crowding', *Journal of Economic Behavior and Organisation*, 68 (1): 273–81.

Rogers, B. D. and McCurdy, C. L. (1974) 'Metropolitan Reform: Citizen Evaluations of Performance in Nashville-Davidson County, Tennessee', *Publius: The Journal of Federalism*, 4 (4): 19–34.

Rothstein, B. (2005) *Social Traps and the Problem of Trust*, Cambridge, UK: Cambridge University Press.

Rudel, T. K. (2008) 'Meta-Analyses of Case Studies: A Method for Studying Regional and Global Environmental Change', *Global Environmental Change*, 18 (1): 18–25.

Sally, D. (1995) 'Conservation and Cooperation in Social Dilemmas: A Meta-Analysis of Experiments from 1958 to 1992', *Rationality and Society*, 7 (1): 58–92.

Samuelson, P. A. (1954) 'The Pure Theory of Public Expenditure', *Review of Economics and Statistics*, 36(4): 387–89.

Satz, D. and Ferejohn, J. (1994) 'Rational Choice and Social Theory', *Journal of Philosophy*, 91 (2): 71–87.

Schank, R. C. and Abelson, R. P. (1977) *Scripts, Plans, Goals, and Understanding: An Inquiry in Human Knowledge Structures*, Hillsdale, NJ: Lawrence Erlbaum Associates.

Schelling, T. C. (1960) *The Strategy of Conflict*, Oxford: Oxford University Press.

— (1978) *Micromotives and Macrobehavior*, New York: Norton.

— (1984) *Choice and Consequence: Perspectives of an Errant Economist*, Cambridge, MA: Harvard University Press.

Schlager, E. (1990) 'Model Specification and Policy Analysis: The Governance of Coastal Fisheries', PhD diss. Indiana University.

—   (1994) 'Fishers' Institutional Responses to Common-Pool Resource Dilemmas', in E. Ostrom, R. Gardner and J. Walker (eds) *Rules, Games, and Common-Pool Resources*, Ann Arbor, MI: University of Michigan Press, pp. 247–65.

Schlager, E. and Blomquist, W. (2008) *Embracing Watershed Politics*, Boulder, CO: University Press of Colorado.

Schlager, E. and Ostrom, E. (1992) 'Property-Rights Regimes and Natural Resources: A Conceptual Analysis', *Land Economics*, 68 (3): 249–62.

Scott, A. (1955) 'The Fishery: The Objectives of Sole Ownership', *Journal of Political Economy*, 63 (2): 116–24.

Selten, R. (1990) 'Bounded Rationality', *Journal of Institutional and Theoretical Economics*, 146 (4): 649–58.

Sen, A. K. (1977) 'Rational Fools: A Critique of the Behavioural Foundations of Economic Theory', *Philosophy and Public Affairs*, 6 (4): 317–44.

—   (2009) *The Idea of Justice*, Cambridge, MA: Harvard University Press.

Shivakoti, G. and Ostrom, E. (eds) (2002) *Improving Irrigation Governance and Management in Nepal*, Oakland, CA: ICS Press.

Simon, H. A. (1955) 'A Behavioural Model of Rational Choice', *Quarterly Journal of Economics*, 69 (1): 99–188.

—   (1981) *The Sciences of the Artificial*, 2nd edn, Cambridge, MA: MIT Press.

—   (1995) 'Near Decomposability and Complexity: How a Mind Resides in a Brain', in H. J. Morowitz and J. L. Singer (eds) *The Mind, the Brain, and Complex Adaptive Systems*, Reading, MA: Addison-Wesley, pp. 25–44.

—   (1990) 'The Potlatch between Economics and Political Science', in J. E. Alt, M. Levi, and E. Ostrom (eds) *Competition and Cooperation: Conversations with Nobelists About Economics and Political Science*, New York: Russell Sage Foundation, pp. 112–19.

Skoler, D. L. and Hetler, J. M. (1971) 'Government Restructuring and Criminal Administration: The Challenge of Consolidation', in *Crisis in Urban Government. A Symposium: Restructuring Metropolitan Area Government*, Silver Springs, MD: T. Jefferson.

Smith, V. L. (2003) 'Constructivist and Ecological Rationality in Economics', *American Economic Review*, 93 (3): 465–508.

—   (2010) 'Theory and Experiment: What Are the Questions?', *Journal of Economic Behavior and Organisation*, 73 (1): 3–15.

Smith, V. L. and Walker, J. M. (1993) 'Rewards, Experience and Decision Costs in First Price Auctions', *Economic Inquiry*, 31 (2): 237–45.

Stewart, J. I. (2009) 'Cooperation When N Is Large: Evidence from the Mining Camps of the American West', *Journal of Economic Behavior and Organisation*, 69 (3): 213–25.

Sugden, R. (1986) *The Economics of Rights, Co-operation and Welfare*, Oxford: Blackwell.

Tang, S. Y. (1992) *Institutions and Collective Action: Self-Governance in Irrigation*, San Francisco: ICS Press.

— (1994) Institutions and Performance in Irrigation Systems', in E. Ostrom, R. Gardner and J. Walker (eds) *Rules, Games, and Common-Pool Resources*, A. Arbor, MI: University of Michigan Press, pp. 225–45.

Terborgh, J. (1999) *Requiem for Nature*, Washington, DC: Island Press.

Toonen, T. (2010) 'Resilience in Public Administration: The Work of Elinor and Vincent Ostrom from a Public Administration Perspective', *Public Administration Review*, 70 (2): 193–202.

Trawick, P. B. (2001) 'Successfully Governing the Commons: Principles of Social Organization in an Andean Irrigation System', *Human Ecology*, 29(1): 1–25.

Tucker, C. M. (2008) *Changing Forests: Collective Action, Common Property, and Coffee in Honduras*, Berlin: Springer.

Uphoff, N. T., Ramamurthy, P. and Steiner, R. (1991) *Managing Irrigation: Analysing and Improving the Performance of Bureaucracies*, New Delhi: Sage.

Walker, J. and Ostrom, E. (2009) 'Trust and Reciprocity as Foundations for Cooperation', in K. S. Cook, M. Levi and R. Hardin (eds) *Whom Can We Trust?: How Groups, Networks, and Institutions Make Trust Possible*, New York: Russell Sage Foundation, pp. 91–124.

Warren, R. O. (1966) *Government of Metropolitan Regions: A Reappraisal of Fractionated Politica Organization*. Davis, CA: University of California, Institute of Governmental Affairs.

Webb, E. L. and Shivakoti, G. (eds) (2008) *Decentralization, Forests and Rural Communities: Policy Outcomes in South and Southeast Asia*, New Delhi: Sage India.

Weissing, F. and Ostrom, E. (1993) 'Irrigation Institutions and the Games Irrigators Play: Rule Enforcement on Government- and Farmer-Managed Systems', in F. W. Scharpf (ed.) *Games in Hierarchies and Networks: Analytical and Empirical Approaches to the Study of Governance Institutions*, Frankfurt, Germany: Campus Verlag, pp. 387–428.

Weschler, L. F. (1968) *Water Resources Management: The Orange County Experience*, Davis, CA: University of California, Institute of Governmental Affairs.

Williamson, O. E. (1975) *Markets and Hierarchies: Analysis and Antitrust Implications*, New York: Free Press.

— (1986) 'The Economics of Governance: Framework and Implications', in R. N. Langlois (ed.) *Economics as a Process: Essays in the New Institutional Economics*, Cambridge, UK: Cambridge University Press, pp. 171–202.

Wilson, J. A. (1990) 'Fishing for Knowledge', *Land Economics*, 66 (1): 12–29.

Wilson, J. A., Acheson, J. M., Metcalfe, M. and Kleban, P. (1994) 'Chaos, Complexity, and Community Management of Fisheries', *Marine Policy*, 18 (4): 291–305.

Wilson, W. (1885) *Congressional Government: A Study in American Politics*, Boston: Houghton Mifflin.

Wollenberg, E., Merino, L., Agrawal, A. and Ostrom, E. (2007) 'Fourteen Years of Monitoring Community-Managed Forests: Learning from IFRI's Experience', *International Forestry Review*, 9 (2): 670–84.

Yamagishi, T. (1986) 'The Provision of a Sanctioning System as a Public Good', *Journal of Personality and Social Psychology*, 51 (1): 110–16.

Yandle, T. (2007) 'Understanding the Consequence of Property Rights Mismatches: A Case Study of New Zealand's Marine Resources', *Ecology and Society*, 12 (2) http://www.ecologyandsociety.org/vol12/iss2/art27/

Yandle, T. and Dewees, C. M. (2003) 'Privatizing the Commons [...] Twelve Years Later: Fishers' Experiences with New Zealand's Market-Based Fisheries Management', in N. Dolsak and E. Ostrom (eds) *The Commons in the New Millennium: Challenges and Adaptation*, Cambridge, MA: MIT Press, pp. 101–27.

Part Three

Epistemic and Social
Philosophical Perspectives

Chapter Seven

Beyond Positivism[1]

Elinor Ostrom

Some intellectual eras come to an end with a bang. Others end with a whimper. Those that end suddenly are swept out by the rapid acceptance of a new theory or a major finding that makes the continuation of old beliefs impossible. Most intellectual eras in the social sciences may end with a whimper – with a vague sense of unease that not much progress has been made for all the efforts of able and hardworking scholars. My personal sense is that we are coming to an end of an era in political science, a slow, whimpering end.

The signs of the demise of an old era include a level of disquietude among the practitioners of a discipline. This volume contains essays written by some of the more able practicing empirical theorists in the country. Most of them indicate some dissatisfaction with the current status of political science. [G. R.] Boynton (Chapter Two) is concerned that the 'most glaring weakness in our program has been the discontinuity between theory and research'. [J. Donald] Moon (Chapter Six) indicates that 'one of the major shortcomings or problems of political science is the apparent confusion and diversity of standards in our field'. [Roger] Benjamin (Chapter Three) argues that 'as soon as we begin to achieve some success in apprehending an important political process, diachronic change occurs in such fields as modernization to render our models obsolete'.

Signs of dissatisfaction with the discipline are not new, however. Since World War II, major confrontations have occurred within political science. Some have occurred in the literature (MacIntyre 1967; Winch 1958; Feyerabend 1970; Falco 1973; Goldberg 1963; Laslett *et al.* 1972).

However, many of the arguments have been fought as departments made recruitment and curricular decisions. The 'quantitative versus nonquantitative' dispute has surfaced in many departments each time a new faculty member is hired as colleagues debate about the appropriateness of the approach taken by candidates. Designing undergraduate or graduate curricula is another process likely to invoke a similar conflict. Those taking the antiquantitative position have argued that studying relationships using quantitative data does not provide an adequate understanding of the political world. Advocates of a more quantitative approach to political science have argued that without careful measurement and

---

1. Introductory Chapter, 'Beyond Positivism: An Introduction to this Volume', in Ostrom, E. (1982) *Strategies of Political Inquiry*, edited by Elinor Ostrom, 11–28, Beverly Hills, CA: Sage Publications.

the use of analytic techniques, one does not have a basis for knowing anything. In some subdisciplines of political science, specialized fields of inquiry have been identified by their stance in the quantitative versus nonquantitative dispute quantitative international relations is one example.

While strong feelings have been triggered, the quantitative versus nonquantitative dispute did not generally touch fundamental issues of importance to understanding political phenomena. When couched as a fight between those who quantify and those who do not, the dispute does not touch the central question of what are the basic processes occurring in different political systems in different eras. Rather, the dispute has centred on the way variables are coded and the type of statistics used as criteria to establish that a relationship between one variable and a second variable exists. It has been, to a large extent, an intellectual confrontation over how to represent descriptions of the world, rather than an argument about different organising principles for understanding the world. Both camps have remained fundamentally descriptive in their approach to the study of political phenomena.

The disquietude reflected in the essays in this volume differs from the discontent articulated by those scholars pushing for a more quantitative approach to political science. The concern here is that after several decades of far more rigorous empirical research, the hoped for cumulation of knowledge into a coherent body of theory has not occurred. This is a lament from those who have been, as Boynton phrases it, 'in the research camp'.

The central theme of the essays in this volume is the need for the development of theory as the basis of our discipline. Benjamin (Chapter Three) concludes after assessing the state of comparative political inquiry that 'we should be concerned again with opening up new concepts, reworking old questions, developing new puzzles, junking old theories and developing new ones, rather than developing and applying methodologies'. While political scientists have been asserting that theory should be the basis of our discipline throughout the post-war era, the definition of what constitutes proper theory is used differently here from the definition of theory articulated by logical positivists and accepted by many scholars in the discipline.

To some extent the heavy emphasis on descriptive, empirical, quantitative work may have resulted from the naive acceptance of a particular school of philosophy of science. The books that had the most influence on our conception of what theory should be were for many years those by Brodbeck (1968), Hempel (1965), Nagel (1961) and Rudner (1966).

At the time these authors accepted the logical positivist position on the type of scientific method to form the foundation of the social sciences. In a critique of rational choice theories from a covering law perspective, Moe (1979: 216) aptly describes the central belief system of the logical positivist's approach.

There is a fundamental unity of scientific method across the natural and social sciences; in both, the purpose of science is the explanation of events and the nature of explanation is nomological. An event is explained when a statement of its [...] occurrence is deductively subsumed under lawlike statements and statements of initial conditions; and these logically prior statements, the theoretical premises, must be well-confirmed by the available evidence, since it is the presumed truth of the premises that logically justifies the expectation of the event's occurrence. Scientific progress hinges on the discovery of well-confirmed lawlike statements and on their integration into increasingly general and comprehensive theoretical structures.

If in order to have a theory admitted to the hallowed halls of science, the theory had to be based upon well-accepted empirical laws, then indeed the major effort in the discipline had to be to go out and discover empirical laws. Since scholars were trying to find empirical regularities, the major focus for political scientists doing research was on questions of method – of how to operationalize variables adequately and of the proper kind of statistical test to use to assert relationships between variables. These are essential questions of an empirically based political science. But their dominance during the past several decades places the questions of how to describe political relationships in a quantitative manner above how to gain an adequate understanding of the processes involved in the relevant world of inquiry.

Further, the positivist perspective on the necessity of building political science anew, based on a rock bottom of quantitative empirical research, dominated the instruction given to graduate students in our discipline. Given the recruitment pattern into the discipline, entering students have frequently evinced shock when presented with this perspective on the nature of the discipline. High school students are rarely exposed to anything called political science until their junior or senior year. By that time most students have already taken mathematics, science, history, literature, and languages. Many students select a college major early from one of the subjects they took in high school and found interesting and challenging. Students who enjoy abstract thinking and mathematics may have already selected mathematics or a science that allows them to pursue these interests prior to any introduction to political science (*see* Lave and March 1975).

The first introduction to political science qua high school civics does not attract the more theoretically and mathematically inclined students either. The focus on current events in high school civics courses associates political science with the study of current events for many students. This association is reinforced in college. At many universities large numbers of freshmen take an introduction to American government course where the emphasis is on the current structure and political behavior of American national government. Given the clientele and texts available, most of these courses are descriptive and include a heavy dose of current events.

Students who are interested in power struggles and learning the inside story related to current world crises are attracted. Students who are interested in more abstract intellectual endeavours are turned off. Majoring in political science does not alter the picture. Students can major in political science and never be introduced to political philosophy or the rigorous development of any type of modern political theory. Few of our undergraduates take more than minimal requirements in logic, philosophy, mathematics, or economics; and few take statistics as undergraduates.

Students entering graduate school with this type of background react to logical positivism in an extremely bimodal fashion. Some students vehemently reject the position. They either drop out of political science during their first year or simply develop a graduate program that does not require them to use theory rigorously or to learn quantitative methods. These students tend to ally themselves with faculty who are still fighting the antiquantitative war. Other students may have accepted the position too naively and wholeheartedly. If the position is accepted totally, what does this mean to a young colleague in political science?

The belief system includes the following propositions. For a discipline to be a science, it must have certain types of theories. For a set of logically connected statements to be a theory, they must start with a well-known empirical law. For a statement to be considered an empirical law, quantitative data must be gathered and analysed, and clear-cut and consistent patterns must repetitively be found. For students exposed to this position early in their careers, the import of their new scientific religion was that political science had no theory. David Easton (1953: 4), for example, asserted that:

> Clearly, if political science could arrive at [...] at general theory, the understanding of political life that it would give would be both profound and extensive. There is no need consequently to point out that such a theory would be desirable because of its utility. The only thing that is not apparent, however, is that the formulation of such a theory is a possible and necessary step along the road to reliable and perceptive knowledge about politics.

No such theory is visible on the horizons of political research in the United States today.

For some political scientists, political science itself began in the 1950s. In a paper I read this past spring, for example, repeated references were made to the classical work in the field. All of the works cited were written after 1960!

With the 'rock bottom' approach, as Popper (1965) calls it, scientific theories could not be constructed until political science had undertaken substantial hard-nosed empirical work to find the empirical laws to become the bedrock of the discipline. With missionary zeal, several generations of young colleagues went forth to collect data so that a political science could be constructed using their empirical findings as the foundation. Many of the early generations in this revolution were armed for the foray with minimal statistical training and no training in mathematics or logic. Changes slowly appeared in our journals. First, a few cross-tabulations were interspersed among what previously had been predominantly textual material. Correlation matrices appeared next. Multiple regression techniques were then introduced. More recently, a whole spectrum of advanced multivariate statistics has been displayed.

As methods have become more sophisticated, graduate students of more recent times faced even more perplexing problems. Those who did not reject the mainstream approach realized that they must acquire substantial methodological training just to read the major journals. Given that our recruitment pattern into the discipline has not fundamentally changed, most entering graduate students still have no philosophical, logical, mathematical, or statistical training as undergraduates. Consequently, in order to gain minimal levels of quantitative training, many graduate students take heavy course loads in statistics and methods and fewer courses where they might be exposed to the development of systematic substantive theories.

The combined effect of this recruitment process interacting with this type of socialization may have produced a 'know nothing' era in the discipline. Many scholars who presumed they were building our new empirical foundation did indeed know very little about substance and about the relationship of the statistical languages they used to the absence of theoretical models to which the language of data analysis should have been related. The criteria for what would be accepted as 'facts' became a significant correlation coefficient or a high R2, even when it meant the acceptance of nonsense or the rejection of long-established knowledge.

It is, of course, hard to characterize political science as being of one piece. Contained within the same discipline are so many individuals following such different approaches. However, during the past several decades, a number of young political scientists considered themselves to be in the vanguard of the discipline. They saw themselves creating the empirical foundation for the final development of a science. They rejected the work of those who had gone before them. It is their work that largely dominated our major journals.

During the 1960s many political scientists accepted, for example, the frequently repeated statement that 'political structure doesn't matter'. As Dye (1966: 297) expressed it, 'political variables do not count for much in shaping public policy'. The fact that political variables accounted for a small proportion of the variance in government expenditure levels after economic and social variables had first been entered in multiple regression equations was taken as 'proof' that institutional variables did not matter and should not be the subject of a mature science (*see* Dawson and Robinson 1963; Hofferbert 1966, 1972).

The way a process is conceptualized should affect the analytical techniques to be used for estimating statistical parameters in empirical models of that process (Wright 1976; Stonecash 1978; Johnston 1972; Hanushek, Jackson 1977). Multiple regression techniques were first developed to examine the independent effect of land, labour, and fertilizer in agricultural productivity (*see* Ezekiel and Fox 1959). Since each of these variables was conceptualized as *independent* and its effect on productivity was *additive*, the general linear model underlying multiple regression was the appropriate theoretical language for stating how these variables would be related to a dependent variable. I seriously doubt that one could find many statements in Hobbes, *The Federalist*, or Tocqueville that conceptualized the effect of institutions in a manner similar to that of fertilizer added to labour and land to produce corn (*see* V. Ostrom 1980, 1982). In the last decade, as models of how political structure affects the pattern of relationships among economic, social, and technological variables have been formulated and tested, scholars have found important structural effects (*see* Carmines 1974; Wright 1976; Frey and Pomerehne 1978; Summers and Wolfe 1977; Phillips and Votey 1972; E. Ostrom and Whitaker 1973; Parks 1979; Parks and E. Ostrom 1981).

The languages of data analysis and method have dominated the languages of theory construction during much of the past two decades. As Sprague points out in Chapter Four, reliance on certain methods, because they are perceived to be more scientific, can coerce political scientists to ignore important theoretical questions. He is particularly concerned with the overreliance on *national* probability samples. Without adding contextual variables to individual records of a national sample, scholars can only examine how individuals, who have been plucked from their environments, acquire political attitudes. Important theoretical questions, relating political learning to context, cannot be pursued using most of the massive data sets already collected about the American electorate.

It is essential for empirical researchers to learn the languages of data analysis and to learn them early in their careers. Our undergraduate programs could all be strengthened by advising students of the importance of mathematics and statistics to an undergraduate major in political science. But a central task of the coming era is to reverse this domination so that the development of theory precedes the choice of appropriate methods to test a theory.

Fortunately, many scholars in the discipline, including the authors of chapters in this volume, are taking major steps to reestablish the priority of theory over data collection and analysis. Moreover, theory has also come to mean for many political scientists a set of logically connected statements without the requirement that assumptions used in a theory have themselves *already* been established as empirical laws. The covering-law perspective has not been replaced with another dominant philosophy of science. Among the important alternative views are those of Kuhn (1970), Lakatos (1971) and Habermas (1973). Among the authors who have provided useful overviews of the different traditions and important attempts at synthesis are Moon (1975), Toulmin (1977) and Shapiro (1981).

The essays in this volume reflect the subtle change occurring across political science and the sister disciplines of economics, sociology, and psychology. The first essay in this volume, by G. R. Boynton, is inspired by the work of Susanne Langer. Boynton argues that scientific advances have come when theorists have found principles by which they can order events that appear incommensurable and relate these events to one another. This places the focus for scientific advance on theoretical breakthroughs. The most important part of a theoretical breakthrough, according to Boynton, is an organizing principle. Terms are defined for the purpose of the relevant organizing principle. Proper names are no longer used. If events that were thought to be incommensurable are included within the same theoretical classification, it may also be the case that empirical references that share similar names may not be included in the same set when looked at from a theoretical perspective.

Boynton's chapter can be viewed as an inquiry into what is the 'right type of law' for social scientists. The right type of law, he argues, is highly specific and relates a limited number of variables to each other under stated conditions. The conditions of a theory state the values of other variables that must be closely approximated for the posited theoretical relations to hold among explanatory variables. The 'other' variables condition the type of relationships among the explanatory variables stated in the theory. By stressing the importance of stating the essential conditions for an organizing principle to operate, Boynton urges social scientists to try to understand the logic of relatively contained situations where the conditions structuring a situation are specified. His notion, therefore, of theory pertains to the organizing principles used to understand particular types of situations structured in specific ways (*see also* Barry, Chapter Five).

The importance of structuring conditions is central to the argument made by Roger Benjamin concerning the historical nature of social-scientific knowledge Benjamin argues that the relationships found *within* political systems may vary across historical time periods. Different historical periods are for Benjamin what the concept of a laboratory is for Boynton. Within a laboratory the scientist structures an experiment to study dynamic change while carefully controlling other variables. Whenever the scientist changes the fundamental structure of the experiment, the scientist produces diachronic change in the laboratory.

As Boynton points out, the concept of a laboratory is a mental frame. Social scientists, studying the on-going stream of events within real political systems, cannot set the parameters of variables that structure political processes. In times of relative political and social stability, the 'experimental conditions' remain unchanged. However, in times of major societal development, the level of diachronic change may be so great as to make the study of dynamics futile until the consequence of change in structure can be examined.

Benjamin compares the prevalent theories used to explain political processes within industrial societies in the 1960s, with the theories used in the 1980s. He reasons that new theories will be needed to understand the macro- and microeconomic forces at work in post-industrial as contrasted with industrial systems. Four theories are currently evolving that Benjamin (Chapter Three) feels will be the source of our understanding of behavior in the remainder of the twentieth century. The four theories are (1) Mancur Olson's recent theory of stable societies and economic decline, (2) the product cycle theory, (3) the collective goods theory, and (4) critical theory. Benjamin concludes from his review of these diverse theories that 'it is not business as usual in post-industrial societies'. This leads him to argue that political scientists must understand the changing macro political-economic structure before they can explain regularity in microbehaviour. Further, he argues the regularity in microrelationships in one historical period may be dramatically different in another.

John Sprague (Chapter Four) also examines the relationship between broader social structure and microanalysis. However, while Benjamin is interested in international political economies as they have an impact on political relationships within nation-states, Sprague is interested in the structure of neighbourhood-level political attitudes as they may affect the determinants of individual political attitudes. Both ask how microrelationships can be examined within a macrostructure; however, the levels of their analyses differ dramatically.

The fundamental theoretical question that Sprague addresses is, 'What are the mechanisms that connect microenvironments with individual political behavior? Or, more boldly put, how does social structure coerce individual behavior?' This is an interesting question for Sprague to address, because he has been interested for many years in macro processes. Sprague develops an organizing principle to answer the puzzle of how the environment impinges upon relationships among individual political-attitude variables. His organizing principle differs from the model of the individual using the traditional assumptions of neoclassical economics. Rather, he posits a model of information processing in the individual that structures the processes through which individuals acquire political attitudes. His work exemplifies a nonrational choice model that is based on a foundation of methodological individualism.

While Boynton draws on the work of Susanne Langer for inspiration about how to develop coherent theory in political science, Brian Barry (Chapter Five) relies upon Mill. Mill, according to Barry, stresses the problem that social scientists face given the multiplicity of causes simultaneously affecting the processes of interest. By isolating some relatively simple cases, in a process similar to the mental laboratory that Boynton posits, Mill argues that one may be able to ascertain how some small systems operate when isolated from the impact of other confounding variables. However, such findings about one micro-system may not hold over time and place if structuring variables change dramatically. While we may be able to establish empirical trends, 'we cannot use them with any confidence as a basis for prediction unless we have reason to expect the underlying conditions to remain unaltered' (Mill, quoted by Barry, Chapter Five). Benjamin's stress on the importance of history is also consistent with Mill's analysis.

The cumulative effect of the chapters by Boynton, Benjamin, and Barry should lead to a sense of humility on the part of social scientists concerning what it is possible to do. All three scholars argue that when conditions are well specified and isolated, it is possible to develop rigorous theory for how some variables interact with others. However, the number of variables in the conditioning requirements may be large. Gaining a hold on how all those variables interact, if major diachronic change occurs, may be beyond our capabilities. Barry argues that this may leave a limited role for the social scientist, but he also argues that it would be 'absurd to reject it in the pursuit of something more ambitious but actually useless'.

The advantage of economics, according to Barry, has been its focus on a confined part of social life where institutions tightly structure the set of available options for participants and the range of effects. Given some simple behavioural laws about how individuals value outcomes, it is possible to develop relatively well-supported theory about the behavioural tendencies, given the nature of immediate situations. Barry then asks what kind of theory may enable social scientists to understand nonmarket processes. He turns to the work of Mancur Olson and shows how it has been applied by Popkin to a different setting with considerable fruitfulness. He also illustrates how Hardin has reexamined the underlying model of the individual to develop a more general theory than originally developed by Olson.

Barry further addresses the question of whether there is a necessary ideological content to an assumption of methodological individualism. Methodological individualism does not require any particular assumptions about individual motivation; rather, it simply insists that an adequate level of motivation be developed. Barry argues that there is nothing ideological about the methodological principle even though some applications are ideological. Sprague illustrates in his chapter a micro theory of motivation that is *not* an economic theory. Sprague demonstrates what Barry says can be done. Kiser and Ostrom also return to the same theme in the last chapter.

J. Donald Moon (Chapter Six) further explores the questions of how individuals make decisions and what types of theory enable scholars to advance understandings of political phenomena. Two fundamental strategies used by political scientists are identified by Moon: the interpretative approach, which he argues does not draw upon general laws and theories, and the theoretical approach, which does. Moon reexamines the situation facing European leaders in the 1930s and their decision concerning macroeconomic policies. In this case, macrostructural variables do not appear to account for the difference in policy decisions made by Sweden and Germany compared to Britain. Within systems that were relatively similar in structure, one set of leaders adopted a theoretical explanation for how the economic world operated that differed from the economic theory used by the other sets of actors.

Kiser and Ostrom (Chapter Seven) present a metatheoretical framework for the analysis and synthesis of a large body of political-economy literature. The microinstitutional political-economy literature they examine explains individual actions and aggregated results occurring in decision situations affected by institutional rules, the nature of goods, and the type of community. Further, they present the key aspects of this approach as a series of component working parts. In any particular theory, a scholar in this tradition will make implicit or explicit assumptions about the specific attributes of each of the working parts. What distinguishes this approach from that used by macropolitical economists is the prominence of a model of the individual at the central core of any particular model. Kiser and Ostrom return to the theme developed earlier by Barry and Sprague, that many different models of the individual are consistent with the principle of methodological individualism.

In their framework, any model of the individual will include assumptions about the individual's level of information, the individual's valuation, and the individual's calculation process for selecting among alternative actions or strategies. Thus, the narrow rational choice model of the individual used in neoclassical economics and by some formal theorists of political behavior is characterized by assumptions that the individual possesses complete information, the individual values a single, externally measurable value (such as profits or the probability of being re-elected) and the individual selects that strategy which maximizes this value. A model of the individual drawing on the work of Herbert Simon would instead posit an individual with limited information and bounded capacities for processing information, with multiple goals, and with a calculation process involving limited search for satisfactory outcomes. The type of model of the individual that Sprague presents is characterized by an individual with incomplete information, multiple goals (political goals plus a desire to please those with whom he or she interacts regularly) and a learning strategy based on rewards or punishments meted out for the political attitudes expressed.

The Kiser and Ostrom framework thus provides for comparing political and economic theories that use the individual as a basic unit of analysis. There is a whole family of such theories. At times the 'family' resemblance is difficult to discern. Some of the debates among proponents of one or another model of the individual have also tended to mask the fundamental similarity in the broad structure of these theories. The broad framework presented in the last chapter should enable scholars using different theories of individual behavior more closely to identify where their similarities and differences are. If we are ever to develop more general theories related to the political and economic world, we must be able to step back from the advocacy of any particular theory to examine how specific assumptions combined together make a difference and produce different explanations. It is hoped that the framework presented in this chapter will enable readers outside and within the tradition to identify some fundamental similarities in the work described.

This introduction began with the speculation than an era was ending in political science. Personally, I feel this may have been a necessary but unpleasant era in the discipline's growth, somewhat like adolescence. The tendency to reject the work of our predecessors and adopt new languages and new technologies in an effort to start over is an important phase of a discipline gaining maturity. But real maturity comes when the worth of past efforts is recognized and new languages and technologies are integrated with the best work of former times. In these chapters one finds many references to and uses of the work of political philosophers, a recognition of the importance of history, an awareness of diverse philosophies of science, a basic concern with the central place of theory in the development of the discipline, the use of formal models, and a recognition of the importance of rigorous methods in data analysis. While pessimism about the discipline has permeated the literature of political science during the past few decades, we may be moving into a more optimistic era. As theory precedes empirical work, and empirical studies help to refine our theoretical understanding of the world, the hoped-for cumulation in that understanding may finally occur. However, if we take the warnings of Boynton, Barry, and Benjamin seriously, the cumulation we do achieve will be limited in scope to specific types of theoretically defined situations rather than sweeping theories of society as a whole.

References

Brodbeck, M. (ed.) (1968) *Readings in the Philosophy of the Social Sciences,* New York: Macmillan.

Carmines, E. G. (1974) 'The mediating influence of state legislatures on the linkage between interparty competition and welfare policies', *American Political Science Review,* 68:1118–1124.

Dawson, R. E. and Robinson J. A. (1963) 'Enter party competition, economic variables, and welfare policies in the American states', *Journal of Politics,* 25 (May): 265–289.

Dye, T. R. (1966) *Politics, Economics, and the Public,* Chicago, IL: Rand McNally.

Easton, D. (1953) *The Political System,* New York: Knopf.

Ezekiel, M. and Fox, K. A. (1959) *Methods of Correlation and Regression Analysis,* New York: John Wiley.

Falco, M. J. (1973) *Truth and Meaning in Political Science,* Columbus, OH: Merrill.

Feyerabend, P. K. (1970) 'Against method: outline of an anarchistic theory of knowledge', in M. Radner and S. Winokur (eds) *Minnesota Studies in the Philosophy of Science,* (Vol. 4), Minneapolis: University of Minnesota Press, pp. 17–130.

Frey, B. S. and Pommerehne, W. W. (1978) 'Toward a more theoretical foundation for empirical policy analysis', *Comparative Political Studies,* 11 (October): 311–336.

Fry, B. R. and Winters, R. R. (1970) 'The politics of redistribution', *American Political Science Review,* 64 (June): 508–522.

Godwin, R. K. and Shepard, W. B. (1976) 'Political processes and public expenditures: a reexamination based on theories of representative government', *American Political Science Review,* 70 (December): 1127–1135.

Goldberg, A. S. (1963) 'Political science as science', in N. W. Polsby, R. A. Dentler and P. A. Smith (eds) *Politics and Social Life,* Boston: Houghton Mifflin, pp. 26–36.

Habermas, J. (1973) *Theory and Practice,* Boston: Beacon Press.

Hanushek, E. A. and Jackson, J. E. (1977) *Statistical Methods for Social Scientists,* New York: Academic Press.

Hempel, C. G. (1965) *Aspects of Scientific Explanation,* New York: Free Press.

Hofferbert, R. I. (1966) 'The relation between public policy and some structural and economic variables in the American states', *American Political Science Review,* 60 (March): 63–82.

—— (1972) 'State and community policy studies: a review of comparative input-output analyses', in J. A. Robinson (ed.) *Political Science Annual,* (Vol. 3). Indianapolis: Bobbs-Merrill, pp. 3–72.

Jacob, H. and Lipsky M. (1968) 'Outputs, structure, and power: an assessment of changes in the study of state and local government', *Journal of Politics,* 30:510–538.

Johnston, J. (1963) *Econometric Methods,* New York: McGraw-Hill.

Kuhn, T. F. (1970) *The Structure of Scientific Revolutions,* 2nd edn, Chicago: University of Chicago Press.

Lakatos, I. (1971) 'History of science and its rational reconstructions', in R. F. Cohen and M. W. Wartofsky (eds) *Boston Studies in the Philosophy of Science,* (Vol. 8), New York: Humanities Press, pp. 91–136.

Laslett, P., Runciman, W. G. and Skinner, Q. (1972) *Philosophy, Politics, and Society* (fourth series), Oxford: Blackwell.

Lave, C. A. and March, J. G. (1975) *An Introduction to Models in the Social Sciences,* New York: Harper & Row.

MacIntyre, A. (1967) 'The idea of a social science', *Proceedings of the Aristotelian Society,* suppl. 41:112–130.

Moe, T. (1979) 'On the scientific status of rational models', *American Journal of Political Science,* 23 (February): 215–243.

Moon, J. D. (1975) 'The logic of political inquiry', in F. I. Greenstein and N. Polsby (eds), *Political Science: Scope and Theory*, (Vol. 1). Reading, MA: Addison-Wesley, pp. 131–228.

Nagel, E. (1961) *The Structure of Science: Problems in the Logic of Scientific Explanation,* New York: Harcourt Brace Jovanovich.

Ostrom, E. and Whitaker, G. P. (1973) 'Does local community control of police make a difference? Some preliminary findings', *American Journal of Political Science*, 19 (February): 48–76.

Ostrom, V. (1980) *Leviathan and Democracy,* Bloomington: Indiana University, Workshop in Political Theory and Policy Analysis.

—— (1987) *The Political Theory of a Compound Republic* (rev. ed.). New Brunswick, NJ: Transaction.

Parks, R. B. (1979) 'Assessing the influence of organization on performance: a study of police services in residential neighbourhoods', Bloomington: Indiana University, Workshop in Political Theory and Policy Analysis.

Parks, R. B and Ostrom E. (1981) 'Developing and testing complex models of urban service systems', in T. N. Clark (ed.) *Urban Policy Analysis: Directions for Future Research*, (Vol. 21), Beverly Hills, CA: Sage Publications, pp. 171–200.

Phillips, L. and Votey, H. L., Jr. (1972) 'An economic analysis of the current effects of law enforcement on criminal activity', *Journal of Criminal Law, Criminology and Police Science*, 63 (September): 330–342.

Popper, K. R. (1965) *The Logic of Scientific Discovery,* New York: Harper & Row.

Przeworski, A. and Teune, H. (1970) *The Logic of Comparative Social Inquiry,* New York: John Wiley.

Rudner, R. S. (1966) *Philosophy of Social Science,* Englewood Cliffs, NJ: Prentice-Hall.

Shapiro, M. J. (1981) *Language and Political Understanding: The Politics of Discursive Practices,* New Haven, CT: Yale University Press.

Stonecash, J. (1978) 'Local policy analysis and autonomy: on intergovernmental relations and theory specification', *Comparative Urban Research* 5 (213): 5–23.

Summers, A. A. and Wolfe, B. L. (1977) 'Do schools make a difference?', *American Economic Review,* 67 (September): 639–652.

Toulmin, S. E. (1977) 'From form to function: philosophy and history of science in 1950s and now', *Daedalus,* 106 (3): 43–162.

Uslaner, E. M. and Weber, R. E. (1975) 'The 'single politics' of redistribution: toward a model of the policy-making process in the American states', *American Politics Quarterly,* 3 (April): 130–170.

Winch, P. (1958) *The Idea of a Social Science,* London: Rutledge & Kegan Paul.

Wright, G. C., Jr. (1976) 'Linear models for evaluating conditional relationships', *American Journal of Political Science* 20 (May): 349–373.

Chapter Eight

A Conceptual-Computational Logic for Federal Systems of Governance[1]

Vincent Ostrom

Those of us who are concerned with the study of federal systems of government confront some fundamental methodological problems in deciding how to proceed in our inquiries. By fundamental methodological problems, this writer is referring to the basic conceptions that are used to frame our inquiries. We are required to confront this issue as we raise questions about the nature of political and social phenomena. If human beings, at least in part, create their own social realities, we need to raise the question of whether there is only one way to create such realities.

To the degree to which choice is possible and alternative possibilities are available, we might anticipate that different conceptions may be used to design, construct, and maintain different social realities. This principle applies to all forms of artisanship. Different conceptualizations can be used by architects, for example, in the design and construction of various types of buildings. Different types of architecture depend both upon different conceptualizations and different computational logics for putting together different types of structures. Knowledgeable architects presumably use a language that enables them to communicate in a coherent way about the conceptual-computational patterns of thought that are an essential part of a theory of architecture.

In considering the question of whether there is a computational logic associated with the conception of a federal system of government that is different from unitary systems of government, we need to take a step backward to view the analysis in the constitutional era of the seventeenth and eighteenth century. The analyses offered in Walter Bagehot's *The English Constitution* and in both Woodrow Wilson's *Congressional Government* and his essay on 'The Study of Administration' have dominated political analysis in the twentieth century. Bagehot's theses about parliamentary government and Wilson's theses about bureaucratic administration in a unitary structure as being the principles of good administration that apply to all governments alike have left us with an intellectual heritage where a combination of parliamentary government and bureaucratic administration is presumed to be the appropriate form for any modern system of democratic government.

1. Chapter initially published in *Constitutional Design and Power Sharing in the Post-Modern Epoch*, D. J. Elazar (ed.) (1979), 2–22, Lanham, MD: University Press of America.

In this formulation no justification exists for a federal system of governance. It is only as we step back to intellectual discourse in the seventeenth and eighteenth centuries that we can recapture the structure of contending arguments and account for differences in the concepts and the computational logics that are inherent in federal and unitary systems of governance. We need to consider the basic challenge to those arguments during the nineteenth century in order to begin a reassessment of the relevance of those arguments for the political conditions of the contemporary world.

The computational logic associated with unitary and federal systems of government are best represented in Hobbes' theory of sovereignty and in the efforts of Montesquieu, Hamilton, Madison, and Tocqueville to establish a computational logic that is appropriate to republican or democratic institutions in a federal system of governance.

Hobbes' theory of sovereignty

Hobbes' *Leviathan* represents a remarkable achievement in laying out the computational logic that applies to the constitution of a system of governance in human societies. There are at least four sets of computations in Hobbes' analysis: 1) his analysis of man in a state of nature; 2) his formulation of the conditions of peace as expressed in some nineteen laws of nature; 3) his theory of sovereignty; and 4) his specification of a sovereign's accountability to God. The first two sets of computations will be briefly characterized because these provide a foundation that is as applicable to a federal system of governance as it is to a unitary state. After indicating the radical asymmetries in his theory of sovereignty, the computations that apply to a sovereign's accountability to God and how these pertain to the sufficiency of Hobbes' argument will then be briefly noted.

Hobbes' analysis of man in a state of nature, where conditions of scarcity prevail, provides us with a zero base for political analysis. A state of nature is conceived to be devoid of any political conditions or political constraints. It is a political void. There is no law, no authority, no 'mine' nor 'thine', everyone is free to take what he can get and defend what he has got. Each individual is essentially equal to any other and is motivated to seek his own good. The result of this situation yields conflict, and conflict in the absence of any constraint escalates into a condition of war of each individual against every other individual. The computational conclusion of this thought experiment is that an unconstrained pursuit of self-interest is an inadequate basis for human society.

The inherent contradiction between being motivated to seek one's own good and realizing misery instead poses for Hobbes the computational task of specifying the conditions of peace. In chapters 14 and 15 of *Leviathan*, Hobbes specifies some 19 'natural laws' as establishing the necessary conditions for peace as an alternative to war. Those will not be enumerated here, because Hobbes indicates that the basic computational logic inherent in each of these 'laws' can be understood by reference to a single summary rule: 'Do not that to another which thou wouldest not have done to thyself' (Hobbes 1960: 103; his emphasis). The golden rule, for Hobbes, provides a method of normative inquiry that is characterized by a fundamental symmetry in computing the basic structure of order in human societies. I act in relation to others as I would have them act in relation to me. The rule can be generalized if I put myself in the place of others, and others in my place so that my 'passions' and 'self-love' add nothing to the weight. Then we can come to understand the grounds for a community of relationships established by reference to shared standards of value that serve as criteria of choice in human societies. All law has reference to standard setting, standard using, and standard enforcing; and the method of normative inquiry enables human beings to make interpersonal comparisons that are sufficient for specifying the standards that serve as criteria of choice and provide the basis for jurisprudential reasoning and economic calculations.

The conditions of peace are, however, an insufficient basis for the organization of human societies. They are but rules – sets of words; and rules are not self-formulating, self-maintaining, and self-enforcing. They persuade in the sense of obliging one's conscience, but they do not necessarily compel or control one's actions. Temptations arise and reign in human actions. Unless rules can be enforced they cannot be made binding in human relationships. Without enforceable constraints, some may be tempted to act at variance with rules, and men of conscience become the prey of others.

Making rules binding in human relationships requires Hobbes to address the basic asymmetries inherent in the ruler-ruled relationships. Hobbes' resolution of this problem is based upon a presupposition that a unity of power is necessary to the unity of law and that the unity of power and of law is necessary to the peace and concord of commonwealths. He expresses his presumption in this way: 'For it is the unity of the representer, not the unity of the represented (i.e., ruled), that maketh the person (i.e., commonwealth as a personated aggregate of individuals) one' (Hobbes 1960: 107). The unity of the commonwealth depends upon a unity of power. This is the basic presupposition that applies to unitary systems of governance.

Hobbes' theory of sovereignty is an articulation of the basic computations that follow from this presupposition. A unity of power entails a monopoly over the powers of governance including the powers of the sword that are necessary to the maintenance and enforcement of rules of law. Such a conception necessarily implies that rulers are the source of law; as such they are above the laws that they promulgate; and rulers cannot themselves be held accountable to a rule of law by other human beings in a commonwealth. From this formulation it follows that the prerogatives of rulers are unlimited, inalienable, absolute, and indivisible. These are the basic attributes of sovereignty that apply to the internal structure of a commonwealth, and these apply in any organization of authority relationships that has the character of a monopoly. Whenever we define a state as a monopoly of the legitimate exercise of force in a society, Hobbes' attributes of sovereign authority necessarily apply as a manifestation of monopoly. Unity of power implies a monopoly of authority relationships in a society.

How, then, does Hobbes attempt to reconcile the basic symmetry inherent in the conditions of peace with the radical asymmetry between rulers and subjects in his theory of sovereignty? This issue is addressed in Chapter 31, 'Of the Kingdom of God by Nature', in *Leviathan*. There he identifies his laws of nature as being God's law (Hobbes 1960: 235) in the sense that they are 'immutable and eternal' (Hobbes 1960: 104). He earlier had asserted that the 'cause, whereof there is no former cause, but is eternal; which is it men call God' (Hobbes 1960: 68). How then do human beings avoid the circumstance of offending against the laws of God by too much civil obedience or of transgressing the laws of the commonwealth through fear of offending God (Hobbes 1960: 232)? Hobbes' resolution is to specify that the radical asymmetry inherent in his theory of sovereignty is subject, or subordinate to, the fundamental symmetries of his laws of nature which he views as the laws of God in the sense that they are immutable and eternal. The logical sufficiency of his political theory turns critically upon the accountability of those who exercise sovereign prerogatives to God. In the absence of that condition the natural punishments will prevail, and the peace and concord of commonwealths cannot be sustained.

In presenting his theory of sovereignty, Hobbes sees his formulation as 'the only way' to constitute a commanding power sufficient to maintain order and security in a commonwealth. There could, then, only be unitary states. He recognizes that the forms of government may vary to include reference to monarchies, aristocracies, and democracies. But, in the case of a democracy, it too would be a unitary state where one assembly of all citizens would exercise the prerogatives of government. Citizens in this case would be both rulers and subjects, but unity of power would be preserved by having but one assembly where binding decisions could be made by a plurality of votes. A majority, in such circumstances, would be the smallest plurality to yield an exclusive decision. It is in the working out of the relationship of democracy to constitutional rule and to federalism that Montesquieu and the American authors of *The Federalist* provide us with an alternative to Hobbes' theory of sovereignty.

Democracy, constitutional rule, and federalism

Hobbes' characterization of democracies as rule by assemblies of all citizens who will come together neglects a crucial consideration pertaining to the governance of a democracy. In order to have rule by assemblies, it is logically necessary to have a shared common understanding and agreement about the rules of assembly and what it means to rule by assembly. There is a set of calculations of what it means to govern by assembly that must be taken into account in the organization of an assembly and in the conduct of its proceedings. These require stipulation in establishing the terms and conditions of governance in an assembly in much the same way that the articles of peace might be specified as the basis for the organization of relationships in a society. We might then distinguish those rules that apply to terms and conditions of assembly as against those rules enacted by an assembly to apply to the ordinary exigencies of life. The former would be constitutional in character, and if enforceable with regard to the exercise of governmental prerogatives, might be regarded as constitutional law. The latter might be characterized as ordinary law, i.e., laws that apply to citizens as subjects of law.

Within a formulation that might apply to a simple, direct democracy, important issues arise both in relation to the proceedings of an assembly and the assignment of authority to those who act on behalf of an assembly. Matters pertaining to eligibility for membership, setting the time and place of meetings, a quorum, voting rules, order of proceedings, etc., all establish the terms and conditions of assembly. The assignment of specialized authority to direct the proceedings of an assembly, to exercise interim authority, to act on behalf of an assembly in the discharge of executive prerogatives, to represent an assembly in external affairs, and to provide for the common defence involve agency relationships where a democratic constitution requires that such authority be limited and accountable to an assembly as a public trust. The prerogatives of an assembly are limited by rules, and the prerogatives of those who act on behalf of an assembly are also limited by rules.

There is a puzzle that arises in direct, simple democracies that long led to the conclusion that democracies were confined to a very limited domain. First, the territorial domain is limited by the distance citizens can travel to participate in an assembly. Second, all democratic assemblies are subject to strong oligarchical tendencies. The first condition requires no explanation.

The oligarchical tendencies inherent in all deliberative assemblies, explained by Madison in *Federalist* 55 and 58, arise from the biological constraint that human beings can listen to and understand only one speaker at a time. This means that orderly proceedings in any group beyond a very limited size depend upon the exercise of leadership prerogatives to set the agenda, recognize speakers, and order the proceedings of a deliberative assembly. As assemblies increase in size the prerogatives of the leadership become increasingly dominant and the voice of the ordinary member becomes more and more confined. There comes a point, probably confined to a very few hundred participants, where coherent debate becomes difficult, and the prerogatives of the leadership become predominant. This problem can be alleviated somewhat by moving to representative institutions, but problems of size still pose difficulties. This problem is resolved in the British House of Commons, for example, by confining debate largely to those who exercise leadership positions among the major parties. The rules allocating debate to each member for a fixed number of minutes in the U.S. House of Representatives means that debate there is of limited coherence. The U.S. Senate, as the smaller body, conducts the more coherent debate.

Simple, direct democracies, then, were always exposed to institutional failures arising from the usurpation of authority by those who exercised leadership prerogatives. If the people acquiesce in the usurpation of authority by a dominant leader, Hobbes argues that this means the death of democracy. A democracy survives only so long as the rule of assembly is maintained with effective limits upon those who exercised leadership prerogatives.

Limits upon size, also, carries a correlative vulnerability to aggression by powerful neighbours. Montesquieu recognized this basic relationship when he observed, 'If a republic be small, it is destroyed by foreign force; if it be large, it is ruined by internal imperfection' (Montesquieu 1977: 181). If both small and large republics are destined to failure, the viability of democratic republics is severely limited.

Montesquieu conceived of confederation as a way of resolving this problem. Small republics might join together in a confederation until they had aggregated sufficient strength to defend themselves against foreign aggression. By retaining small republics within a confederate republic, the virtues of small republics could also be maintained. If corruption arose in some part of a confederate republic, remedies could be sought through alternative instrumentalities of government. Montesquieu, thus, viewed confederation as a way of 'withstanding an external force' and of preventing 'all manner of inconveniences' that arise from 'internal corruption' (Montesquieu 1977: 182).

The American effort to draw upon Montesquieu's conception of a confederate republic to organize the United States of America was, however, accompanied by serious problems of institutional failure. This problem was diagnosed by Alexander Hamilton, and an alternative conceptualization was advanced which shall be referred to as a federal republic.

Hamilton argues, consistent with Hobbes, that government implies a capacity to make rules binding as enforceable laws. A confederate assembly, which depends upon member republics to enforce law, is not a government in the proper signification of that word. Its resolutions are not binding as rules of law but constitute mere recommendations to member republics. If a confederate republic as a 'government' mobilizes sanctions to enforce its resolutions in relation to a member republic, it could do so only by an exercise of sanctions against a collectivity. Reliance upon collective sanctions implies that sanctions are being exercised against innocent bystanders as well as those who are culpable of wrongdoing. Reliance upon sanctions against collectivities is, thus, contrary to the requirements of justice. Justice can only be done if the prerogatives of government are exercised with reference to individuals. Thus, a federal system of government requires that each unit of government be constituted with reference to the persons of individuals. A government of governments is, for Hamilton, an absurdity that is contrary to the essential requirements of government. Hamilton's analysis is of far-reaching importance, and his formulation of the principle that individuals are the basic units in the constitution of order in human societies is deserving to be treated as one of the most fundamental theorems in political theory.

In light of this formulation, the task that the Philadelphia convention of 1787 faced was to constitute a limited national government that extended its jurisdiction to all individuals in its domain in the context of a more general federal system of government. A limited national government exercises governmental prerogatives that are confined to its domain, concurrently with limited state governments that exercise independent powers of government within their domains. The states, in turn, might exercise a limited prerogative with reference to local units of government which in turn exercise limited, independent governmental prerogatives with reference to local affairs. Both Montesquieu's confederate republics and Hamilton's federal republics were compound republics, not simple, unitary republics.

The compound nature of a federal republic requires what Hamilton refers to as a general theory of limited constitutions so that limits to the prerogatives of each unit of government might be maintained by reference to a general system of constitutional law. The computations that apply to the constitution of a federal republic require reference to quite a different formulation than Hobbes specifies in his theory of sovereignty. The strong emphasis upon subordination, or subjection as Hobbes calls it, is indicated by his formulation that each sovereign has the exclusive, unlimited, inalienable, and indivisible powers of rulership; 'and everyone besides, his SUBJECT' (Hobbes 1960: 112; Hobbes' emphasis). By contrast, Montesquieu articulates the basic structure of a republic that is capable of maintaining liberty as depending upon using power to check power (Montesquieu 1977: 200). Madison articulates the same principle by saying that constitution of a popular system of government depends upon using the principle of 'opposite and rival interests' through 'the whole system of human affairs' including 'the supreme powers of the state' (Hamilton, Madison, and Jay, n.d.: 337–338; author's emphasis).

The basic computations that apply to a general theory of limited constitutions in organizing a federal republic can be conceptualized in the following way. Each unit of government is subject to the terms and conditions as specified in a constitution which serves as a legal character specifying the way that authority is distributed and shared in that unit of government. Specifying the terms and conditions of the constitution is subject to distinguishable processes of constitutional decision-making so that those who exercise governmental powers cannot on their own authority establish or alter the terms and conditions of a constitution. The mark of a democracy turns critically upon the capacity of the people through processes of constitutional decision-making to control the basic sharing of power by provisions of constitutional law. If power is to be shared on the basis of opposite and rival interests then all persons must have access to some powers of government and no one can be in a position to exercise unlimited powers. Conditions of asymmetry must be met so that law can be effectively enforced, but the inequalities must be limited so that everyone has a voice in the processes of government, and no one exercises an unlimited voice.

Citizens in federal republics have as recognizable roles in the exercise of rulership as they would within the assembly of simple, direct democracies. These are specified through rules assigning the authority of citizens to participate in processes of constitutional choice, in establishing limits upon the authority of government, and in specifying the means by which citizens participate, directly or indirectly, in the processes of government. The basic architecture of a limited constitution, then, has reference to the authority of individuals and limits upon the authority of government, a distribution of the powers of government among diverse decision structures assigning both powers and limits to the exercise of those powers, and specifying the conditions for the direct or indirect participation of people in the powers exercised by the different structures of governments. Each of these sets of calculations shall briefly be reviewed.

Constitutional provisions that are traditionally referred to as 'bills of rights' typically specify limits upon governmental authority and assign authority to individuals as persons or citizens. These usually refer to freedom of communication, protection of property, the enforcement of contracts, rights of association including religious association outside the confines of government control, rights to due process of law, etc. It should be strongly emphasized that these are not private rights but public rights exercisable by individuals. Freedom of speech and press have their significance in maintaining an open public realm for discourse among people in a democratic society about public affairs, not subject to control by governmental authorities. Such freedoms are essential to an independent exercise of the public prerogatives of citizenship and are not confined to purely private relationships and matters of individual conscience. A right to due process of law, in turn, implies that citizens have the authority to command the services of officials – judges – to enforce demands that other officials, including judges, discharge their prerogatives in a proper, nonarbitrary way. A right of due process of law, in turn, implies lawful limits upon the exercise of governmental prerogatives by officials. A right to trial by jury, in turn, implies that the judicial process must include provision for juries, and, thus, for the direct participation of citizens in the judicial process. The enforceability of contracts implies that individuals can enter into arrangements for specifying rules that are binding and enforceable in their mutual relationships. This means that individuals can establish terms and conditions of association that are binding upon one another in governing their mutual affairs. Individuals have authority to govern their own affairs under mutually agreeable arrangements which allow for substantial spontaneity in constituting social relationships. Constitutional guarantees of the right to bear arms clearly implies that no monopoly over instruments of coercion can exist in such a society.

The architecture of constitutional arrangements in federal republics also calls for a separable assignment of authority among distinct decision structures in each unit of government. Distinguishing legislative, executive, and judicial instrumentalities of government clearly imply the existence of a division of labour and a separation of powers in the exercise of authority in any society where those distinctions occur. The critical constitutional issue turns upon the way that such structures are linked to one another. Where limits occur, one would anticipate that those limits imply checks, and where a reciprocal set of limits exists it would be proper to conceptualize a separation of powers as being accompanied by 'checks and balances'. If there are limits to the exercise of legislative authority, if executive officials are confined to rules of law in the exercise of executive prerogatives, and if judges can exercise independence in adjudicating disputes pertaining to the application of law, something like a system of checks and balances exists. *Power is then used to check power* through *opposite and rival interests,* and we can suppose that such a society is equilibrating relationships among the members of that society by references to rules of law that have reference to both constitutional and ordinary law. Rules of law, then, serve as media for the ordering of relationships in such societies.

The third set of provisions usually entailed in the architecture of a democratic constitution provides for ties that link the exercise of authority by citizens to the exercise of authority in governmental decision structures. These provisions specify how citizens participate, directly or indirectly, in the structures and processes of the diverse decision structures of government. Provision for jury trials imply that citizens participate directly in judicial decision-making. The same principle applies to the exercise of the investigatory authority of grand juries. Elections become ways that citizens either participate indirectly in the exercise of governmental authority by selecting those who do exercise governmental prerogatives in legislative or executive instrumentalities of government or directly in processes of government through various forms of initiative and referendum. These participatory ties anchor the exercise of governmental authority to the same community of people who exercise the prerogatives of individuals that allow for significant degrees of spontaneity in the organization of society at large. The structural characteristics of custom and law are meshed one with the other by the way that the constitutional prerogatives of individuals have an autonomous standing apart from the prerogatives of government and individuals participate, directly or indirectly, in processes that pertain to the formal decision structure of government. The participatory links are means by which distributed authority is shared in the governance of society. Individuals govern their own affairs, participate in the spontaneous governance of relationships with one another in the society at large and in the more formalized institutions of governance. In these circumstances custom, convention, and law become consonant with one another under conditions where it is possible to think of societies as being self-governing. Members of the society rule through a variety of different instrumentalities of government rather than simply being *subjects* where *the state rules over* society. Principles of self-governance prevail in place of Hobbes' principles of sovereignty and these principles of self-governance require both that power be used to check power and power be shared in accordance with rules of law.

Where principles of constitutional choice can be reiterated to specify an appropriate charter for all different units of government in a federal system of government, we can appreciate the merit of Montesquieu's suggestion that a confederate republic might avoid the exigencies of failure that were associated with both small and large republics. The reformulation advanced in fashioning a federal republic in 1787 was of fundamental importance in establishing the viability of Montesquieu's conception. The computational logic that applies to the design of a federal republic is radically at variance with the computational logic of Hobbes' theory of sovereignty. There is an alternative way for structuring the necessary asymmetries inherent in the rule-ruler-ruled relationships such that individuals as citizens might share in the prerogatives of rulership where both citizens and officials are subject to the rule of law. Tocqueville, a devoted student of Montesquieu, recognized the intellectual achievement that had occurred in the organization of the United States as a federal republic when he observed in the concluding paragraph to the first chapter of *Democracy in America*:

> In that land the great experiment of the attempt to construct society upon a new basis was to be made by civilized man; and it was there for the first time, that theories hitherto unknown, or deemed impracticable, were to exhibit a spectacle for which the world had not been prepared by the history of the past (Tocqueville 1945: I, 25).

Coping with counterintuitive relationships

If citizens in a democratic society were ignorant of the principles of self-governance, we would expect the use of power to check power through opposite and rival interests to yield stalemate and then to escalate to a point where the various opposite and rival interests in a society were at war with one another. A different outcome can, however, be expected when people come to expect that conflicts require recourse to processes of conflict resolution so that conflict situations become the basis for inquiry about the sources of conflict and how conflict situations have the possibility of being transformed into a mutually productive community of relationships if it is possible to reconstitute human relationships through properly conceived principles of association. This does not foreclose failure to resolve conflict. Possibilities of failure can be reduced where conflicts are to be processed through arrangements for conflict resolution which allow for a due process of inquiry in a due process of law.

Human institutions are, unfortunately, subject to counterintuitive relationships that pose a serious challenge to common sense in a democratic society. If common sense were sufficient to cope with problems in this world, we might expect people intuitively to understand what would be required in coping with any situation. Our common-sense intuitions are clearly unsatisfactory, and we must go to substantial effort to establish counterintuitive relationships that occur in many problematical situations. The significance of any science turns upon its capacity to clarify that which is counterintuitive. This problem is especially great in any system of governance that depends upon the use of power to check power by opposite and rival interests. The equilibrating tendencies in such a system of relationships may be seriously distorted if counterintuitive relationships become manifest in key linkages. Under those circumstances, equilibrating tendencies can be transformed into patterns of dominance that permit some to exploit others.

Such problems have reoccurred in American society. This analysis will focus only upon the rise of machine politics and boss rule because this development stands at a critical juncture that was marked by Woodrow Wilson's rejection of federal theory and influenced the turn to a model of parliamentary government and bureaucratic administration as the appropriate model for a democratic system of governance. This model fits a unitary state. Federal systems are superfluous in such a conception of social reality.

Elections have a critical role in any democracy where people are presumed to have a voice in the system of governance. A due dependence on the people calls for people to elect representatives who act on their behalf in a system of representative government. Any system of elections is likely to entail counterintuitive relationships. First, elections imply that some will win and some will lose. This involves strong conflict situations.

There are grounds for initially presuming that strong conflict situations have the danger of tearing a community apart into rivalrous factions that diverge increasingly from one another. The single-member-district electoral system that Americans borrowed from their British heritage has the opposite tendency. Where the candidate securing the largest number of votes wins an election to represent that constituency, a strong disadvantage accrues to additional candidates when more than two candidates compete for election. Further, there is an advantage for the two leading candidates to target their appeal to the median voter when only a majority vote guarantees victory. This means that candidates jockey themselves into positions that have strong tendencies toward convergence rather than divergence. If this process is carried too far, opportunities for added candidates to enter the electoral competition may occur and give voters a choice in relation to contending policy positions against a choice only of alternative candidates who stand for much the same policies.

Since strong conflict focuses upon the rivalry between candidates for particular offices, a further incentive exists to form coalitions with candidates who are contending for other offices. This is the basis for the organization of political parties. A party is a coalition among all candidates who are not in direct conflict with one another for particular offices. Where a strong strategic advantage accrues to only two contending parties, an incentive exists for someone to assume leadership in slating candidates, running the election campaign, and getting voters to the polls. If one party wins most offices and if the leadership can control all of those who won election on its slate, the leader, or 'boss', can achieve two critically important results. First, the boss has the possibility of controlling decisions in all of the different instrumentalities of government – legislative, executive, and judicial – where his slate was successful in winning control. Successful election of a winning slate enables the boss to override a constitutional separation of powers and dominate all of the separate decision structures of government controlled by his slate. A constitutional separation of power fails, and a 'boss' rules like a sovereign.

This possibility of controlling all of the different instrumentalities of government further gives the boss a capacity to control decisions, and take advantage of public jobs, the public treasury, and public powers to mobilize resources, strengthen his machine, and increase his dominance as a political entrepreneur.

This process was developed early in American political experience with the rise of Tammany Hall and a variety of similar organizations in larger American cities. The process continued to mushroom in the late nineteenth century until political machines came to dominance in most state legislatures and in national politics as the U.S. Senate became a club of bosses elected by the machine-controlled legislatures in most states. Machine politics and boss rule overrode the constitutional separation of powers as articulated by Montesquieu and as further elaborated by Madison.

Woodrow Wilson's book on *Congressional Government* and his essay on 'The Study of Administration' were first published in 1885 and 1887 against the background of events that were associated with the development of machine politics and boss rule. He rejected the theses advanced in *The Federalist* as 'literary theories' and 'paper pictures' which did not account for the 'living reality' in the American system of government of his time (Wilson 1956: 30–31). The system of checks and balances had been replaced by 'a scheme of congressional supremacy'

(Wilson 1956: 28). Furthermore, 'this balance of state against national authorities', in a federal system of government, 'had proved, of all the constitutional checks, the least effectual' (Wilson 1956: 34).

Wilson viewed these tendencies not as a pathology but as the manifestation of a 'natural' tendency in any system of government to move to a single center of ultimate authority that would exercise a position of absolute supremacy in the governance of society. Somehow the boss might be made responsible if the people could exercise a choice between bosses through processes of election. He fails to consider what a theory of sovereignty implies in the absence of a respectful and worshipful obedience by rulers to God's law, and the ease with which the terms and conditions of election can be altered to create one-party systems where no choice is available to citizens as electors.

Wilson's presumption about the 'natural' tendency of a system of government to move to a unitary system of government is consistent with Hobbes' conception that there is only one way to constitute a commonwealth as a monopoly of authority relationships. An alternative approach would be to entertain a conjecture that machine politics and boss rule manifested counterintuitive relationships which yielded pathological consequences requiring both a diagnostic assessment and a formulation of institutional modifications of remedial proportions.

The best diagnostic assessment of machine politics and boss rule is offered by Moisei Ostrogorski, a European scholar, in the second volume of his work on *Democracy and the Organization of Political Parties*. With a century of hindsight, we can begin to appreciate that constitutional changes introduced among the American states made sufficiently important changes in the organization of electoral processes, the interposition of limits upon the exercise of state legislative authority, and the extension of federal principles of organization to units of local government, to place radical constraints upon the opportunities for political bosses to dominate the slating process and exercise control over diverse decision structures across multiple units of government in the American federal system. Perhaps the most important single change was the introduction of public primary elections that allowed any member of a political party to challenge any other potential candidate for a position on a party's slate. This has meant that bosses can no longer control the slating process, and party leadership can no longer maintain disciplined control over party ranks in taking governmental decisions. The equilibrating tendencies of a federal system of governance constituted on principles of opposite and rival interests where power is used to check power were reestablished by the constitutional revisions achieved during the Progressive reform movement.

Beyond the twentieth century

Political discourse in the twentieth century has been dominated by a presupposition that 'natural' tendencies exist in systems of governance where models of government are assumed to be unitary in character and the method of the natural sciences apply to the investigation of political phenomena. There is no point to intentionality in construing the meaning of political experience if that experience is viewed as only manifesting natural tendencies. If political experience is conceived to be artifactual (i.e., created by reference to human knowledge), then elements of intentionality and knowledgeable calculations need to be taken into account in construing the 'living realities' that exist in the political realm.

Human beings as artisans conceptualize alternative possibilities and work through the computational logics that enable them to realize different possibilities. The conceptualization of a federal system of government as formulated by Montesquieu and Hamilton entails a computational logic that was best formulated in the analyses offered by Hamilton and Madison in *The Federalist*. That logic is, best taken into account in Tocqueville's analysis of *Democracy in America* in contrast to his incomplete study of France in *The Old Regime and the French Revolution*.

The application of natural science methods to the study of political phenomena during the twentieth century has meant the abandonment of any serious preoccupation with the critical problems of constitutional choice and the conceptual-computational logics that inform the artisanship inherent in the design and alteration of systems of governance as these are constituted and reconstituted. Political science in the twentieth century has become a science without an explicit understanding of the critical role of theory as a system of conceptual-computational logics that applies to the design of different systems of government. The use of the method of the natural sciences has transformed the conceptual-computational logics available to political artisans into something that is identified as 'ideologies'. Ideologies are then treated as a form of false consciousness, and the practitioners of a positive political science have become an intellectual community of know-nothings. Nothing was salvaged from destruction by using the methods of the natural sciences to study 'living realities' in the governance of human societies.

The challenge facing us in exploring the problem of 'constitutional rule and shared power' is to reconsider the epistemological and metaphysical grounds on which we stand. Human beings have been agents in an extraordinary transformation of the world of nature into an artifactual realm. This artifactual realm uses the materials and processes of nature and transforms them through the use of human knowledge and artisanship to serve human purposes. The earth has been transformed into a human habitat that is a visibly different 'reality' than the earth in its 'natural' condition. Pierre Teilhard de Chardin characterizes this transformation as a noosphere, a sphere shaped by human knowledge which has its analogue in the biosphere, a sphere shaped by the existence of life. Artifacts cannot be understood as natural occurrences. In explaining artifactual constructions, we are required to account for human artisanship and the conceptual-computational considerations that entered into the design and creation of artifactual constructions.

These relationships were well understood by major political thinkers who were concerned with the knowledge that informed political artisanship during the constitutional eras that followed the English, American, and French revolutions. Serious problems arise from the discrepancy between intentionality and the consequences that were yielded from conscious efforts to fashion diverse social realities. This requires an acknowledgement of the insufficiency of common sense and the burden that human beings must necessarily assume in accounting for Counterintuitive relationships. The existence of counterintuitive relationships necessarily implies that artisanship is subject to error. A discrepancy between intentions and outcomes in fashioning artifacts is indicative of a potential for error.

When Tocqueville wrote *Democracy in America*, he recognized that a new conceptual-computational logic was required for the constitution of democratic societies if human beings under conditions of increasing equality were to achieve and maintain substantial freedom in their relationships with one another. He was persuaded that alternatives were available so long as human beings might have recourse to a science of association in the conceptualization and design of human institutions. People might, then, appreciate the utility of forms and procedures in constructing a due process of inquiry bounded by a due process of law.

This implies that on the eve of the twenty-first century, we are first required to relearn what Hobbes, Locke, Montesquieu, Rousseau, Hume, Hamilton, Madison, Tocqueville, and a host of others have to teach us about the conceptual-computational logics that apply to the design, creation, and study of systems of governance as artifactual constructions. When we recognize, as Tocqueville did, that human beings have the possibility of fashioning creations that exhibit spectacles 'for which the world has not been prepared by the history of the past' (Tocqueville, 1945: I, 25), we can understand what has occurred only by reference to the computational-conceptional logics that inform the design of those spectacles. We have as much to learn when the spectacles are of disastrous proportions as when they achieve successful performances. If we learn how to avoid disasters and enhance successful achievements, we might then learn how to address problems of constitutional rule and shared power again. Once we relearn the computational logics used to inform constitutional inquiry in the seventeenth, eighteenth, and nineteenth centuries, we shall be better prepared to face the twenty-first century. The disasters of the twentieth century can yield their lessons for what to avoid and remind us to be wary of the potential for error when commonsense intuitions fail to account for counterintuitive relationships.

References

Bagehot, W. (1964) *The English Constitution*, London: C. A. Watts.

Hamilton, A., Jay, J. and Madison, J. (n.d.). *The Federalist*, New York: The Modern Library.

Hobbes, T. (1960) *Leviathan or the Matter, Forme and Power of a Commonwealth Ecclesiastical and Civil,* Oxford: Basil Blackwell.

Montesquieu, C. L. de Secondat (1977) *The Spirit of Laws*, Berkeley: University of California Press.

Ostrogorski, M. (1964) *Democracy and the Organisation of Political Parties, Volume II: The U.S.,* Garden City, New York: Anchor Books.

Tielhard de Chardin, P. (1961) *The Phenomenon of Man,* Harpers Torchbook edition, New York: Harper and Row.

Tocqueville, A. de (1945) *Democracy in America*, New York: Alfred A. Knopf.

— (1955) *The Old Regime and the French Revolution,* Garden City, New York: Doubleday.

Wilson, W. (1887) 'The Study of Administration', *Political Science Quarterly,* Vol. 2 (June): 197–200.

— (1956) *Congressional Government*, New York: Meridian Books.

Chapter Nine

Epistemic Choice and Public Choice[1]

Vincent Ostrom

At the intersections of anthropology, economics, law, political science, public administration, and sociology, a sufficient body of literature had accumulated from interdisciplinary research efforts by the mid-1960s to support a new approach to the study of public decision making. Those inquiries were stimulated by a growing awareness that problems of institutional weaknesses and failures in market arrangements could not be corrected simply by recourse to governmental decision processes that were themselves subject to serious limits. How did we develop a better understanding of the structure of decision making and performance in the 'public sector'? What were the limits applicable to collective choice and its relationship to collective action? Now, in the presence of three or four decades of cumulative efforts in the Public-Choice tradition, how does one assess the prospects for the next generation?

My conclusion is that the most important potentials have been associated with diverse thrusts on the peripheries of work in the Public-Choice tradition rather than with efforts at the core of the tradition to apply 'economic reasoning' to 'nonmarket decision making', as the Public-Choice approach has been conceptualized by the mainstream of Public-Choice scholars. The 'core' of the Public-Choice tradition involves economic reasoning that places primary emphasis on a *nontuistic, self-interested, rational actor* approach to *methodological individualism. Nontuism* implies *not* taking account of the interests of others; *self-interest* implies taking account of one's own preferences. *Rational actors* in economic theory seek to maximize their own net advantage. *Methodological individualism* involves taking the perspective of hypothetical individuals in choice situations. By 'thrusts on the peripheries', I refer, for example, to Gordon Tullock's (1965) focus on the way that bureaucracies filter and distort the transmission of information to create systemic propensities for deception and for error, to James Buchanan's (1979a) emphasis on the artifactual character of human individuality, to Douglass North's (1990) insistence that ideas and institutional arrangements are important, and to James Coleman's (1990) concern that norms are important sources of productive potentials.

---

1. Initially published in Vincent Ostrom's *The Meaning of Democracy and the Vulnerability of Democracies: Response to Tocqueville's Challenge*, 89–116. Ann Arbor: The University of Michigan Press, 1997.

Work on the peripheries is where important advances at the frontier are most likely to occur. The leading contributors to the Public-Choice tradition have never confined themselves to a 'core' built on extreme rationality assumptions. A. K. Sen's article on 'Rational Fools' (1977), Karl Popper's essay on 'Rationality and the Status of the Rationality Principle' (1967) and Brian Barry and Russell Hardin's collection of essays on *Rational Man and Irrational Society?* (1982) are indicative of some of the social dilemmas and puzzles that pervade human societies. Perhaps the important challenge for Public-Choice scholars is to address how basic anomalies, social dilemmas, and puzzles can be resolved in human affairs, rather than to apply economic reasoning, narrowly construed, to nonmarket decision making.

A question of some importance is whether these efforts at the periphery of the Public-Choice approach are only miscellaneous idiosyncratic accretions. In that case, the literature will exceed human cognitive limits and become fleeting fads among Towers of Babel. Or are there ways that these cumulative inquiries can be ordered as contributions to diverse elements, foci, and levels of analysis that are complementary to one another and that meet standards of scientific warrantability? This, too, is a matter of 'public' choice at an epistemic level about what is worthy of inclusion in the corpus of knowledge. The attribute of publicness as applied to the corpus of knowledge is not confined to collective choice implicating institutions of government. Rather, the public-good character of knowledge evokes important potentials for economic and political development – in all aspects of market and nonmarket decision making. The public-good character of knowledge is not decided by Governments but by those who are artisans engaged in the creation and uses of knowledge. Public choice need not be decided by elections and coalitions claiming popular mandates. Furthermore, the principles of choice applicable to the warrantability of knowledge are different than the principles of choice applicable to a choice of goods in market and public economies. These are different than the principles of choice applicable to the constitution of rule-ordered relationships in accordance with standards of fairness. Principles of consensus among participants can apply to each, but the criteria of choice vary among different types of choice.

If an intellectual apparatus can be developed to give complementarity to the diverse thrusts in inquiries pursued over the last three or four decades, we might also expect to achieve a greater coherence among much longer traditions of inquiry in the social or cultural sciences. Edwin Haefele, for example, called attention to an assertion made by Aristotle – 'For that which is common to the greatest number has the least care bestowed upon it' (Aristotle 1942, bk. 2, chap. 3, sec. 3 – to reject Plato's argument about the ideal polity expounded by Socrates in *The Republic*, a title that is itself a misnomer drawn from the Latin language. Aristotle's assertion indicates a long-standing awareness of collective-action dilemmas. If a public facility or service were to be collectively provided, any narrowly rational actor would take advantage of what became freely available, while declining to bear responsibility for a proportionate share of the burdens and costs. Under these circumstances, levying a tax through some instrumentality of government would serve as a proxy for a market price. People could not be expected to pay taxes voluntarily.

A new approach not only opens potentials for future work but allows for a better appreciation of how to select from and build on prior achievements. Problems of epistemic choice – the choice of conceptualizations, assertions, and information to be used and acted on in problem-solving modes – must necessarily loom large. If the Public-Choice approach will continue to contribute to the advancement of knowledge, that future depends on meeting the requirements of epistemic choice. In this chapter, I first give attention to the problem of epistemic choice and then relate that problem to the arraying of elements in a framework implicit in the Public-Choice tradition.

The problem of epistemic choice

Fundaments of epistemic choice

Thomas Hobbes, David Hume, Adam Smith, and others give us foundations for dealing with language, learning, knowledge, communication, artisanship, and moral judgment in the exercise of choice. In considering the problem of epistemic choice, the contingencies of language and their relationships to knowledge, choice, and action are at the focus of attention. The conceptions formulated, the words used, and the assertions made are all significant because symbolic expressions stand for referents. Symbols used in interpersonal communication refer to events in the world: elements [things named] and relations [motions, action tendencies, transforms] functioning in subject-predicate-object relationships, in hypothetical if-then relationships, and in factor-function-product relationships. Distinctions relate to classificatory schema that identify sets and subsets in patterns of associated relationships.

Three criteria can be used for establishing the warrantability of assertions: (1) logical coherence among complementary assertions in bodies of knowledge presuming a unity of knowledge; (2) empirical warrantability – hypothetical assertions withstand critical scrutiny in light of experience – and (3) public reproducibility – empirical results, achieved by some, can also be replicated by others if assertions are appropriately formulated and acted on. The important associations between linguistic formulations and referent events are accompanied by parallel associations occurring in the patterns of thought characteristic of inferential [if-then] reasoning. This is complemented by thinking associated with the use of the imagination to array speculative what-if conjectures. Human thought may evoke fictions of the mind that differ substantially from those sets of assertions that withstand the tests of logical coherence, empirical warrantability, and public reproducibility.

In an epistemic context, I find Thomas Hobbes's analysis 'Of Man' ([1651] 1960: 7–108) to be far more helpful for establishing the conceptual foundations for human understanding than Jeremy Bentham's formulation, which emphasizes something Bentham called 'utility' ([1823] 1948). Hobbes argued that speech [language] is the factor that distinguishes *Homo sapiens* from other creatures, like lions, bears, and wolves. Science is a 'knowledge of consequences' associated with hypothetical assertions. Thought permits the arraying of alternative possibilities. Choice involves a weighing of those alternatives in relation to internal indicators of individuals reflecting their appetites and aversions [preferences]. Hobbes asserted that 'The POWER [action potentials] *of a man,* to take it universally, is his present means, to obtain some future apparent good' ([1651] 1960: 56, Hobbes's emphasis). I conceptualize Hobbes's definition of power to equate purposive action with artisanship – the use of present means to obtain some future apparent good. His basic postulate is then formulated, 'So that in the first place, I [Hobbes] put for a general inclination of all mankind, a perpetual and restless desire of power after power, that ceaseth only in death' (Hobbes: 64). I interpret that assertion to indicate that the general inclination of all mankind is a continual striving to use present means to obtain some future apparent good, in successive efforts that cease only with death. Saints, for example, presumably strive through prayer and meditation to bring themselves closer to God, rather than maximizing their net assets in a system of financial accounts. Scholarship need not be concerned with maximizing wealth, even though scholars, like everyone else, need to meet the economic requirements of life. Languages, then, not only act as devices that enable human beings to convey signals to one another but are the means for constituting knowledge, organising thought, arraying alternatives, ordering choice, and taking actions in arranging present means in appropriate ways to realize future apparent goods. Choice is mediated by human cognition and action potentials articulated through language. But language can, unfortunately, also be used to fool oneself and others.

Hobbes's Man in a State of Nature is, I believe, a hypothetical thought experiment of presuming human beings to be *devoid of speech* and, thus, comparable to animals like lions, bears, and wolves. In referring to the frailties of the mind in Chapter Thirteen of *Leviathan,* Hobbes proposed 'setting aside the arts grounded upon words' (Hobbes: 80). Individuals would seek their own good; but, in the absence of speech, in the presence of scarcity and the existence of others, they would end up fighting with one another. Fighting is a recurrent and persistent phenomenon among *Homo sapiens.*

The precariousness of conflict situations is indicated by Kenneth Boulding's essay 'Toward a Pure Theory of Threat Systems' (1963). Boulding presumes speech; but an exchange of threats involves a form of speech in which someone demands, '*You* do something *good* for *me* or *I* will do something *bad* to *you*'. The person confronted with a threat is presented with a choice between two bads because doing something good for the other will require a cost to oneself. To defend oneself in such a circumstance, an even stronger counterthreat is easily made. Threats, as such, are mere words. The vulnerable point in an exchange of threats occurs when the credibility of a threat is made a matter of honour. One or the other is required to follow through and make his or her threat credible or to apologize for being offensive. Conflict involving an exchange of threats has a very strong tendency to escalate into violent confrontations yielding more destructive effects than were intended by those who initiated an exchange of threats. Destruction can easily escalate into uncontrolled violence.

Toward a lawful order and a culture of inquiry

In adopting a problem-solving mode as an alternative to fighting, Hobbes explored a set of principles that would be constitutive of Peace as an alternative to War. Achieving peace requires taking account of the interests of others; nontuism does not work in that context. Rather, Hobbes argued that a method of nonnative inquiry grounded in the rule *'Do not that to another, which thou wouldest not have done to thyself'*([1651] 1960: 103, Hobbes's emphasis) is necessary to the achievement and maintenance of peace. As a method of inquiry, Hobbes suggested that such a rule can be made 'intelligible even to the meanest capacity' by using the following approach.

> [If,] when weighing the actions of other men with his own, they seem too heavy, [...] put them into the other part of the balance, and his own into their place, that his own passions, and self-love, may add nothing to the weight; and then there is none of these laws of nature [articles of peace] that will not appear unto him very reasonable. (*Ibid.*)

A method of normative inquiry grounded in the Golden Rule is available for reconsidering one's own preferences in relation to the preferences of others when interdependent interests require *impartiality* in arriving at a judgment pertaining to joint interests. John Harsanyi (1977) and Reinhard Selten (1986) have adopted a similar approach as a broader foundation for evaluating rules of action and not simply action alone. I summarize the set of principles Hobbes derived from this method of normative inquiry in Table 9.1. These can be viewed as necessary conditions for the constitution and reform of human communities in accordance with basic normative precepts taught in the Jewish, Christian, and Islamic traditions. Similar precepts prevail in other civilizations. They are steps to be pursued in the resolution of conflict as a way of peacefully resolving problems in human relationships. Conflicts associated with interdependent individual interests suggest commonalities that require attention to how individual interests relate to communities of interdependent interests. A method of normative inquiry in a problem-solving mode is available among members of speech communities to explore options for resolving conflict in relation to all different forms of choice.

This method of normative inquiry is a way of making interpersonal comparisons and arriving at rules of reason. Hobbes viewed these rules of reason as accessible to anyone who draws on his or her fundamental resources as a human being, mediated through the use of language, to build shared communities of understanding. Mutual trust is established by performing covenants made. For Hobbes, a fool would deny such rules of reason without appreciating the destructive potentials involved. The terms *nature* and *natural* are associated with different meanings when referring to man in 'a state of nature' and to 'the laws of nature'. This tension reflects puzzles about the place of language in 'human nature' and the place of culture in human societies. Rules of right reason are presumed to be expressive of human nature even though they accrue as human cultural achievements and are not evoked by genetic reproduction alone.

David Hume (1948) and Adam Smith ([1759] n.d.) relied on a sentiment of sympathy, modified by the generality of language in human communication, to arrive at a standard of justice for mediating human relationships. In 'An Enquiry concerning the Principles of Morals', Hume wrote:

> The distinction, therefore, between the species of sentiment [i.e., sympathy or fellow feeling in contrast to those connected with any other emotion or passion] being so great and evident, language must soon be moulded upon it and must invent a peculiar set of terms in order to express those universal sentiments of censure and approbation which arise from humanity or from views of general usefulness and its contrary. Virtue and Vice become known; morals are recognized; certain general rules are framed of human conduct and behavior; such measures are expected of men in such situations. This action is conformable to an abstract rule; the other contrary. And by such universal principles are the particular sentiments of self-love frequently controlled and limited. (1948: 254)

Table 9.1: Hobbes's Laws of Nature [The Way to Peace]

1. That one seek peace and follow it, but be prepared to defend oneself.

2. That one be willing, in the quest for peace, when others are willing, to lay down one's right to all things and be content with so much liberty against others as one would allow others against oneself.

3. That individuals perform their covenants made.

4. That one act in relation to others so they will have no cause for regret.

5. That everyone strive to accommodate oneself to the rest.

6. That upon caution of future time, a person ought to pardon the offenses past of them that, repenting, desire it.

7. That in retribution of evil for evil, persons look not at the greatness of the evil past but at the greatness of the good to follow.

8. That no one by deed, word, countenance, or gesture declare hatred or contempt of others.

9. That everyone acknowledge another as one's equal by nature.

10. That at the entrance into the conditions of peace, no one reserve to oneself any right which one is not content should be reserved to every one of the rest.

11. That if one be trusted to judge between one person and another, one deals equally between them.

12. That such things as cannot be divided, be enjoyed in common,
    if it can be, and if the quantity of the thing permit, without stint,
    otherwise proportional to the number of them that have right.

13. That such things as cannot be divided or enjoyed in common
    require that the entire right to the whole thing, or else,
    making the use alternative, be determined by lot.

14. That distribution by lot be determined by an agreement
    among the competitors or by first seizure.

15. That all who mediate peace be allowed safe conduct.

16. That they that are at controversy submit their
    right to the judgment of an arbitrator.

17. That no one is a fit arbitrator of one's own cause
    in relation to the interest of another.

18. That no one in any cause ought to be received for arbitrator
    to whom greater profit or honour or pleasure apparently
    arises out of the victory of one party rather than another.

19. That in controversies of fact those who judge should give no more
    credit to one witness than to another but should call additional
    witnesses until the question is decided by the weight of evidence.

Summary Rule: *Do not that to another, which thou wouldest not have done to thyself.*

Source: Hobbes [1651, 1960, chaps. 14 and 15].

The moral quality arises from fellow feelings expressed as general rules: 'Virtue and Vice become known; morals are recognized; certain general rules are framed of human conduct [...]; such measures are expected of men in such situations. This action is conformable to an abstract rule; the other contrary'. Hume was emphasizing the *coevolutionary* and *configured* development of sentiments, languages, the foundation of morals, the articulation of meaning, and the basic foundations of law as these might apply to epistemic choice and other forms of choice.

Following his well-known passage about distinguishing 'is' and 'ought' statements, Hume indicated that it is necessary to 'look within' to find the standards for rendering moral judgment. Those standards are ascertainable by the use of methods of normative inquiry to make interpersonal comparisons mediated through speech. Without a background of common knowledge, a shared community of understanding about making appropriate normative distinctions, a system of social accountability for monitoring and enforcing rules, and a substantial degree of public trust that rule-ordered relationships will be adhered to, there is no basis for assigning autonomy to individuals to exercise responsibility for the actions they take in the governance of their own affairs and in relating to others. The conditions stipulated in Hobbes's laws of nature are the foundations for both a lawful order and a culture of inquiry. The use of extreme rationality assumptions in economic theory runs the risk of stripping away and ignoring essential epistemic and moral considerations that are constitutive of human affairs.

The basic epistemological problem

Walter Eucken ([1940] 1951), the German economist associated with the development of *Ordnungstheorie* [theory of order], writing in the late 1930s, called attention to what I regard as the basic epistemological problem in the cultural and social sciences. Eucken asserted that economic theorists rely on a single, simple, general model that is presumed to have universal application in the conduct of economic analysis. By so doing, he argued that economists increasingly distanced themselves from economic 'reality'. Abstractions lose meaning, theory is confined to doctrine and lacks contact with 'reality'. Hans Albert (1984), a German philosopher concerned with problems of epistemology in the Popperian tradition as applied to economics and the social sciences, refers to this as a problem of model-thinking. A fully specified model bounded by limiting assumptions is presumed to have universal applications. Model thinking may serve the purposes of rigorous mathematical reasoning but neglects empirical 'realities' and problematics in human affairs. Eucken contrasted the empirical inquiries of economic historians of his time as heaping facts on facts without relevance to economic theory. The result was a 'great antinomy': abstract doctrine on the one hand, and the accumulation of facts, on the other, without critical attention to how theory and facts – ideas and deeds – relate to one another in establishing the warrantability of what was being asserted. Eucken's 'great antinomy' yields a basic incoherence in discourse about human affairs. Contemporary work by Douglass North (1990) and Harold Berman (1983) and a virtual flood of similar inquiries represent major advances in this regard. The ambiguous and pervasive uses of the term *model* among economists and among many social scientists, however, leave me grasping for words to gain understanding.

At this point, it is important to recall Hobbes's assertions about the use of language that might make one 'excellently wise' by acting on scientifically warranted conceptions in contrast to 'excellently foolish' when acting on absurd doctrine – 'senseless speech' ([1651] 1960: 22). In Hobbes's judgment, being excellently foolish was worse than simple ignorance. People of simple ignorance do not indulge in genocide and holocausts. Rather, those who engage in such conduct are presumably infected with some form of intellectual 'virus', so to speak. Prudence, which Hobbes associated with experience, is a way of distinguishing sensible from senseless uses of language. Absurd doctrines can meet standards of logical rigor and mathematical proof but yield disastrous consequences when used to inform actions. Human action needs to draw on general principles that can be applied to particular time and place exigencies that vary with ecological and cultural circumstances.

Eucken presumed that different systems of economic order exist in different times and places. His concern was how to identify and develop basic elements and relationships so that a commensurate framework could be used to specify structured variants – morphologies – to allow for comparative assessments of performance. He presumed that all systems of economic order require planning – the uses of knowledge and information. His concern was with the differences in planning processes that occurred, for example, in contemporary 'market' and 'command' economies, rather than with a presumption that there are some 'planned' and other 'unplanned' economies. He further presumed that all economic orders function in a context of political orders.

Eucken's presumption that planning takes place in all economic activities is commensurate with Hobbes's presumption that all action is grounded in thought. This poses an issue with regard to Friedrich von Hayek's use of the concept of 'spontaneity' (1973: 36–54) and Adam Smith's concept of the 'hidden hand' ([1776] n.d.), in the creation and maintenance of social orders. Are such terms to be applied to relationships viewed as 'brute facts' or 'institutional facts' that reflect self-organising and self-governing capabilities among knowledgeable and intelligible human beings? Can 'hidden hands' be expected to work spontaneously in the constitution of order in human societies viewed as systems of natural order – 'brute facts'? If Hayek's spontaneity and Smith's hidden hand depend on the intelligent use of the arts and sciences of association among the members of societies, we in the Public-Choice tradition bear a substantial burden in elucidating and making use of the sciences and arts of association. Coming to terms with problems of institutional weaknesses and failures depends on the development of analytical capabilities commensurate with the sciences and arts of human association.

Neoclassical economic theory relies on a 'model' presuming a perfectly competitive market economy in which fully informed actors participate as buyers and sellers when a price equilibrium is achieved at a point where demand at that price equals the supply offered at that price. With an indefinitely large number of market participants, the actions of particular buyers and sellers will not alter the price equilibrium. So price provides crucial information about economic opportunities. Market decisions about price are nontuistic in the sense that a perfectly competitive market would determine price on an impartial basis without regard for others. A rational actor in such circumstances would act in a way that maximizes individual self-interest.

Social dilemmas arise, however, when individuals select strategies to maximize their own gains that diverge from the aggregate gain that might have been realized. Each individual acting on the basis of a best response without regard for others need not achieve the highest joint benefit (common good). Individual success in acquiring wealth is not the appropriate measure of a contribution to 'society', 'civilization', or 'human welfare'. Many human relationships are not monetized exchange relationships. Individual rationality in maximizing 'utility', as Bentham used that term, could yield Sen's 'Rational Fools' and Barry and Hardin's 'Irrational Society'.

As a purely abstract intellectual enterprise, neoclassical economic theory in the Anglo-American tradition has considerable merit; but it is bound up with seriously limiting assumptions. Among these are fully informed actors whose actions are governed by law and order. Ordinary theft, violence, and the expropriation and seizure of property are assumed away. The *necessary* conditions for the constitution and operation of a market economy depend on establishing conditions approximating these assumptions by reference to the proper operation and performance of a political system, an epistemic [knowledge and information] system, and a moral order. These patterns of order operate concurrently. Habituated patterns of conduct are not sufficient. Self-conscious awareness of the way that economic, political, epistemic, and moral contingencies may work in complementary ways is necessary to the sustainability and reformability of patterns of order in human societies.

The emphasis on maximizing 'utility' or 'wealth' means that primary attention is being given to preference orderings; other aspects of the political economy of life are excluded from the focal attention of inquiry and swept into the background. The principle of maximizing Utility, also referred to by Bentham as the 'happiness principle', presumably applies universally to people everywhere for choosing among bliss points without regard to language, culture, or the constitution of order in particular societies and ways of life. The place of knowledge and of information, the place of a moral order as constitutive of fiduciary relationships, the place of law and the requirements of justice, and the requirements of intelligibility in human artisanship are treated as outside the focus of inquiry. Such circumstances are susceptible to self-deception. If attention is given only to preferences, there is a danger that the 'whole moral and intellectual condition of a people' will be reduced to 'intellectual dust', as Tocqueville asserted ([1835–40] 1945, 1:299, 2:7).

Continuing to adhere to an orthodox way of applying 'economic reasoning' to nonmarket decision making does not allow for learning to occur. An openness to uncertainty, social dilemmas, anomalies, and puzzles as presenting problematics, allows for learning, innovation, and basic advances in knowledge to occur. This is why all scholarship in the social and cultural sciences needs to be sensitive to the artifactual character of language and the intellectual constructions that are used to frame inquiry. The existence of conflict should serve as a reminder that our intellectual constructions may be at fault. Recognizing different ways of conceptualizing problematics may be the key to the achievement of conflict resolution. Different ways of conceptualizing the intellectual enterprise within and among the social and cultural sciences is of basic importance in working out the essential relationships of ideas to deeds in human societies.

The problem of lawful order

If we recognize that Jeremy Bentham, the early exponent of the concept of Utility as a single, linear scale of values, was a philosopher with a strong interest in jurisprudence, we can begin to appreciate some of the difficulties that can arise in applying economic reasoning grounded only in Utility theory to nonmarket decision making. Bentham's concept of Utility served as a single summary measure for preference orderings implying a single selection principle applicable to all human choices. Both Hume and Adam Smith used the term *utility* to mean 'usefulness' rather than a summary measure for all values. Maximizing Utility for Bentham also meant the achievement of the greatest good for the greatest number.

Bentham's way of addressing the problem of rule-ordered relationships was to presume that men of goodwill could know what would provide the greatest good for the greatest number and, thus, what was good for others. Such men could be relied on to establish a rational code of law that would avoid the irrationalities of relying on the Common Law, an accretion of precedents derived from the accidents of historical decisions accumulated from the past. The problem of representative government could be resolved by the selection of an assembly of men of goodwill rather than of aspiring politicians seeking to win elections and form governing coalitions to enjoy the fruits of victory. The criminal law for Bentham was the core of the law because it established the bounds of lawful conduct and was, presumably, made effective by enforceable sanctions. A fear of punishment rather than a sense of justice motivates men to obey rules. Bentham's solution to the problem of men governing men placed reliance on principles of command and control, in contrast to Madison's solution of using power to check power in a search for conflict resolution in accordance with principles of freedom and justice. If potentials for deception and self-deception prevail in human societies, a way to cope with such ambiguities is to rely on principles of contestation among opposite and rival interests. Checks and balances are necessary to make such systems work. But then the question is how to achieve commonalities.

We face a puzzle posed by Hobbes of whether the unity of commonwealths turns on the unity of the Sovereign *representative* or the unity of the *represented*. Hobbes presumed that the unity of the commonwealth could only be achieved by the unity of the Sovereign representative. The American federalists, by contrast, presumed that the application of covenantal methods to conflict and conflict resolution was the appropriate way to create the conditions of common knowledge, shared understanding, social accountability, and mutual trust that were viewed as essential to self-governing communities of relationships and to the achievement of the conditions of peace and other public goods.

If command and control by a single power are not the key design principles, how do we devise the rules for a fair game? These rules require the experience of communicating and relating to others in the context of a prior background of common knowledge, shared understanding, social accountability, and mutual trust. Human beings are always drawing on prior experiences, but they need not be the slaves of precedents. Systems of rule-ordered relationships depend on change, adaptability, and reformulation. What methods of normative inquiry should be applied to the construction and alteration of rule-ordered relationships?

Hobbes presumed that standards of fairness depend on informed consent: 'It is in the laws of a commonwealth, as in the laws of gaming: whatsoever the gamesters all agree on, is injustice to none of them' ([1651] 1960, 227). This assumption implies standards achieved through informed consent – general agreement, not majority rule. Hobbes warned that 'Unnecessary laws are not good laws; but traps for money' (*Ibid.*, 227–28). Adherence to the Golden Rule as a method of normative inquiry is an appropriate way to devise the rules of a fair game that are consistent with rules of equity and informed consent. If the Common Law of England had been constructed by relying on the principles of equity inherent in God's law, the Common Law might then be revised by relying on principles of equity appropriate to a search for equitable solutions. Covenantal methods are constitutive of covenantal societies. This would be an alternative to Hobbes's sovereign or to Bentham's reliance on men of goodwill to formulate a rational code of law presuming criminal law to be the core of positive law.

The cost calculus introduced by Buchanan and Tullock (1962), emphasizing expected decision costs as time and effort expended on the making of decisions and expected external costs as the deprivations likely to be suffered from adverse decisions – or the mutual advantage gained from favourable decisions – goes some distance in taking account of factors that would enter into a method of normative inquiry appropriate to the formulation of rules for a fair game. Their cost calculus is an effort to array expected costs consistent with Utility calculations. Estimating 'costs' applicable to both monetized and nonmonetized relationships does not provide the basis for formulating a fair set of rules as such. Jurisprudence still has its place. A cost calculus is a useful mode of computation in estimating what is worth doing, as a complement to other standards of performance.

Human choice involves contingent relationships grounded in knowledge *plus* the capacity to weigh and choose among alternatives in relation to criteria of choice. The important contribution by Buchanan and Tullock was to recognize that the logic of choice applied to the choice of rules is different than the logic of choice applied to the selection of persons to serve in positions of political authority or the expenditure of money to buy vendible services and products. How to select 'men of goodwill' is always problematic. How to achieve equitable resolutions by using power to check power turns critically on the achievement of a culture of inquiry to pursue a problem-solving mode of inquiry applicable to conflict and conflict resolution.

Eucken's critique and the analyses offered by Hobbes, Montesquieu, Hume, Adam Smith, and others addressing similar questions in the seventeenth and eighteenth centuries have led me to conclude that the requirements of epistemic choice cannot be met by universal models alone. Differently conceptualized systems of order in human societies do exist. Such systems are constituted in different ways. Establishing commensurability for treating variable characteristics requires reference not to an infinite plenitude of 'facts' but to common elements in a framework that can take on variable characteristics.

Features of an Analytical Framework

In my judgment, the innovative thrust in early Public-Choice efforts was to bring together concerns about 'methodological individualism', 'the nature of goods', and 'decision-making arrangements' (institutions) as distinct elements to be taken into account in addressing market and non-market decision making (V. Ostrom [1973] 1989). These were elements of a general framework that could be used to specify the logic of prototypical situations in human societies. An epistemic element – the place of common knowledge and communities of shared understanding in decision situations – was neglected. The accompanying schematic in Figure 9.1 is a representation of such a framework.

Figure 9.1: A Framework of Elements and Stages in Institutional Analysis and Development

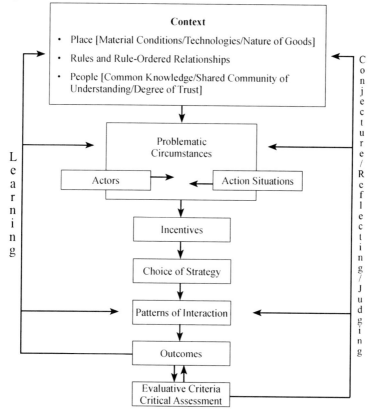

Actors perceive *incentives* (opportunities and constraints) in *problematic circumstances* in light of the structure of *action situations* set in a more general *context*. These incentives affect their *choices* of *strategies* in *interactions* affecting *outcomes*. These processes are evaluated through *conjecturing, reflecting,* and *judging*. Individuals in such situations learn to modify the structure of the situation or their strategies in an emerging or destabilizing system of order. (For similar frameworks, *see* Kiser and E. Ostrom 1982; E Ostrom 1990; and Oakerson 1992).

Unlike a universal model that is presumed to apply to human experience everywhere, a framework uses basic elements that can be brought together to conceptualize different patterns of order in human societies. By drawing on human agents to be the active elements that make the system work, it is possible to consider competing hypotheses about differently conceived systems of order, provided that people in human societies are willing to engage in the experiments. Criteria applicable to epistemic choice might then be applied to conjectures about different systems of political order. It would be appropriate to conjecture whether societies of men [and women] might constitute 'good governments' by reflection and choice, provided that they are willing to specify their standards of judgment. Under these circumstances, the 'political doctrine' used to formulate 'basic demands and expectations' typically set forth in constitutions, charters, and formal declarations, as expounded in Lasswell's formulation, might be treated as relevant hypothetical conjectures within 'political science' and the related cultural and social sciences.

Tocqueville used a similar framework for his study in *Democracy in America*. Before addressing himself to the institutional arrangements characteristic of the American system of governance, he explicitly considered the physical circumstances of the North American continent, where the Anglo-Americans had settled and lived in relation to the aboriginal population. The origins – historical background – of the Anglo-Americans and their general social condition were also considered as the context for specifying the institutional arrangements characteristic of their system of governance. His analysis of the particular factors that contributed to the maintenance of the American federal republic turned explicitly on the elements in his framework:

I.   The peculiar and accidental situation in which
     Providence has placed the Americans.
II. The laws [rules and rule-ordered relationships].
III. The manners and customs of the people. ([1835] 1945, 1:288)

The analytical problem, then, is how contextual elements fit together to create action situations that are relevant to the choices being made by actors who are acting with reference to that situation. The more fully the situation can be specified, the less burden needs to be placed on the particular rationality postulates being asserted for hypothetical actors. A postulate of complete or perfect information can be avoided if situational conditions pertaining to common knowledge and shared communities of understanding can be specified. Thus, Tocqueville presumed that manners and customs of the people apply to moral and intellectual conditions that are characteristic of those who are participants in action situations. The weaker form of such a postulate would be a combination of Hobbes's conception of power as the use of present means to obtain some future apparent good when combined with the assertion of 'a perpetual and restless' striving that persists so long as life endures. Active agents are motivated to act in ways that will leave them better off, rather than worse off, as they conceptualize the importance of fundamental values, including peace, knowledge, freedom, justice, and well-being, but not necessarily limited to those values.

A framework is necessary in specifying the features that need identification in any analytical effort. Indicating how some activating factor can be used to drive transformations to be achieved is a way of specifying hypothetical if-then contingencies to account for cause and effect relationships. This is a way of formulating theoretical explanations. Moving toward a more precise specification of the necessary and sufficient conditions for achieving a transformation is the specification of a model. Working with frameworks, theories, and models is necessary for achieving general explanations in the cultural and social sciences and in such fields of study as history, journalism, jurisprudence, and public administration. Model thinking alone is not sufficient. The intellectual enterprise requires moving back and forth across frameworks, theories, and models so as to appropriately fit limiting conditions, opportunities, and hypothetical contingencies into the multidimensional facets characteristic of the artifactual nature of human habitation.

The rudiments for such a framework can be built by drawing on the early work of Public-Choice scholars. Methodological individualism is a way of postulating active agents. These agents act in light of knowledge and information and in relation to material conditions and technologies, to affect the nature of the goods that function in the economy of life. Relationships are mediated by decision-making arrangements set within the moral and intellectual conditions that affect how individuals relate to each other.

Methodological individualism

I use the term *methodological individualism* to presume, as Lasswell did, that the fundamental feature of human societies is 'acts performed by individuals who are not merely biological entities but persons who have an individual 'ego' and a social 'self' embedded in a cultural heritage (Lasswell and Kaplan 1950: 3). Individuals, as egos and social selves, function in the social and cultural context of normative processes with an autonomous sense of personal existence, without being confined to the extreme rationality assumptions of microeconomic theory. Self-interest considered in light of the interests of others is a way of reaching shared communities of understanding. Calculations pertaining to warrantable knowledge, standards of fairness, other normative considerations, and material well-being are deserving of complementary attention. Collectivities may act in concert and function as actors, but group actions are always to be understood as patterned forms of individual actions.

I presume that the perspective of methodological individualism is necessary in the cultural and social sciences, even for inquiries in societies that do not recognize the autonomous standing of individuals in the constitution of those societies. We, as individuals, use our own resources as human beings to attempt to understand others, presuming as Hobbes did that there is a basic similitude of thoughts and passions characteristic of all mankind. Confucian societies, for example, have not traditionally recognized the standing of individuals apart from family units (Yang 1987). Any such conception has consequences that are important, as individuals act either with reference to family ties and the webs of obligation and opportunities among kin or as outcasts required to come to terms with radically different conditions of life. Outcasts, for example, can associate together in secret societies, organised as brotherhoods, and function at the margin of society, engaged in some combination of organised crime and as enforcers for those who cannot rely on the formal system of authority relationships. It is entirely possible for such outlaw societies to achieve an honourable place in societies with repressive regimes, as did Robin Hood and his men. Political realities include reference to Mafias of diverse nationalities, implying universal tendencies.

Whether 'lawful' or 'unlawful' regimes best serve the interests of 'people' is an open empirical question. Where indiscretions of speech are treated as high crimes, as in the characterization of imperial Russia by Marquis de Custine ([1839] 1989), standards of legality lose their relationship to standards of moral judgment. Former inhabitants of prison camps in the Soviet Union testify that professional criminals were treated as the elite among the prisoners and cooperated with camp authorities to maintain 'order' within the camps in return for opportunities to prey on political prisoners. Mafias were being nurtured in the confines of prison camps. State authorities who view 'private property' as an evil might also view ordinary theft with ambiguity about who is the offender – the 'thief' or the 'victim'. Under such circumstances, individual entrepreneurship would be difficult to distinguish from organised crime; and 'lawful' activity may be difficult to distinguish from theft. Those issues can only be resolved by determining who is preying on whom with reference to basic standards of moral judgment. *Who* has standing with regard to *what* is a critical question in establishing patterns of order in human societies. Economic orders turn on moral contingencies. A proper economic order would, presumably, be a moral economy (Scott 1976; Popkin 1979).

The place of moral contingencies in the constitution of a moral order needs to be understood in relation to the patterns of character structure that affect individual choice in the context of more extended patterns of human association. This is why Tocqueville identified religions as political institutions in American society even though religious institutions took no direct part in the function of governmental institutions as such. The question remains whether human beings can use their resources as human beings to understand how other human beings can be expected to draw on a cultural heritage, with its ontological, moral, and epistemological contingencies, to anticipate what choices actors would be prepared to make in hypothetically specified situations. We are still dealing with hypothetical actors confronted with the problem of making choices in hypothetical situations.

Knowledge and information

Factors pertaining to common knowledge and asymmetries of knowledge and information are among the reasons why 'applied theoretical' economists concerned with the empirical investigation of industry structures do not undertake studies of markets in general but focus on particular markets involving closely substitutable goods in which commensurable bodies of knowledge and technologies occur in a nexus of market relationships. We are back to Eucken's problem of whether a single, simple, abstract, universal model of a perfectly competitive market allows comparisons to be made; again we must identify how exogenous parameters and endogenous variables function in establishing the empirical warrantability of theoretical conjectures.

Competitive markets are important 'public' institutions. They play a significant evolutionary role in generating common knowledge about the place of price as a measure of value, for equilibrating supply and demand [production and use] and for establishing conditions of individual rationality. The experience of buying and selling in competitive market economies evokes levels of information and common knowledge placed on a scale of value expressed in prices that is not only advantageous to buyers and sellers but informative to any entrepreneur who may seek to take advantage of opportunities that are available. Anglo-American economic theory emphasizes the equilibrating features of competitive market economies. Austrian economists emphasize the information-generating features and their role in entrepreneurship (Kirzner 1973). When the latter is combined with innovation and advances in knowledge and technologies, equilibrating tendencies are continuously being challenged by disequilibrating tendencies that are affected by advances in knowledge, skills, and technologies, including the institutional arrangements that serve as modes of production, exchange, and consumption or use (Dosi 1984).

The problem of common knowledge and asymmetries applicable to the generation and use of knowledge and information occur in the context of speech communities, in the crafts and professions, in the context of individual and collective choice, and generally in relation to whatever human beings do. The assertion of private property rights and their enforcement depend on communities of shared understanding. Common knowledge is of fundamental importance for coordinated activities in human societies. All knowledge conditions cannot be directly resolved by market exchange. Complementary criteria are required to supplement benefit-cost analysis. Presuppositions of methodological individualism need to be related to communities of shared understanding as fundamental elements in a framework for the analyses of decision situations (Kiser and E. Ostrom 1982; E. Ostrom 1990; Oakerson 1992).

Material conditions, technologies, and the nature of goods

Material conditions as they are transformed by technologies and institutional arrangements have a decisive effect on the conditions of life as these affect the nature of goods. Two sets of variables that pertain to exclusion and to subtractability or jointness of use can initially be used to construct a typology of goods as illustrated in Table 9.2. Other factors related to domain and scope add further dimensionality.

The *exclusion* principle has long been recognized as a criterion essential to the feasibility of market organisation. Two sets of criteria – difficulty of exclusion;

Table 9.2: Types of Goods

	Jointness of Use	
Exclusion	Alternative Use	Joint Use
Low Cost	*Private Goods*: bread, shoes, automobiles, haircuts, books, etc.	*Toll [Club] Goods*: theatres, night-clubs, telephone service, toll roads, cable TV, libraries, etc.
High Cost	*Common-Pool Resources*: water pumped from a groundwater basin, fish taken from an ocean, crude oil extracted from an oil pool, etc.	*Public Goods*: peace and security of a community, national defence, mosquito abatement, air pollution control, fire protection, weather forecasts, etc.

Source: V. Ostrom and E. Ostrom 1977: 12.

jointness of use – have been variously used in efforts to conceptualize public or collective goods as distinguished from private goods (Head 1962; Olson 1965). I emphasize jointness or sub-tractability of use rather than rivalry or nonrivalrousness of Utility considerations. Treated as variables, these two sets could be conceived as independent of one another; and dichotomizing the sets with on yes or off [no] settings could be used to create a two-by-two matrix, including private goods, toll [club] goods, common-pool resources, and public goods.

This simple logical construction reflects abstractions put into dichotomized logical sets. The logical construction is used to clarify sets of distinctions. In practical circumstances, factors pertaining to potentials for exclusion and to use or consumption are likely to represent continua of more or less and in some combination. For example, excludable goods and services are amenable to market organisation, but competitive markets allow open access to buyers and sellers who make joint use of market arrangements. Open competitive markets themselves have the characteristics of public goods, while trading in markets applies to private goods. Discrete markets or shopping centres with assigned locations have the characteristics of common-pool resources. Money as a medium of exchange has the characteristic of a private good; money as a unit of account in a monetary system is a public good. The set of logical categories needs to be used with caution in addressing the exigencies of human experiences. These categories provide ways of addressing essential elements in an analytical schema available to scholars in the cultural and social sciences.

In addition to factors pertaining to exclusion and those pertaining to subtractability or jointness of use, other factors of basic importance pertain to domain and scope, implying multidimensional matrices. Domain bears on factors of territoriality [space], ranging from small third-party neighborhood effects to those of global proportions, as in the case of fallout from nuclear explosion or cumulative changes in the chemical composition of the atmosphere and stratosphere. *Scope* pertains to the independence of one or another type of good or service so that units of a good or service are distinguishable from other goods and services. If the state of affairs subject to joint use and consumption implicates a domain of small magnitude, the relevant public – those affected – might be organised with regard to something appropriately called 'neighbourhoods'. There is no necessary identity between the domain of Nation-States and the domain characteristics either of natural phenomena [e.g. watersheds] or of the way that human habitation is accompanied by neighbourhood effects.

Scope contingencies apply to functional specialization, leading to distinction among goods and services. Both water and electricity have the characteristics of common-pool, flow resources that must be kept isolable from one another. Electrical engineering requires careful attention to 'insulation'. Flows of storm water, sewer water, and domestic water require separable consideration. Diverse opportunities exist in how enterprises associated with such services might be put together in ways that are accountable to the people being served, to develop a consciousness of the interdependencies among productive, distributive, and consumptive aspects of a public economy in contrast to a private market economy. Where considerable autonomy exists in the exercise of self-organising and self-governing capabilities, various combinations might be achieved in which the character of specialization is resolved by complementary sets of decisions worked out within particular collectivities and in the interrelationships among particular collectivities. Such arrangements are open to mutual accommodation depending on the problematics arising in discrete situations; we need not presume that uniform rules apply to Society as a Whole.

Critical problems arise for the organisation of joint consumption aspects among communities of users in public economies. Diverse opportunities available for organising production functions allow for the creation of quasi-market conditions in a public economy, depending on the alternatives that are available. Scholars with strong applied and theoretical interests in the Public-Choice tradition have faced many of the same problems as applied theoretical economists in industrial organisation. Problems confronting fishers are quite different than those confronting irrigators, even though fisheries and irrigation systems both have characteristics associated with common-pool resources (E. Ostrom 1990; Schlager and E. Ostrom 1992). Furthermore, the interface between the resource base and its use implies that common-property relationships are closely bound up with the 'private' property rights of individual users. Variations in the scope and domain of toll goods, common-pool resources, and public goods have substantial implications for how communities of relationships are affected and for what standing those communities have within systems of governance for exercising collective choice and taking collective action. We could expect to find multitudes of collectivities operating in systems of governance that simultaneously function as public economies (V. Ostrom, Tiebout, and Warren 1961; Bish 1971; Advisory Commission on Intergovernmental Relations 1987).

The relationships of private property to public thoroughfares, such as sidewalks, streets, and highways, are closely correlated. How the interests of diverse publics are to be taken into account is of substantial importance. Collective organisation on a small scale is essential to the interest of smallholders because collective organisation enables them to better articulate their joint interests rather than acting as isolated individuals in relation to State authorities. The relationship of the property rights of individuals to complementary forms of social ownership, including various forms of cooperative associations and private, municipal, and public corporations, is of substantial proportions in all human societies (Grossi [1977] 1981; Netting 1993; E. Ostrom 1990).

Decision-making arrangements

The great diversity of potential public goods and common-pool resources, where exclusion of individuals may be difficult to achieve and where variable patterns in jointness of use may prevail, implies many communities of interests of varying scope and domain. Efforts to escape these complexities by reference to the concept of 'the State' are inevitably confounded by the diversity of decision-making arrangements applicable to choice in human societies. The specter of simplified allusions to 'the Market' and 'the Government' [State] haunts a large proportion of the work in Public-Choice theory. Such uses of language evoke allusions to 'Capitalism' and 'Socialism' under circumstances in which I cannot understand whether the term capitalism refers to what Adam Smith meant by free trade or mercantilism or both. An allusion to something called 'the Government' does not clarify what the term refers to. If the reference implies that the instrumentalities of collective action are organised as a single firm – the Government – occupying a monopoly position with regard to (1) authority relationships and (2) the legal instruments of coercion, we are conceptualizing Public Choice as occurring under conditions specified in Hobbes's theory of sovereignty. Eucken's conjectures about different ways of conceptualizing systems of order would suggest that alternatives of economic, epistemic, and political significance may exist. Concepts of 'States' and 'Markets' are not effective ways of articulating the intellectual revolution that is stirring in our midst. As intellectual constructs, they are too gross to be useful; they run the risk of being misleading and are the source of serious forms of deception and misconceptions.

To make rules binding, criteria grounded in moral distinctions must be enforceable, and enforcement may depend on imposing deprivations [punishment] for failure to conform to rules. There are thresholds of choice where coercion is a necessity for the maintenance of order in human societies. As a consequence, I expect no human society to exist without coercive capabilities. Should the exercise of coercive capability be based solely on a power of command without contestability or on some other way of constituting authority relationships?

One way of coping with a theory of sovereignty is to sort out diverse levels of choice. Buchanan and Tullock's *Calculus of Consent* (1962) began that important task by distinguishing between constitutional choice and collective choice. They argued that a base rule of *conceptual unanimity* is important in establishing consensus about the terms and conditions applicable to the exercise of collective choice. There are situations where a rule of unanimity might be relaxed by unanimous agreement to prefer other, less encompassing decision rules in light of the time and effort required to achieve unanimity and the strategic opportunities available to holdouts. The operational significance of coerced choice can be subject to levels of mutual understanding and public scrutiny that achieve informed consent or voluntary agreement in establishing standards of legitimacy. Distinctions can be made among constitutional, collective, and operational choices as the necessary and continuing complements to one another if standards of legitimacy are to prevail. Standards of legitimacy, conceptual unanimity, and informed consent mirror one another, but they need not function through single collectivities applicable to whole societies. If constitutional choice is exercised by military coups or revolutionary struggles and if collective decisions are made by ruling elites engaged in predatory exploitation of others, we would expect very limited opportunities to be available for choice in organising ways of life. A unitary power of command implies servitude for subjects, not choice for persons and citizens.

Efforts to achieve binding effects by putting words on paper take us back to conceptual-epistemic problems. Words by themselves do not convey meaning but depend on communities of shared understanding among members of speech communities. The language of the Constitution of the United States has been used to draft constitutions in other parts of the world but without much effect. This has led many scholars to conclude that constitutions are meaningless fictions or, at most, positive morality, not positive law. The problem cannot, however, be resolved at that level. Statutory enactments and administrative rules and regulations are also words on paper. What are the grounds for legitimacy? Officials can command; but individuals do not necessarily obey. Patterns of deception and self-deception may pervade human relationships. We are back to problems of publicness in language, communication, meaning, common knowledge, consensus about basic norms or criteria of choice, and social accountability. In the absence of consensus, conflict is possible. In the presence of conflict, a problematic situation may exist requiring the adoption of a problem-solving mode of inquiry to reestablish shared communities of understanding. Such circumstances suggest that epistemic difficulties exist and that problems of epistemic inquiry about the relationship of concepts and information to problematic situations have priority in deciding what is to be done. A single, universal, comprehensive, and workable code of law applicable to all mankind is an empirical impossibility. So is a single, simple, universal 'model' of 'economic' reasoning applied to 'nonmarket' decision making.

Back to epistemic and cultural factors

Words in the realm of science and technology do not convey meaning apart from knowledgeable, skilled, and intelligible individuals who know how to act with reference to the meaning assigned to words. No experiment can be appropriately conducted by uninformed experimenters or 'strategic opportunists' who wish to rig the results to their own advantage. The conduct of any viable enterprise depends on knowledge, skill, and intelligibility among those who constitute the enterprise. Any viable enterprise, public as well as private, turns on the use of knowledge in whatever gets done, set in a context of economic potentials mediated by patterns of rule-ordered relationships as essential complements to one another.

The importance of epistemic and cultural factors in the constitution of different patterns of order can be illustrated by contrasting the republican character of covenanting [federal] societies with despotic systems of order. The concept of *res publica* – the public thing – implies an open public realm in which public affairs are openly considered and decisions are reached through open public deliberation. Cooperative activities depend on undertaking contingent agreements subject to plausible commitments. The promises made need to become binding commitments consistent with contingent agreements. If some participants are played for suckers, trust is broken and a moral offense has been committed. Openness of deliberation in processes for mediating conflict and achieving conflict resolution need to be designed to elucidate information, articulate arguments bearing on contending interests, and reach resolutions in light of mutual and public consideration of complementarities. Individual interests need to be understood as having commonalities bearing on shared communities of interest.

How individual interests relate to common interests needs to be clarified through processes of conflict and conflict resolution that serve the correlative purposes of generating common knowledge and shared communities of understanding that create a consciousness of complementary social identities. The structure of incentives needs to be such that the quest for cooperative endeavours is reinforced in ways that are compatible with fundamental values, such as peace, enlightenment, liberty, justice, or wellbeing; such values should have the potential for becoming universal public goods. Incentives compatible with 'republican virtues' need to be the basis for the design of decision structures that give expression to decision processes consistent with the enlightenment of the open public realm.

In autocratic systems of order, which are constituted with reference to a single centre of Supreme Authority and which rely on law as command uniformly applicable to people under diverse ecological conditions, the pursuit of cooperative endeavours runs the risk of violating the letter of some legal formulation having the proclaimed force of law. Instead of plausible commitments to be resolved by commonly accepted standards of enlightenment and justice, advantage is likely to accrue by pursuing a strategy of plausible ignorance. Resolutions are sought through secret accommodation. These circumstances occur where regulatory prohibitions are subject to granting conditional licenses and permits by administrative methods. The confidential character of administrative methods encourages favouritism. Regulatory measures become potential sources of corruption and traps for money. Administrative methods that focus on legalities become destructive of a rule of law. Under such circumstances, each individual's task becomes a lifelong endeavour of achieving special connections to cope with the problems of life. The standard response is to plead ignorance rather than trying to be helpful to others and acquiring a public reputation for being helpful to others.

What Tocqueville refers to as 'the whole moral and intellectual tradition of a people' accrues in the course of living a life. Problems are worked out through time, in structures mediated by processes at work in everyday life. In this way, people form habits of the heart and mind with less than conscious awareness of the changes that transpire in the course of time. Yet the viability of democratic societies depends on continuing the function of the *res publica* conditions, while maintaining the continuities of a rule of law that is itself subject to change through time, and while meeting the requirements of freedom and justice. Incentives to seek special advantage through the art of manipulation always exist. Random solutions will not suffice. Instead, knowledgeable, skilled, and intelligible creatures confront the challenge of learning how to correct errors and how to respond to problematic situations in constructive ways.

Viable democracies are neither created nor destroyed overnight. Emphasis on form of government and the binding character of legal formulations are not sufficient conditions to meet the requirements of democratic societies. The moral and intellectual conditions of those who constitute democratic societies are of essential importance. This is why building common knowledge, shared communities of understanding, patterns of accountability, and mutual trust is as essential as producing stocks and flows of material goods and services. The epistemic and cultural contingencies of life are at least as important as the economic and political conditions narrowly construed.

My sense is that the more innovative contributions to the Public-Choice tradition of research have come from contributors who were concerned with a better understanding of basic anomalies, social dilemmas, or paradoxes, rather than with applying a single abstract model of economic reasoning to nonmarket decision making. The latter concern becomes an exercise in the application of an orthodox mode of analysis in price theory; the former opens important new frontiers of inquiry.

Conclusions

Language and its place in the articulation of knowledge is the most fundamental source of productive potentials in human societies. No human mortal can be presumed to know the Truth. The conditions for establishing the warrantability of what we presume to know are the foundations for developing a culture of inquiry appropriate to addressing ambiguities and unknowns in efforts to identify and resolve that which is problematic. The future of Public Choice will be determined by its contributions to the epistemic level of choice in the cultural and social sciences and to the constitution of the epistemic order with which we live and work. Increments to knowledge in research programs require conceptual ordering for what is to be taught. All processes of choice are mediated by languages that enable human beings to acquire capabilities not achieved by lions, bears, and wolves.

Rationality is affected by access to knowledge and communities of shared understanding; every individual is fallible; and everyone endures the costs of choices made under ignorance, misconceptions, deceptions, and strategic manipulations.

Both the systems for making epistemic choices and those for making market choices contribute to the elucidation of knowledge and information essential to systems for making public choices. I cannot imagine a modem society without some form of exchange arrangements characteristic of market organisation. A key question is how variable structures among market arrangements affect conduct and performance. If the range of inquiry is extended to the epistemic realm, our concern is with how variable conceptions [ideas] affect the design of structures, the organisation of processes, patterns of conduct, and performance. The concept of a perfectly competitive market can serve as an important conceptual yardstick and an initial point of departure. Whether such a conceptualization serves as an adequate basis for discriminating observation about different types of market structures is questionable.

That problem is made more difficult by the potentials for strategic collusion between economic entrepreneurs and political entrepreneurs in setting the rules of the political and economic games to facilitate the dominance of the few in relation to the many. Potentials for collusion and intrigue are greatly enhanced when political orders are constituted as monopolies in the exercise of rulership prerogatives and in control over the instruments of coercion in societies. The application of economic reasoning to public choices cannot be advanced very far using the postulates of perfectly informed actors participating in competitive markets operating in unitary States directed by a single centre of Supreme Authority. Equilibrating tendencies under those circumstances are likely to sacrifice market rationality to bureaucratic rationality and both market rationality and bureaucratic rationality to corruption. We need to go back to basics to reconsider the human condition and what it means to be a human being relating to other human beings in the world in which they live.

References

Advisory Commission on Intergovernmental Relations [Ronald J. Oakerson] (1987) The Organization of Local Public Economies, Washington, D.C.

Albert, H. (1984) 'Modell-Denken und historische Wirklichkeit', in H. Albert (ed.), Oekonomisches Denken und sociale Ordnung, Tiibingen: J. C. B. Mohr (Paul Siebeck).

Aristotle (1942) Politics, trans. Benjamin Jowett, New York: Modern Library.

Barry, B. and Hardin, R. (eds) (1982) Rational Man and Irrational Society?: An Introduction and Sourcebook, Beverly Hills: Sage.

Bentham, J. (1823; 2nd edn 1948) An Introduction to the Principles of Morals and Legislation, New York: Hafner.

Berman, H. (1983) Law and Revolution: The Formation of the Western Legal Tradition, Cambridge, Mass.: Harvard University Press.

Bish, R. L. (1971) The Public Economy of Metropolitan Areas, Chicago: Markham.

Boulding, K. E. (1963) 'Toward a Pure Theory of Threat Systems', American Economic Review 53 (May): 424–34.

Buchanan, J. M. (1979a) 'Natural and Artifactual Man'' in What Should Economists Do? Indianapolis: Liberty, pp. 93–112.

Buchanan, James M. and Tullock, Gordon (1962) The Calculus of Consent: Logical Foundations of Constitutional Democracy, Ann Arbor: University of Michigan Press.

Coleman, J. S. (1990) The Foundations of Social Theory, Cambridge: Harvard University Press.

Custine, M. de (1839; 2nd edn 1989) Empire of the Czar: A Journey through Eternal Russia, New York: Doubleday.

Dosi, G. (1984) Technical Change and Industrial Transformation, New York: St. Martin's.

Eucken, W. (1940; 2nd edn 1951) The Foundations of Economics, Chicago: University of Chicago Press.

Grossi, P. (1977; 2nd edn 1981) An Alternative to Private Property: Collective Property in the Juridical Consciousness of the Nineteenth Century, trans. Lydia G. Cochrane, Chicago: University of Chicago Press.

Harsanyi, J. C. (1977) 'Rule Utilitarianism and Decision Theory', Erkenntnis 11 (1) (May): 25–53.

Hayek, F. von (1973) Rules and Order, vol. 1 of Law, Legislation and Liberty, Chicago: University of Chicago Press.

Head, J. G. (1962) 'Public Goods and Public Policy', Public Finance 17 (3): 197–219.

Hobbes, T. (1651; 2nd edn 1960) Leviathan or the Matter, Forme and Power of a Commonwealth Ecclesiasticall and Civil, Oxford: Basil Blackwell.

Hume, D. (1948) Hume's Moral and Political Philosophy, New York: Hafner.

Kirzner, I. M. (1973) Competition and Entrepreneurship, Chicago: University of Chicago Press.

Kiser, L. L. and Ostrom, E. (1982) 'The Three Worlds of Action: A Metatheoretical Synthesis of Institutional Approaches', in E. Ostrom (ed.) *Strategies of Political Inquiry*, Beverly Hills: Sage, pp. 179–222.

Lasswell, H. D. and Kaplan, A. (1950) *Power and Society: A Framework for Political Inquiry*, New Haven: Yale University Press.

Netting, R. McC. (1993) *Smallholders, Householders: Farm Families* and *the Ecology of Intensive, Sustainable Agriculture*, Stanford: Stanford University Press.

North, D. C. (1990) *Institutions, Institutional Change, and Economic Performance*, New York: Cambridge University Press.

Oakerson, R. J. (1992) 'Analyzing the Commons: A Framework' in D. W. Bromley *et al.* (eds) *Making the Commons Work: Theory, Practice, and Policy*, San Francisco: Institute for Contemporary Studies Press, pp. 41–59.

Olson, M. (1965) *The Logic of Collective Action: Public Goods and the Theory of Groups*, Cambridge: Harvard University Press.

Ostrom, E. (1989) 'Microconstitutional Change in Multiconstitutional Political Systems', *Rationality and Society* 1 (1): 11–50.

—— (1990) *Governing the Commons: The Evolution of Institutions for Collective Action*, New York: Cambridge University Press.

Ostrom, V. (1973; 2nd edn 1989) *The Intellectual Crisis in American Public Administration*, Tuscaloosa: University of Alabama Press.

Ostrom, V. and Ostrom, E. (1977) 'Public Goods and Public Choices' in E. S. Savas (ed.) *Alternatives for Delivering Public Services: Toward Improved Performance*, Boulder, Colo.: Westview, pp. 7–49.

Ostrom, V., Tiebout, C. M. and Warren, R. (1961) 'The Organization of Government in Metropolitan Areas: A Theoretical Inquiry', *American Political Science Review* 55 (Dec.): 831–42.

Popkin, S. (1979) *The Rational Peasant*, Berkeley and Los Angeles: University of California Press.

Popper, K. (1967) 'Rationality and the Status of the Rationality Principle' in E. M. Classen (ed.) *Le fondements philosophiques des systems economiques: Textes de Jacques Rueff et essais rediges en son honneur*, Paris: Payot pp. 145–50.

Schlager, E. and Ostrom, E. (1992) 'Property-Rights Regimes and Natural Resources: A Conceptual Analysis', *Land Economics* 68 (3) (August): 249–62.

Scott, J. C. (1976) *The Moral Economy of the Peasant: Rebellion and Subsistence in Southeast Asia*, New Haven: Yale University Press.

Selten, R. (1986) 'Institutional Utilitarianism', in F. X. Kaufmann, G. Majone, and V. Ostrom (eds), *Guidance, Control, and Evaluation in the Public Sector*, Berlin and New York: W. de Gruyter, pp. 251–63.

Sen, A. K. (1977) 'Rational Fools: A Critique of the Behavioral Foundations of Economic Theory', *Philosophy and Public Affairs* 6 (summer): 317–44.

Smith, A, (1759) *The Theory of Moral Sentiments*, Indianapolis: Liberty.

—— (1776) *The Wealth of Nations*, London: Ward, Lock, and Tyler.

Tocqueville, A. de (1835; 1840; 3nd edn 1945) *Democracy in America,* New York: Knopf.

Tullock, G. (1965) *The Politics of Bureaucracy*, Washington, D.C.: Public Affairs Press.

Yang, T.-S. (1987) *Property Rights and Constitutional Order in Imperial China*, PhD diss., Indiana University, Bloomington.

Index

Page numbers in *italics* refer to material in figures and tables.

contextual variables *191*, 194, 218, 256
  see also under common-pool
    resources; social dilemmas
cooperation 46, 123, 124–5, 134,
  135–6, 137, 139, 143–4, 193
  communication, role in 134, 145, 186
  conditional and 125
  failure of 123
  game theory and 136
  microsituations affecting and 193
  reciprocity norms and 139–41, 143
  structural variables and 124, 168, *191*
  theory development and 136
  tongue-lashing, use of and 146
  trust and 135, 143, 144, 146
coordination 35, 123, 259
  experiments/games and 132n.13,n.14
co-production, theory of 83
corruption 46, 56, 126, 152, 232, 264, 266
Cox, M. 182, 183
crime 35, 101, 152, 258
critical theory 219
culture 80, 247, 252, 257, 258, 265
  of inquiry and 250, 254
  patterns of order and 264
cycle theory 219

Dawes, R. M. 133, 142
decentralization 189
decision making 29, 243, 255, 257
  citizen participation and 235
  costs involved in 29–30, 254
    calculation of 254
  decision situations and 259
  economic reasoning and 243–4,
    252, 253, 263, 265
    utility theory and 253
  epistemic level and 244
  moral/intellectual conditions and
    252, 257
  risk and uncertainty in 26–7
  see also governance systems; public
    choice theory
deliberation 264
democracy 47, 57, 86, 125, 153, 230,

236, 265
  accountability in 73
  citizen empowerment and 149
  conceptual-computational logic and
    239, 240
  direct democracy and 231, 233
  elections, role in 236
  Hobbes's theory of 62, 230
  logical foundations of 61, 63, 64
  rational citizens, image of and 125
  see also constitutional theory;
    federalism
design principles 84, 134, 182–3, 253
division of labour 234
Djilas, M. 65
Downs, A. 102, 104, *105*
duty *see* norms
dynamic change 65, 219

economic order 5, 48–9, 251, 258
  competition and exchange in 48–9
  moral contingency and 258
  political order and 251
  see also markets
economic theory 220, 221, 222, 250,
  251–2
  economic reality and 250
  as model thinking 250, 251, 257
  individual, model of in 221, 222, 251
    nontuism and 243, 251
    as rational actor 243, 251, 257
  neoclassic and 251, 252
    assumptions of 252
    utility maximization and 251, 252
  see also methodological individual-
    ism; rational choice theory
efficiency-pricing principle 74
Elazar, D. J. 16
election arena 101, 102
  citizen preference studies and 102
  plurality vote and 102
elections 56, 58, 64, 110, 235, 236–7,
  244, 253
electoral theory and procedures 30,
  102, 103, 238

sanctioning systems and 135
see also cooperation; reciprocity
Tullock, G. 3, 7, 23, 29, 31–2, 61, 64, 80, 109, 243, 254, 262

uncertainty 26, 27, 127, 252
United Kingdom 231
United States
    Alaska constitutional convention and 61
    Constitution of 62, 263
    democracy in 45, 236
        boss rule and 237, 238
    federalist system in 45, 47, 54, 55, 56, 57, 58, 62, 232–3, 235, 236, 238, 256
        coalition formation and 55
        House of Representatives and 231
        as polycentric ordering 55, 56, 57, 58–9
        primary elections and 56, 238
        Senate and 231, 237
        Supreme Court and 54
    machine politics and 236, 237
    Philadelphia convention (1787) and 232
    Progressive Reform Movement 56, 65, 238
    Tammany Hall and 237
    water resource management in 61
USSR 57, 65
    classless society and 65
    communist anticipation in 65
utility 169, 252, 253
    maximization of 253

van de Kragt, A. 133
Villamayor-Tomás, S. 182, 183
virtue 63, 248, 249
von Hayek, F. *see* Hayek
von Wright, G. H. 100
voting behaviour 77
Waldo, D. 23
Walker, J. 130
warfare 57, 62, 122, 152, 153, 228, 236, 247

see also conflict
Warren, R. 46, 170
water resources 78–9
water services industry 170, 173
    Californian study 167, 170, 171
    as a common property resource 179
    irrigation systems analysis 84, 178–9, 195, 261
Weber, M. 35, 46
Weingast, B. R. 109
White, L. D. 24
Williams, A. 35, 188
Williamson, O. E. 32, 33
Wilson, R. 132
Wilson, W. 23–4, 34, 227, 236, 237–8
Workshop in Political Theory and Policy Analysis 1, 67, 173, 178

Yamagishi, T. 135

Lightning Source UK Ltd.
Milton Keynes UK
UKOW04f0754270514

232354UK00007B/455/P